Legal Education and Legal Profession During and After COVID-19

C. Raj Kumar · S. G. Sreejith
Editors

Legal Education and Legal Profession During and After COVID-19

Springer

Editors
C. Raj Kumar
Jindal Global Law School
O. P. Jindal Global University
Sonipat, Haryana, India

S. G. Sreejith
Jindal Global Law School
O. P. Jindal Global University
Sonipat, Haryana, India

ISBN 978-981-19-2567-2 ISBN 978-981-19-2568-9 (eBook)
https://doi.org/10.1007/978-981-19-2568-9

This Springer imprint is published by the registered company Springer Nature Singapore Pte Ltd.
The registered company address is: 152 Beach Road, #21-01/04 Gateway East, Singapore 189721, Singapore

Preface

The idea of this book was born out of the conference, "*Reimagining and Transforming the Future of Law Schools and Legal Education: Confluence of Ideas During and Beyond COVID-19*", organized virtually by Jindal Global Law School, O. P. Jindal Global University from 25 to 27 November 2020. The Conference brought together 100+ educational leaders from all over the world to deliberate on ways and means to sustain legal education during the pandemic and to imagine the way forward.

The Conference was organized 10 months into the pandemic, which, today as we turn back, we sense, was one of the most terrible times in human recorded history. Established thought fell apart from practice, leaving a vacuum in terms of ideas, which were most essential not only to survive and sustain but also to push on. It was a state akin to what one of Elena Ferrante's characters feels in *My Brilliant Friend*, of "dissolving margins", the sudden disappearance of outlines of people and things, a violation of known and established edges of memory and imagination. We had to reclaim the many forms and frames of our existence, things which made sense to us until the pandemic shut the world before us.

During the Conference, we heard many notes of imagination—thoughts of optimism, pronouncements of determination, display of courage, and of course, tales of loses and extraordinary experiments. Each such expression fell on minds as rain on arid lands. It was a torrent of ideas on rediscovering the world and using legal education as a means for that rediscovery.

We thought it worthwhile to capture the profoundest of such ideas by way of a historical record of the efforts of the legal education community to restore the normal, if not build a new normal against the tyranny of the COVID-19 pandemic. This bunch of thoughts on legal education, expressed when world got reversed to its beginnings, nullifying every idea and structure, would, we hope, become part of the essential ideas on legal education.

Sonipat, India

C. Raj Kumar
S. G. Sreejith

Preface

Contents

Editors and Contributors

About the Editors

Prof. C. Raj Kumar, a Rhodes Scholar, is the founding Vice-Chancellor of O. P. Jindal Global University, Sonipat, Haryana, India, and Founding Dean of Jindal Global Law School (JGLS) of the same university. He has academic qualifications from the University of Oxford, Harvard University, University of Hong Kong, University of Delhi and Loyola College. He served as a faculty member at the School of Law of City University of Hong Kong, where he taught for many years. Professor Kumar is an accomplished legal scholar and works in the fields of human rights and development, comparative constitutional law, terrorism and national security, corruption and governance, law and disaster management, legal education and higher education. He has seven books and over 150 publications to his credit and has published widely in peer-reviewed journals, law reviews in Australia, Hong Kong, India, Japan, Singapore, UK and the USA.

Prof. S. G. Sreejith is Executive Dean, Jindal Global Law School (JGLS), O. P. Jindal Global University. Prior to joining JGLS, he worked with reputed intuitions like the Arctic Centre; the University of Lapland; National University of Advanced Legal Studies (NUALS); and the University of Kerala. He has also published in journals like *Third World Quarterly*, *San Diego International Law Journal*, *California Western International Law Journal*, *Journal of Space Law*, *Journal of Air Law and Commerce*, *San Joaquin Agricultural Law Review*, *Air and Space Law*, *Space Policy*, *Journal of Law and Social Deviance*, *Indian Journal of International Law*, *Journal of the Indian Law Institute*, to name few. He sits on the editorial board of the *Indian Journal of International Law*. He has also served as special issue editor of *Journal of Human Values* and *Jindal Global Law Review*. His areas of interest are public international law, heterodox approaches to international legal thought, and air and space law.

Contributors

Sonsoles Arias holds a Bachelor degree in Law (2005), and a Ph.D. (2015). She practiced law for several years since 2005. She currently teaches Constitutional Law and Administrative Law at IE University as a full-time professor.

Her research interests lie in the field of Comparative Constitutional Law, more specifically in the vertical separation of powers, unitary and federal systems, direct democracy in federal countries and clinical legal education. She is the co-author of the *Blueprint on the Global Legal Education*, presented by the International Bar Association and the Law Schools Global League (https://www.ibanet.org/MediaHandler?id=B372104C-690D-4EEE-B7F2-47A18C563E38). She has also published a number of op-ed related to the exercise and the restriction of fundamental rights in the context of the 2019 pandemic, as well as the role of executive powers in times of crisis.

She has been a visitor researcher at the University of Cambridge (United Kingdom), Harvard Law School (United States), Bucerius Law-School and Ludwig-Maximilians Universität (Germany). Her doctoral dissertation—*The Constitutions of the Länder of Germany: Content, guarantees and position in the German legal system*, CEPC, 2015, obtained the national recognition of the Centro de Estudios Políticos y Constitucionales, Ministry of the Presidency of Spain, in 2015.

Soledad Atienza is the Dean of IE Law School and has an extensive academic experience and a global vision of legal education. Prior to that, she practiced law at the leading Spanish law firm Pérez-Llorca for 5 years.

She earned her Ph.D. in Social Sciences from IE University and is currently a law professor. Her expertise includes the areas of comparative law and legal teaching methods. Soledad has an Executive MBA degree from IE Business School and a Certificate in European Studies from the European Institute of the University of Saarland in Germany. She was a visiting student at Cornell University in New York and holds a law degree from the CEU San Pablo University in Spain.

Soledad Atienza is Co-chair of the Commission for the Future of Legal Services of the IBA (International Bar Association) and has co-directed the "Blueprint on global legal education". She is also co-director of the Pérez-Llorca/IE Chair of Business Law and author of the book "Enseñar Derecho. ¿Puede servirnos la experiencia de Estados Unidos?" ("Teaching Law: Can the U.S. experience help us?"), published by Editorial Aranzadi.

Jorge Cerdio is a Full Professor at The Instituto Tecnológico Autónomo de México's Law School (ITAM). He was Dean from 2009 to 2020. He is also head of the Center for Access to Justice, which provides legal aid and counsel to underprivileged persons and promotes social awareness among the legal community through an extensive clinical education program. In addition, he has designed or implemented nearly a thousand initiatives in legal education, including courses, entire curricula for undergraduate and graduate degrees in Law, and training courses on instructional design and applied pedagogy. He has designed the domain ontology and the training sets for the Legal Search Engine used by the Mexican Supreme Court and the Interamerican Court of Human Rights. He also designed and currently maintains the semantics for Tirant Online Mexico, the largest Legal Document Database in Mexico. He is the Academic Director of the Laboratory on Cybersecurity for the American States Organization. He has served as an expert to the Policy Development Group that elaborated the feasibility study for the regulation on AI and Human Rights, for the CAHAI—Ad Hoc Committee on Artificial Intelligence under the Council of Europe, where he was also the Co-Drafter of the Human Rights, Democracy and Rule of Law Impact Assessment Methodology.

Vesna Crnić-Grotić, member and a former chair of the Committee of Experts of the European Charter for regional and minority languages of the Council of Europe. She is a professor of International Law and dean of the Faculty of Law, University of Rijeka, Croatia. She was the chair of the Main Commission for Law of the National Council for Science in Croatia and the chair of the expert panel for legal science of the Croatian Science Foundation. In 2013–2014, she was the Agent for Croatia at the International Court of Justice, Case Concerning the Application of the Convention for the Prevention and Punishment of the Crime of Genocide, Croatia v. Serbia). In 2003 and 2012, she was a candidate for the judge of the European Court for Human Rights. She is a member of the COST Association Human Rights Network, the International Law Association and the Croatian Academy of Legal Sciences.

Sandhya Drew, MA (Oxon), is a practicing barrister and academic based in London. She is a Senior Lecturer at City, University of London specializing in Labour Law and Business and Human Rights Law. She has been Assistant Dean at City, responsible for international exchanges and she jointly organized a successful online Summer School with Jindal in Summer 2021. The online Summer School model is being continued in other initiatives. She is joint Blog Editor for the Business and Human Rights Journal (CUP). She is Visiting Professor in Employment Law at the University of Paris Nanterre. She is of dual English-Indian heritage, which enriches her perspective.

Achilles C. Emilianides is a Professor, Dean of the School of Law at the University of Nicosia, and a practicing advocate, senior partner of the law firms Achilles and Emile, Constantinos Emilianides LLC, and A&E C. Emilianides, C. Katsaros and Associates LLC. He holds a Ph.D. in Law and an LL.M from the Aristotle University of Thessaloniki and an LL.M from Leicester University. He has been elected as a founding member and first Secretary-General of the Cyprus Academy of Sciences, Letters and Arts, and as a member of the European Academy of Sciences and Arts. He is also the national representative to All European Academies (ALLEA), the Chair of the Royal Commonwealth Society Cyprus Branch, and a board member to a number of scientific organizations and journals. He has been involved in high-profile civil litigation, as well as legal consultancy and funded research. Recent publications in the IEL series include: Tort Law in Cyprus (Kluwer, 2020), Civil Procedure in Cyprus (Kluwer, 2020), Religion and Law in Cyprus (3rd ed., Kluwer, 2019), Constitutional Law in Cyprus (2nd ed., Kluwer, 2019), Family and Succession Law in Cyprus (2nd ed., Kluwer 2019), Labour Law in Cyprus (2nd ed., Kluwer,

2019), and Media Law in Cyprus (2nd ed., Kluwer, 2019), Competition Law in Cyprus (Kluwer, 2021).

Marina Feferbaum Ph.D. (2016), Master (2009) and Bachelor (2006) of Law from the Pontifical Catholic University of São Paulo (PUC-SP). Learner designer (Kaospilot), coordinator of the Teaching Methodology and the Center for Teaching and Research in Innovation, both at FGV Sao Paulo Law School. Her research lines cover human rights, African legal system, Brazilian legal education, teaching methods and technology. At FGV Sao Paulo Law School, she also coordinated the Observatory on Legal Education and FGV Law programs. She was a professor of scientific methodology and internationalization of legal areas of the Lato Sensu Graduate Programs. She has published and organized several articles on human rights, legal education and participatory teaching methodologies. She also participated in teacher training courses throughout Brazil.

Dr. Rachel Hews is a Senior Lecturer at Queensland University of Technology, Australia. Her primary interest is in supporting students to develop the graduate skills and capabilities they need to build better legal futures. Rachel's teaching focus is in law and design thinking—also known as legal design—where she supports students to develop creative and entrepreneurial mindsets, a design thinking methodology, how to apply this approach to complex legal problems, and ways of preparing for careers in the future of law. Since 2019, Rachel has fulfilled a range of course coordination and curriculum roles in the QUT Law School. Her research interests include legal design, legal education and the future of legal work. Rachel is currently leading and working on several legal education and design thinking research projects with cross-disciplinary and cross-institutional collaborators. In 2021, Rachel was shortlisted as a finalist for both the Australia Law Awards Academic of the Year and the Women in Law Awards Academic of the Year. She is a Senior Fellow of the Higher Education Academy.

Raveena Lalit is an advocate, presently associated with the competition law practice at Shardul Amarchand Mangaldas & Co., New Delhi. She completed her BA LL.B from Jindal Global Law School in 2017, and her LL.M from the University of Cambridge in 2017–18 as a Justice Pratibha M. Singh and Cambridge Trust Scholar. Apart from her work at the firm, she is associated with Her Forum, a platform connecting women in law, and runs a not-for-profit initiative she co-founded in 2022. She often contributes to various legal and non-legal publications and projects as well.

Shreeyash U. Lalit is an advocate practicing in the Supreme Court of India, various High Courts, tribunals and other fora. He completed his B.Tech. from IIT (Guwahati) in 2014, and thereafter, completed his LLB from the University of Delhi in 2017. He pursued his LL.M from the University of Cambridge in 2017–18 as a Tata Trust, Narottam Sekhsaira, and Cambridge Trust Scholar. He was also awarded the Pegasus Scholarship while at Cambridge, which gave him an insight into various barristers' chambers in the UK. Presently, Shreeyash works across a wide range of civil, commercial and criminal matters, representing the Union, certain state governments and private clients. He often contributes to various legal and non-legal publications as well.

Sabrina Shizue McKenna of the Hawai'i Supreme Court grew up in Japan and the Philippines, attending U.S. schools. She received a B.A. from the University of Hawai'i at Manoa (UHM) and a J.D. from UHM's William S. Richardson School of Law (WSRSL), serving as editor-in-chief of the law review. She was a practicing attorney, served as general counsel to a Japan-based company making international investments, taught business law at the UHM College of Business, and was an Assistant Professor at the WSRSL. From 1993 to 2011, she was a Hawai'i state trial court judge and presided over thousands of trial matters. In 2011, she was appointed one of five justices of the Hawai'i Supreme Court, and she has written many opinions regarding constitutional, civil, criminal and family law issues. She has been a faculty member for the National Judicial College and is also a Judicial Advisory Board member for the George Mason University Antonin Scalia Law School Law and Economics Center's Judicial Education Program. She has been honored by the American Bar Association with the Stonewall Award, by Jindal Global Law School as an Eminent Jurist and Honorary Adjunct Professor of Law, by the Association of Corporate Counsel Foundation as a Global Women in Law and Leadership Honoree, by the National Asian Pacific American Bar Association with the Daniel K. Inouye Trailblazer Award, by the Hawaii Friends for Civil Rights with the Dr. Martin Luther King, Jr., Friends Award, and by the University of Hawai'i as a Distinguished Alumnus.

Prof. Judith McNamara is the Dean of Law at the University of Adelaide and was previously the head of the Queensland University of Technology Law School. Professor McNamara has published extensively in legal education and has expertise in curriculum design and learning and teaching pedagogies. She has undertaken several legal education research projects including as a Chief Investigator on an Australian Learning and Teaching Council category 1 project investigating the capstone experience in law. During the COVID-19 pandemic, she led a rapid shift to fully online delivery of all programs in the QUT law school. She is currently researching how higher education institutions can adopt a more responsive and empathetic approach to student engagement. The project seeks to gain deep insights into student learning experiences to understand how higher education institutions can recognize students' individual needs and experiences and provide support that promotes high-quality learning. Professor McNamara is a Senior Fellow of the Higher Education Academy.

Zoe Nay is a Doctor of Philosophy candidate at the University of Melbourne Law School. Her research is part of the Melbourne Climate Futures research center—a multidisciplinary climate initiative established by the University of Melbourne to contribute to greater action on climate change. Zoe's primary research interests are in the fields of international law, climate change governance and socio-legal studies. In her doctoral research, Zoe examines international legal responses to climate change loss and damage in the Pacific region. Before commencing her Ph.D., Zoe worked as a Research Assistant at Queensland University of Technology. She was engaged in several research projects, including this study on student engagement.

Prof. Pip Nicholson is DVC (People and Community) at the University of Melbourne, Australia. She served as Dean of the Melbourne Law School from 2018 to 2022 and as the Director of the Asian Law Centre before that. For over 20 years, Pip's research has focused on the Vietnamese legal system and comparative approaches to socialist legal change and development aid. She has held national research grants focussing on drugs and the death penalty in Southeast Asia and the impact of international development aid, particularly as it impacts legal institutions. As a former barrister and solicitor of the Supreme Court of Victoria and the High Court of Australia, Pip worked as a commercial lawyer and for the Legal Aid Commission of Victoria. Together with Prof. Farrah Ahmed, Pip introduced the teaching of *Law and Legal Practice in Asia,* which originally focused on the practice of law in India.

Prof. Suzanne Rab is an Independent Barrister at Serle Court Chambers in London. Suzanne has two decades of wide experience of competition law, regulatory law, data protection and EU law. Suzanne's practice has a particular focus on the interface between innovation, trade and economic regulation. She acts in disputes involving governments, regulators and businesses across the regulated sectors including in the financial services, energy/environmental, healthcare/pharmaceuticals, infrastructure, TMT and natural resources sectors. Suzanne has significant experience at the interface between intellectual property rights and data protection. In private practice as a solicitor prior to joining the bar, she has held positions at leading international regulation and trade practices. She has been a partner and head of regulatory practice with a leading US law firm. She has also held the role of director at PricewaterhouseCoopers working within its strategy, economics and regulatory teams. Suzanne maintains an active academic practice concurrently with her barrister practice. She is a Professor of Commercial Law and holds the Practice Chair at Brunel University, a law lecturer at Oxford University and a Visiting Professor at Imperial College, London (IPR and competition). Suzanne maintains a number of public sector advisory and expert panel roles in law and regulation. She is a board member of the Legal Aid Agency, a board member and senior research associate at the Oxford-based Regulatory Policy Institute and an expert panel member of the UK Regulators Network. She has significant research interests in the areas of technology, innovation and artificial intelligence.

Prof. (Dr.) Managay Reddi is Dean and Head of the School of Law, University of KwaZulu-Natal. She holds the degrees of BA (Law) and LLB from the University of Durban-Westville, a Master of Laws (LLM) degree from the University of Natal, and a Doctoral degree in Law (LLD) also from the University of Durban-Westville. Professor Reddi is an Advocate of the High Court of South Africa and a past President of the South African Law Deans Association (SALDA). She also served as a member of the Executive Council of the South African Judicial Education Institute (SAJEI). Her 2-year-long membership of the National Forum on the Legal Profession ended when the Forum dissolved at the establishment of the Legal Practice

Council of South Africa. Professor Reddi is currently a Board member of the African Ombudsman Research Centre (AORC), which is the research and training arm of the African Ombudsman and Mediators Association (AOMA). Her research interests and publications focus on South African Criminal Law; Criminal Procedure, International Criminal Law, Gender and the Law, and Human Rights. Apart from being a regular reviewer for various South African law journals, Professor Reddi also serves as an editor of the *South African Judicial Education Journal* and the *South African Criminal Justice Journal.*

Giorgio Resta, Ph.D. University of Pisa (1999), is Full Professor of Comparative Law at the University of Roma Tre (Italy). Senior Wainwright Fellow at McGill Law School, he taught courses as Visiting professor—among other Universities—at the McGill Law School (2010–2011; 2014–2015), Ecole des Hautes Etudes en Sciences Sociales (2008, 2009, 2014), Nagoya Faculty of Law (JP) (2018).

Associate member of the International Academy of Comparative Law, fellow of the European Law Institute, honorary member of the Italian Association of Civil Lawyers, and co-founder of the Italian Academy for the Internet Code, he served as a member of two Legislative Reform Committees appointed by the Italian Ministry of Justice, and of the Study Group on the legal and ethical implications of COVID-19, established within the Superior Institute of Health (the authority in charge of epidemiological surveillance of COVID-19 in Italy). He has been included on the list of legal experts for the provision of independent legal expertise to the European Parliament in the fields of comparative law and private law. He received special funding and scholarships from various institutions, and among them the Max Planck Institute for Intellectual Property, the Max Planck Institute for Comparative Law, the Canadian Government, the Italian Ministry of University and the Italian National Center of Researches.

He is the author of about 160 publications in the field of personality rights, data protection, biomedicine, as well as general private and comparative law. In 2021, he co-edited a major commentary to the GDPR and the Italian Data Protection Code for the publisher "Giuffré-Francis Lefebvre".

Among his books are *Data protection in the context of Covid-19. A short (hi)story of tracing applications*, Rome: RomaTrE-Press, 2021 (coauthored with E. Poillot—G. Lenzini—V. Zeno-Zencovich); *Le persone fisiche e i diritti della personalità* ("Human persons and rights of personality") (coauthored with G. Alpa), Trattato di diritto privato diretto da R. Sacco, 2nd ed., Wolters Kluwer 2020; *Dignità persona mercati* ("Dignity, person, markets"), Giappichelli, 2014; *Trial by Media as a Legal Problem: A Comparative Analysis*, Editoriale Scientifica, 2009; *Autonomia privata e diritti della personalità* ("Freedom of contract and personality rights"), Napoli, 2005. He co-edited (with Fausto Caggia) *I diritti fondamentali in Europa e il diritto privato* ("Fundamental rights in Europe and Private Law"), RomaTrEpress, 2019; (with Carlo Petrini and Alberto Gambino), *La ricerca su materiali biologici di origine umana: giuristi e scienziati a confronto* ("Research on human biological materials: a dialogue between jurists and scientists"), DIMT, 2018; (with Vincenzo Zeno-Zencovich) *La protezione transnazionale dei dati personali: dai Safe Harbour Principles al Privacy*

Shield ("Transnational data protection: from Safe Harbour to Privacy Shield), Roma-TrEpress, 2016; *Il diritto all'oblio su Internet dopo Google Spain* ("Right to be forgotten in Internet after Google Spain").

Prof. Yubaraj Sangroula is Executive Director and Professor at Kathmandu School of Law, Nepal. He is also visiting professor at various Asian Law Schools. He teaches Jurisprudence, Philosophy and International Law. He is the current Chair of the Asian Association of Law Professors. Previously, he has served as the Attorney General of Nepal.

Martin Škop is an associate professor at the Department of Legal Theory, Faculty of Law, Masaryk University, Brno, Czech Republic (Ph.D. in 2004 at Masaryk University in Theoretical Legal Sciences). Martin Škop, as a teacher, participates in teaching legal philosophy, legal theory, sociology of law and media law. Among his scientific interests belong critical legal studies, law and literature, and sociology of statutory drafting. He published four monographs in Czech (Law and Violence; Law in Postmodern Situation; Law and Passion; …Law, Language, Narrative) and many peer-reviewed articles. He was chairing Argumentation conference organized in Brno every 2 years with WoS indexed proceedings. For years 2019–2023, he was appointed to the dean's office of law faculty.

Oscar Vilhena is the Dean of the School of Law at São Paulo of the Getulio Vargas Foundation (FGV Direito SP), where he teaches Constitutional Law, Human Rights and Law and Development, besides to coordinate a FGV multidisciplinary research team in socio-environmental damages in the cases Rio Doce environmental disaster. He has a B.A. in law from the Catholic University of Sao Paulo, a LL.M. from Columbia University in New York, a M.A. and Ph.D. in political science from the University of São Paulo, and post-doctoral at the Centre for Brazilian Studies—St. Antonies College, at Oxford University. He served as state attorney for São Paulo, was executive secretary of the United Nations Latin American Institute in Brazil, executive secretary of the Teotonio Vilela Commission for Human Rights, legal adviser for the Center for the Studies of Violence of the University of São Paulo, participated the board of Open Society Foundation to Human Rights and Latin America Initiatives. Nowadays, he is member of the board on Ethos Institute, Fair Trials Organization, and Institute for Integrated Transitions. He also was founding member of Conectas Human Rights, Pro Bono Institute and former president of Law Schools Global League (LSGL). Oscar was Global Fellow at Brazil Institute of the Woodrow Wilson International Center for Scholars. He is founding and member of the board of Arns Comission for Human Rights and active pro bono lawyer in several human rights cases. Oscar Vilhena has written several books throughout his career and is columnist at one of the most important newspaper in Brazil.

Prof. Ibibia Lucky Worika holds a Ph.D. in *International Environmental and Comparative Petroleum law and Policy* from the University of Dundee in Scotland, UK under a Commonwealth Academic Staff Scholarship administered by the Commonwealth Scholarship Commission between 1995 and 1998. He was a post-doctoral researcher at the Centre for Energy, Petroleum and Mineral Law and Policy, at the University of Dundee, Scotland, UK between 1999 and 2000. He holds an LL.M. as well as an LL.B (Hons) degrees from the University of Lagos in 1989 and 1986, respectively; and was called to the Nigerian Bar in 1987. He is currently a Professor of Law and Dean, Faculty of Law, University of Port Harcourt (Uniport). Until his assumption of duty at Uniport, in 2014, he was a *Senior Legal Adviser* at the Commonwealth Secretariat in London, providing expert legal counsel to member governments of the Commonwealth under the Commonwealth Fund for Technical Co-operation (CFTC) in the area of natural resources policies, laws, contracts, institutions and governance. Between 2004 and 2011, he was first, Senior Legal Counsel and later, *General Legal Counsel* of the Organization of Petroleum Exporting Countries (OPEC) in Vienna, Austria. In these positions, Prof. Worika (then Dr. Worika), provided specialist expert legal advice to the Secretary General, Senior Secretariat Management and Governing bodies of OPEC Member Countries (MCs), producers of two-thirds of the World's oil-based in the Middle East, Africa and South America on legal matters that impacted the organization and its Member Countries.

Introduction

Recording the New Renaissance: Legal Education and Legal Profession During and After COVID-19

C. Raj Kumar and S. G. Sreejith

> *The tale ... could not be one of a final victory. It could be only the record of what had had to be done, and what assuredly would have to be done again in the never-ending fight against terror and its relentless onslaughts, despite their personal afflictions, by all who, while unable to be saints but refusing to bow down to pestilences, strive their utmost to be healers.*
> —*Albert Camus, The Plague* (1948)

1 Introduction: Fighting the Monster

COVID-19 is a deadly pandemic that has impacted all walks of human life. As we write this editorial, the traces of coronavirus still continue to remain in the world amid many continuing human efforts to wipe them out. Although the light of hope—the luminosity of freedom—is brimming on the horizon, it only consoles the soul. The sigh of relief is far off. Losses caused by this deadly monster have been countless—of lives, health, peace, love, protection, care, and security. Everyone's heart goes out to the other—we are human, after all. But that's not the best we can do in our fight against the Pandemic. We need to battle the malady. We need to gather the fragments strewn by the blow of the Pandemic and secure them from further destruction. We need to renew our creative energies. We need to renew our collective willing and acting.

It struck mildly, but soon spewed its venom all over the world, paralyzing human thought and action. We waited for it to abate, and as it did not abate, we resisted. It spread its ferocious wings, and as it threatened our existence, we decided to fight it. This willing and acting resulted in one of the most remarkable human efforts

C. Raj Kumar · S. G. Sreejith (✉)
O.P. Jindal Global University, Sonipat, India
e-mail: sgsreejith@jgu.edu.in

C. Raj Kumar
e-mail: crk@jgu.edu.in

C. Raj Kumar and S. G. Sreejith (eds.), *Legal Education and Legal Profession During and After COVID-19*, https://doi.org/10.1007/978-981-19-2568-9_1

at response and resilience. Our healthcare and frontline workers fought valiantly, leading us from the front. The spirit of their fight ignited a revolution of resistance all over the world. Wherever they perished, hundreds of thousands of new warriors rose from the embers of the dying fire. The sentiment that the world we have built is too precious to be surrendered before a deadly virus was prevalent.

The world over had the awakening against the perils of coronavirus. The awakening was also to the reality that there is dawning a new epoch, reminiscent of history.[1] The world has been reconstructed over and over again in the past—after wars, genocides, revolutions, pestilences, and even from a proverbial "end of history". Hence, the awakening against the Pandemic was also an awakening to the hidden and innate potential of humankind, as Philip Allott writes, recalling histories and referring to the COVID-19 Pandemic: "Suddenly human beings had become conscious of their capacity for self-improvement using the power of ideas".[2]

As the action unfolded from the self-confidence and courage of humanity, the years of accumulated wisdom, scientific knowledge, and technological *savoir-faire*—what Yuval Noah Harari considers as having culminated in "the merger of biotech and infotech"—facilitated all efforts. The world found an alternative to the material geographies in the meta-geography of the Internet. Social and cultural production continued in the seamless World Wide Web, with a larger amount of success, although not fully free of challenges. While the story of success is a story of sustenance and resilience, some of the knock-on effects of the online-shift include social isolationism, impact on mental health, loss of income, digital divide, and privacy and security concerns.

Whatsoever, the move online was a solution accepted worldwide—it was a natural transition to the next, and perhaps the only available alternative. All sectors ranging from information technology to local businesses, and all domains of function from international organizations to local administration resumed functions online. Leaders in these sectors and domains, irrespective of the diversity of their social roles and their share in the social production, had the responsibility to create regimes of resilience such that social functions continued to be performed.

While every such leader and their teams deserve praise for their resistance, fight, and rebuilding, this book is meant to account for the efforts of the leaders in legal education and legal profession. We pay tribute to their efforts in their fight against the Pandemic by submitting their ideas and stories of resilience in this volume. While heroically fighting the Pandemic, they re-oriented, re-organized, re-discovered, and re-invented—first themselves, and then the systems they were governing. They experimented with time, innovated approaches, improvised strategies, and imitated best

[1] Philip Allott, "From Eunomia to Eusophia: Planning a Better Future for the Human World", *EJIL: Talk*, *available at* From Eunomia to Eusophia: Planning a better future for the human world—EJIL: Talk! (ejiltalk.org).

[2] Philip Allott, "Making Humanity Greater Again: Self-evolving and Self-perfecting", *EJIL Talk*, *available at* Making Humanity Greater Again: Self-evolving and self-perfecting—EJIL: Talk! (eji ltalk.org).

practices. They explored imaginative possibilities in policies and supportive potentialities in regulations. They optimized resource allocation, reassessed their core-strengths and core-competencies, and drew up stakeholder concerns—all in adherence to their core-values. The narratives we submit in this volume, on many of the above said responses and actions, through the voice of leaders in legal education and legal profession, evince courage, confidence, optimism, and hope.

2 Losing the Normal in Legal Education and Legal Profession

2.1 The Old Normal

Law that is imparted through legal education is disciplinized through an epistemological revolution, a jurisprudential movement that has witnessed the ebb and flow of various schools of legal thought. Law in law school—otherwise known as "law in books"—therefore, is a set and many sub-sets of discourses: Contracts, Torts, Transfer of Property, Antitrust, Intellectual Property, and so on and so forth. By narrating the origins and evolution of law and the social circumstances which led to the acceptance of law, the discourses help produce legitimacy for law. Some other sets of discourses account for the application of law in prior contexts of dispute settlement. More often than not, social morality, cultural particularities, collective self-interest, and ideologies become part of these discourses.

These discourses are in fact quite rich, as they help students understand the society's historical evolution, the present state of affairs, and the future course of social progress. They also help students get a deep sense of the social architecture and the socio-cultural discursivity. But legal education is not all about mastering discourses and the art of making them. Legal education also provides certain qualities to learners, which include objectivity, rationality, inquisitiveness, certain sensitivities, critical mind, dialectical ability, reformist spirit, professionalism, and respect for rule of law.

The law school also provides opportunities to students for extension and outreach. The legal knowledge—the knowledge of social constitution and function—is put into the creation of frameworks for the participation and enablement of the local communities in social production through various community outreach programmes and legal clinics. Through such participation, students develop a sense of empathy for local communities. In many legal systems, such participation is also in fulfilment of constitutional and statutory duties. Clinics and other outreach programmes further help students assimilate, internalize, and uphold the cardinal value of access to justice.

As part of skill-education, law schools provide opportunities for mooting, trial advocacy, client counselling, and mediation and negotiations. These activities help students develop the basic skills of the game, e.g., reasoning, analysis, heuristics, dialogue, and dispute avoidance/settlement. It is nothing less of the skill-basedness of law that was meant by Lewis Carroll, when he sardonically wrote in *Alice's Adventures in Wonderland*,

> In my youth, [...], I took to the law,
> And argued each case with my wife;
> And the muscular strength, which it gave to my jaw,
> Has lasted the rest of my life.

Through competitions testing the oral and written skills of students, law schools highlight the importance of skills in competitively succeeding in the legal profession. This blend of skills and knowledge that law schools impart is correspondingly closer to the Aristotelian virtues of *techne* and *phronesis*.

Considering that professional legal education is also the holistic development of individuals, which includes the development of loyalties, empathies, and sensibilities, law schools create frameworks for students for intercultural and cross-cultural experiences through international collaborations in the form of student and faculty mobility, short-term study programmes, and dual and joint degrees. These programmes also help students appreciate diversity and develop the spirit of inclusiveness.

Law school also makes the transition to the legal profession easier. As they teach the functions of law in society, students also obtain a sense of the "legal" and the possible roles the legal has in social production.[3] This sense enables them to find the "locus" in the profession and thereby their situationality amid the diverse possibilities offered by the profession. Internships and short-term placements help students develop desirable pre-conceptions—as if enablement—before entering the profession, and in choosing the "ideal role" in social production.

Once the transition is complete, the identity of law students—who we liken, although cautiously, with the embattled, beleaguered, weather-beaten sailor triumphantly reaching ashore; rather than the Shakespearean schoolboy with the "shining morning face"—get transformed into a professional identity. A new sense of responsibility and professionalism sets in as they start to see justice through the interests of clients and the causes they represent. Court or law firm becomes their site of belonging and contestation. Employing the knowledge and skills learned from the law school, they start new roles afresh in social production.

That being the idea of law school, legal profession is a natural transition from law school to the various domains of the functions of law. Legal profession is, therefore, a means for the fulfilment of the legal functions of society. It is upon the profession to uphold the values of social justice and guarantee citizens their rights and freedoms, be that their constitutional rights or their rights in performing various trade and commercial activities. Every case before a court of law has the breach of one or other legalized social convention, and every breach is a disruption of the social process, and lawyers and legal professionals are problem-solvers who help in restoring social

---

[3] We have the idea of the "legal" becoming a function from the celebrated article by Prof. Karl Llewellyn. *See* Llewellyn [1].

systems. It is these indefatigable efforts of the lawyers that Justice William O. Douglas referred to as "the tough inexhaustible energies of the practising lawyer".[4]

Further, all state guarantees—be that in the forms of rights or privileges—to its citizens are implemented through the legal profession, if ever and whenever the state fails. Legal profession also has an advisory role in helping individuals and institutions in fulfilling necessary legal formalities, mostly relating to highly specialized contractual and commercial matters. In such cases, the profession assumes a highly institutional character by mobilizing talents and resources under a contractual arrangement like a partnership or corporation. They mostly work with the economistic leitmotif of helping to reduce transaction costs of parties in the many high-profile deals, e.g., by creating simplified procedures, envisaging measures for dispute avoidance, and setting up means for dispute settlement.

2.2 *The Fall of the Normal*

COVID-19 Pandemic fell the above said old normal. The fall had everything therein back to the primordial stage, a forced return to the Eden as the world and its public spaces were shut. Humans were siloed to live unconnected from others with haunting memories of the fallen world. The world moved to the meta-geography of the Internet to perform essential social functions. We know that story, which is our own.

Amid the fall and associated losses, legal education, in particular, met with the loss of its educational essentials—the physical classrooms, live Socratic sessions, and means and avenues for real-time teaching of skills: courts, chambers, and communities (students, clients, and subjects). As in everywhere and with everything else, the instant response to the *loss* was to connect remotely through "virtual socializing". However, succumbing to the diffusion of the Pandemic, law schools soon realized that although initial reactions have helped the systems from falling apart, its sustenance needs larger re-imagination, re-invention, and bold experiments in resilience.

Things were no different in the legal profession which is the professional space, that in a classical sense, is a natural extension of legal education. Many courts, based on the health advisories issued by the governments, suspended proceedings. However, they would soon resume proceedings virtually, prompted by the supreme judicial responsibility to oversee the sustenance of rule of law and to provide continued access to justice. While the sense of social responsibility of the legal profession prevailed over all other concerns, many particular things were reimagined, e.g., the case-listing priorities, mode of filing, nature of hearings in courts and in chambers, and lawyers' attires. Amid these transformations in the legal profession, people all over the world have shown increased faith in the judiciary and other constitutional machineries by way of overcoming the fear and insecurity caused by the Pandemic.

---

[4] Douglas [2, p. 674].

Extraordinary levels of optimism were displayed by the members of legal education and legal profession that extraordinary turn of events can be handled with extraordinary will and determination. Against the odds of time, law schools as well as the bar and the bench stood resolute, and became extraordinarily resilient—many times defying conventionalities, making unpopular decisions, and travelling uncharted roads.

In the cyberspace and through its seamless network, law schools found that the "space" essential for performing their functions can be reclaimed. They realized that discourse-making through the culture of dialogue does not need material spaces; rather, it needs a sense of community and bonding. Although the computer screens can be limiting in the said regard, the digital world which unfolds from it is neither "inverted" nor has Jabberwocks and Jubjub birds dwelling therein. Rather, the same participants inhabit that space as subjects with the same qualities as earlier.

The fall of material spaces also has law schools losing access to communities. The communities, wherein all extension and outreach activities were carried out, were never means for law schools; rather, they were the ends—the ends which have justice meeting social vision. Every law school considered community services through legal aid as a progress towards the vision of access to justice. Whether materially accessible or not, the communities continued to exist, and in a never before manner, they needed legal aid as the COVID-19 pandemic and the resulting loss of health, livelihood, and economic stability deprived them of their self-reliance. Many law schools responded to the situation by connecting with community representatives, NGOs, paralegals, and volunteers positioned within the communities to run clinics under the mentorship and aegis of law schools, while in-house law school clinics continued functioning online. Student training in clinical skills like mooting, negotiations, client counselling, and drafting was carried out through video-recorded interactions, online simulations, and case files.

COVID-19 was a time when law schools connected to each other in an exceptional way. While making certain that students do not lose out on the intercultural experiences—an essential element in legal education—through online student and faculty exchanges, law schools also advanced the possibilities of international collaborations through resource exchange and online mobility. The seamless online-connect helped many institutions in the periphery to benefit from the world-class institutions through joint webinars and guest lectures. Many professional guilds like the International Association of Law Schools (IALS), American Association of Law Schools (AALS), and Law School Global League (LSGL) provided platforms for law schools to get united and share their online experiences for mutual learning and collaboration.

During the Pandemic, the communication channels between legal academia, profession, and industry got strengthened. Such communications in the form of round tables and conclaves helped each domain understand and appreciate others' efforts at resilience. The dialogues have resulted in resilient measures like law firms and offices offering virtual internships (of course, with necessary online protocols); members of the legal profession offering courses on trial advocacy, witness examinations, and judging in lieu of in-court apprenticeship; and law schools helping profession and industry with various studies and reports on e-courts and e-transactions. This collective action through mutual support is a remarkable case of collective resilience.

One of the biggest challenges faced by the legal profession during COVID-19 was apropos of providing access to justice to all, which was due to the loss of physical spaces caused by social distancing norms. Moving online was only a means to minimize the impact that COVID-19 had on the timely delivery of justice; much less was it a viable alternative, especially considering the digital divide in society. The stalling of many social functions due to lockdowns also heightened the need for larger judicial overseeing as social maladies were on the increase. However, despite the many limitations of cyberspaces, courts explored the possibilities of maximizing online services by increasing the legitimacy and scope of Alternative Dispute Resolution (ADR). Judiciaries in many countries shifted their priorities to matters of social and collective importance for achieving the larger good during the Pandemic. Many judicial systems voluntarily subjected their action plans and responses to periodic reviews by departments of disaster management, technology evaluation, and public health to safeguard the system from errors and failures.

Capturing all such responses is not within the scope of this editorial (although it is certainly of this book and has been done by the learned authors in its many pages). However, what is striking about the responses is that although the move online was a quick fix to sustain systems, the *spatial* potential of cyberspace was soon uncovered. It was, as Sherry Turkle referred to as, the discovery of the "second self".[5] Turkle summarizes this long-drawn process of self-discovery,

> In cyberspace, we are learning to live in virtual worlds. We may find ourselves alone as we navigate virtual oceans, unravel virtual mysteries, and engineer virtual skyscrapers. But increasingly, when we step through the looking glass, other people are there as well.[6]

Law schools and legal profession did find the lost communities in the meta-spaces and the cross-cutting multiple realities of the internet. Those and that which were present there were different in themselves, as meaning and identity therein are formed "in terms of multiplicity and flexibility".[7] It is these meanings and identities and the many complexities and heterogeneities which became the possibilities of resilience. Perhaps it is the case that more than the extent of the appropriateness of cyberspace to material space, the move online marked a symbolic discovery of a new world and everyone had the consolation that we will rebuild this new world.

3 The Book

This edited volume is an effort to record the amazing transformations brought about by the leaders in legal education and legal profession. The volume aims to capture

---

[5] Turkle [3, p. 643].

[6] Ibid.

[7] Ibid.

experiences and experiments in the governance of law schools and the legal profession during the Pandemic as case studies; ideas that helped in resilience and which could show the way forward; the psychological, philosophical, and sociological aspects of the transformation; and the spiritual and material sources of motivation of the leadership.

3.1 The Idea of Law School and Legal Education

When COVID-19 had us back to the primeval, humanity fell into a collective vertigo—a senselessness, déjà vu of the fall of modernity, and the rise of postmodern conditions. The decontextualized self was searching for its situationality in alien conditions. Quite naturally, the earliest efforts were to abstract the Pandemic as a temporal phenomenon before even the fallen ideas—of law school and legal education—can be re-abstracted. Giorgio Resta in his chapter entitled, "*Overcoming the Boundaries of Legal Education: How to Make Sense of the Pandemic*" submits such a blueprint, for both re-claiming the lost sense of historical time and re-imagining law school and legal education. He holds that COVID-19, while in itself isolated societies, was an intervening force of change to break a classical "isolation" in which legal education has been functioning. First, the "territorial isolation", an overly localized/spatialized imagination and existence. Second, a "methodological isolation", a separation of law and its environment. The ideal solution for the temporal isolation existed in the approaches of "empire"—the transnational way of the local staying relevant in global conditions—and, "cosmos"—the global looming large in every legal imagination as a universal. Apropos of methodological isolation, what is needed is a well-ordered interdisciplinarity—certainly not a free interplay of disciplines to deny law its ontological purity. Then again, the law should also transcend its classicism of epistemological autonomy to be in perpetual conversation with disciplines in a framework of disciplinary pluralism.

Resta makes the point that while these approaches existed as ideal solutions, if not as options, in legal scholarship, for the problem of isolation, there was never a spatio-temporal condition that prompted the change until COVID-19 struck the world. COVID-19 and the move online have necessarily created a meta-geography without the classical walls and exposing the global to the isolated communities, which is in addition to the many interdisciplinary and multidisciplinary conversations between law and other disciplines which the Pandemic has prompted. Resta has the optimism that the new idea of legal education that has been emerging will have an inherent humanism in it, thanks to the insights from all around.

In a similar vein as Resta, Jorge Cerdio in his chapter, "*Assume and Not Postpone: Effective Education and Also Digital*", explores the possibilities in the newer conditions. He presents the two options which were before the law schools, both of them were formed by the reactions of the academic community to the move online caused by the Pandemic. The first was a resistance to the move online, as there was a predominant myth that the online mode of education is a supplementary means for "Continuing Education" or as means to augment the overall learning experience of students in colleges and universities. This resistance was exacerbated by the conventional practices of professors and the expectations of students and parents. Such academic communities consider the Pandemic as transitory and have a reason for waiting for the "old normal" to return. The second option before the law schools was to accept the change as inevitable and that it has given the opportunity to reorganize academic policies and practices and develop "effective education models for law schools" which are digital. Emphasizing the need to make stronger and resilient academic communities, Cerdio develops the "digital model" of education for best outcomes. The model will be based on the values of transparency, fairness, and participation.

Resta and Cerdio jointly lay the foundation for the book to unfold. The tone they set is of optimism, confidence, determination, and courage. The project of reform they propose is based on a thorough understanding of the historical conditions in which legal education existed. Both of them, in their own respective ways, provide a juxtaposition of legal education models prior to and during COVID-19. Their vision for the present and future gets profoundly united—Cerdio's digital model will help transcend the isolation Resta has problematized, as much as Cerdio's values-based approach to the model matches squarely with Resta's hope for a humanist model of legal education.

As online becomes the new site (even the time–space) of legal education, the phenomenology of cyberspace becomes significant. What does it mean to get educated online? What outcomes can online education obtain? Judith McNamara, Rachel Hews and Zoe Nay in their chapter, "*Student Engagement, Online Learning and COVID-19: A Law School Perspective*" deal with the said theme and questions. Upon situating student sensibilities in the postmodern global context, McNamara, Hews, and Nay point out that despite the potential of technology in advancing legal education, there was less motivation among law schools to go for technology, primarily due to the misplaced focus on the worst outcomes of technology like "'massification' of legal education and 'death by PowerPoint'". There were, however, visible signs of a transformation before the Pandemic prompted a rapid shift to online learning.

To understand the shift and the student engagement online, the authors submit the findings of a study conducted among students of law at the Queensland University of Technology. Some of the benefits of online engagement, as identified by the participants of the survey, include flexibility and the work–life balance which comes with it, effective workload management due to asynchronous times, and authenticity of online information. The negative side of online learning includes the absence of the sense of presence as in synchronous learning, absence of real-time interaction and feedback, and the killjoy of online protocols and policies. McNamara, Hews, and Nay emphasize that there are, however, certain essential elements of online life, which include the ability to use the skills necessary to perform online. Once the teaching community recognizes these potentials and adequately trains teachers, the sense of loss that students feel in online classes will be addressed.

The approach of McNamara, Hews, and Nay to know the online world in its totality is akin to the reclamation of spaces of production through cyberspace that we discussed earlier in this chapter. Once the space and its potential are known in their totality, the space gets an alternative experience of time. This renewed sense of time in cyberspace can transform the teacher–student engagement to obtain better learning outcomes. The authors' study and observations are quite motivating, especially their underlying faith in technology as a means for human excellence.

After the study-based chapter by McNamara, Hews, and Nay, the book has an empirical research. In the chapter entitled, "*Legal Education and Legal Profession During and Beyond COVID-19: Studying Law During the COVID-19 Pandemic*", Suzanne Rab submits the report of an empirical study on the "law students' perceptions, expectations and experiences of studying in the time of COVID-19". The study aims to contribute, in the words of Rab, "to the existing and emerging global knowledge about the behavioural and psychological aspects of law students' functioning in a crisis and what measures can be taken to support students in this situation". The timeline of the study is 1 year since March 2020 which gave all the subjects—at various levels of legal education—who participated in the study adequate experiences of the various experiments carried out during the first year of the Pandemic. The study tested all aspects of student engagement in legal education ranging from classroom experience to careers and placements.

The study reports major concerns surrounding the well-being of students—on the one hand, the spreading malady causing gloom and despair in society, and on the other hand, the anxiety about the loss of regular studies and opportunities. However, the latter were primarily due to an unfair comparison of the experiences during the Pandemic with experiences earlier. The decision to defer and wait for the Pandemic to abate, the same approach Cerdio has presented as seen among some institutions, was seen as optimal by a few students. The move online was seen as an alternative, ersatz though, despite their acknowledgement of many of the highs of online education. One concern that particularly eclipsed the highs of online education is whether the Pandemic has altered industry expectations or not, and if not, what level of acceptance and appreciation of online education can students expect from the industry. The study reveals that student perception of the Pandemic is largely shaped by their "psychological reactions, their emotions and fears".

Rab's concluding observation is that the "views expressed by students can be explained overall by a concept of professional identity whose roots can be grounded in humanism, existentialism and phenomenology". It is this element of her study which makes it an outstanding empirical verification of the correctness of law schools' response to the Pandemic, expressed earlier in this chapter as a return to the fundamental ideas on legal education. The larger re-imagination, and the rebuilding thereof, should also thus include the idea of "student" and their role in legal education such that they can be situated as essential constituents of the idea of law school and legal education. The findings of the study and inputs thereof are excellent resources for building frameworks of resilience.

3.2 Experiences from Countries

The second part of the book captures the experiences and experiments from various parts of the world. We divide these accounts into experiences generally and on particular areas of legal education, e.g., law school accreditation, international and industry collaborations, legal aid clinics, and student well-being.

In the chapter, "*A Case of Law Teaching in Brazil During the COVID-19 Pandemic: The Response of FGV Law SP to the Pandemic*", Oscar Vilhena and Marina Feferbaum report the steps taken by the São Paulo Law School (FGV Law SP) to make the transition to online education smooth. What enabled such a transition, however, is the dynamism of the School in keeping itself prepared for renewal and transformation in the highly dynamic global landscape. Both maximization of technological possibilities and interdisciplinarity were part of the School's plan. Hence, the Pandemic did not catch the School by surprise.

Midway through the Pandemic, FGV Law SP conducted a survey among students and based on its outcomes, the School augmented its online learning system so as to broaden the learning experience. What is noteworthy about the approach of FGV Law SP is that rather than seeing students as a collective, it abstracted students as an individual-whole such that there is a holistic approach to the well-being of students, as Vilhena and Feferbaum note, it is necessary to "value the student as an individual, working on emotional aspects of confining or social distancing, so as to minimize harms to mental health, which can be as incapacitating for learning as the use of inadequate teaching methodologies for remote teaching." The success that FGV Law SP has achieved owes primarily to its thought, preparedness, positive action, and most importantly, its humanitarian approach.

In the chapter, "*Legal Education During and After COVID-19*", Achilles C. Emilianides presents the experiences of Cyprus in dealing with the challenges posed by COVID-19. Cyprus is an interesting case in point, as Emilianides points out, "due to its experiment of mixing legal traditions" in legal education. When the Pandemic struck, as every other law school, Cypriote law schools too transitioned to online education. This was somewhat challenging given the lesser emphasis online education had on the Cypriote education system. Yet, timely and proper regulatory guidance and quality assurance standards helped law schools make the transition successfully. The university and student federations like the Cyprus Rectors' Conference and the Pancyprian Federation of Student Unions provided the necessary inputs to create a common framework for all universities.

What differentiates the response of Cyprus from other regions is the outstanding promptness of regulatory bodies. Their timely response to the crisis and periodic reviews of action taken on matters ranging from attendance to pedagogy, from evaluations and assessments to examinations, helped law schools overcome the unfamiliarity with online education. Emilianides observes that if the collective action and consultative process seen in Cyprus by state agencies, regulatory bodies, and universities can be repeated in the post-Pandemic world, Cyprus would be advancing to the highest excellence in legal education.

Yubaraj Sangroula provides the South Asian experiences through a representative case study of Nepal in the chapter, "*Legal Education and Legal Profession in a Post-COVID-19 World: South Asian Context with Specific Emphasis on Nepal*". Nepal is an excellent case in point to understand the impact of COVID-19 on a country the economic aspirations of which are closely connected to higher education. A state like Nepal, as many other South Asian states, considers higher education as a means for achieving economic prosperity and well-being.

One of the major challenges faced by law schools in Nepal was to provide digital access to students, especially to those belonging to the socio-economic margins. Despite the determination and vision of many educational leaders to build online alternatives to regular classes, they faced the problem of severe infrastructural and resource deficits, which thwarted prompt action. The absence of regulatory guidance made law schools grope in the dark.

Sangroula considers the extraordinary challenges Nepal faced in implementing the alternatives as part of a larger systemic problem in South Asia, problems that go deeper into the social, economic, and political conditions in the region. He critiques a "detachment" prevalent in the legal system in the region from social and economic contexts and realities, an approach he refers to as "legalist-centralist" approach (a colonial leftover), which renders law isolated and alienated from the socio-economic contexts. Legal systems perpetuate this alienation and forge a forgetfulness of the mission of social justice from legal consciousness. Law schools have also fallen into this framework of perpetuation. Failure of law schools in the region to effectively respond to COVID-19 has to be hence approached diagnostically and pathologically. What makes Sangroula's observations persuasive is that he makes them after many rigorous historical analyses.

In all his honesty and candidness, Sangroula refuses to tell us a success story, as there is none so profound. Rather, he uses the response to COVID-19 by the law schools all over the South Asian region as a reason to approach legal education critically, although he is very conscious of the obvious exceptions. As much as systemic problems defeated an effective transition to online alternatives, law schools too contributed to that failure by not being prepared—they had neither the sense of the local nor the global. All they had was a false consciousness of the legalist-centralist approach and a parochialism which accompanied the said approach. The story of inaction and failure told by Sangroula has enough food for thought for any reimagination and reinvention of the new normal.

Ibibia Lucky Worika captures the Nigerian scenario in his chapter, "*Legal Education and Legal Profession During and After COVID-19 in Nigeria*". The Pandemic produced similar patterns of events in Nigeria as in other parts of the world—a nationwide lockdown, closure of educational institutions, the temporary suspension of functions, and then the move online wherever possible. However, the need for increased reliance on technology was a test, a test of resilience in which law schools with better financial resources, most of them in the private sector, emerged triumphantly. This exposed certain stark inequities in the system of legal education in Nigeria which, until then, remained dormant.

Loss of physical spaces badly impacted the legal profession as well, as client–lawyer interactions, which are cardinal to the delivery of legal services, got affected. Soon, law firms and law offices moved online based on their affordability. Judicial proceedings also were conducted online, although many judicial and legal functions remained unfulfilled either due to unfeasibility or due to lack of online efficiency. Even the Nigerian courts had to obtain a constitutional assent to hold court proceedings online. Whatsoever, the Pandemic revealed the lag between the legal profession and the rapid advancement of technology.

Considering the lack of technological readiness, Nigerian law schools have been preparing for the physical reopening of campuses by putting in place systems and protocols for making campuses safe from the spread of COVID-19. Many federations and associations— e.g., the Academic Staff Union of Universities and the National Association of Nigerian Students—and university leaderships and public and private corporations have joined hands to keep campuses clean and safe. This Public–Private Partnership (PPP) model for reclaiming the lost physical spaces is quite unique.

As online education remains a privilege due to the socio-economic conditions in Nigeria, the country has found the alternative in safe campuses. The new normal therein is regulated and controlled campuses that place emphasis on hygiene and public health such that the traditional mode of education can be continued therein. However, Worika has the optimism that the lessons that the Pandemic has taught in the form of the need for certain "essentials" will prompt the country to invest more resources in enhancing the technological potential in legal education and legal profession.

The chapters by Worika and Sangroula present the stark realities in the less privileged parts of the world, and the socio-economic peripheries. The alternative imaginations prevalent in many parts of the world sound like a luxury for many institutions and countries in South Asia and Africa. The debate therein is not about the imperfections of online education, but about how to make online education possible and without major digital divides. However, Worika and Sangroula support re-imagination and re-invention, but they have a caution that historical mistakes should not be repeated. As we rebuild, beware, as Lucille Clifton reminds in "*I am Accused on Tending to the Past*"

> [T]he past was waiting for me
> when I came,
> a monstrous unnamed baby
> and I with my mother's itch
> took it to breast
> and named it
> History

They consider the Pandemic as an opportunity to annihilate imposed histories—the oppression of monsters—and create one's own history in the self-image of society's lived experience.

Then we get to hear yet another story from Africa, particularly from South Africa, in the Chapter, "*Teaching Law in the Time of COVID-19: Experiences from the University of KwaZulu-Natal, South Africa*" by Managay Reddi. The University of KwaZulu-Natal (UKZN), after a phase of effective preparation, made the transition to online legal education. The preparation was also an enabling one, as the more the understanding of the online ecosystem, the better will be the utilization of online possibilities. The framework of the enabling set up by UKZN, included *inter alia* capacity building, continued training and grievance redressal, and geo-mapping and surveys for assessing "staff and students' ICT and skills". The "distribution strategy" within the framework based on mapping and surveys helped UKZN address the problem of the digital divide and deficit, which would become a model for the country.

There was a complete reimagination of teaching and pedagogy, and evaluations and assessments. The UKZN was also able to obtain approvals for the revised approaches. The approach taken by the Council on Higher Education, the accreditation body in South Africa, for granting approvals for the alternative plan was a progressive step in regulatory reforms. Finally, when the school did make the transition to online education, the primary effort was to guarantee that the resilient approach does not diminish the standards of education, lower the integrity of assessments, and compromise the health and well-being of the university community. As part of striking the work–life balance in online spaces, UKZN has restricted online engagements of its personnel to office hours such that there is a sense of "break" so as to overcome screen fatigue and get rejuvenated for the next day at work. For students, the university provided counselling services and individualized support on even matters beyond academic affairs.

Reddi senses that the remarkable reimagination during the Pandemic will not wane—not simply due to the possible memories of experiences, but due to the degree of impact of those imaginations. Although steps taken during the Pandemic were in the spirit of resilience, they advanced the idea of a better law school. It prompted law schools to shed the many inhibitions they had about the use of technology and co-opt it as an element of excellence.

All the six chapters in this part of the book are inspiring—they not only make us feel good about the remarkable achievements of our counterparts, but also make us think deeply and critically. There is certainly a pattern in the way law schools responded to the Pandemic, as all of them had common challenges. Everyone holistically approached the issue, deeming the problem as a historical problem—a fall faced by humanity. The Pandemic was also a test of our consciousness, which has revealed many of our false convictions and imperfections. Either way, it informed us of our plight, indicted us of our faults, and instructed us of our potential.

3.3 Experiments in Resilience

The third part of the book is "Experiments in Resilience". Herein, we have some of the responses by law schools on a particular area of function or a particular activity of law schools. These responses help us understand the many experiments, innovations, improvisations, and strategies of law schools made as part of the larger transformations discussed in the previous section.

Vesna Crnić-Grotić in the chapter entitled, "*Legal Education and Legal Profession During and After COVID-9: The Shifting Idea of Law School—Systems and Processes*" discusses how the University of Rijeka sustained an ambitious legal aid clinic during the Pandemic. The legal aid clinic, established with the support of the European Social Fund, was threatened due to the fall of physical space and loss of communities caused by the lockdown and social distancing. Collective participation by students was one of the highlights of the clinic, which was also threatened due to the move online. The clinic, as many other clinics, was meant to evoke a sense of responsibility among students towards communities and societies. It was also a means for improving students' practical skills including interpersonal skills, client counselling, mediation, and dispute settlement.

The School responded to the situation by connecting to the communities through NGOs which already had a physical presence in the communities. Student volunteers were also posted in communities. The rest of the members of the clinic including faculty members, students, lawyers, and judges provided all essential inputs for functioning to the volunteers through video conferencing and online lectures. The system of "Clinical Hubs" which provided simulations of clinics and the case-based classes under the "Incubator Programme" became excellent alternatives to on-site training.

What made the University of Rijeka to succeed in sustaining the legal aid clinic was its outcome-orientedness. Instead of letting the clinics—which required physical spaces and strong physical presence—to fall, the University made use of the online alternatives. Realizing the inevitability of online life, it searched for possibilities in the online spaces, designing innovative schemes and projects and thereby obtaining the same outcomes as would have been obtained in physical spaces. Such an approach becomes possible only when legal aid is understood in its totality—as a service/aid, as a mentality, and as a learning in clinical legal education—and the University of Rijeka deserves appreciation for that understanding and internalization.

Another particular function of law school, which has been threatened due to physical barriers—the closure of national borders—is student mobility through internationalization of universities. The formula for the sustenance of this function is discussed by Sandhya Drew in her chapter, "*New Landscapes on Student Exchange*". Drew initially articulates the classical model of student mobility, which is the "parallel physical moves of students between universities" which is primarily meant to provide students with intercultural spatio-temporal experience, inter-institutional classroom experience, and multiple contexts of knowledge. However, this experience comes with a price—for travel, maintenance, and tuition fee—and limits the experience based on affordability. As the Pandemic has foiled this model of mobility, Drew proposes a viable alternative model.

Quite interestingly, in proposing the alternative, Drew's approach is coincidentally similar to how the University of Rijeka approached clinical legal education—that is, viewing a function in its totality rather than on technicality. Delving deeper into the concept of university, drawing on historical wisdom, situating university in the spatio-temporality of globalization, and capturing the dynamics of the Pandemic conditions, Drew submits that the true function of internationalization is to connect universities intellectually for the exchange of ideas and to collectively stand for global causes. The Pandemic has given us that opportunity and broken the classical image that internalization is the movement of students across the borders. In the conversation between institutions—the exchange of ideas—students certainly play a pivotal role. Apart from the alternative imaginations in her chapter, Drew provides many illustrations and successfully tested frameworks of alternative models of internationalization.

We then get to read an altogether new, and much lesser explored, area which is that of the accreditation standards for law schools during the Pandemic. In the chapter, "*Law School Accreditation During COVID-19: Transparency, Agility and Trust and the Australian Experience*", Pip Nicholson presents the Australian experience in accreditation and how adherence to certain values helped make the process of accreditation effective during the Pandemic.

Accreditation, according to Nicholson, is the "process by which tertiary law courses are reviewed and deemed suitable to satisfy [certain] 'specified academic qualification' criterion". Accreditation is done mainly based on the nature of the course for which accreditation is sought, duration of the course, learning outcomes of the course, course contents, eligibility to teach the course, and mode of assessments. The applicant institution should demonstrate that it satisfies all these criteria in order to get accredited. However, during COVID-19, fulfilment of many of these criteria became difficult especially when assessed against the standards of accreditation set by accrediting bodies. In the chapter, Nicholson particularly tells the story of how Melbourne Law School continued to satisfy the accreditation criteria through various reimagination and re-adaptations.

What made the accreditation process possible and successful during the Pandemic, according to Nicholson, is the adherence of the Law School and the accrediting bodies to the three core values of transparency, agility, and trust. *Transparency* in reporting by law schools helped avoid site visits by the accrediting body during lockdowns. *Agility* in the process and procedures of accrediting agencies helped law schools manage the shifting global social and public health conditions and actor and stakeholder expectations. And, trust between law schools and regulatory bodies helped them empathize with each other's respective roles and make the accreditation process easier.

The case presented by Nicholson is a case in point for the reformist spirit of regulatory bodies and law schools and their efforts to reinvent their mutual relationship. It helps us dispel the classical impression of regulatory bodies being slow and sluggish and excessively controlling. However, the case of accrediting bodies in Victoria and

New South Wales illustrates the shifting sensibilities of regulatory bodies towards the law schools and the latter's efforts in resilience.

What is interesting about the law schools' particular functions—be that student mobility or legal aid clinics or getting accredited—during the Pandemic is that they are viewed by all the authors in a holistic perspective, as parts of a larger whole. No one has considered or suggested heuristic techniques or makeshift arrangements by way of a response to the Pandemic. They have all been loyal to the project of reinvention. Or perhaps it is that the Pandemic itself is a painful revelation of the many human fallacies glorified in our systems and processes. As the Pandemic relegated us to Eden, we started to think full and think big, and re-inventing ourselves in the image of truth.

3.4 The Impact of the Pandemic on Legal Profession

In Part IV of the book, we shift our focus to the legal profession and its response to COVID-19. The Part has two chapters dealing with the judicial response to the Pandemic, the legal profession's experiments with technology, and concerns surrounding accreditation standards for legal practice. The three chapters are representative of the progressive and critical thinking in the legal profession. In the chapter entitled, "*COVID-19 and Courts: How 'Remote' Should the Future Be?*", Sabrina Shizue McKenna discusses the relevance of online court proceedings in a post-Pandemic world. Like every other institution in the world, courts in the United States too went partly online during the Pandemic. The primary motivation for such a move was to continue to uphold the cardinal value of access to justice and to let rule of law prevail even in the worst of conditions.

In the same vein, the courts in the State of Hawaii, which is the case in point for the chapter, after a brief pause during the earlier days of the Pandemic, resumed oral hearings through video conferencing. In the interest of access to justice for all, even for those who do not have digital access, the judiciary established "kiosk in the Supreme Court Law Library, as well as by creating a guide to online access and a map of free Wi-Fi hotspots". However, cases, which have evidentiary requirements in the form of physical testimony and deposition and constitutionally guaranteed confrontational rights, were postponed until physical hearings could be held.

However, the crux of the chapter is the author's reflections on the future of virtual remote proceedings. As expedient and beneficial as they may be, as they have been proven to be during the Pandemic, can virtual remote proceedings become a regular, if not alternative, mode of judicial proceedings? Evaluating multiple considerations, McKenna observes that while constitutional breaches remain on one side, remote hearings at the cost of due process can detrimentally affect the outcomes of criminal cases. There is a sense of credibility associated with the "active presence" of witnesses in the court, what McKenna refers to as "perceptions of credibility", which can never be reproduced in virtual hearings due to the potential for digital distortions and possibilities of digital disruptions. The perceptions of credibility can be particularly significant in matters requiring "demeanor evaluations" by judges.

Although, according to McKenna, there is no strong case for remote hearings to become "the normal" in judicial proceedings, there are certain areas of function where remote hearings are viable, e.g., appellate oral arguments, cases involving minor infractions like road traffic violations, and "pre-trial or post-trial status conferences or hearings involving attorneys arguing legal or procedural issues only". On balance, the author holds that in determining what type of proceedings can qualify for remote hearing and what cannot, consideration should be on the socio-legal value of access to justice.

After this very interesting discussion, which is motivated by judicial values and ethics and the commitment to access to justice, we get to hear the story from India in the chapter, "*The New Normal in Legal Profession: Embracing Technology*" by Shreeyash U. Lalit and Raveena Lalit. This narrative becomes important especially given a deep-rooted traditionalism in Indian juridical practices which is either a colonial thing or an obsession with the tangible—Lalit and Lalit refer to this traditionalism as a "paper-heavy" culture. However, there has been a tiny heartbeat of change since globalization in the form of increased digitalization of documents. In the recent past, video conferences and virtual hearings were also held under special circumstances, although more as a matter of judicial discretion and less as an established procedure.

Lalit and Lalit provide us with detailed and impressive accounts of the various measures taken by the Supreme Court of India for the continuance of its own proceedings and proceedings of other courts in the country during the Pandemic, which include measures like e-filings, virtual hearings, and live streaming. They also suggest possible ways and means for rectifying the imperfections of the measures taken and for streamlining the digital practices relied on during the Pandemic. But what is most noteworthy in the chapter is the legal and ethical questions surrounding some of the digital practices, e.g., the legality and ethicality of live streaming of judicial proceedings. The authors address this question by providing the thoughts of the Supreme Court of India on this matter through the Supreme Court's own jurisprudence, through the observations of the e-committee of the Supreme Court, and through a brief comparative review of practices in select other countries. These inputs are extremely valuable in deciding the extent of digitalization of courts in a post-Pandemic world.

It is obvious from the accounts of Lalit and Lalit that, in India, the Pandemic has given the judiciary an opportunity to experiment with its technological competency. In the past, even when holding on to a juridical system that is deeply traditional, the Supreme Court has expressed its technological modernism through its judgements, while being conscious of the potential misuse of technology. This sense of balance was quite apparent in the response of the Indian judiciary to the Pandemic. In fact, we sense a fine correlation between McKenna's reservations about a complete technological take-over of judicial proceedings to that of the balanced approach of the Supreme Court of India apropos of the use of technology by the judiciary as finely captured by Lalit and Lalit.

3.5 The Way Forward

The Pandemic has taught us many things. They have become inputs and imaginations for designing the future of legal education and legal profession. Hence, the last part of this book captures some of the finest ideas of re-imagination and re-building. The chapter by Soledad Atienza and Sonsoles Arias, entitled "*A Blueprint on Global Legal Education: The European Perspective*" contains thoughts of a law school federation, the Law School Global League (LSGL). The eruption of the Pandemic coincided with the release of a Report by LSGL—"A Blueprint on Global Legal Education"—which aimed to ascertain the standards of legal education all over the world and take steps to revitalize legal education. The Report, which was prepared region-wise under the coordination of the law schools from the regions, did not in fact have COVID-19 as a major element in it, although certain COVID-19 related perspectives were added to the Report at a later stage. However, the Report and the measures suggested therein have the scope to re-organize legal education during challenging times like the Pandemic and even beyond.

Atienza and Arias explain that scope from the perspective of Europe, one of the regions studied in the Report. The Report identifies limited use of technology by law schools which is primarily due to the heavy investments that law schools are required to make to digitalize legal education. However, many of the participants and the Report itself identified the potential of technology to transform the landscape of legal education. As if a self-fulling prophesy, the recommendations in the Report for law schools to maximize technology use through "official channels of collaboration with governmental agencies, private companies, and legal organisations", became extremely relevant during the Pandemic.

Other recommendations in the Report for the need to upskill students, reduce the gap between legal education and legal profession, and create an ecosystem of happiness and well-being of the law school community, started to get implemented during COVID-19. The authors, drawing on the Report, urge to continue focusing on technology, skill, internationalization, and well-being for re-organizing legal education beyond the Pandemic and thereby facilitating a collective march towards excellence. Atienza and Arias consider the Pandemic as a revelation—a unique moment in time—when an old normal, from which legal education ought to have risen—has fallen, giving way to a new normal. The Report of the LSGL provides an appropriate orientation to rebuild the new normal in legal education.

Next in the order of futuristic visions and framework is the chapter by Martin Škop, entitled "*Potential Changes in Law School Teaching in Central Europe After the Pandemic*". In a characteristic postmodern-*esque* analysis, Škop reverts to the ontology of law and extracts the essential elements of law's socio-cultural functions. Legal education is such a function of law in the social and cultural self-becoming of society. That, according to Škop, however, is the classical impression that has been altered by the Pandemic—the Pandemic's social impact has transformed the foundations of legal education, and has created newer conditions and scenarios.

They are legalization (of remote learning), democratization (trans-spatial accessibility), modernization (digitalization), socialization (limited actual presence), and discipline (social restrictions). Škop considers the first three as positive scenarios and the remaining two as negative scenarios in legal education.

Considering these five scenarios as the future context in which legal education has to be provided, Škop suggests that alternative methods and approaches should be developed. He recommends fiction as such an alternative. Apart from its ability to enhance many skills associated with law, e.g., imagination, correlation, text-making, and storytelling, fiction can also help reclaim the social time and space infested by a virus thanks to fiction's power of creating alternative realities. These mind realities later become the idea for the material reinvention of society. This message by Škop is quite powerful—it has the foundations of Platonic idealism and the spirit of reconstruction in Lévi-Strauss. The spirit and essence of that vision are succinctly verbalized by Allott

> Imagination generates connections within the contents of our minds, making available to us a series of connections from among the infinity of possible connections ... Thus imagination is the mind in its creative aspect, creating itself from itself, combining and constructing and co-ordinating, providing the contents of the process of consciousness.[8]

The last chapter in this part, which is the last chapter of this book, by Suzanne Rab is very special, as it not only provides a vision for the future, but also provides for a confluence in the vision of legal education and legal profession through collective and concerted efforts at rebuilding. Rab appropriately titles the chapter, "*Legal Education and Legal Profession During and Beyond COVID-19: Building Bonds between Academia and Practice*".

Rab makes certain that she informs the reader what "voice" she is, through which the joint vision for legal education and legal profession is submitted. Her identity of being a law professor and a barrister and mediator, situated in the intersections of both legal academia and legal profession, has given her enabling perspectives on both the academia and the profession to formulate a joint vision. The author focuses on a certain "connectedness" that has started to appear of late—academia and industry, industry and profession, academia and profession. This connectedness stems from a desire to speak to each other and understand everyone's experiences in resilience, and particularly in the case of legal academia and legal profession, the desire to connect has been quite intense, as they complement each other in social production.

The chapter has many empirical and analytical information on the state of affairs in legal education and legal profession. The quality of information is quite rich. The scope of the information is quite comprehensive. The author also highlights the complementarity in the responses of legal academia and legal profession to the Pandemic.

As legal education and legal profession stand today, it is essential that the rebuilding is collective and mutual with a greater understanding of each other's expectations. In legal education, Continuing Legal Education and Blended Learning, which

---

[8] Allott [4, p. 7].

do not support spatial confinement, help legal education to become a public good accessible to students and professionals in their early careers. Assessment and evaluation of students could be more personalized and customized, rather than a one-size-fits-all approach. Finally, legal education should adopt a humanist approach by putting in place necessary checks and balances—in the form of policies, laws, and regulations—against the oppression of technology and power. It is certain that a humanist legal education will have its positive impact on the legal profession.

Rab concludes with optimism and assurance that the Pandemic was a test of time for humanity on how its members relate to each other in "academic, business and personal environment". The change, which is happening, was destined to happen. We have the opportunity to turn that change for the better.

4 Conclusion

We wonder whether COVID-19 is the only ordeal for us in the nearest history. Perhaps, one may say that history recurred exactly a hundred years after the onslaught of the Spanish Flu. But barring pandemics and pestilences and many other maladies which produced destruction and desolation for humanity, was there a moment in postmodernity when challenges were not part of our lives? We had the fall of modernity, which trigged a barrage of "unknown" phenomena—the annihilation of space by time (globalization) and a new mode of production (capital mobility), the millennium bug (Y2K), terror attacks, climate change, Global Financial Crisis, political parochialism and virulent nationalism, reverse globalization, and more recently, the AI revolution and the threatening human irrelevance. Weren't we dwelling in "chaosmos", as Deleuze and Guattari refer to the loss of the totality of harmony, evolving through the uncanny fecundity of crises? If that is in fact the case, we fought the Pandemic due to the inbuilt resilient capacity in us. When it is combined with our resolve and collective willing and acting, we have our destiny getting transformed, and the world has us individually and collectively shaping our own reality.

In this book, we have captured the tale of a coming-to-consciousness and the reality-making. We, the editors of this book, consider ourselves fortunate and honoured to have become the accounters of that awakening by the legal community—yet another renaissance in the eternal recurrence of time. We submit this volume to the readers, in all praise for all COVID warriors, reciting Tennyson,

> When can their glory fade?
> O the wild charge they made!
> All the world wondered.
> Honor the charge they made!

References

1. Llewellyn, K.N.: The normative, the legal, and the law-jobs: the problem of juristic method. Yale Law J. **49**(8), 1355–1400 (1940)
2. Douglas, W.O.: Law in eruption: a concept of lawyers' duty in a time of change. Am. Bar Assoc. J. **34**(8), 674–676 (1948)
3. Turkle, S.: Cyberspace and identity. Contemp. Sociol. **28**(6), 643–648 (1999)
4. Allott, P.: Eunomia: New Order for a New World. Oxford University Press, Oxford (1990)

The Idea of Law School and Legal Education

Overcoming the Boundaries of Legal Education: How to Make Sense of the Pandemic

Giorgio Resta

Abstract The COVID-19 pandemic has confronted most Universities, and in particular Universities in Continental Europe, with the necessity to critically revise some of the most traditional aspects of legal education. This paper argues that we strongly need to overcome two forms of "isolation" that characterized the orthodox model of legal education: (a) territorial isolation, deriving from the idea that the law that has to be taught and learnt is primarily the law of the territory; (b) methodological isolation, represented by the idea of a necessary cleavage between law and its environment. The pandemic experience, among other factors, has put such elements under strain, insofar as it abolished the physical borders through the massive recourse to digital technologies (platforms for legal education and open access) and the methodological ones as a result of the increasing resort to the law as an instrument of social governance in a time of emergency. The pandemic may be a trigger for a more humanist form of legal education, one that locates the law—to recall a famous essay by Justice Kasirer—within the dimension of the "cosmos", rather than that of the "empire".

1 Introduction

The COVID-19 pandemic has challenged conventional wisdom on various important issues and will certainly have long-lasting consequences on various aspects of social life. Legal education is not an exception. It has been strongly affected by a year-long isolation period, distance research and teaching, and emergency-based adjustments to the curriculum. What have we learnt from this experience? Taking a European viewpoint, I will argue in this paper that the pandemic has accelerated the pace of an already ongoing process of critical rethinking of the epistemological bases of the legal science, with important consequences on the design of the curriculum and teaching methodologies. In particular, the pandemic has prompted us to overcome two main pillars of the traditional (and self-imposed) isolation of legal science: the idea of jurisdictional boundaries as the natural working space for the jurist and the

G. Resta (✉)
Department of Law, University of Roma Tre, Rome, Italy
e-mail: giorgio.resta@uniroma3.it

C. Raj Kumar and S. G. Sreejith (eds.), *Legal Education and Legal Profession During and After COVID-19*, https://doi.org/10.1007/978-981-19-2568-9_2

idea of disciplinary boundaries as the proper methodological framework for legal teaching and learning.

The transition to various forms of remote teaching and the use of digital platforms has considerably enlarged the "public" of legal training, making it possible to connect teachers with students located in various parts of the globe (I had this experience in my courses, attended by international students, as soon as the pandemic broke out) and with other colleagues physically located in other countries (the global conference on legal education organized by the Jindal Global Law School is a clear example on the point).

Similarly, the socio-economic upheaval triggered by the COVID-19 emergency has brought to the fore the need to interact more systematically and carefully with extra-juridical disciplines, such as medicine, epidemiology, psychology, and sociology.

These are not ephemeral changes, but evolutions that have already been underway for many years and can be traced back to a well scrutinized series of factors such as: (a) the crisis of the state monopoly on legal sources and the increased importance of supranational and transnational law, as well as non-state sources [14]; (b) the loss of centrality of statutory law-making to the benefit primarily (but not only) of judge-made law; (c) the disappearance of the traditional link between law and national language: legal documents are increasingly multilingual, binding judicial decisions are frequently issued in languages different from the municipal one (one might only think at the case-law of the European Court of Human Rights) [4]; (d) the impact of information and communication technologies on many social phenomena regulated by law, as well as on the methods of teaching, transmission and application of legal knowledge; (e) the increased international competition among universities, which significantly changes the potential pool of users of legal training services; (f) the growing importance of the phenomenon of "juridification" of social processes, which makes it more urgent a stable communication between law and neighbouring disciplines.

The pandemic has only accelerated, or at least brought to the fore such transformations. It is, therefore, time to reflect more closely on what it exactly means and implies—to overcome the boundaries of law.

2 Challenging the "Isolation" of Legal Science

Among other forms of conventional wisdom, the pandemic has seriously challenged the traditional paradigm of "isolation" of legal science, which for many has been a boast and for others a limitation of the modern positivistic conception of law. Hermann Isay, for instance, spoke expressly of the "Isolierung" of German legal culture in the aftermath of the defeat in the First World War [9], with an acute analysis, which was later resumed and further developed by one of the founding fathers of modern comparative legal science, Ernst Rabel [16]. The *Isolierung* to which reference was made at the time was the other side of Jhering's *Begriffshimmel*:

extreme technicality as an end in itself, the self-referentiality of a science devoted to working on a system that axiomatically defined itself as closed, as well as the ill-concealed sense of superiority of German legal science over other legal cultures.

The isolation that today we need to overcome is the one based on two of the fundamental pillars of the positivist paradigm. The first pillar is constituted by the link between law and territory, and therefore by the conception of the norm as an artifact of the nation-state [14]. Hence the corollary that the study and teaching of law should primarily focus on the rules positively in force in a given territory, and therefore mainly on national law. The second pillar is represented by the idea that the task of legal science is to develop a "neutral knowledge of existing law without confusion with the desired law" [19]. Hence, the acceptance of a deliberate epistemological closure, which has traditionally prevented both the study and the teaching of law from deep "contaminations" with other forms of knowledge, either belonging to humanities or to social sciences.

It is not surprising, therefore, that many critical proposals and reform processes underway at a global level are aimed at achieving one of the following purposes: the "internationalization" of legal education [17, 10], and the accentuation of its "interdisciplinary" dimension [21, 20]. What is less clear is what such formulas actually mean and what they practically entail.

Therefore, it is worth asking: which internationalization, and for which interests? Which interdisciplinarity and under what conditions?

3 Overcoming Territorial Boundaries

The fundamental terms of the problem of the internationalization of legal studies have been masterfully clarified way a few years ago by Justice (and former Dean of McGill Law School) Nicholas Kasirer, in an essay written in the wake of the introduction of the new "transsystemic" program at McGill [11]. Kasirer contrasted two main models of internationalization of legal education: one inspired by the logic of the "empire" of law; the other inspired by the idea of law as a "cosmos".

3.1 The Logic of the "Empire"

The first model looks at the problem of internationalization, basically, as a problem of control and management of a growing mass of legal information, directly resulting from the proliferation of globally relevant regulatory nodes. If domestic law tends to be increasingly integrated, enriched, and often replaced by supranational sources, if the globalization process increases the importance of transnational law in all its dimensions, if therefore the jurist is entangled in a network of rules coming from different (and often boundless) territories and from sources that are no longer originating from the nation-state, then the course of study and teaching must be carefully modified in order to adapt it to the changes that have taken place on the deeper level of the structures of normativity. This approach has a markedly instrumental connotation. It does not intend to revoke in doubt the traditional physiognomy of legal education, which remains preordained to instruct good technicians by teaching the rules positively in force, in space and time, but simply to adapt it to the new conditions, also in order to make it more attractive to the lords of global law. Internationalization of the curriculum and of legal education, therefore, essentially means increasing the number and weight of courses that study phenomena with cross-border relevance, adding more "information" to the consolidated pedagogical path, whose aims and methods are not intended to be questioned.

3.2 The Logic of the "Cosmos"

The second model, on the other hand, has a more ambitious goal, as it intends the internationalization of legal education not in a quantitative sense but in a qualitative one. To internationalize the curriculum does not mean, from this perspective, adding new courses that have as their object regulatory processes of a supranational or transnational character. It means, rather, rejecting the very significance of the idea of border and territory for the understanding of legal processes, and looking at the multiplication of sites of normativity as a real opportunity for cultural enrichment through the development of critical, dialogical, and pluralistic thinking. What this approach specifically intends to contest is the assumption that the law can be reduced to the complex of formal rules set by state (or supranational) authorities specifically appointed to do so, and its corollary that every legal system has to be regarded as a whole, cohesive, and ontologically distinct from other systems. The paradigm of reference is rather that of legal traditions as connected networks and intertwined in several points, which are constantly modified by continuous interaction, mutual dialogue, and hybridization. From this perspective, internationalizing the curriculum means putting aside the conceptual filter of the national legal system as a necessary key for accessing, understanding, and teaching the law. Training the jurist in the "cosmos" therefore means to abandon the purely instrumental concept of acquiring more extensive technical skills, through the learning of multiple "laws", and to embrace instead the idea that the entire pedagogical model must be aimed at training critical and responsible jurists, through a constant exploration and comparison of different normative conceptions, in their assumptions and implications [13]. In the words of Judge Kasirer, "the justification turns not on what law is perceived to be in force, or is understood to be useful to problem-solving in the practice of law, but what the law represents as an intellectual tradition, and what that tradition reveals of the nature of legal knowledge in a changing world" [11]. In other words, not only more information for good technicians, but better knowledge for jurists destined to operate in a dimension of "global citizenship".

The first model described above is representative of the way in which topics related to European law have been integrated into the curriculum of many continental universities: the addition of new teaching subjects, either in the area of public law, or in the area of private law, but not hybridization of models and cultures (as it has been done, for instance, in some Dutch universities) [7].

The aforementioned McGill transsystemic program responds, by contrast, to the second model. It has completely reset the structure of the curriculum envisaged by the old National Law Program [12], replacing the parallel treatment of civil law and common law in a given sector of the legal system with an integrated model, whereby the teaching is conducted simultaneously on study materials drawn from a plurality of legal traditions (civil law and common law of course, but also chthonic traditions, religious laws, etc.) [15]. Having had the privilege of teaching one of the first-year integrated courses at McGill, I regard it as a successful example of what the de-positivization of legal education should look like.

4 Overcoming Disciplinary Boundaries

Several years ago, the Italian legal philosopher Uberto Scarpelli noted, with a touch of bitterness, that "non-jurists often consider legal studies a branch of culture in the process of drying up, or at least a quiet lake, a bit marshy, on the edge of the great rapid and tumultuous river of contemporary culture" [19]. One of the reasons for such a (perhaps too) merciless judgment is that the value of the autonomy of law and the purity of its science (in a Kelsenian sense) has traditionally been pursued in such a manner as to largely obstruct the channels of communication between the law and other sciences (or arts). The jurist, therefore, felt authorized to disregard the acquisitions made in other disciplines, condemned in the limbo of "non-law", keeping a gaze on reality centered solely on the points of view and conceptual tools offered by the *scientia iuris*, and consequently producing a form of knowledge that is difficult to export or usable elsewhere. Such an attitude of epistemological closure is slowly disappearing: on the one hand, the complexity of social phenomena is such that the law is no longer able to understand and govern the underlying reality without the help of the skills developed by other sciences; on the other hand, the growing "Americanization" of legal culture has brought with it—among other aspects—the widespread diffusion of the various currents belonging to the law and … movement [20]. As a consequence, interdisciplinarity is increasingly regarded as a necessary tool to strengthen the conceptual baggage of the jurist, and therefore as an objective to be pursued in a decisive manner.

The problem, however, is to establish on what basis this interdisciplinarity has to be built and how it should be employed for the aims of legal education, without running the risk of a "colonization" of the study of law by other scientific disciplines [1].

5 Resisting the Colonization of the Law

Two different approaches may be distinguished, following the arguments proposed by Guido Calabresi in his book "The future of law & economics" [2]. Calabresi notes at the outset that, when asked about the seminal minds of the century, John Stuart Mill gave two names: the poet Samuel Taylor Coleridge and the philosopher Jeremy Bentham. Speaking of Bentham, Mill observed that he used to approach all ideas with the attitude of a foreigner and, if they did not satisfy his test (the utility test), he immediately dismissed them, as "vague generalities". Mill added that what Bentham could not understand was that "these generalities contained the whole unanalyzed experience of the human race." In Calabresi's reading, Bentham epitomizes the approach of the "economic analysis of law", whilst Mill personifies the perspective of "law & economics".

This dichotomy between the two versions of the economic law approach is interesting, because it sums up the reasons for the gap between two opposite interpretations of interdisciplinarity.

According to the first, the whole gamut of rules, institutions, and legal doctrines must be analyzed and assessed on the basis of parameters external to the legal system, such as social justice, gender equality, or Pareto efficiency. Bentham did exactly the same when he applied the utility test to any existing rule or institution, inferring a judgment of rationality or irrationality. The economic analysis of law *à la* Posner is seen by Calabresi as an ideal continuation of this approach. In fact, it subjects the existing legal framework to an efficiency test. If it conforms to it, this means that the structure itself is rational and must be preserved; if it does not conform to it, it deserves first to be criticized, and then reformed. The policy-oriented attitude of economic analysis is actually aimed at tilting the balance of interests underlying the creation or application of legal rules solely from the side of maximizing the expected economic benefits. In so doing, as aptly pointed out by Calabresi, the economic analysis of law is no different from the Marxist approach or from all other approaches that analyze, evaluate, and criticize the law in conformity with parameters of exogenous origin, adopting a purely instrumental conception of the normative dimension.

According to the second reading of interdisciplinarity, legal institutions should be the focal point of a plurality of perspectives, all legitimate and capable of contributing, as a whole, to a better understanding of the phenomena observed. Mill would embody its spirit, due to the methodological reservations expressed towards Bentham's approach, and in particular his disregard of all forms of rationality other than the utilitarian one. Thus, to go back to the initial example, the law and economics approach (of which Calabresi himself can rightly be considered the epigone) approaches the legal phenomenon first in an agnostic way, acquiring the information and explanations provided by the jurists themselves, to then verify whether it can be also explained on the basis of orthodox economic categories. If it finds a discrepancy between the forecasts of the economic theory and the solutions adopted by the law, it does not automatically conclude—as in the previous approach- for the irrationality of the legal framework, but it follows two alternative routes. In the first place, one should ask whether the way in which jurists present the underlying normative reality is really convincing or whether a different explanation of the same structure could be given, one that could result in conformity with the chosen heteronomous parameter and its rationality. Secondly, if the answer to this first question is unsatisfactory, one should inquire whether the analytical tools used—and in particular the tools of neoclassical economics—are themselves in need to be modified and fine-tuned, based on the empirical evidence gathered from the observation of the legal phenomenon. This, typically, is what happened when economists started to use experimental and laboratory tests to check the validity of their traditional axioms, that is, when the behavioral approach began to join forces with the more abstract and deductive analysis.

The apparent economic "irrationality" of some legal rules and principles (just think of the discipline of the gift in classical civil codes) has thus taken on a different light, becoming instead an important clue to insinuate doubts on the effective epistemological stability of the REMM (resourceful, evaluative, maximizing) model of rationality and therefore it contributed to a modification and enrichment of the same analytical baggage of economic theory. If then the same enriched version of the economic model is not able to explain the content of legal rules or doctrines, two further avenues would open: either recourse to the interpretative aid of other disciplines, such as cultural anthropology or history, or the acknowledgment of the inadequacy of the rule, as, for example, a relic of a socio-economic context that has been definitively overcome, and therefore of the need for a legal reform.

This second version of interdisciplinarity is the one that appears most promising and convincing. In fact, it is based on the idea of a true, mutually profitable dialogue between law and other branches of knowledge and does not sacrifice legal reason to other forms of rationality, incorporated into different systems of thought. It embraces the ideal of methodological pluralism, which is the true distinctive feature of the social sciences [5]. Dialogue on an equal footing, it was said, is profitable for both sides. The jurist works, to a large extent, as an engineer of social structures: she creates devices and models, i.e. infrastructures, to facilitate the peaceful cooperation of human beings, to prevent or reduce the risk of conflicts, and to promote harmonious and virtuous social relationships [8]. To build a stable material infrastructure, no engineer may ever ignore mathematics, physics (in its various forms), materials science. These sciences are essential components, but they do not exhaust the theoretical task of the engineer, who is called upon to filter them and use them selectively to achieve the results prescribed by her own discipline.

Likewise, the jurist, in constructing or implementing efficient social infrastructures, cannot ignore all those sciences, which contribute to a better understanding of the phenomena awaiting to be regulated, and in the first place of the behavior of persons and groups, and their social context. Therefore, human sciences, social sciences, and natural sciences: all offer essential points of view to better understand, and therefore better regulate, and this is exactly what Raymond Saleilles meant when he wrote that the jurist, unlike other intellectual professionals, must necessarily be the master of "universal science" [18]. But in turn, legal science, although it cannot have a "colonizing" attitude, also due to the essential link that associates theory and practice, does not operate, nor has it ever operated, as a mere vector for the importation of models developed elsewhere. The basic reason is that juridical knowledge presupposes, together with a specialized language, a logic with its own specificity, which leads to a reading of the surrounding world functional to the inner needs of the law and that cannot be conflated with those pursued by other subsystems [3, 6]. Precisely because of its specificity, which obviously is not inscribed in the nature of things but is simply the result of the stratification of experience, juridical wisdom represents in turn a model to be preserved and—why not?—to be offered to other disciplines as the oldest and still one of the most powerful instruments of observation and theoretical rationalization of social reality.

References

1. Balkin, J.M.: Interdisciplinarity as colonization. Wash. Lee L. Rev. **53**(3), 949 (1996)
2. Calabresi, G.: The Future of Law & Economics: Essays in Reform and Recollection. Yale University Press (2016)
3. Dedek, H.: Stating boundaries: the law, disciplined. In: Dedek, H., Van Praagh, S. (eds.) Stateless Law: Evolving Boundaries of a Discipline, p. 9. Routledge (2016)
4. Gambaro, A.: A proposito del plurilinguismo legislativo Europeo. Riv. Trim. Dir. Proc. Civ. **58**(1), 295 (2004)
5. Glenn, H.P.: Against method? In Adams, M., Heirbaut, D. (eds.) The Method and Culture of Comparative Law: Essays in Honour of Mark Van Hoecke, p. 177. Hart (2014)
6. Harner, M.M.: The value of 'thinking like a lawyer'. Maryland L. Rev. **70**, 390 (2011)
7. Heringa, A.W.: European legal education: the Maastricht experience. Penn State Int. Law Rev. **29**, 81 (2010)
8. Howarth, D.: Is law a humanity: (or is it more like engineering?). Arts Hum. Higher Educ. **3**(1), 9 (2004)
9. Isay, H.: Die Isolierung der Deutschen Rechtsdenkens Ein Vortrag. Franz Vahlen (1924)
10. Jamin, C., Caenegem, W.V. (ed.): The Internationalisation of Legal Education. Springer (2016)
11. Kasirer, N.: Bijuralism in law's empire and in law's cosmos. J. Legal Educ. **52**, 29 (2002)
12. Macdonald, R.A.: The national law programme at McGill: origins, establishment, prospects. Dal L J **13**(1), 211 (1990)
13. Macdonald, R., Glover, K.: Implicit Comparative Law. 43 R D U S 123 (2013)
14. Michaels, R.: Was ist nichtstaatliches Recht? Eine Einführung. In: Calliess, G.-P. (ed.), Transnationales Recht: Stand und Perspectiven, p. 39. Mohr Siebeck (2014)
15. Morissette, Y.M.: McGill's integrated civil and common law program. J. Leg. Educ. **52**, 12 (2002)
16. Rabel, E.: Aufgabe und Notwendigkeit der Rechtsvergleichung. In Rabel, E. (ed.) Gesammelte Aufsätze III, p. 1. Tübingen (1967)
17. Sacco, R.: L'internationalisation de la formation juridique. In: Gambroo, A. (ed.) Rapports nationaux italiens au XIXe Congrès international de droit comparé Vienne 2014, p. 67. Giuffrè (2014)
18. Saleilles, R.: Les méthodes d'enseignement du droit et l'éducation intellectuelle de la jeunesse. Rev Intern de L'enseignement, 313
19. Scarpelli, U.: L'educazione del giurista. Riv. Dir. Proc. **1** (1968)
20. Smits, J. M.: Law and interdisciplinarity: on the inevitable normativity of legal studies. Crit. Anal. Law **1**, 75 (2014)
21. Vogliotti, M.: Pour une formation juridique interdisciplinaire. In: Sueur, J. J., & Farhi, S. (eds.) Pratique(s) et enseignement du droit: L'épreuve du réel (LGDJ 2016), p. 277

Assume and not Postpone: Effective Education and also Digital

Jorge Cerdio

> *Be careful, because there are those who still think that this will pass, that it will be a nightmare overcome and that we will continue where we had left off, perhaps that is why they have only postponed ... Meanwhile, those who have not been able to send words of encouragement in time or out of time, those who have not made sensible calls, those who have not written to get closer, those who postpone meetings while keeping the issues pending ... all of them are useless to face the new world to which we are heading.*
> *(Sor Gemma, Dominican Congregation)*

Abstract University teaching in times of the COVID-19 pandemic has been exposed to new challenges and requirements. The fundamental challenge is to show that the educational quality of the institutions designed and rooted in a face-to-face model can offer the same educational quality in a digital format. The challenges appear in the form of students, who do not see added value in digital distance education and, on the other hand, employers and families who strongly question the price they are paying in terms of tuition and human resources educated now remotely. Faced with this problem, there are two opposite attitudes: wait or assume. The institutions that have decided to wait believe that this passage is temporary and that the adjustments they will have to make rest on presenting a mitigation plan with the hope to return to normal face-to-face. Other institutions have decided to assume that the changes are more profound, and that the pandemic is an opportunity to restructure and rethink their educational model. This paper presents some routes to go through this second attitude through a model called Effective Education also Digital (EED).

J. Cerdio (✉)
Academic Department of Law, Academic Division of Economics, Law and Social Sciences, Instituto Tecnologico Autonomo de Mexico, Mexico City, Mexico
e-mail: jcerdio@itam.mx

C. Raj Kumar and S. G. Sreejith (eds.), *Legal Education and Legal Profession During and After COVID-19*, https://doi.org/10.1007/978-981-19-2568-9_3

1 Introduction

In these past months that have elapsed, universities have had to adopt different strategies in the face of the global pandemic of COVID-19. In general terms, the strategy seems unique: add some tools for lecturing or remote collaboration to the design, pedagogy, and content that had been a rapid response against the pandemic. In other words, professors and students had to interact in the same way as before, only now with a different medium, before in person, now digitally. Firstly, in the situation of a global sanitary emergency, parents, students, professors, and society, in general, all understood that the reactive measures of the universities occurred with a degree of urgency: to mitigate a clearly abnormal situation. The collective compassionate attitude has been reflected in the students' evaluations and the actions of most professors, who have shown leniency and flexibility and have exchanged solidarity ties in what all of the parties have understood as a joint effort to continue classes disrupted by the pandemic. However, there have also been voices that demand a decrease in tuition payments. At the end of 2020, and the beginning of 2021 students in different parts of the world asked questions about how their training would be continued in the context of a pandemic that seems not to return us to the known normality and, at best, in most cases, it might force us to have intermittent periods of lockdowns for the foreseeable future.

An Art & Science Group LLC survey of 1171 high schools in the United States showed a symptom of the generation's concerns that saw their education interrupted at the beginning of the pandemic: 60% of them were not interested in being educated remotely. The class of 2020, faced with the decision to enroll for the first time in college education in the United States, had the idea that it was better to wait a year before actual enrollment.[1] The numbers, depending on the source consulted, showed that between 15 and 20% of that graduated class did not enroll[2]—but the distribution among subjects could be much higher. In addition, the Council of Education of that country calculated that during 2020 the universities lost 25% of international students.[3] In Mexico, informally, among directors of different schools and universities, some programs expect to have 70% less enrollment registered by August 2021. Moreover, many parents seriously questioned paying for an education that is not comparable to what their children would otherwise receive in person.[4] On the other hand, international students who travel to universities in other cities want to be closer to their families, and these families, in turn, are not equally willing to let their children go to study far from home.[5] In the United Kingdom and the United States—but also in other parts of the world—we see how universities are lowering recruitment standards, looking to all people on the waiting list to offer them to choose any career regardless of admission score or even giving them considerable discounts; all to

[1] Gallagher [10].

[2] Ref. [16]; Simpson [39].

[3] Ibid.

[4] Ref. [1].

[5] Kim [21].

attract them towards the inscription in the following dates. According to UNESCO, the pandemic has affected 9.8 million students in Africa and universities have had to negotiate with internet companies to obtain free access to the web (Rwanda, South Africa, and Tunisia). It argues that 5.3 million students are at risk of not returning to school in Saharan Africa.[6] Also, the World Bank estimates that COVID-19 may increase the risk of school dropout in Latin American countries, such as Brazil and Argentina, which before the current health crisis already had dropout rates of 20% and 15%, respectively, among higher education students.[7]

Universities have built their business model and their system of symbols around face-to-face events: classrooms, commencement speakers, fraternities and sororities, social and business networks, extensive libraries, student centers, dormitories, and graduation ceremonies. In its simplest form: getting a college education is an experience formed from human contact. On the other hand, institutions and programs that offer online courses remotely have focused their attention on a market of people who, due to their work constraints, time availability, or financial situation, see a value in the asynchronous distance training without the need for face-to-face attendance. Families, students, and employers have discriminated between the types of training in a university in person and the types of training in distance education. This discrimination now plays a relevant role in the attitudes of students and families who are not willing to pay the same price for the face-to-face experience only now behind a screen. In an informal survey carried out among more than a dozen groups of students at ITAM, they recognized screen fatigue and fatigue that they are not willing to continue extending for two or three more semesters. It is, therefore, a case in which the student population previously did not consider remote online education their valued choice, but now, specifically, how face-to-face education has been simulated through remote screen interactions seems even less valuable to them and exhausting. The difference between planning remote education versus face-to-face education should be brought back here. In remote education, the students' workloads are thought to be compatible with other activities, to have a form of self-learning, and in a complementary way, professors have secondary roles in facilitating content understanding. The sum of hours in a remote program is key to its pedagogical and terminal effectiveness. The accounting of screen times established activities, and the way to facilitate and accompany those activities have not been present in the colleges and Law Schools that in the semesters during the pandemic decided to add some tools to transplant the in-person experience to the digital world. The result has been the wear and tear of the students.

In our Law School, some fearful professors, and perhaps with little confidence in the use of digital tools, threw a massive workload on students without considering the class that preceded or the next class or the aggregate of hours that students would have to invest in completing that number of exercises by their means. On the other hand, this reflects a crucial flaw in the credit system in our Law Schools and universities. If we currently calculate how many hours each student should dedicate

[6] UNESCO [43].

[7] World Bank [46].

to taking a semester of six courses in which each subject has an average of six credits, that calculation would produce an unhealthy schedule by any wellness standard. The underlying expectation of that unhealthy schedule is that students will put themselves through countless hours of exercises, data, and lectures sourced in the classroom. We have defined the successful student as one who can pass the semesters under excessive loads of misdirected work without proof of effective learning. Our ineffective assumptions about students' workload became evident in these semesters of face-to-face transplants to the digital realm. In this lies the complaint that the semesters have been exhausting. There were very few—albeit remarkable—cases where professors understood how a learning experience in a digital ecosystem should be generated instead of producing the "same face-to-face experience now in digital media." It was the minority of professors who already had training in transferring their programs and the class script to a digital ecosystem. The challenge for some professors has not been to know a digital tool in particular or to know how to operate it but to have the ability to adapt the first-person point of view, the point of view of the student who will have a new learning experience. More precisely, most professors have exhibited a lack of creative empathy; they have not been able to put themselves in the students' shoes to imagine learning milestones, concrete capacities, learning activities, and effective feedback reports using a digital ecosystem. Furthermore, the fact is that this state of affairs is very natural: many professors have learned their teaching trade in an imitative way, through oral presentations, lectures, repeating groups of exercises, and repeating, in the best of cases, a histrionic self-presentation style of lecture. When the digital world demands doing things with information in unaccompanied segments and with more hours of individual reflection, a professor used to listen to herself or, looking at her writing in front of the blackboard, fails bluntly. Faced with this accumulation of challenges and difficulties, most Law Schools have adopted the attitude of postponing any radical change to their educational model.

The postponement attitude is based on the fearful idea that the pandemic is transitory, that students and their families can bear the adjustments, and that the market will not discriminate against graduates of this hybrid era between digital and face-to-face—which is, by the way, a potential source of discredit: that Law Schools welcome professionals with a lower academic profile than in past generations; and, finally, that their financial structures will be able to withstand the expected drop in enrollment. Around the world, from Edinburgh to California or Colombia, these attitudes are palpable. They have translated into either offering during the semesters of the Covid-19 pandemic the discourse that students "will be able to continue advancing towards obtaining their academic degrees through digital platforms (Janet Napolitano, UCAL-System)" or that there will be a hybrid accommodation where small rotating groups will have sanitized contact in the classrooms, while another cohort of students will do it remotely, alternating face-to-face education with digital. The postponement attitude is the most fragile and vulnerable to the challenges and difficulties that I have described above; and as time passes the situation will become more serious.

Note that as of now, May 2021, only 0.3% of the 1.84 billion vaccine doses have been administered in low-income countries.[8]

The second attitude is to assume. Assuming that we are facing a radical change that forces us to take with both hands the challenge of adding value to the digital experience in order to return to society, families and individuals, who entrust their education to us a higher standard than the one obtained before face-to-face. To assume that it is possible to have a better educational model for Law Schools redesigned from the challenges that education is experiencing today, generate new profiles of professionals who know how to be productive in this new world with intermittent alternation between their physical and digital contact.

Both attitudes certainly have costs and are ultimately investment decisions for universities and Law Schools. I believe that the best bet investment is the attitude of assuming because, paraphrasing Blaise Pascal, if it turns out that everything returns as before, if there never will be another pandemic like Covid-19 and this was a nightmare overcome, we will have added better capacities to our institutions, to our teaching staff, and the educational, legal model. Furthermore, if the nightmare came to transform the grounds of our society, we will be able to show others the way; in both cases, it is a rationally winning bet to assume the challenge posed by the pandemic. It is, therefore, convenient to outline the broad lines of action of what indeed in each Law School-University should be a more detailed plan and with the concurrence of many minds-voices, but, above all, spirits convinced that only collective action could lead us to a better state of affairs. The first line of action begins with a better understanding of the cognitive and pedagogical structures that work better in the digital world (2) and then designing a concrete action plan that sets a guideline for us to overcome difficulties present and future, face challenges and add a new value to our educational offer (3).

2 Structure and Digital Understanding

In some sense, it is true that technological tools by themselves, and the way we use them, do not represent a way of teaching, nor do they translate into a specifically digital method of learning. However, it is also true that how we structure the ways of transmitting ideas and the objectives that we set ourselves as professors can be obstacles to a digital education of real and added value to our students. Let us take an example. A professor presents a philosophical or a doctrinal text in a face-to-face situation. She gives the task of making an argument from a text according to her initial presentation of critical ideas. She encourages dialogue and debate, and at the end, she elaborates on Socratic corrections so that the class takes a more orderly picture of the core ideas of the text. The learning objective is the understanding of abstract ideas that students can translate the philosophical–doctrinal ideas through

---

[8] Mathieu et al. [31].

their minds and in their own words. The professor uses students' voices as a beatbox, where each participant echoes their classmates' ideas to restructure and rework their initial thoughts. Taken to a digital domain, a linear transposition of the learning method—where students meet in a virtual classroom with video and audio, where the professor presents the text again, perhaps now with the help of a slide show—leads to a resounding failure of the initially set learning outcomes. Each student is not experiencing their classmates perceptually, live; nor can they process the ideas of the virtual discussion in the same way to produce the introspection that the Socratic method proclaims. The cognitive process that occurs in face-to-face versus digital learning environments is different, and yields different modes of apprehension, attention and cognition[9]; there is a radical difference that professors should always have in mind. Nevertheless, our hypothetical professor, unknowing of the different cognitive processes when using digital media, continues to speak to the screen and requires her students to participate in the same way as they did before, in the classroom, face-to-face. Our imaginary professor will generate anguish in her students, followed by total boredom from losing concentration on the screen. The attention routine, adequate concentration time to one or more voices on the computer's audio channel, and real-time attention to the image transmitted in a video conference are radically less than face-to-face.[10]

The previous example assumes the ideal conditions of the instructor's performance. Unfortunately, the usual conditions are far from ideal. These past semesters, our students have seen some professors who do not adequately handle their interventions to be attentive to the digital hands raised during the sessions. They do not realize that the cadence of their voice and the digital transmission has a delay. Communication has interruptions in its bandwidth that yield students continuously requesting the professor to repeat the last communication. In the middle of a fragmented communication, the feedback to students' questions is also of lesser quality, and sometimes confusing because of the ongoing chat conversations in the virtual classroom.

To sum up, we must say that the pedagogical structure (e.g., a Socratic class) counts to be a facilitator or an obstacle to learning in the digital domain.

On the other hand, a structuring that we find helpful in facilitating the transition to learning in the digital domain distinguishes between the pedagogical triad (2.1) and the fundamental learning triad (2.2); and from this distinction incorporates the sense of balance in our teaching (2.3).

2.1 The Pedagogical Triad

The learning outcomes that a professor sets at the beginning of a course should be equivalent to a contract whose central tenet would be expressed as follows: "you will acquire such and such capabilities through such and such activities, and I assure

[9] Hou et al. [17, pp. 84–94].

[10] Geske and Bellur [12, pp.399–423].

you that it will be so because I will take such and such actions to help you make these activities effective so that you obtain the capabilities that I offer you here".[11] Let us give an example again for a course with philosophical–doctrinal content. The professor offers the capability to explain a complex and abstract idea that is typically found in philosophical texts. The expected capability is for the student to be able to explain a philosophical text. The professor's activities should be suitable to obtain the capability to explain a philosophical text. For example, she can design the activity of actively analyzing the structure of the text: to find the main ideas, secondary ideas, the structure of the arguments, the vocabulary of the text, the problem presented in the text, the consequences of the thesis held by the author. After actively showing students how to analyze the structure of a philosophical text, the professor can challenge them to imitate the analytical identification they made before with her guidance, but with a new text. To ensure that the activity is carried out correctly, the professor should plan a cycle of interactions among the students, the text, and her. So, when a student, or a group of them, try to analyze the text in the exemplified manner, the professor provides effective, precise feedback. When this has been successful, she can now progress to new texts so that students gain confidence to apply what they have learned by analytical imitation of the professor. Moreover, once they have gained more confidence in simple texts, the professor can now progressively introduce more complex texts and repeat the learning cycle until she judges that the capability has been acquired to the degree that she determines satisfactory. Through this technique, students develop not only the capability to acquire vocabulary but also to detect structures at a prosodic level of philosophical language, identify structures of thought in the text in order to provide coherence to their explanatory discourse about the text, to increase their reading comprehension; all of which translates into a better philosophical understanding. After this process, students read philosophy more fluently—it is a process very similar to the one that takes place with prosodic structures in the development of essential reading.[12]

The triad of capacities, activities, and performance based on the learning activities should be explicit for the students and the entire class and criteriologically determined. It should be clear under what criteria the activity is carried out successfully, and the degree to which the capacity has been reached in connection to that activity carried out; in this way, each professor's intervention makes sense to students. It is not perceived as a trial-and-error dynamic. The role played by the professor in accompanying the students to achieve the capacity offered in each activity becomes intelligible to the student. A pedagogy planned from the triad described above can be taken advantageously to the digital world by translating this triad into three fundamental learnings: the acquisition of vocabulary, the application of concepts, and the development of creative reasoning.

[11] Bain [24].

[12] Whalley and Hansen [45, pp. 288–303].

2.2 The Triad of Fundamental Learning

The acquisition of the vocabulary necessary to interact in any discipline, be it formal such as the use of symbolism in Mathematics, or in a more technical way, as in the case of Finance or Law, is undoubtedly one of the first learning capabilities that we promote as professors and that employers value. A person has been professionally formed when she is inserted into a symbolic universe determined by using a particular vocabulary—and even knowing a word is cognitively associated with processes of identity and belonging much more profound than merely the professional.[13] Nowadays, ensuring that students have the appropriate vocabulary and understand it to return it with relevance in the appropriate contexts of professional use is fundamental learning that has to occur entirely in a digital domain. The identification of a list of keywords; searching for similar paragraphs in different documents; research exercises from documents where keywords have been removed; or even discussion forums to find better definitions between different concepts in a discussion thread are all examples of activities that have long been part of pedagogical resources in education performed in the digital world. The activities can be developed alone, in groups outside of class time, as challenges during class time, or as part of a collaborative document construction project: Wikipedia, collaborative thesaurus, or frequently asked questions (FAQ). The records produced by the performance of these and other activities in the digital environment help the professor understand the level of acquisition of the students' vocabulary and better gauge the progression of the learning outcomes and capabilities. Incidentally, in all the activities mentioned above, the professor has an active role in providing feedback, guiding, and facilitating the learning process.

Nevertheless, vocabulary acquisition is merely the previous step to using—in a proper way— concepts in a professional context. The concept of income is used to calculate the due amount of an income tax, the concept expressed in the vocabulary of family law to establish parenthood between two people, the concept of skepticism expressed in the philosophical vocabulary is used to be able to reason about the abstract ideas of an author. In all these scenarios, what we want from students is that they can appropriately generalize a concept expressed by the vocabulary to apply it concretely in specific situations. It is what has been termed the enabling ability to solve problems.[14] The key in the digital world is learning through the persistent reuse of examples: group discussions on the application of the resolution of a paradigmatic case, the presentation of poorly resolved or poorly justified cases to find the variants of use of the same concept; the use of anomalous cases that show the vagueness of a concept—as in the funny case of SEALAND, an oil platform abandoned on the high seas that a person declared a country and issued passports, visas, and citizenship; the investigation of files that collect news that exemplify the vocabulary and that can be of a journalistic nature or academic articles. Showing paradigmatic examples of applying a concept and reusing those examples already worked on is an effective

[13] Wagner and Sence [44, pp. 1–14].

[14] Abdullaeva et al. [2].

way to acquire problem-solving skills.[15] Each of these activities is carried out in small groups with an active and participatory voice because this is how learning problems are best solved, and examples are built by similarity. The digital world, in this sense, can bring many benefits to developing collaborative problem-solving skills and effective soft skills of teamwork.[16]

We want students who have developed an understanding of vocabulary and the ability to apply it in specific situations to expand that ability to new contexts. We want students to be creative with their learning skills. We want them to have the capacity to extrapolate past solutions to new cases. To manage the complexity of new situations by moving concepts from their domain of use to different ones. We want students to be creative because creativity helps handle uncertainty and complexity. For example, the contractual forms of deposit, leasing, served several decades for solving problems in applied bioethics. Digital tools developed as an expression of problem-solving based on design-oriented methodology, visual data representation managers, but also social collaborative applications (to produce collective knowledge) are formidable enhancers of creative abilities. What is required is that each student realizes that they have a potential for invention within their reach; that their potential can be increased with the development of specific digital activities, and that it can be used daily to solve any difficulty (“*to tap into their inventive potential at will*”). Contrary to popular belief, the digital world has tools and applications for the experiential approach (“*hands-on*”), to carry out activities that have more than one solution (“*open-endedness*”) and, in this sense are not determinative; digital learning through these applications has proven results in increasing student’s confidence in their design processes and in generating new solutions.[17]

Returning to the example of our hypothetical professor who wanted to generate text explanation capabilities in her students, this professor should now sit down to design learning activities and feedback-evaluation interventions for each of the three fundamental learning components in the digital world. She must generate activities for the acquisition of vocabulary, also create activities for the application of concepts and problem-solving, and she must sit down to generate activities that promote the inventive capacity of her students so that at the end of carrying out these activities, her students are capable of explaining other philosophical texts of a certain level.

At this point, we must note that both the pedagogical triad and the triad of fundamental learnings that we have just outlined can live both in a face-to-face world and in a digital one but that, with advantage, the tools currently available for digital teaching promote student’s awareness of the added value that the digital tool brings in their training. Like the skills–activities–assessment contract, all digital activities must be put into a schedule beforehand as a tour. The learning script is a necessary condition for any conscious learning. We must exalt the student’s point of view, the point of view of the learning experience as a journey of interactions. As with any road trip, the stops on the learning road should show them in advance the difficulties they

[15] van Gog and Kester [13, pp. 1532–1541]; van Gelder [11, pp. 41–48].

[16] Leman [28, pp. 804–820]; Schunn et al [38, pp. 407–432].

[17] Lewis [29, pp. 255–268].

will have with vocabulary acquisition-understanding. The type of interactions they will have with others, in working groups, and for what purposes, to attain what objectives, using what tools how much time, and the reasonably expected results should also be highlighted. Finally, there is also the description of the interactions with the professor throughout the entire journey, emphasizing how students can resort to different resources for self-correction, validation and accompaniment.[18] The presentation of the journey that crosses the triad of fundamental learnings in the digital world is far from being a mere academic program and is transformed more into an anticipated living blog of intellectual travel.[19]

It is also important to note that the class and the time allocated must be at the complete service of both triads. There will be sessions in which the professor focuses on making specific presentations; others in which she must manage workgroups through the use of specific applications; or spend most of the time reviewing and doing horizontal collaborative work; perhaps, finally, in other sessions, she should have brief interventions to present paradigmatic examples. All the activities described above, as possibilities, must be accommodated to a greater or lesser extent to an agenda that keeps a gentle learning curve, a reasonable progression of activities designed in the digital world, and not the other way around as it has been the case in pandemic times. The accommodation of the instructional design is flexible and dynamic. In that regard, the techniques to calibrate the group's commitment (engagement) to detect the learning progression in the asynchronous workload, are techniques that already exist in the online teaching world and that should now be taken into account in a meaningful way.[20] The amount of time lecturing loses weight before the notion of balance in the learning process, balance between the fundamental learnings described above.

2.3 *Balance in Learning*

One of the biggest challenges in instructional design is to balance learning activities before, during and after each class in conjunction with the matrix of courses that a student takes per semester. In our Law School, our credit system does not reflect effective learning time; each credit does not represent the actual work it takes for a student to prepare, on average, for their classes adequately. Nor does it consider the distribution of students' different skills require in courses with different disciplinary contexts (e.g., Law and Economics, Jurisprudence, Legal Clinic, Legal Writing). If we take as an example the average semester of any student who will take about six courses each of three hours per week, and we assume that they should dedicate one hour of preparation for each hour of lecture taken and another two hours later for reinforcement and exercises-reading, it would be equivalent to a dedication of 5 h a

[18] Clark [5, pp. 598–604].

[19] Krause et al. [27, pp. 158–170].

[20] Kalyuga [22, pp. 387–399]; Kapp [23]; Strother [41].

day, seven days a week. This distribution is fictitious for several reasons. The first is that most courses have a syllabus with mandatory literature that disregards the reading demand of other courses in the same academic term. Professors create the number of exercises that consider necessary to reaffirm what they have lecture, and design the grading assignments of the course. Each professor's judgement regarding the amount of material to be read and the activities to be carried out within their courses never takes into account the distinction between the time before, during, and after class. The estimated hours it will take an average student to prepare for each class, and perform each activity, does not appear in any syllabus. In addition, no professor regards the calculation of hours dedicated to her course and the hours required by other courses during the same semester term. From another point of view, the calculation of hours reflected in a credit system is not realistic either. Let us take the number of pages that an average college student can read per hour. On average, a college student can read around 19 pages per hour.[21] The average number of pages per class for some courses in our Law School is 50, while in others, it can be 125 for each session, and in the case of subjects such as Jurisprudence, this calculation can be as high as 200 pages; which gives us an average of 125 pages for each class, multiplied by six classes, and taking into account the average reading time, the student would need about 39 h to read the texts that are required fully. It is not surprising that students have developed strategies to overcome these difficulties: they focus on detecting the criteria of relevance that each professor exposes in their classes, the references they make, and the answer to the questions that interest the professor the most. All this is synthesized in the mode of notes passed down from A-grade students to the next generation. It is an imitation game as much as a cognitive strategy to detect the relevance of a task that would otherwise be impossible to carry out. In short, there is no rational system that relates credits by course with the actual capacities for meaningful learning.[22]

However, the lack of balance in credit systems that do not consider students' actual work has an even more significant and systemic flaw: they do not take into consideration the balance that students must learn to attain in their lives if they are to have a good life. Students should have study time management skills in balance with the different aspects of their lives to be successful and well-rounded individuals professionally and personally. The so-called wellness management techniques are already part of the credit systems of the best universities in the world; they provide students with soft skills that have proven to be a palliative to reducing bad academic habits, bad sleep habits, bad eating habits, and, in this way, produce professionals with better chances of facing situations of stress, complexity and uncertainty.[23] Law Schools and Universities that have adopted the well-being perspective into their credit system have added human value to their academic programs. A vast body of literature currently studies and associates these credit systems with graduate students with a more active social and cultural rol. They are professionals more willing to get

[21] Streichler [40].

[22] Prasuhn [35, pp. 4–13].

[23] Howell [18], pp. 1–13].

involved with their communities; they have remarkable resilience. A credit system oriented toward students' well-being generates a body of more motivated students and, above all, improves their cognitive learning abilities.[24]

The planning approach for professors must focus on managing the fundamental learnings of vocabulary, problem-solving and creative reasoning in a balanced way with soft skills for well-being. They should encourage forms of responsible self-management on the part of the students and adjust the expectations of learning outcomes accordingly for the capacities that they want their students to acquire throughout the academic term. Balance and equilibrium should be at the center of every professor's instructional design decisions.[25]

The absence of equilibrium and balance as guiding axes of teaching planning and instructional design in face-to-face systems was frontally evident with the transplantation of face-to-face classes to a digital format during the pandemic time, which was aggravated by a combination of attitudes of some professors and a lack of understanding of how to produce sensitive learning in a digital educational space. On the one hand, some professors, distrustful of the effectiveness in the digital domain and fearful of a decline in the educational quality of their courses, engaged in poor instructional practices. They saturated students with recurring tasks—without feedback or grading rationale—; they placed tests at random without correlation with the syllabus progression or more frequently asked questions than usual. It was a collection of control tools so that they did not lose the class dynamics, so that they did not lose authority in the (virtual) classroom. This attitude only increased the already stressful environments for students. On the other hand, some professors did not realize that the mental workload is an indicator that must be permanently verified in the digital space to avoid mental fatigue; as well as emotional indicators such as empathy and commitment—that is, the enthusiasm that students have for each activity must be permanently monitored.[26] A strategy that is certainly not consciously present in face-to-face teaching environments. Under an effective learning digital environment, everything is about implementing permanent strategies to monitor the information processing workload and promote engagement of *affective attitudes* towards the course content—for this, supervision mechanisms and dynamic indicators are developed.[27]

At this point, it is convenient to take stock of what has been presented so far. Effective education is based on the pedagogical grounds of study programs that develop capacities through activities supervised in a persistent, progressive way, with helpful feedback towards the student. The role of the professor becomes central in the creation of the activities, in the elaboration of rubrics, support notes, and qualitative systems so that students understand in a very transparent way at the beginning of the course the manner how they are acquiring degrees of the capacities offered. The professor has to translate this skills training program into a digital support strategy

---

[24] Conner [6]; Checkoway [4, pp. 6–11]; Keyes [25, pp. 95–108].

[25] Baird et al. [3], pp. 11–20].

[26] Pimenta et al. [34, pp. 25–32].

[27] Happy et al. [15]; Clark (n 18).

through three fundamental learnings enhanced by a varied ecosystem of tools that allow the acquisition of vocabulary, the application of concepts and problem solving, and the strengthening of inventive capacities.[28] The planning of the class scripts is given by interactions in these three levels of fundamental learning, and time must be used to produce a balance, a balance in which the mental workloads, the attention of the students, and their well-being are permanently the center of the dynamic class setting. We should embrace dynamic, flexible, and emotionally oriented instructional learning by design.

Effective learning in a digital environment has a genuinely beneficial and powerful expected effect on the Law School-University in generating a change in the profile of the students in the profile of future professionals. Indeed, the tools we choose must train them in a new way of working in their discipline, collaborating digitally, generating a portfolio of clients, and adding value to the institutions where they work. Therefore, the selection of digital tools should never be episodic or temporary to the learning task; in contrast, we should choose the tool that is either the standard for the industry in which we want to insert the student or is a widely extended tool for professional tasks. For example, project management applications exemplify the first case that large and small firms use to tackle simple or complex projects for their clients. A second example is that data mining applications for legal discovery and document searching are the standard for the performance of professional tasks such as legal auditing or preparing complex arbitration trials (they are mature software applications). The third example would be generic collaborative tools, information visualization tools, content editing tools, programming tools, database interconnection tools, document standardization, and collaborative writing tools. Once mastered, they are applications that produce a new workflow for legal professionals. In short: we will be able to generate a new, hitherto unknown profile so that our students can be influential professionals in the new digital environment that they will have to face.

Each Law School-University should calculate the investment in time and human resources, and indeed, there are different ways of implementing the view that we have sketched so far. However, we would like to present an action plan that will lead us to a swift implementation within a horizon of months of this change that I consider urgent for institutional survival in an aggressive, uncertain environment and of greater competition in the market of legal education.

3 Action Plan

I believe that a hybrid methodology inspired by the agile methodology for implementing prototypes, combined with a development methodology focused on the student's experience, could be the most appropriate to carry out an intervention

[28] Huang et al. [19, pp. 354–357].

within months promptly.[29] The implementation plan then only sets the general lines to quickly generate actions that can be feedback, corrected, and adjusted in a short time. The action plan focuses on two coordinated and parallel actions: the insertion of teaching champions (reengineering of the programs and the teaching attitudes of the faculty) (3.1) and the insertion of a new educational message (positioning speech, marketing, and persuasion of effective and digital education towards the relevant stakeholders) (3.2).

3.1 Propagating Teaching Leaders

In the past 11 years, as dean of ITAM'S Law School, I have seen a minimal capacity of high-level professionals interested in teaching to translate their knowledge and experiences in terms of a learning program with objectives, capacities, activities, and feedback actions (evaluation). There area several reasons for the limited capacity; one is that instructional design is a lengthy process that takes 6–8 months. However, the most potent limitation is the lack of introspection of law professionals to design the activities that produce the valuable capacities for the legal services market. As a result, most lawyers cannot create valuable and concrete learning activities that transcend the mere informative presentation. The second constraint is the time that law professionals can spend training themselves to develop a learning program guided by the best practices of digital instructional design. The eight months' time is drastically reduced when there is already a course program that has gone through the method of adaptation to pedagogy oriented to the triad of capabilities–activities–feedback. In my experience, a syllabus redesign using the triad has certain topical neutrality that allows them to be recycled for other courses; this occurs with the course rubrics (micro-level), and at the level of the structure and presentation of the capacities and activities (macro-level). So, we will have to start the first phase with a group of professors to recreate syllabus and their teaching approach using the triad of capabilities-activities-feedback; to translate it into the digital world.

Nonetheless, redesigning current syllabuses to balance the time allocated to the three fundamental learnings has imminent challenges. On the one hand, there is a generation gap between some professors, whose attitudes towards using digital tools are very different [37], especially in a Law School. On the other hand, there is sound evidence that the adoption of digital tools in education occurs best when they are vertically established in the organization and horizontally reinforced by the success cases through the voice of students.[30] In the past months, we have seen an example of the former, a vertical imposition in adopting remote platforms for teaching and collaborating with students. Professors had no choice but to adopt a videoconferencing platform to lecture and interact with their students. This institutional action has bought us time because it has produced a quick adoption of interaction tools. What

[29] Fox et al. [9].

[30] Tondeur et al. [42, pp. 134–144]; Zhou and Xu [47].

is still needed is recognizing the students that this experience is more enriching than the face-to-face one. We have to achieve the students' recognition that their professors have become digital facilitators of their learning. On the contrary, it would seem that the perception of the students is relatively poor in relation to the benefits that the use of this tool has brought and the value-added that it generates compared to the traditional face-to-face classes.

Given that the critical organizational factor in succeeding in the implementation of an educational methodology and, at the same time, of digital learning tools is to lower the costs of self-learning through groups of collaborators and to intensify the coordination mechanisms between this groups[31]; then that will be the direction of the first phase of the implementation plan.

It will then begin with a group of professors who, over the past five years, have adopted the pedagogical triad to formulate standardized scripts of the functional learnings, with specific tools suitable for each of these functional learnings: vocabulary formation, problem-solving, and inventiveness. Time accounting rates will be developed to balance the tasks before, during, and after the class within each course and between courses in the same semester. This work will be done individually and then in small groups to generate an ecosystem, a digital social community of mutual support. Best practices indicate that this should be an intense phase that generates sympathies of affiliation with the project and whose learning focuses on generating "collective knowledge," so new professors are invited to join a club-like mechanism.[32] The expected product will be a series of course templates, activity scripts, lines of action related to specific applications, and digital tools, which have a high capacity to be reused through different domains and topics; that is, through different courses. Indicators and supervision mechanisms will also be created to ensure that all professors pursue the same pedagogical strategy, the same type of fundamental learning, and carry out frequent controls to adjust mental burdens and emotional commitments to the courses dynamically. It is key to success to generate sustainability of the process to achieve long-term implementation.[33]

In a second phase, the working group will be extended to four times the size of the initial group to reach at least one group in each of the courses offered in the following semesters. Following the logic of the horizontal effect that winning the audience has, we must reinsert the best professors to show their leadership in front of other groups, to remove the resistance that will naturally exist among other professors, and, at the same time, to generate an active change in the qualitative perception of the digital learning process in students.

The first and second phases have an intermediate review and adjustment time in an agile way, both the implementation program and the expected results. At the end of each phase, there is also a review of the digital materials, tools, and their specific results. In other words, the implementation will generate a digital repository

[31] King and Boyatt [26, pp. 1272–1780].

[32] Liu et al. [30].

[33] Nichols [32, pp. 598–609].

of the implementation experience that could advantageously be transferred to other departments and schools within the university outside the Law School.

On the other hand, the program's implementation needs to be accompanied by the discursive collaboration of other actors who are central for the strategy to be successful, mainly students, parents, and employers.

3.2 *Insertion of a New Discourse*

The first policy of this program is absolute transparency with the student body. Let them know by every channel available with particular messages what is the reason for this change, how it will benefit them, how it will give them a comparative advantage and add value to their training, and how the learning experience will improve compared to last semester. More generally, we must show them that they are being trained in a highly competitive way in relation to their peers in other Law Schools-Universities, precisely because of the digital skills they acquire in the professional context. We must convince them of this certitude: that effective and digital education will shape them as better professionals to face the future. The main message to the student body should be that the department or Law School will constantly be monitoring the execution of all the phases describe above. However, it should be clear that it is not an experimental product. It is a mature product that will admit all the improvements hand in hand with the adequate feedback from them throughout the semesters.

Centrally, we must remind them of what makes us different: the academic quality of the Law School-University and its professors and its contents. We must convey in practice and discourse that the difference with a purely digital online university is grounded in the speed of skills acquisition. We must outline the unique view of the experts who lecture them and who select texts and materials. There must be a message that the combination of the expert knowledge of the professors and the materials are combined with digital learning activities makes our educative experience singular. Finally, that we distinguish ourselves by the priority we give to qualitative feedback, focused on making them progress and improve professionally and humanely.[34] If we do not manage to make it clear in practice and discourse that this is our differentiating factor, a methodological change in digital pedagogy will be useless. Furthermore, this very idea that academic quality will now be enhanced towards a new digital profile, but also from solid foundations of our humane view of education, the message that we must transmit to parents. The families who trust their resources and their expectations in the Law School-University to carry out the life plans they have for their children; we will have to generate differentiated informative material for that specific audience.

[34] Strother (n 20).

The third group within the audience of stakeholders is employers. Here are two lines of action. The first line is collaborative, and the other is informative. The collaborative line of action is that public and private institutions cannot stop operating in a recurring pandemic or in a context where less open social contact is required. They are now working but by other means; and in this "function by other means," the Law School-University is called to offer joint participation; we must approach professional firms, civil organizations, companies, and public institutions to have digital modalities of professional practices, clinics, cases of study, joint projects and strategic participations. All of them should occur in the context of our classes and also digitally. The second line of action is informative in that we will show them that the profile of our graduates is uniquely adapted to their current and future needs and that it adds value to organizations that now face the challenge of being more productive in a changing and uncertain environment. This line of action, which is communicative but also substantive, requires today more than ever the dedication of personal time by directors of centers and department heads to make personal and direct contact with the key actors that surround the professional ecosystems of our programs. It is a time of persuasion and a time to bring them to this new vision of professional education so that they can see how there is a heading and a palpable leadership.[35] The best way to prove that we are leading the way is to show them how digital capabilities enhance our well-known professional quality. Here we will have to provide the critical actors with concrete examples linked to the interests of their organization: the ability to have a better form of remote negotiation (to an arbitration and negotiation office); the use of collaborative tools for large projects for the creation of legal audits (of a corporate consulting firm); the ability to analyze large legal databases in the preparation of cases to identify relevant precedents (to a litigation firm); the use of collaborative tools for the creation and writing of digital content in different formats and structures (to the legal services of public institutions); to mention a few.

I trust that the conjunction of these two projects can be executed with the reorientation of resources that Law Schools-Universities already have available, with the sum of the wills of professors who are willing to change, and with the investment of time and dedication to arrive prepared for the subsequent semesters. With the hope that we will assume the challenge imposed upon us and that we will be able to reap more vital institutions in the coming years, and to be recognized for our ability to innovate in a context where Law Schools-Universities seem to be stunned, waiting.

Bibliographic Notes

In (Petersson et al. [33]) it is highlighted, for example, how the perception of students in relation to the assistance and feedback of the professors did not change when received in an online format; also, the results of the study show that students were less satisfied with their performance.

---

[35] Kapp (n 20).

References

1. 14th Annual State of College Savings survey. College Savings Foundation (2020) https://www.collegesavingsfoundation.org/members-only-area/surveys/. Accessed 9 July 2021
2. Abdullaeva, B., et al.: Developing critical thinking and problem-solving skills. Int. J. Psychosoc. Rehab. **24**(1) (2020)
3. Baird, J., et al.: Researching balance between cognition and affect in science teaching and learning. Res. Sci. Educ. **20**(1) (1990)
4. Checkoway, B.: New perspectives on civic engagement and psychosocial well-being. Liberal Educ. **97** (2011)
5. Clark, D.: Psychological myths in e-learning. Med. Teacher **24**(6) (2002)
6. Conner, J.: When does service-learning work? Contact theory and service-learning courses in higher education. Michigan J. Commun. Serv. Learn. **23**(2) (2017)
7. Corey, G.: Theories and Practices of Counseling and Psychotherapy. Thomson Brooks/Cole (2009)
8. Duschl, R.: Science Education in Three-Part Harmony: Balancing Conceptual, Epistemic, and Social Learning Goals. Rev. Res. Educ. **32**(1) (2008)
9. Fox, D., Sillito, J., Maurer, F.: Agile methods and user-centered design: how these two methodologies are being successfully integrated in industry. In: IEEE Agile Conference, Toronto, pp. 63–72 (2008). https://ieeexplore.ieee.org/document/4599453. Accessed 9 July 2021
10. Gallagher, K.: More Cause for Concern about Fall Enrollment. Art & Science, 28 April 2020. https://www.artsci.com/news/2020/04/28/private-polling-offers-another-warning-sign-about-college-admissions. Accessed 9 July 2021
11. Gelder, T.: Teaching critical thinking: some lessons from cognitive science. College Teach. **53**(1) (2005)
12. Geske, J., Bellur, S.: Differences in brain information processing between print and computer screens. Int. J. Advertis. **27**(3) (2008)
13. Gog, T., Kester, L.: A test of the testing effect: acquiring problem-solving skills from worked examples. Cogn. Sci. **36**(8) (2012)
14. Hanley, G.: Teaching critical thinking: focusing on metacognitive skills and problem solving. Teach. Psychol. **22**(1) (1995)
15. Happy, S.L., et al.: Automated alertness and emotion detection for empathic feedback during e-learning. In: IEEE Fifth International Conference on Technology for Education, Kharagpur, December 2013. https://www.computer.org/csdl/proceedings-article/t4e/2013/5141a047/12OmNyOHG0N. Accessed 9 July 2021
16. Higher Education Community Requests $46.6 Billion for Students and Institutions in Fourth Supplemental Package, Proposes Tax Changes. Acenet, 10 April 2020. https://www.acenet.edu/News-Room/Pages/Higher-Education-Community-Requests-$47-Billion-for-Students-and-Institutions-Proposes-Tax-Changes.aspx. Accessed 9 July 2021
17. Hou, J., Rashid, J., Lee, K.: Cognitive map or medium materiality? Reading on paper and screen. Comput. Hum. Behav. **67** (2017)
18. Howell, A.: Flourishing: achievement-related correlates of students well-being. J. Positive Psychol. **4**(1) (2009)
19. Huang, Y., Wang, C., Liu, Y.: A study of synchronous vs. asynchronous collaborative design in students learning motivation. Int. J. Inf. Educ. Technol. **5**(5) (2015)
20. Scott, J.: Colleges could lose up to 20 percent of students. Inside Higher Ed, 29 April 2020. https://www.insidehighered.com/admissions/article/2020/04/29/colleges-could-lose-20-percent-students-analysis-says. Accessed 9 July 2021
21. Kim, H.: COVID-19 and US Higher Education Enrollment: Preparing Leaders For Fall. McKinsey & Company (2020). www.mckinsey.com/industries/social-sector/our-insights/covid-19-and-us-higher-education-enrollment-preparing-leaders-for-fall. Accessed 9 July 2021
22. Kalyuga, S.: Enhancing instructional efficiency of interactive e-learning environments: a cognitive load perspective. Educ. Psychol. Rev. **19**(3) (2007)

23. Kapp, K.: Winning E-Learning Proposals the Art of Development and Delivery. J Ross Publishing (2003)
24. Ken, B.: What the Best College Teachers Do. Harvard University Press (2004)
25. Keyes, C.: Promoting and protecting mental health as flourishing: a complementary strategy for improving national mental health. Am. Psychol. **62**(2) (2007)
26. King, E., Boyatt, R.: Exploring factors that influence adoption of e-learning within higher education. Br. J. Educ. Technol. **46**(6) (2014)
27. Krause, U., Stark, R., Mandl, H.: the effects of cooperative learning and feedback on e-learning in statistics. Learn. Instr. **19**(2) (2009)
28. Leman, P.: How do groups work? Age differences in performance and the social outcomes of peer collaboration. Cogn. Sci. **39**(4) (2014)
29. Lewis, T.: Creativity in technology education: providing children with glimpses of their inventive potential. Int. J. Technol. Des. Educ. **19**(3) (2008)
30. Liu, Q., Geertshuis, S., Grainger, R.: Understanding academics' adoption of learning technologies: a systematic review. Comput. Educ. **151** (2020)
31. Mathieu, E., et al.: A global database of COVID-19 vaccinations. Nature Human Behav. (2021)
32. Nichols, M.: Institutional perspectives: the challenges of e-learning diffusion. Br. J. Educ. Technol. **39**(4) (2008)
33. Petersson, J., Hatakka, M., Chatzipetrou, P.: Students Perception on Group Workshops: A Comparasion Between Campus-Based and Online Workshops. ECEL, Berlin (2020)
34. Pimenta, A., et al.: Mental Workload Management as a Tool in E-Learning Scenarios, pp. 25–32. PECCS (2015)
35. Prasuhn, F.: Credit hours with no set time: a study of credit policies in asynchronous online education. Am. J. Distance Educ. **28**(1) (2014)
36. Russell, C.: A systemic framework for managing e-learning adoption in campus universities: individual strategies in context. ALT-J **17**(1) (2009)
37. Schrum, L., et al.: Understanding tech-savvy teachers: identifying their characteristics, motivation, and challenges. Int. J. Technol. Teach. Learn. **4** (2008)
38. Schunn, C., et al.: What Makes Collaborations Across A Distance Succeed? The Case Of The Cognitive Science Community. MIT Press (2002)
39. Simpson Scarborough: Higher Ed and COVID-19: National Student Survey (2020). https://f.hubspotusercontent30.net/hubfs/4254080/SimpsonScarborough%20National%20Student%20Survey%20.pdf. Accessed 9 July 2021
40. Streichler, R., Lewis, K., Staeck, J.: Reading Speed Charts (2012). https://mla.hcommons.org/?get_group_doc=222/1370658266-CreditHourPolicy.pdf. Accessed 9 July 2021
41. Strother, J.: An assessment of the effectiveness of e-learning in corporate training programs. Int. Rev. Res. Open Distrib. Learn. **3**(1) (2002)
42. Tondeur, J., et al.: Preparing pre-service teachers to integrate technology in education: a synthesis of qualitative evidence. Comput. Educ. **59**(1) (2012)
43. UNESCO: How Many Students are at Risk of not Returning to School? 30 July 2020. https://unesdoc.unesco.org/ark:/48223/pf0000373992/PDF/373992eng.pdf.multi. Accessed 9 July 2021
44. Wagner, R., Sence, C.: Vocabulary Acquisition. Guilford Press (2007)
45. Whalley, K., Hansen, J.: The role of prosodic sensitivity in children's reading development. J. Res. Read. **29**(3) (2006)
46. World Bank: Acting Now to Protect the Human Capital of Our Children: The Costs of and Response to COVID-19 Pandemic's Impact on the Education Sector in Latin America and the Caribbean (2021). https://openknowledge.worldbank.org/handle/10986/35276. Accessed 9 July 2021
47. Zhou, G., Xu, J.: Adoption of educational technology ten years after setting strategic goals: a Canadian University case. Austral. J. Educ. Technol. **23**(4) (2007)

Student Engagement, Online Learning and COVID-19: A Law School Perspective

Judith McNamara, Rachel Hews, and Zoe Nay

Abstract During the COVID-19 pandemic, law classrooms around the world underwent a major shift to transition rapidly to online learning as a result of campus closures and lockdowns. Learning in Law Schools was (and in some places still is) largely being undertaken online. This chapter will explore the impact of 'emergency remote teaching' on law student engagement and present the findings of a project undertaken in 2020, during a period during the pandemic when students were learning wholly online, which sought to understand how student engagement was impacted by online learning. It provides insights into how law teachers and law schools can learn from the experience to enhance the law curriculum by adopting student-centred and innovative approaches to online teaching.

1 Introduction

This chapter investigates the impact of the COVID-19 pandemic and the shift to online learning on law student engagement. The pandemic led to closures of higher education campuses in most countries resulting in a sudden paradigm shift for Law Schools from on-campus teaching to remote learning supported by online technologies. This change provides an opportunity to understand how students learn in an online environment by exploring the impact of 'emergency remote teaching' on student engagement. The effectiveness of learning and teaching strategies is best measured by levels of student engagement, which is a strong predictor of student

J. McNamara (✉)
School of Law, Queensland University of Technology, Brisbane, Australia
e-mail: j2.mcnamara@qut.edu.au

R. Hews (✉)
Faculty of Business and Law, School of Law, Queensland University of Technology, Brisbane, Australia
e-mail: rachel.hews@qut.edu.au

Z. Nay (✉)
Queensland University of Technology, Brisbane, Australia
e-mail: z.nay@qut.edu.au

C. Raj Kumar and S. G. Sreejith (eds.), *Legal Education and Legal Profession During and After COVID-19*, https://doi.org/10.1007/978-981-19-2568-9_4

learning outcomes in all modes of delivery. Engagement, put simply, refers to the effort a student puts into learning, and is generally considered to have behavioural, psychological and emotional dimensions. Bond and others provide a broad definition of engagement:

> Student engagement is the energy and effort that students employ within their learning community, observable via any number of behavioural, cognitive or affective indicators across a continuum. It is shaped by a range of structural and internal influences, including the complex interplay of relationships, learning activities and learning environment. The more students are engaged and empowered within their learning community, the more likely they are to channel that energy back into their learning, leading to a range of short and long-term outcomes, that can likewise further fuel engagement.[1]

Understanding the enablers and barriers to student engagement during the pandemic provides an opportunity to inform innovation in legal education towards a more student-centred, outcomes-focussed curriculum.

Law Schools in the twenty-first century have been facing increasing pressure to reform the legal curriculum to better meet the needs of students. Even before the pandemic, socio-political events were impacting how students learn in higher education[2] and the availability of technology and social media meant educators were already competing for students' attention both within and outside the classroom. Students themselves have also changed. Today's students have different learning styles, different cultural and social perspectives, they are generally technologically savvy, have access to vast amounts of information, and they are impacted by different economic forces. Accordingly, they have different learning needs. Twenge argues that today's students need more structured and interactive learning, specific instructions, frequent feedback, explanations of relevance of materials, strict rule-following and delivery of material in shorter chunks.[3]

Over the past 20 years, there have been significant shifts globally in approaches to learning and teaching in higher education with an increasing focus on student-centred learning, alignment of assessment to desirable outcomes and attainment of meaningful graduate outcomes.[4] While legal education is not immune from this shift, it has lagged behind other disciplines, particularly in relation to online learning, with continued emphasis on traditional approaches.[5] Despite calls for law schools to update their approaches to become more student-centred[6] and to embrace technology to 'enliven curriculum reform'—both to improve the student experience and better prepare graduates for future legal practice[7]—law schools largely continue to rely upon traditional approaches. Wolff and Chan suggest that law schools have been reluctant to use technology, arguably as a result of limited resources and lack of

---

[1] Bond et al. [2].

[2] Kahu [14].

[3] Twenge [27].

[4] Glofcheski [9], p. 135.

[5] Kennedy and Cosby [16].

[6] Glofcheski (n 4).

[7] Shackel [24], p. 204.

training and experience.[8] Where technology has been used, it has been argued that it has been for little more than 'massification' of legal education and 'death by PowerPoint'.[9] As Schwartz notes, legal educators tend to elevate the benefits of in-person teaching and imagine online learning in all its worst potential.[10]

Despite this reticence, there is growing evidence of innovation in legal education with increasing use of online, blended and flipped approaches.[11] Kohn predicts that quality legal education can be delivered online, and that online legal education will promote innovation and improve access to justice.[12] Recently there has been an increasing exploration of online learning, particularly since the lifting of American Bar Association restrictions on online legal education in the United States.[13] There has however been limited research into how online learning can be utilised in legal education to achieve these outcomes.

The pandemic forced a rapid pivot to online learning with little opportunity for preparation or planning. While the resulting 'emergency remote teaching' or 'emergency online pedagogy' does not provide a model experience, it does provide an opportunity to learn how law teachers can embrace innovation and harness technology to take a more student-centred approach and respond to the needs of current students.

2 Methodology

To better understand how COVID-19 and the move to online learning affected law student engagement, we conducted an extended online focus group with student participants over a 2-day period. Our focus group comprised 10 participants who were undertaking a Bachelor of Laws (Honours) or a double degree including the Bachelor of Laws (Honours), in Semester 1, 2020, at the Queensland University of Technology, an Australian university, who were all impacted by a rapid transition to wholly online learning during COVID-19. We undertook a thematic analysis of the data to identify common themes. These themes provided rich insights from our students and provided a clear sense of how students perceived their learning and engagement experiences during the pandemic. Our study showed the pandemic had a considerable effect on student engagement, which varied depending on students' individual circumstances.

8 Wolff and Chan [29, pp. 2–3].

9 Denvir [5], p. 4.

10 Schwartz [23], p. 116.

11 Kennedy and Cosby (n 5); Shackel (n 7) 209–10.

12 Kohn [17].

13 Ibid., 1.

3 Findings and Discussion

3.1 Flexibility

Technology can improve students' learning experience by affording greater flexibility and one clearly positive outcome of online learning experienced during the pandemic was greater flexibility and better ability for students to manage their own workload.[14] As Wolff and Chan note students can 'choose between a synchronous setting, where participants are present at the same time (though not necessarily at the same location), or an asynchronous setting when the participants are not present at the same time, or place.'[15] This flexibility is particularly beneficial in supporting access to education to those from 'non-traditional backgrounds'[16] and those whose ability to participate in live classes might be limited by factors such as the need to financially support themselves, caring responsibilities, location or mobility issues. This flexibility was particularly important during the pandemic which exacerbated external stressors such as work commitments, caring responsibilities, and mental and physical health. For example, one student suggested that their personal circumstances caused conflicting pressures on their time and this required them to reprioritise: *Some weeks this semester I have had to prioritise other activities like work and family over uni[versity].* The flexibility of online learning enabled students to make strategic choices about how they learned, such as allowing them to study intensively by engaging with multiple weeks of content over a short period, especially when an assessment was due. It also provided the option, for example, of pausing or re-watching class recordings and taking notes, or taking breaks to consult other resources and clarify concepts.

For students who are intrinsically motivated or disciplined, the flexibility of online learning allows them to better manage their time and conflicting commitments. In our study, the students who responded to the shift to online learning most positively and enthusiastically were those who had completed a previous degree, had previously studied remotely, or who were already balancing a combination of study and work. One mature aged student commented: *I enjoy managing my own hours and days – I've worked that way for decades. So, the independence and self-motivation required to study online, is something that I have been doing for about 10 years part-time, getting my last degree.* This finding is consistent with findings of other research that engagement during the emergency remote learning of the pandemic was positively correlated with having previous e-learning experience and greater self-efficacy.[17]

Various studies have suggested that flexibility of learning modalities should be retained in educational models (e.g., Green, et al.; Muller).[18] Muller found that

[14] Martin [19, pp. 7–8].

[15] Wolff and Chan (n 8) 4.

[16] Butcher and Marr [4].

[17] Ekici and Ekici [7, pp. 134–135].

[18] Green et al. [11, p. 867]; Müller et al. [21].

while teachers expressed a preference for on-campus learning, they accepted that e-learning would continue to be part of their future teaching practices where it would be appropriate to meet educational goals, with some expressing a preference for a hybrid model.[19] This preference was shared by students in our study who, when asked about their ideal learning environment moving forward, indicated a hybrid approach, including in-person plus both synchronous and asynchronous online learning, would be ideal. Participants suggested this hybrid approach would provide flexibility when learning online, which would allow them to personalise their learning experience by managing their own time and effort. In this way, it would accommodate their need for flexibility, including *prioritis[ing] other activities like work and family over university* when necessary.

While flexibility was strongly valued by students and has the potential to promote access to education it can also be a factor that leads to disengagement. Flexibility makes it convenient for students to make choices about their learning that reduce their engagement. Most students in our study reported that they chose to watch both lectures and tutorials asynchronously in preference to attending live classes. This resonates with Thornton's research that suggests law teachers perceive students to not appreciate the value of class interaction or critical discourse.[20] However, students in our study reported choosing not to participate in Zoom tutorials even though they did appreciate the benefits of synchronous learning. This may have been, at least in part, due to students' lack of preparedness for online learning and the use of e-learning tools which is discussed below. Engagement in learning is a shared responsibility of students, teachers and institutions and as such law schools need to seek ways to demonstrate the value of synchronous learning and class discussion.

3.2 Workload

Students at Australian higher education institutions reported an increase in workload due to the shift to online learning and more difficulty in managing their own time and workload.[21] Online learning requires a greater degree of independent learning and students can become overwhelmed with the amount of content available to them if they do not have the study skills to navigate the online environment. This was true for some students in our study. One student commented: *To be honest, I think the format QUT are using in their on-line forum is challenging, and at times overwhelming with the workload – but it is still enjoyable.* Another student noted they needed to take a day off every week and limit the number of hours per day studying in order to stay motivated. One aspect of online learning that may have contributed to the perception of increased workload was the availability of multiple different learning activities without the benefit of in-person guidance to assist students to manage their learning.

[19] Müller and others (n 18) 10.

[20] Thornton [26], pp. 87–88.

[21] Martin (n 14) 11.

Students who had not yet developed independent learning skills found it particularly challenging. One first-year student commented: *the workload to [sic] high in the early weeks – especially taking into consideration the amount of new information coming at me from every source. ie; website, discussion board, live tutorials – all new to me – I didn't realise the length of time it would take to learn a new 'law language'.* Students need support to develop the independent learning and time management skills needed to succeed in an online learning environment.

3.3 Authentic Learning

Tai and others found that 'authenticity and relevance of learning tasks were strongly associated with engagement.'[22] Students in our study also noted increased motivation when completing practically orientated assessment, as opposed to theoretical tasks. They described some of their best learning experiences prior to COVID as those that involved practical learning such as legal research and 'learning by doing'. When asked what their ideal future online learning experience would include, many students pointed to the need for relevant learning and practical skills. Students reported being motivated by practical assessment and developing transferable skills. For example, one student suggested: *technology that lets students practice practical skills in an interactive way.* Developing effective technologies to support the development of practical skills and replicating authentic environments should be considered as part of future research into online learning and Muller notes that efforts are being made 'to transfer practical learning experiences from physical classrooms into digital spaces'.[23] In law, increased use of technology-based simulations for learning, combined with authentic projects undertaken with industry partners, would provide students with a combination of safe, low-risk, and fail-proof environments (simulations) as well as opportunities to make connections and build networks to support career development (industry projects).

3.4 Synchronous Learning and Feedback

Ekici and Ekici found that synchronous online learning resulted in higher levels of engagement.[24] Several students in our study specifically noted that in comparison to asynchronous learning, the learning benefits of in-person or synchronous online tutorials included a significant improvement in their attention and focus, as well as allowing them to ask questions as they arose, and providing a source of accountability

[22] Tai et al. [26].

[23] Müller and others (n 18) 12.

[24] Ekici and Ekici (n 17) 135.

to stay on task. Students appreciated the ability to communicate verbally and non-verbally in Zoom tutorials. This is consistent with the experience of teachers reported in other studies that the lack of live feedback available in asynchronous learning left them 'to wonder how cognitively engaging their asynchronous learning material and activities are.'[25]

Where students relied solely on asynchronous learning, they reported a negative impact on their capacity to deeply understand course content and receive feedback on learning:

> Where lectures are delivered online, it would also be nice to see lectures being delivered live (e.g., through BB Collaborate), and then recording this live lecture so people have the option to watch it later. This may help with engagement, because then students can ask questions as the lecture is happening, rather than having to email someone after the fact, and potentially not getting a response for a few days.

Another student commented: *[D]uring the live tutorials, I participate and listen - and find I get confirmation that I am on the right 'track' with my study that week - or redirection to the right way of doing things - in a constructive manner.*

Even where students participated in synchronous classes, they reported a diminished sense of belonging and connection which led to reduced levels of engagement. Lack of interaction with teaching staff is a factor that is identified in several studies as having a negative impact on engagement during the pandemic, including informal interaction before and after classes (e.g., Martin; Muller, and others).[26] Teachers also reported difficulty maintaining student engagement even in synchronous online classes because they did not receive the same degree of verbal and non-verbal feedback from students and because online classes lacked the same degree of spontaneity, support, and individual connection.[27] This is in part because the physical presence of teachers enables them to respond to student reactions and provide instant feedback[28] and also due to the dialogic role of interaction with peers and teachers.

As a result of the limited feedback received from formal and informal teacher interactions, students in some studies have suggested there instead needs to be more timely feedback on submitted work.[29] Participants in our study suggested feedback be provided through quizzes, guidance on group assessments, rapid return of marked assessment, and individual feedback on tutorial questions. By far the most common theme in relation to feedback, however, was that it is best provided in live classes.

---

[25] Müller and others (n 18) 8.

[26] Martin (n 14) 10; Müller and others (n 18).

[27] Müller and others (n 18) 8.

[28] Jones [12, pp. 76–77].

[29] Martin (n 14) 10.

3.5 Physical Learning Environments

Physical and digital learning environments affect engagement by impacting whether students feel like they are part of a broader campus culture, and how they are able to receive support from staff and peers.[30] Even prior to the pandemic, Jones and others, found that studying online was a 'powerful determining factor' in law student well-being.[31] For participants in our study, the physical on-campus environment was a significant aspect of most students' experience. In commenting on their best learning experiences prior to the pandemic, students commonly drew upon examples of spontaneous interactions with peers and professors, as well as the capacity to interact through extra-curricular activities. Activities outside the classroom that were noted to enrich the student experience included faculty-specific clubs, sports teams, career and networking sessions, support groups, and informal study groups in campus libraries.

The physical environment changed significantly during the pandemic, as a result of isolation, a change of study space, and physical surroundings. For many students, this change to their physical spaces led to psychological and emotional distress which limited their ability to engage productively.[32] The change to the physical environment was a particular challenge for students with a lower socio-economic status,[33] particularly those in developing countries, who may have home environments unsuitable for study and a lack of access to technology and the Internet.[34] Ekici and Ekici reported that high levels of engagement were positively correlated with personal computer ownership, household internet connection, and having one's own room.[35] The change to the physical learning environment was an issue for many of the participants in our study even though they were studying in Australia and had good access to technology. Several study participants identified that COVID19 had considerable effects on their mental health and well-being, which affected their engagement and learning. As one student summarised: *My engagement is... heavily influenced by work and mental health.* Another noted that: *I find it challenging to study solo though as I can get quite agitated.* For another, this meant they *needed to take one day off every week - regardless of what I was doing* and for another they elected to study only one subject that semester.

Learning remotely from campus also reduced students' sense of belonging. Students emphasised the role of campus culture prior to COVID-19, including co-curricular activities, in shaping their learning experiences and promoting a sense of belonging and community. During the pandemic, students missed the informal on-campus meetings with friends and peers.[36] In our study, early year students, in particular, emphasised the importance of belonging and the negative impact of remote

---

[30] Zhao and Kuh [30].

[31] Jones [19], p. 14.

[32] Pokhrel and Chhetri [22, p. 135].

[33] Martin (n 14) 9.

[34] Pokhrel and Chhetri (n 32) 136.

[35] Ekici and Ekici (n 17).

[36] Martin (n 14) 10.

learning. For example, one student thought that shifting early-year law lectures to podcasts feels like *just being talked at* and that *building a class community is fairly important in early years.*

For some students, their engagement was negatively impacted due to the reduced level of interest stimulated by the attention, effort and effect of participating in an online class compared to that of an on-campus class.[37] One first-year student highlighted that the modified online course work differed from the collaborative and immersive environment they had envisioned for their law degree: *while flexibility is a strength and being able to catch up on material missed online is a bonus, missing out on live engagement either physical or online is not always a positive. Occasionally, this can affect aspects of how you choose to approach work.* This shift is consistent with several studies that demonstrate there were broad reductions in situational interest in education at the time of the transition to online learning due to COVID-19.[38] One possibility for offsetting this decrease in interest, is to seek to make 'online teaching creative, innovative and interactive through user-friendly tools'.[39]

In contrast to these negative impacts of the changed physical environment, for some students there were positive outcomes, because forced isolation meant they were no longer commuting or attending as many social events, creating more time in their day for study. For others, it allowed them to focus their time, energy, and attention on discrete tasks which served as a positive coping strategy during COVID-19.

3.6 Digital Learning Environments

The success of online learning is impacted by the expertise of teachers and students in using the available technologies.[40] As Wolff and Chan note, there are a range of online tools used to deliver education, e.g., 'webcasts, video feeds/video link, podcasts, discussion forums, dialogs/chats, blogs, wikis, quizzes, and student's online assessment'.[41] In addition, learning management systems 'allow teachers to upload digital teaching material to the web for around the clock availability resulting in an increased and flexible access to education'.[42] During the pandemic, a range of these online platforms and e-learning tools were used by educators.[43] At QUT, the online delivery during the pandemic mirrored the approach taken previously, which was generally 'flipped', with learning resources such as case and other readings and

[37] Krapp et al. [18].

[38] Garris and Fleck [8]; Wong et al. [28, p. 5].

[39] Pokhrel and Chhetri (n 32) 139.

[40] Ibid., 135.

[41] Wolff and Chan (n 8) 4.

[42] Ibid.

[43] Pokhrel and Chhetri (n 32) 135.

podcasts provided to students prior to small group tutorial classes. For first-year subjects, the approach also included on-campus face-to-face lectures. During the pandemic, the small group tutorials were facilitated online via Zoom and all lectures were recorded and delivered asynchronously. Thus, teachers delivering the course and students undertaking it were familiar with most of the technology and e-learning approaches adopted, other than the use of Zoom for tutorials. First-year students, however, had only been studying for a few weeks prior to the lockdown and they were, therefore, less experienced with the tools and the approach to learning and teaching used in the course.

Studies have shown that engagement with e-learning is stronger where students are familiar with the e-learning tools being used and with the process of e-learning (e.g., Ekici and Ekici; Muller and others).[44] Given the flipped classroom approach adopted in the course in which our study participants were learning, the use of synchronous classes (tutorials held on Zoom) was an essential element of the learning design intended to deepen learning, problem-solving skills, and critical analysis through discussion. Students generally did not have experience participating in this type of discussion in an online environment and some students found aspects of online participation uncomfortable and disconcerting which meant they were reluctant to participate during class. Indeed, most students reported that they chose to watch tutorials asynchronously, in preference to attending synchronous classes. Even where they did participate, they may not have fully utilised the e-learning tools available. For example, they were reluctant to turn on their video[45] or to use audio to ask questions. They also may not have known how to use text-based chat, or other platform affordances such as buttons for 'raising your hand' or 'liking' something. One student observed that they *...really have not enjoyed zoom tutorials, as I find many tutors quite strongly push students to switch on cameras and microphones, which is not something I'm generally comfortable with* .... However, as noted by Martin, failing to fully participate and to use the video component of an online class reduces the benefits to students.[46]

It should be noted that the discomfort of participating in online classes was not felt by all students. Some, particularly those who might typically be less vocal during on-campus classes, stated that it could be easier to participate in online classes than on-campus. As one participant in our study noted, for them online learning was an *equalizer for different personalities*, promoting equity through the capacity to *communicate verbally and non-verbally in class through the use of Zoom.* This is consistent with Muller's findings that some students who were less willing to ask questions in on-campus classes were more open to seeking clarification by asking questions through the Zoom chat function.[47] A question for the future is whether technologies can be used in on-campus classes in a similar way to the Zoom chat function in order to draw these students into the discussion.

[44] Ekici and Ekici (n 17) 136; Müller and others (n 18).

[45] Martin (n 14) 13.

[46] Ibid.

[47] Müller and others (n 18) 7–8.

Just as the ability of students to use technology in learning environments is important to the success of online learning, so too is the ability of teachers to effectively use e-learning tools. Ekici and Ekici argue that 'teachers need to know how to fully take advantage of readily available tools and platforms for online learning, and they need to develop a skill-set'.[48] The majority of higher education institutions already offered online and blended courses and so were better placed than other education sectors to transition to fully online learning.[49] Even so, the shift to online learning during the pandemic was sudden and unexpected and teachers were forced to embrace the e-learning tools available to them. Many were ill-prepared for such a fundamental change to learning and did not have time to prepare or to learn how to use e-learning tools. This presented a 'real challenge ... because online teaching and learning require[s] a completely distinct skill-set'.[50] Students in our study affirmed the importance of teachers being able to use e-learning tools. One student noted, 'Tutors and Lecturers need to be fully comfortable in the technological tools that they're provided to teach'. The best tutorials use tech to enhance their presentations and allow the class to participate in answering or working through the subject matter. For online learning to be successful, teachers need to be provided with professional development and support to confidently and effectively use the e-learning tools available.

3.7 *Teacher Empathy*

A factor that is critical to fostering a sense of belonging and that contributes to student engagement is the warm and respectful disposition of the teacher.[51] According to Kahu and Picton, caring is a marker of good teaching.[52] Anderson and others found that students perceive good teachers 'as people who show they care about their discipline or subject matter, teaching and students'.[53] Further, students describe teachers as demonstrating care about students 'through attentiveness, openness, awareness of students' lives and other commitments, responsiveness to students' learning needs and investment in students' well-being and learning'.[54] Grant-Smith and Payne argue that connection and care are at the heart of good pedagogy and that institutions must support teachers to provide caring practices.[55] Our study affirmed the importance of empathetic teachers and caring personal relationships, particularly for students

[48] Ekici and Ekici (n 17) 138.

[49] Ibid., 128.

[50] Ibid.

[51] Bryson and Hand [3, pp. 349–362].

[52] Kahu and Picton [15, p. 31].

[53] Anderson et al. [1].

[54] Ibid., 11.

[55] Grant-Smith and Payne [10].

who reported experiencing overwhelm, isolation, or other negative impacts of the pandemic. For example, one student emphasised:

> My ideal future in online learning would focus around student and professor relations, with more engagement and interaction occurring between the two. I don't expect super deep and personal relationships to develop, but I do think more creative mechanisms for collecting teaching feedback, regular student progress and even mental health can be harnessed.

Bryson and Hand found enthusiasm of teachers is also critical to fostering student engagement.[56] Consistently with other COVID-19 pedagogy research (e.g., Martin),[57] students in our study were understanding of the circumstances facing teachers and where they could see effort and enthusiasm for e-learning and the subject matter on the teacher's part, this too lifted their own engagement. For example, one student, who acknowledged they had not *particularly enjoyed* the transition to an online learning environment, nonetheless stated that one of the most engaging aspects of online learning had been the *spirit and effort* some lecturers invested in their teaching approaches. Expanding on what was meant by *spirit and effort*, students discussed the effort invested into teaching materials, their enthusiasm or excitement for the subject matter, and their willingness to customise the content to fit individual student learning needs. In contrast, disengaged teaching methods had a negative effect on engagement. One student noted:

> One lecturer in particular puts lots of effort into their slides so that they're entertaining, and is always cracking jokes and sounding excited. This makes it much easier to complete long lecture recordings as it keeps me engaged, whereas other recordings … are very long and sound like a script being read out, and I really struggle to focus.

While our study did not investigate the experience of teachers during the pandemic, anecdotally we noted the experience of colleagues appeared consistent with research which has shown that the motivation of many teachers during the pandemics was diminished with nearly 50% of participants in one study reporting negative impacts on their motivation, and 'rather than thriving, seemed merely to have survived'.[58] The lack of personal connection, struggle to engage students, and feelings of a lack of competence are real issues that need to be addressed by institutions planning future online learning. In the Moorhouse and Konke study, even those who were found to have thrived during the pandemic wanted to return to in-person teaching.[59] The impact of online learning on the well-being, satisfaction, and identity of teachers needs to be considered in any plan for online delivery.

---

[56] Bryson and Hand (n 51) 357.

[57] Martin (n 14) 7.

[58] Moorhouse and Kohnke [20, p. 283].

[59] Ibid., 285.

4 Conclusion

The insights from the experience of law students during the emergency remote teaching adopted during the COVID-19 pandemic can help to inform future innovation in legal education. Student-centred approaches to innovation, such as online and blended learning, are needed to ensure law schools meet the needs of students. It is clear that the flexibility of online learning can provide benefits in catering to different learning styles and improving access to education. However, without careful planning and development of effective online pedagogies, online learning can negatively impact student engagement and lead to diminished outcomes.

Engagement is multi-faceted and deeply complex.[60] While institutions and teachers can provide support and learning activities that enhance engagement, ultimately students' ability to engage in learning will be impacted by a range of personal, environmental, cultural, and socio-political factors that are outside the influence of the teacher. As a result, as Pokhrel and Chhetri note, there is 'no one-size-fits-all pedagogy for online learning',[61] individualised approaches are needed to meet the diverse needs of students.

A clear lesson learnt from the COVID-19 pandemic is that students and teachers need to be adequately equipped and supported to learn and teach online.[62] Students need good independent learning skills (time management and self-directed learning) and they need to know how to fully use e-learning tools. The overall design of online courses should incorporate the development of independent learning and time management skills to equip students to navigate the online environment. In order to support students' participation in synchronous online classes, teachers need to create safe and supportive learning environments. In class time needs to be devoted to learning how to engage in online activities, building students' confidence with online learning, creating a sense of community, and building connection between both students and teachers, and students and their peers. Teachers too need professional development to confidently use the e-learning tools available and to design effective teaching strategies.

The disposition of teachers, including their enthusiasm for online learning and their ability to demonstrate respect and care for students, is a critical factor in supporting student engagement. Given many teachers themselves feel less engaged with online teaching than with on-campus teaching,[63] law schools need to develop strategies to support teachers in developing confidence and enthusiasm for online learning. This chapter focusses on the student experience, but it is worth noting that this is critical also for the well-being of teachers.

A challenge for the design of online learning is how to develop interpersonal and social skills, create a sense of belonging and connection, and generate the same interest in learning that is more easily created in on-campus classes and activities.

---

[60] Dismore et al. [6].

[61] Pokhrel and Chhetri (n 32) 135.

[62] Müller and others (n 18) 11.

[63] Ibid.

More support needs to be provided for teachers to learn how to fully utilise the functionality of e-learning tools (e.g., Zoom chat, break out rooms, whiteboards, and polls) and to incorporate other tools like Miro boards that can support collaboration and the development of technology-based simulations for learning.

After the pandemic is over, law schools should encourage teachers to continue to use e-learning tools where they are educationally appropriate in order to provide more student-centred approaches to enhance the law curriculum.

References

1. Anderson, V, et al.: Good teaching as care in higher education. High Educ. **79**(1), 1–19 (2020). https://doi.org/10.1007/s10734-019-00392-6. Accessed 9 July 2021
2. Bond, M., et al: Mapping research in student engagement and educational technology in higher education: a systematic evidence map. Int. J. Educ. Technol. High Educ. **17**(1), 2. (2020). https://doi.org/10.1186/s41239-019-0176-8. Accessed 9 July 2021
3. Bryson, C., Hand, L.: The role of engagement in inspiring teaching and learning. Innovations in Education and Teaching International **44**(4), 349–62 (2007). https://doi.org/10.1080/14703290701602748. Accessed 9 July 2021
4. Butcher, J., Marr, L.: Bend me, shape me: flexible pedagogies to widen participation and deliver on social justice. In: Dennis, C., et al. (eds) Flexibility and Pedagogy in Higher Education: Delivering Flexibility in Learning Through Online Learning Communities, pp. 11–21. Brill (2020). https://doi.org/10.1163/9789004438118_002. Accessed 9 July 2021
5. Denvir, C.: Introduction. In: Denvir, C. (ed.) Modernising Legal Education, pp. 1–17. Cambridge University Press (2020). https://doi.org/10.1017/9781108663311.002. Accessed 9 July 2021
6. Dismore, H., Turner, R., Huang, R.: Let me edutain you! Practices of student engagement employed by new lecturers. High. Educ. Res. Dev. **38**(2), 235–249 (2019). https://doi.org/10.1080/07294360.2018.1532984. Accessed 9 July 2021
7. Ekici, M., Ekici, D.I.: Factors influencing student engagement during COVID-19 emergency remote teaching. In: Bozkurt, A. (ed.) Handbook of Research on Emerging Pedagogies for the Future of Education: Trauma-Informed, Care, and Pandemic Pedagogy, pp. 127–144. IGI Global (2021). https://www.igi-global.com/chapter/factors-influencing-student-engagement-during-covid-19-emergency-remote-teaching/276963. accessed 9 July 2021
8. Garris, C.P., Fleck, B.: Student evaluations of transitioned-online courses during the COVID-19 pandemic. Sch. Teach. Learn. Psychol. (2020) https://doi.org/10.1037/stl0000229. Accessed 9 July 2021
9. Glofcheski, R.: Rethinking teaching, learning and assessment in the twenty-first century law curriculum. In: Legal Education in the Global Context. Routledge (2016)
10. Grant-Smith, D., Payne, R.: Enacting care-ful engagement in the (post)pandemic care-less university. In: Bozkurt, A., (ed.) Handbook of Research on Emerging Pedagogies for the Future of Education: Trauma-Informed, Care, and Pandemic Pedagogy, pp. 169–190. IGI Global (2021). https://www.igi-global.com/chapter/enacting-care-ful-engagement-in-the-postpandemic-care-less-university/276965. Accessed 9 July 2021
11. Green, C., et al.: Preparing education for the crises of tomorrow: a framework for adaptability. Int. Rev. Educ. **66**(5), 857–879 (2020). https://doi.org/10.1007/s11159-020-09878-3. Accessed 9 July 2021
12. Jones, I.M.: Can you see me now? Defining teaching presence in the online classroom through building a learning community. J. Legal Stud. Educ. **28**(1), 67–116 (2011). https://doi.org/10.1111/j.1744-1722.2010.01085.x. Accessed 9 July 2021

13. Jones, E., Samra, R., Lucassen, M.: Key challenges and opportunities around wellbeing for distance learning students: the online law school experience. Open Learn.: J. Open Distance e-Learn., 1–19 (2021). https://doi.org/10.1080/02680513.2021.1906639. Accessed 9 July 2021
14. Kahu, E.R.: Framing student engagement in higher education. Stud. High. Educ. **38**(5), 758–773 (2013). https://doi.org/10.1080/03075079.2011.598505. Accessed 9 July 2021
15. Kahu, E.R., Picton, C.: The benefits of good tutor-student relationships in the first year. Student Success **10**(2), 23–33 (2019). https://doi.org/10.5204/ssj.v10i2.1293. Accessed 9 July 2021
16. Kennedy, A., Cosby, A.: Never mind the platform, here's the pedagogy: e-learning in environmental law. In: Kennedy, A., et al. (eds.) Teaching and Learning in Environmental Law: Pedagogy, Methodology and Best Practice. IUCN Academy of Environmental Law Series. Edward Elgar (2021)
17. Kohn, N.A.: Symposium: online learning and the future of legal education: introduction. Syracuse Law Rev. **70**(1), 1–12 (2020)
18. Krapp, A., Hidi, S., Renninger, K.A.: Interest, learning, and development. In: Krapp, A., Hidi, S., Ann Renninger, K. (eds.) The Role of Interest in Learning and Development, pp. 1–26. Lawrence Erlbaum Associates, Inc (1992)
19. Martin, L.: The student experience of online learning in Australian Higher Education during the COVID-19 pandemic (TEQSA 2020), pp. 1–30. https://www.teqsa.gov.au/sites/default/files/student-experience-of-online-learning-in-australian-he-during-covid-19.pdf?v=1606953179. Accessed 9 July 2021
20. Moorhouse, B.L., Kohnke, L.: Thriving or surviving emergency remote teaching necessitated by COVID-19: university teachers' perspectives. Asia-Pac. Educ. Res. **30**(3), 279–287 (2021). https://doi.org/10.1007/s40299-021-00567-9. Accessed 9 July 2021
21. Müller, A.M., et al.: COVID-19 emergency e-learning and beyond: experiences and perspectives of university educators. Educ. Sci. **11**(1), 19 (2021). https://doi.org/10.3390/educsci11010019. Accessed 9 July 2021
22. Pokhrel, S., Chhetri, R.: A literature review on impact of COVID-19 pandemic on teaching and learning. High. Educ. Future **8**(1), 133–141 (2021). https://doi.org/10.1177/2347631120983481. Accessed 9 July 2021
23. Schwartz, M.H.: Towards a modality-less model for excellence in law school teaching symposium: online learning and the future of legal education. High. Educ. Future **70**(1), 115–142 (2020)
24. Shackel, R.: Navigating e-spaces in legal education and legal practice. In: Gane, C., Huang, R.H. (eds.) Legal Education in the Global Context. Routledge (2017)
25. Tai, J.H.M., et al.: Student perspectives of engagement in learning in contemporary and digital contexts. High. Educ. Res. Dev. **38**(5), 1075–1089 (2019). https://doi.org/10.1080/07294360.2019.1598338. accessed 9 July 2021
26. Thornton, M.: Privatising the Public University: The Case of Law, 1st edn. Routledge (2011) https://doi.org/10.4324/9780203804537. Accessed 9 July 2021
27. Twenge, J.M.: Generational changes and their impact in the classroom: teaching generation me. Med. Educ. **43**(5), 398–405 (2009). https://doi.org/10.1111/j.1365-2923.2009.03310.x. Accessed 9 July 2021
28. Wong, C., et al.: College student meaning making and interest maintenance during COVID-19: from course-based undergraduate research experiences (CUREs) to science learning being off-campus and online. Front. Educ. **5** (2020). https://doi.org/10.3389/feduc.2020.590738. Accessed 9 July 2021
29. Wolff, L.C., Chan, J.: Defining flipped classrooms. In: Wolff, L.-C., Chan, J. (eds.) Flipped classrooms for legal education, pp. 9–13. SpringerBriefs in Law, Springer (2016). https://doi.org/10.1007/978-981-10-0479-7_2. Accessed 9 July 2021
30. Zhao, C.M., Kuh, G.D.: Adding value: learning communities and student engagement. Res. High. Educ. **45**(2), 115–38 (2004). https://doi.org/10.1023/B:RIHE.0000015692.88534.de. Accessed 9 July 2021

Legal Education and Legal Profession During and Beyond COVID-19. Studying Law During the COVID-19 Pandemic

Suzanne Rab

Abstract Professor Suzanne Rab, professor of commercial law and practising international barrister and mediator provides her reflections on a unique study of student experiences of studying during the COVID-19 pandemic. This short study is aimed at an initial exploratory level to seek to fill the gap in the existing literature. It provides the results of a pilot qualitative inductive analysis of the free-form (undisturbed) descriptions of law students' perceptions, expectations and experiences while studying in COVID-19. It is intended at a modest level to contribute to the existing and emerging global knowledge about the behavioural and psychological aspects of law students' functioning in a crisis and what measures can be taken to support students in this situation. The study explores the experiences of students of law in higher education institutions in the UK, reflecting on the situation in March 2021. Through inductive qualitative analysis the study seeks to gain a better understanding of the impact of the pandemic on law students' study experience.

1 Introduction

On 30 January 2020, the World Health Organization declared the outbreak of the coronavirus disease (COVID-19) caused by the severe acute respiratory syndrome coronavirus 2 (SARS-CoV-2) a public health emergency of international concern, i.e., a pandemic at the highest level of alarm. COVID-19 has affected the lives and well-being of every section of society. There are questions about the particular impacts of the pandemic on higher education students, who have found themselves having to ensure that they continue their studies safely but in unique environments and often away from their institutions. Many have had to self-isolate with others they do not

S. Rab (✉)
Serle Court Chambers, London, UK
e-mail: SRab@serlecourt.co.uk

University of Oxford, Oxford, UK

Imperial College London, London, UK

Brunel University, London, UK

C. Raj Kumar and S. G. Sreejith (eds.), *Legal Education and Legal Profession During and After COVID-19*, https://doi.org/10.1007/978-981-19-2568-9_5

know well and have had to adapt ways of working, including online. These factors raise issues about measures to manage the risk of the pandemic's transmission and the impact on the education and wellbeing, both physical and mental, for students studying through COVID-19 and beyond.

COVID-19 reached the UK on or around 31st January 2020, with the first documented case detected in York, North Yorkshire. COVID-19 quickly reached the pandemic level in the UK and, as of 2nd March 2021, there had been 4,188,400 confirmed cases in the UK and sadly 123,296 deaths, the world's fourth-highest death rate per hundred thousand population and the highest number overall in Europe at this time.

There remains a lack of detailed research on the lived-in experience of COVID-19 and many studies are ongoing. A range of research has been published on the impact of the pandemic on students including in the UK through the Student Covid Insights Survey conducted by the Office of National Statistics.[1]

Existing studies in a higher education environment have focused mostly on quantitative assessment including the experience of nursing students in a Middle East respiratory syndrome coronavirus epidemic in Saudi Arabia.[2] Other studies describe sources and ways of informing students during the pandemic and the difficulties.[3] A more recent study has captured the perceptions and experiences of Croatian B.Sc. nursing students at a single institution at the outbreak of the pandemic using qualitative analysis.[4]

The existing and ongoing research initiatives illustrate the importance of capturing the perceptions, experiences, and feelings of students during a crisis of global proportions, whilst also serving to inform the formulation of appropriate responses to provide effective protection and support.

Given that COVID-19 is a recent phenomenon, a review of the available literature has found that there is no currently available research that focuses specifically on the perceptions and experiences of higher education law students. Law students can be considered a prime candidate for a case study for a number of reasons. First, a typical lawyer mindset that is risk-averse means that lawyers and prospective lawyers studying in a pandemic are acutely aware of the need to take protective measures to minimise the risk to health, whilst accepting that compliance with governmental regulations may not be universal.[5] This situation can be very stressful for students with an impact on their mental health and studies. Secondly, the population has been exposed to misinformation about the pandemic. For law students who operate within a rules-based learning paradigm, the lack of available and reliable information can have an impact on their learning and achievement as well as on their mental health. Thirdly, the study of law in higher education tends to be vocational where law students

[1] 'Coronavirus And The Impact On Students In Higher Education In England [6].

[2] Centre for Disease Control and Prevention (CDC) [5].

[3] Irggal et al. [13, pp. 607–612]; Stirling and Harmston [19]; Al-Rabiaah et al. [2]; Hassan [14, pp. 19–26].

[4] Lovrić et al. [12, p. 188].

[5] Shultz and Zedeck [18, pp. 620–661].

intend to practice in the profession. Due to the COVID-19 pandemic and the closure of universities and business, including law firms, many law students have been unable to engage directly with future employers as part of the critical networking, including vacation schemes, that can provide a pathway to their future career.

This short study is aimed at an initial exploratory level to seek to fill the gap in the existing literature. It provides the results of a pilot qualitative inductive analysis of the free-form (undisturbed) descriptions of law students' perceptions, expectations and experiences while studying in COVID-19. It is intended at a modest level to contribute to the existing and emerging global knowledge about the behavioural and psychological aspects of law students' functioning in a crisis and what measures can be taken to support students in this situation. The study explores the experiences of students of law in higher education institutions in the UK, reflecting on the situation in March 2021. Through inductive qualitative analysis, the study seeks to gain a better understanding of the impact of the pandemic on law students' study experience.

2 Methodology

2.1 Theoretical Framework and Key Research Questions

The qualitative study was conducted in England in March 2021, one year on from the first nationwide government lockdown which forced the closure of all UK businesses, including regular university classroom training and necessitating a move to remote learning.

The study is designed to describe the phenomenon of law students' experiences of studying during the pandemic using the method of inductive content analysis.[6] This method is appropriate where there are few accepted theories.[7] The study is exploratory in that it does not have a single theoretical departure point. When set against the background to the study, the findings in other studies that have highlighted the impacts on student mental health and the emerging insights from the relationships between categories or themes, some results can be considered against cognitive theories of emotions. Some results can also be understood from the perspective of personality-type theories.[8]

The study focused on providing answers to the following questions: (1) what were students' expectations of studying before COVID-19; (2) what were students' experiences of studying through COVID-19; (3) what were students' concerns about studying through COVID-19; (4) what was students' use of technology; (5) what were students' perceptions on the impact on employment and career progression; (6) what were students' perspectives on how higher education institutions can best support

[6] Hsieh and Shannon [9, pp. 1277–88].

[7] Elo and Kyngäs [7, pp. 107–15].

[8] Holland et al. [8, pp. 1–12].

students studying remotely (Key Research Questions). A further question was added to allow students to provide comments, if any, not addressed in the responses already provided.

2.2 Participants

The participants in the study were 20 students studying for a qualification in law (or a subject with a law-related module component) at four higher education institutions in the UK. Given the modest and pilot nature of the study, purpose sampling was conducted based on the intended focus of the study.

There were 13 female and 7 male students. Most students were studying for an undergraduate degree (18) with 2 undertaking post-graduate diplomas. The study included 14 students who were studying full-time (up to 36 h per week over a 3-year period) and 6 who were studying part-time (16–18 h per week over up to a 6-year period). This mix was reflective of the fact that full-time students would typically be studying more modules at greater intensity, not be balancing study with work and be undergraduates. Contrastingly, part-time students may be expected to be studying fewer modules at lower intensity, balancing study with work and tend to be post-graduates. 17 participants identified themselves as ordinarily residents in the UK while 3 were residents of Northern Ireland, Hong Kong and Singapore, having enrolled at a UK institution.

The institutions reflected a range of organisational formats including traditional campus-based (3) and one which offers exclusively online tuition as well as mixed online and face-to-face courses. The campus-based institutions were all part of the Russell Group, a self-selected association of twenty-four public research universities in the UK.

The size of the sample was dictated by the pilot nature of the study and its informational needs. The inductive thematic saturation process involved in this study involved the identification of new codes and themes since the study did not have one strict theoretical starting point.[9] The saturated number of 20 respondents in this study is consistent with other studies which suggest that in order to obtain a meaningful insight into the data, the sample should be based on 1–30 participants.[10] The smallest sample size for qualitative interview-based research can be determined at around fifteen.

The criteria for inclusion in the study were: (1) participation in a programme for a qualification in law (or a subject with a law-related module component) in a higher education institution in the UK in the academic year 2020/2021; (2) voluntary participation in the study; and (3) completion of a survey comprising 12 questions (5 screening, 6 substantive, and 1 free-form optional questions). All questionnaires

[9] Bengtsson [3, pp. 8–14]; Saunders [17, pp. 1893–1907].

[10] Bengtsson (n 9); Saunders and others (n 9); Hsieh and Shannon (n 6); Elo and Kyngäs (n 7); Mason [15]; Lovrić [11, pp. 38–44]; Palinkas et al. [16, pp. 533–44].

that were attempted were included in the analysis of results as all were substantively completed in respect of the mandatory 6 substantive questions.

2.3 Data Collection

The data were collected using an online questionnaire containing details of the study, its aims, guidelines for completion and the research questions. The questionnaire was sent by email to maintain confidentiality. Any suggestions from the researcher were avoided. It was emphasised that participation in the survey was on a voluntary and anonymous basis and the results would only be published in an aggregated and non-attributed format.

The six substantive questions were formulated having regard to the need to control for potential biases in a manner that fostered inclusion, regardless of the answer. Non-suggestible, open-ended questions were included.[11] An additional open-ended question (which required participants to provide any other comments not made already) was included to allow students to provide their open responses in an unconstrained manner. There were no constraints on the amount of text to be included in any of the responses and a period of up to ten days was given to complete the survey.

Given the focus of the study to explore perceptions, expectations and experiences and to seek to elicit students' views on responses to dealing with the pandemic itself, the free-form writing approach has advantages over using a structured questionnaire with pre-populated multiple-choice questions and which require further controls for bias.

The written form of expression can be more appropriate than oral as it gives time to think and does not cause stress which can contribute to better quality answers. Incidentally, one student volunteered the information that they found the process of responding to the survey "therapeutic". Another observed that committing their thoughts to writing had helped them with their legal writing skills as they did not need to focus on the underlying legal content. Yet another commented that by contributing to the study they thought they could "also try to help others by getting the message out".

2.4 Ethical Considerations

Students were informed that the purpose of the study is to describe students' perceptions and experiences of studying law in higher education during the pandemic. They were told that the views gathered will provide a student perspective to supplement the learnings from professional legal practice and teaching.

[11] Bengtsson (n 9).

Participation in the study was voluntary and students could elect not to respond to the study. There was no follow-up action required on their part. There were no consequences for taking part or deciding not to take part. The anonymity of responses was ensured as all results were collated in pseudonymised form where information provided by a student was coded to their personal data (provided in response to the screening questions) which was contained in a separate file. Students were informed that any results published would be in anonymised and unattributed form.

Only the researcher had access to the underlying full dataset. The results of the survey and details of participants were not shared with the students' universities as the study was independent of those institutions. The research was conducted in the researcher's own personal capacity and independently of affiliation with any institution, organisation or professional body. The research was conducted on a pro bono (unpaid) basis by the researcher and all time and resources devoted to it were their personal cost. There was no external funding and no payment was obtained for this independent research.

2.5 *Analytical Framework*

This qualitative study used a conventional content analysis of students' open-ended written responses to the survey questions.[12] This involves a subjective analysis of the textual information through structured classification of themes to distil and interpret themes and patterns, through a system of coding based on categories and, where appropriate, sub-categories. This form of analysis can be used regardless of how the data are collated and contributes to a richer understanding of human experiences.[13]

The coding process was performed against the raw textual information where the researcher inductively created codes, categories and sub-categories. The survey questions and resulting codes and categories were peer-reviewed by a public policy expert who has worked with the main researcher on the design of similar qualitative research projects. This was intended to minimise the risk that independent researchers would draw different conclusions when examining the same data and where it is suggested that at least two persons need to code data separately.[14] Once the data were coded, the qualitative material (written reports) was further analysed in accordance with the research questions and overall analytical framework using inductive thematic saturation to provide depth of analysis. The data collection and organisation framework is reproduced in Appendix 1. Selected qualitative material from the students' reports is contained in Appendix 2.

---

[12] Ibid.

[13] Hsieh and Shannon (n 6); Elo and Kyngäs (n 7).

[14] Elo and Kyngäs (n 7).

3 Key Themes and Insights of Study

This limited study provides a qualitative insight into the perceptions, experiences and viewpoints of the UK law students during the time of COVID-19.

Some of the results of the study are not unsurprising and echo findings in other education contexts. These include particularly the ubiquity in terms of the impact on student mental health; the perception of 2020/2021 being a 'lost year' for undergraduates studying at the height of the pandemic; the role of technology in facilitating learning, and student dissatisfaction with the reduced socialisation.

Unsurprisingly, students expressed fears about the infection and its impact on their studies. The fear of illness was interesting as it centred much more on the negative impact of being stuck in a tiny room in isolation than fear of the disease itself (which may be logical given the age and risk profile of at least those students studying at undergraduate level).

No student discounted the significance of the health crisis or said that they did not adhere to the imposed lockdown and social distancing regulations. This responsible approach is consistent with students dealing with crisis events in other studies.[15] These results are also consistent with studies that have found that most students find coronavirus highly contagious and infectious.[16] However, as an academic tutor in a range of institutions the researcher finds that observed behaviour during the pandemic has tended to diverge somewhat from the written responses reported in the study.

The impact of the pandemic on mental health was recounted by all students. This issue was discussed in response to multiple questions as a recurrent theme and even where the question did not directly focus on mental health. This is not surprising and consistent with other studies which link epidemics with fear and high levels of psychological distress.[17] At a general level, fear and stress accompany the psychological, physiological and behavioural conditions that trigger coping mechanisms which combine to deal with unexpected adverse events. The pandemic can be considered a focal stressful event, in that it has occurred suddenly, sporadically and where the participants have little control.

In terms of the impact of students experiencing a disconnect between their expectations and actual experiences of higher education, there is evidence that this dissonance can present a risk of students withdrawing from their studies.[18] There was no overwhelming evidence among the small sample reviewed that students were disengaged with their studies and students showed resilience in dealing with the situation. One student did however note that they had decided to defer but believed that was a good choice for them.

The results indicate that students are divided into the highs and lows of studying in the pandemic. Accepting the sombre context of the study, students were able to appreciate some positive elements, variously documented through actions by universities

---

[15] Hassan (n 3); Irggal and others (n 3).

[16] Al-Hazmi [1, pp. 572–77]; Tork and Mersal [20, pp. 40–44].

[17] Al-Rabiaah and others (n 3); Khalid [10, pp. 7–14]; Wong et al. [21, pp. 657–59].4, pp. 912–920].

[18] Lovrić and others (n 10).

to provide agile online support, compensatory tuition or additional social activities; an ability to focus on other dimensions of university life particularly peer collegiality; a recognition of the importance of people coming together in a time of crisis and feeling a sense of community; greater contact with family; efficiencies from remote studying; and an affirmation that studying in the pandemic was an achievement in itself.

Contrastingly, the lows included a lack of environmental or full university experience; social comparison concerns as a result of peer pressure where students were told by others who had studied in more normalised times that they were 'missing out'; the impact of the infection on their ability to study and achieve; a lack of freshers' experiences; and the imperfect experience of remote learning.

Throughout this evaluation, students' own value and belief systems were apparent, reflected through their recognition of the gravity of the situation. This was revealed through students documenting that they engaged in pro bono activities and that they recognised a need to put community before self; itself a hallmark of courage. This suggests that perhaps a better characterisation would be in terms of the weighting of highs and lows in the face of a serious and adverse threat. That weighting may also be coloured by situation, for example, students electing for an exclusively online or executive (post-graduate) experience tended to view the situation differently from first-time undergraduates in a campus environment who were looking for a more holistic 'bricks and mortar' experience.

Related to the 'lows' students gave fulsome expression to their concerns with studying under lockdown, ranging from academic, health-related, financial and emotional.

With the imposition of remote learning, all students reflected on how technology had supported their education. This was largely viewed positively with opportunities for skills acquisition and development. Students recounted their investments in technology to deal with the pandemic as well as online support from their institutions. This issue in turn raises a question of a digital divide where some students may not have adequate financial resources to access technology. While online learning has developed in ways that may have been scarcely credible pre-pandemic, some students, however, expressed a preference for in-person examinations. The role of technology outside the curriculum was also significant as a partial substitute for student-led initiatives to achieve a sense of community and maintain their social networks.

The relationship between academic study and career prospects and progression yielded mixed and at times nuanced responses. There were concerns about the impact of the pandemic on achievement in examinations linked to the online environment but students did see the experience as supporting skills that would be transferable to the workplace, whether developing resilience or new skills or interests. A recurrent theme was the impact on work experience opportunities caused by limited access to networking opportunities, reduced benefits of online internships/networking and the limitations of interacting online. Students also reflected on the wider impact of the pandemic on the economy and pool of jobs and where wider exogenous factors, coupled with their unique situation, may worsen their prospects. Consistent with the results on the congruence between the expectations and reality of study under COVID-19, the experience of post-graduate students was largely neutral on career progression, explicable by the fact that such students had engaged in study more for pedagogic than social content. For them, the qualification was an end in itself and an adjunct to an existing career whose trajectory was not contingent on attaining the degree itself.

The relationship between themes, categories and sub-categories and, particularly, the nexus between physical and mental health was significant. This suggests that students' expectations, perceptions and opinions are shaped by their physiological reactions, their emotions and fears and which grounds the theoretical basis of this study in cognitive theories of emotions and stress. This may be useful in comparing the reactions of students in other contexts and geographies.

The views expressed by students can be explained overall by a concept of professional identity whose roots can be grounded in humanism, existentialism and phenomenology.[19] Thus, the study has shown that law students develop throughout their lives from their entry and progression in the educational system and continue to develop throughout their careers. It may be that it is precisely through their formative years in higher education and executive education that it is important to provide them with the support to foster resilience. This is where they acquire the knowledge and skills to become professional lawyers.

The study has highlighted a number of strategies that may be adopted to provide a safer and more supportive educational environment at a time of crisis and, potentially, beyond. These included providing effective online support; institutional flexibility in assessment methods; support for students' mental health; sensitivity to special needs including disabilities and carer responsibilities; assistance with tuition fees; greater preventative measures including planning, response strategies and preparedness; consideration of the needs of international students where remote learning should reflect time-zones; greater opportunities for face-to-face contact where permitted by public health regulations; greater coordination of centralised and decentralised communications; and student engagement in the institutional decision-making which affects them. These measures were postulated as a reaction to a dynamic predicament, while recognising the challenges of responding effectively in crisis, acceptance of the uniqueness of the situation and understanding the role of other support networks beyond the institution itself.

Additionally, and anecdotally, the study provides insights on students' perceptions on the effectiveness of institutions' responses in dealing with the unfolding crisis. Here again, opinions are divided. Prompt interventions in providing online support and continuity were applauded and students praised their tutors in dealing with the situation and adapting their delivery and materials. Where criticism was voiced, it was more targeted at the faculty or institutional level. This manifested variously as a need for greater sensitivity to mental health concerns and complaints about a lack of effective centralised communication.

[19] Brooks et al.

Overall, students demonstrated a philosophical approach to the situation sometimes displayed through courage, and overall humanity to others, including their tutors. Even where students put forward critical comments, this was mainly in response to the question asking them to identify how institutions can best support students. This is important because it reflects feedback with a view to changing the *status quo*.

The vast majority of students provided responses that were calibrated against the specific survey questions. Such responses were also largely congruent with the questions asked whilst traversing themes which were all-pervasive. When asked for "other" responses, a respondent highlighted a concern with the level of university fees. Although this was not addressed directly in the written responses, the researcher observes the issue of paying for rent for unused accommodation which has been very galling for many students. This may have given expression to a concern implicit in other comments on the dissonance between expectations and reality; namely, that students did not receive value for money and this imbalance will affect those who are least able to pay:

> While understanding that the costs of running the university largely virtually are high, it is nonetheless frustrating that university fees remain the same/are rising when students are unable to make full use of the facilities and may not even be on campus for much of the time. This will also be the harshest on those who are already suffering more from the pandemic itself.

As far as the researcher is aware this is the first qualitative study in the time of COVID-19 that has been undertaken involving exclusively higher education law students. The study may serve as a catalyst to inform research that can contribute to the design of student support strategies and provide a more effective learning environment during and after a time of crisis. To facilitate better understanding to inform evolving strategies, it is important to have a comprehensive insight into students' dynamic perceptions, feelings and experiences in a crisis. This study could also be an incentive to education institutions and the academic community to undertake further research in this area in the UK and elsewhere.

4 Limitations

This was a qualitative study where the participants included students from only 4 higher institutions in one geography (the UK).

Given that COVID-19 and its variants is a new and dynamic disease, the research takes place against an evolving landscape (at the level of pathology, and responses).

An important factor in the UK study was the sporadic nature of lockdown measures where, at the time of writing in March 2021, the UK is being progressively released from its third lockdown and where the success of its vaccine programme has been significant. The variability of the situation, which is inherent in any global crisis of unprecedented proportions, highlights the need for sensitivity to the fragility of these findings. It further underscores the need to replicate and scale the exercise, repeatedly, in different contexts if meaningful and transferable insights are to be gained.

The study was a pilot only where the sample size was at the lower boundary of statistical significance. As a result, the study is a reflection of the experiences of a small, though saturated group of participants and cannot necessarily represent a generalisation of the viewpoints of all law students in a particular institution, still less those in the UK and internationally.

Any interpretation of the results should, therefore, take account of the expectations for the study, and the fact that it was taking place in real-time where students were living through the experience. During the study, the relaxation of social distancing was in sight but the end point is not clear. It is also necessary to reflect on the specific identities of students of law and the elements of personality which have motivated them to study law in the first place. These include but are not limited to their attitudes to risk, rules-based paradigms, human interaction and social responsibility. It is also necessary to take into account that the effects of the pandemic on the 2020/2021 cohort may only be more comprehensively known many years from now and where the benefit of hindsight may bring added insights.

5 Areas of Future Research

There is comparatively limited study into the impact of global pandemics on university studies. As far as the researcher is aware, there is no comparable study on the impacts on law students. The unprecedented nature of COVID-19 means that there is a lack of experience and understanding of the impacts of the pandemic on many areas of life and there are many ongoing studies. The unfolding and recurring nature of COVID-19 and its variants means that it is imperative to gain an understanding of the impacts in a timely manner.

Potential areas for future research could explore: (1) whether the insights are sensitive to the context or population segment (e.g. undergraduates vs. post-graduates or full-time vs. part-time), type of institution (campus-based and others), geography; (2) the perceptions and experiences of academics, higher education administrators and regulators within a similar frame of reference; and (3) over the longer term, the attainment of the 2020/2021 cohort relative to previous and succeeding generations of law students in terms of academic qualifications and career progression.

6 Conclusion

The aims of the study were modest, namely, to explore law students' perceptions, expectations and experiences of studying during the time of COVID-19 and to obtain their views on how effective student support mechanisms could be adopted.

In so doing, it is anticipated or hoped that the study will further build bridges between the academic and professional practice of law in a changing and more digitised world and at a time of continuing (though staggered) crisis. The study may also expand knowledge about the impact on the student experience at a time of crisis and what steps higher institutions and the academic and professional community can take to provide better support to students.

Overall, this and other studies may contribute in a timely manner to a better understanding of the impact of the crisis on student functioning and aid the development of effective responses to global pandemics.

Appendix 1

Data Capture and Organisation

Main categories	Generic categories	Sub-categories	Codes
1. Students' expectations of studying before and through COVID-19	Academic	Content of curriculum	1. Importance of substantive content 2. Quality of the content
		Delivery of curriculum	3. Online delivery—positive 4. Online delivery—negative
	Non-academic	Interaction with other students	5. Reduced opportunities for socialising 6. Reduction in sporting activities
		The University experience	7. No change 8. Whole university experience 9. Value for money 10. The post-graduate experience 11. The part-time experience 12. Actions by universities

(continued)

(continued)

Main categories	Generic categories	Sub-categories	Codes
2. Students' experiences of studying through COVID-19	Highs		13. Intellectual engagement 14. Focus on other dimensions of university life 15. Collegiality 16. Greater contact with family 17. Efficiencies from remote studying 18. Studying in the pandemic as an achievement
	Lows		19. Lack of environmental experience 20. Peer pressure 21. Impact of the infection 22. Impact on mental health 23. Lack of fresher's experiences 24. Remote learning 25. Sporadic nature of lockdowns 26. Deferral 27. Recognising the personal and public significance
3. Students' concerns about studying through COVID-19	Academic	Examinations	28. Performance 29. Evaluation
		Knowledge acquisition	30. Comprehensivity 31. Access to tutors 32. Reduced intellectual engagement online
	Health	Personal	33. Contracting the infection 34. Impact of screen-time
		Public health	35. Responsibility
		Carer responsibilities	36. Balancing studying with carer responsibilities
	Financial		37. Loss of employment 38. Paying tuition fees

(continued)

(continued)

Main categories	Generic categories	Sub-categories	Codes
	Emotional		39. Sustaining motivation 40. Sustaining concentration 41. Insecurity, doubt and self-criticism
	Student's value system and beliefs		42. Recognising the gravity of the situation 43. Courage in dealing with the situation
4. Students' use of technology	Role of technology	Student behaviour	44. Investing in new technology—Students 45. Opportunities for skills acquisition and development 46. Preference for in-person examinations
		University actions	47. Investment in technology to deal with the pandemic—Institutions 48. Additional support to students 49. Pre-recorded lectures
	Impact of technology	Social	50. Student-led initiatives to achieve sense of community
		Health	51. Impact on physical health 52. Impact on mental health
5. Students' perceptions of impacts	Employment prospects	Examinations	53. Value of examination results 54. Format of examinations
		Marketability	55. Developing resilience 56. Developing new interests
		Networking	57. Limited access to networking opportunities 58. Reduced benefits of online internships/networking

(continued)

(continued)

Main categories	Generic categories	Sub-categories	Codes
		Interviews	59. Limitations of interacting online 60. Benefits of technology
		Economic situation	61. Impact of the pandemic on the economy and pool of jobs
	Career progression		62. Impact on executive development
6. Students' perspectives on how higher education institutions can best support students studying remotely	Academic		63. Online support 64. Institutional flexibility in assessment methods
	Non-academic		65. Support for students' mental health 66. Sensitivity to special needs
	Financial		67. Assistance with tuition fees
	Planning		68. Planning, response strategies and preparedness
			69. Overseas students
	Communication		70. Face to face contact 71. Effective communication 72. Regular student engagement
	Appraisal		73. Recognising the challenges of responding effectively in crisis 74. Recognising the uniqueness of the situation 75. Role of other support networks

Appendix 2

Results

The final categorisation of data is presented in Appendix 1, where 6 main categories were identified corresponding to the substantive Key Research Questions; supplemented with 19 generic categories and 18 sub-categories. This produced a total 75 codes.

Selected examples of students' statements are provided below grouped according to the Key Research Questions and codes. The students' own language has been preserved in its original form, as far as possible, with limited redactions for confidentiality. Grammar errors which do not impede comprehension have not been corrected to preserve the raw authenticity of responses.

A. Students' Expectations of Studying Before and Through COVID-19

Almost all undergraduate students recounted some difference in their pre-COVID expectations and the reality. The differences were most stark where the student was studying full-time in a campus-based institution.

> Studying through COVID-19 has made a drastic impact on my university life these past few months, undoubtedly far from matching my pre-pandemic expectations of university life.
>
> It could not match as expected. COVID-19 brought an element of fear and worry which affected my studies.
>
> It has certainly been different than expected.

1. Importance of Substantive Content

The academic substantive content of the curriculum is a driver of student satisfaction.

> The pandemic has not, relative to other students, had too great of an effect on my expectations, because I am still learning [ ], and I am still on track to attain the "badge", even though the experience has not been what it would normally be.

2. Quality of the Content

Some students affirm the quality of the curriculum despite the challenges of the pandemic.

> The quality of education has not fallen below my pre-pandemic expectations.
>
> The same as ever - the other students at a rigorously selective institution and a world class faculty make for a potent heady mix.
>
> [Institution 1] is still [Institution 1] and [a degree] is still [a degree].

3. Online Delivery—Positive

More than half of students identify some positive aspects of their online experiences.

> Online learning was actually more accessible than I had expected and allowed me to more readily plan my day and lectures in a more convenient manner.
>
> I am used to studying remotely on my laptop so nothing has changed here. The online tutorials are still the same. Zoom and Microsoft Teams have been brilliant for extra drop in tutorials.
>
> I am already studying in distance learning model, which I prefer. It has made more courses accessible to me.

4. Online Delivery—Negative

Online delivery is the most frequently cited area where students' experiences fall short of expectations for those who had chosen campus-based or mixed online/physical programmes.

> It was all remote which is disappointing.
>
> The lack of day schools and constant concerns regarding COVID-19, [ ] has resulted in less enjoyment during studies.
>
> It has not been the same, online tutorials are not as effective as day schools and there has been less interaction with peers.
>
> It has been very different from that of my pre-pandemic expectations, in that, there was no face to face tutorials which meant it was entirely online.
>
> The largest difference between my pre-pandemic expectations of studying and the reality of studying through COVID-19 is that of in-person teaching.
>
> Online teams meetings work well but there is no substitute for meeting a tutor in person and having a lively discussion.
>
> I was expecting/hoping to meet more students and tutors face to face in tutorials and be able to have discussions with them in tutorials and outside of tutorials. The pandemic resulted in all contact being either audio only (or in some students' cases, text only) with no use of the video facility.
>
> Studying through COVID-19 has meant that my study is more independent and isolated in comparison to pre-pandemic where I had access to face-to-face tutorials and was able to discuss ideas with other students.

5. Reduced Opportunities for Socialising

More than half of students report concerns about reduced social interaction.

> The social aspect of the university experience has been very disappointing vis-à-vis pre-pandemic expectations.
>
> It is very different in the social aspect - having no clubs, bars or pubs means that making friends and more importantly, maintaining friendships you already have is quite a more difficult task. Walks have become the new 'nights out'.

6. Reduction in Sporting Activities

Some report disappointment about the reduction in sporting activities.

> The cancellation of most (if not all) social events, as well as sporting events, have been disappointing to say the least.

7. No Change

For around a quarter, however, the pandemic had no material impact. These observations were made by those who had elected to take exclusively or mainly online courses and/or study part-time.

> Fully matched.
>
> To me it was a normal year like ones before.
>
> It feels the same as it's away from an institution.
>
> It has been fairly similar to the previous year's study in that a lot of my studying has been based online and I like it that way. Whilst I did attend a couple of face to face tutorials prior to the pandemic, this was more for the social aspect of studying and I do not feel not being able to do these have made much of a difference.
>
> The same as I usually did as [Institution 4] has always done it remotely.
>
> Covid has not really affected my study to a great degree. It has not changed the expectations I had pre pandemic due to choosing remote learning initially. Studying with [Institution 4] has been greatly beneficial throughout Covid.

8. Whole University Experience

Almost all those studying at a campus-based university feel that they have lost out on the full university experience.

> The main low for me is that I like to be "in the environment" e.g. actually staying in [Institution 2] and attending live lectures, which I find is how I learn best, and obviously that has not been possible.

9. Value for Money

Two students vocally and directly express concerns that the experience does not represent value for money.

> That said, I am aware that other members of the [2020/21] cohort very much felt that they had paid for the "experience", including networking opportunities.
>
> While understanding that the costs of running the university largely virtually are high, it is nonetheless frustrating that university fees remain the same/are rising when students are unable to make full use of the facilities and may not even be on campus for much of the time.

10. The Post-Graduate Experience

Most undergraduates studying at campus-based universities express some concerns but these are less prevalent for those studying as post-graduates.

> Further, if this had been my undergraduate degree, when the "experience" was more important to me, I would have been disappointed to have been part of the generation that attended university during the pandemic.
>
> In my personal situation I therefore feel that the age factor has played a very important role in determining my response to these questions – if I had been answering these questions whilst an undergraduate, the responses would have been very different.

11. The Part-Time Experience

Part-time students express less disappointment. These perspectives tend to reflect different priorities for study or the accepted benefits of combining study with paid employment.

> Put another way, the university "experience" was less important to me than it was for other students going into the pandemic, and therefore when that experience was not what would normally be expected, that change also had less of an effect.
>
> There has been times throughout covid where I have also been on furlough as well as working and studying. This has been a benefit due to having more time to study when in the first lockdown without worrying too much financially

B. Students' Experiences of Studying Through COVID-19

Highs

Some students could not identify any high points at all.

> It's difficult to think of any particular highs of studying through COVID-19.
>
> There are not many high points.

12. Actions by Universities

Around one-third expressed satisfaction with the steps that their institution had taken to manage the situation.

> The adaptations the faculty have had to make as a result of COVID mean that a lot of resources are more easily accessed online, which I think will carry on and be useful even after the pandemic has ended.
>
> The faculty have been quite good at making sure everything needed is available online so there have been a lot of online academic resources I've used to access books and such.
>
> Tutors appear to have adapted well to the circumstances and have endeavoured to provide us with the best experience possible with additional individual sessions etc.

However, one student was more circumspect where the institution had taken additional support measures in response to complaints.

> The only real high has been the extra attention and "gives" given to [] students.

13. Intellectual Engagement

Many students see the value of opportunities for increased study and intellectual engagement as a consequence of remote education

> The highs have been having more time for studying.
>
> I think my experience has introduced me to more areas of law than I was previously [un]familiar with such as protest law, mental health law, prison law and coronial law which has in turn made me consider different practice areas.
>
> High points of studying through COVID-19 has included having more access to external resources such as webinars by [a barristers chambers], more online events which I have been able to attend alongside work commitments such as the Student conference by JUSTICE and more time to read content not otherwise covered by the modules I am studying.

14. Focus on Other Dimensions of University Life

Students appreciate non-academic aspects of university life.

> There certainly have been highs: exploring a city which is more beautiful than words can describe; interacting with a colourful spectrum of cultures; falling in love with a new academic discipline.
>
> I have also learned about different places I would potentially like to gain work experience which I wouldn't have known about pre-pandemic and most university events are filled with commercial firms which I haven't been interested in.

15. Collegiality

Participants recognise the importance of people coming together in a time of crisis and feel a sense of community.

> I think the pandemic has brought students closer together who can collectively sympathise with the impact the virus has had both on our social and academic lives.
>
> Any friendships made in corona times are really really strong ones, because you spend so much time together.

16. Greater Contact with Family

Students appreciate the benefits in terms of increased opportunities to interact with the family.

> The high points have been staying at home with my family more than usual and approaching my studies in a relaxed environment- as opposed to rushing from one place to another which comes with the everyday work/life balance.

17. Efficiencies from Remote Studying

Some students find efficiencies in studying remotely.

> Studying in my opinion, is all about time management so the effects of the pandemic have actually benefitted me in that I have been able to stay at home more and focus on my studies.
>
> In terms of structure, remote learning has made scheduling freer than expected.
>
> What has been good is having fewer distractions and a less rigid schedule.
>
> Cutting down on travel times has also allowed me to have more meaningful rest incorporated in my schedule.

However, this finding is not universal.

> I have found studying at home to be extremely less efficient compared to studying at University.

18. Studying in the Pandemic as an Achievement

Students reflect positively on the study and academic performance during the pandemic is viewed as an achievement in itself.

> My highs were completing my undergraduate degree during difficult circumstances.
>
> The high has been getting through the first year, without falling.
>
> High point was receiving a mark of 77 for [an assignment] which I started in earnest at 6 am one morning with a deadline of mid-day.

Lows

Most students express lows, although this was not universal.

> I luckily do not have any low points to share.
>
> I have not had any concerns at all and have found that my tutor and the University have been very supportive and accessible when required.

19. Lack of Environmental Experience

Students observe the lack of physical movement and miss the ritual of 'going to' lectures.

> Another aspect that corona has made different is 'going to' lectures.
>
> I used to really enjoy the walk to university as a way to prepare for the day and the walk home as a way to switch off. Whereas now I find that I am sitting at my desk all day, it can be easy to lose focus.
>
> The downsides have been not having the option to do the walk in tutorials which [Institution 4] usually has on offer. I have found previously that being able to attend both online and walk in tutorials has been beneficial.

However, this preference is not universal:

> Studying from home is, at least for learners like myself, a very positive option. I have never found going to lectures particularly helpful.

20. Peer Pressure

Undergraduate students and particularly those in their first year feel they missed out relative to previous years.

> However, from speaking to second- and third-year students, it does appear that we have lost out on the more detailed and personal academic discussion that can be better facilitated by in person tutorials.
>
> Lows - constantly having other years tell us everything we're missing out on !

21. Impact of the Infection

Students describe the fear of contracting and the impact of the infection, often in graphic terms.

> Testing positive for coronavirus and being subjected to a sixteen-day prison sentence in my box room as a result of the failed test and trace programme was certainly a low.
>
> My main, but very strong concern was that it is impossible to predict if one is to fall ill at any time. Considering it is my last year I felt a huge pressure to manage to submit assessments "while I am healthy".

Low point was trying to pick up my studies again after spending the whole of January in bed ill with Covid.

Concern, as above, that I was unable to study during one whole month of the course, and difficulty in restoring motivation after an extended period of illness.

Having to keep up with my studies alongside health concerns and fatigue.

It was also difficult to manage physical illnesses and keep up with studies.

22. Impact on Mental Health

All students express concerns about the impact on student mental health, mostly their own but also that of peers.

My main concerns have been that of mental health.

Isolation during difficult emotional moments where I haven't been able to access support from family and friends.

Being locked up in such a small space was not only awful for my physical health – suffering from cramps due to a lack of movement and the symptoms of coronavirus – but also took a toll on my mental health.

Studying solely online can lead to a sense of isolation and, especially when having to study at home, that can take a very heavy toll.

While studying through COVID-19 I have been concerned about my mental health while also dealing with the mental fatigue of having to work and study from the same space for long periods of time with limited outdoor access.

The mental health side of things and missing the human adult company, meant that studying was sometimes difficult.

Concerns about mental health often elide with concerns about financial insecurity and physical health.

It was a tough time to go through. It affected me financially, my health and mental health as well.

23. Lack of Fresher's Experiences

First-year students describe their regret over the lack of freshers' experiences.

The lack of socialisation between myself and others on my course, especially outside of college.

The lack of social contact as well as not having many of the traditional freshers' experiences.

24. Remote Learning

More than half think that remote learning is a particular low-point.

The lows are that all remote is hard socially and limiting intellectually; losing those en passant conversations in the margins of lectures or over meals is frustrating.

In addition, not being able to attend lectures or tutorials in person.

One of the main lows was having technical issues during one of my January exams which caused a great deal of stress.

25. Sporadic Nature of Lockdowns

Students note the intermittent and 'stop-start' nature of lockdowns in the UK as an exacerbating factor.

> The continuous on and off nature of lockdown policy didn't help; glimpses of the end of this period were provided only to be taken away again.
>
> Another low of this is that all the sporadic lockdowns and changes of corona have meant that sometimes friends have to really suddenly leave and some can't come back for long periods of time - everything is very uncertain.

26. Deferral

Three students considered deferring their studies and one did so.

> And the hardest is having to defer even though I could have just carried on but sought advice from my tutors who were more than willing to refer me to student support for further guidance.
>
> I have had to defer, health wise, causing anxiety when it came to dealing with my university as I have had to reveal personal details about my family to be able to get my deferral.
>
> I was worried to be seen as a time waster due to my circumstances.

27. Recognising the Personal and Public Significance

Students' reveal a value system where they are able to consider both the personal and public significance of the pandemic and consider themselves more fortunate than others.

> Luckily, I was already working as a criminal paralegal before Covid-19 started and although I have been working remotely, we should all be back in the office soon which will be good. This means it has not affected me as much as others.
>
> As everyone is trying to work through Covid, similar covid related problems are true for everyone therefore I do not feel that anything has particularly slowed my career.

C. Students' Concerns About Studying Through COVID-19

28. Performance

Around one-fifth identify specific concerns that studying during the pandemic has affected their academic performance.

> This has impacted my mental and physical health and ultimately, affected my studies.
>
> I feel I could have done a lot better [ ]. My situation and the constant worry during these difficult times has meant I am/was unable to perform to my best ability.

29. Evaluation

Some students think that they would have performed better under normal exam conditions (in person).

> Although happy with my overall module result, I know I could have achieved a higher grade having done the [exam]. (Although I am aware this is taken into account when marking).

30. Comprehensivity

Although most students express satisfaction with the academic content of the curriculum, concerns were expressed that online delivery may not be comprehensive.

> Academically, I've had concerns that perhaps my teaching was not as comprehensive in the pandemic.
>
> [With] time-constrained zoom calls and pre-recorded lectures there is only so much one can ask about, so there has been lesser benefit in online teaching there.

31. Access to Tutors

Students report concerns about not being able to access their tutors as they would pre-pandemic.

> It can sometimes be a worry that its not possible to receive as much support as was available before COVID-19 due to the fact that when you do not see your professors on a daily basis it is harder to have constant support.
>
> Now in order to ask a question, you have to send an email, which can take time to reply to.

32. Reduced Intellectual Engagement Online

Students express concerns that online interaction may reduce opportunities for full intellectual debate and engagement.

> However, the lack of in person interaction with tutors, heated academic debate with other students, and society events has potentially impacted in development of career oriented social skills, e.g. thinking on the spot and networking.

33. Contracting the Infection

While the impact of actually contracting the infection is well-documented one student reports a chilling effect of having to take compensating measures to guard against illness.

> I am compromising my assessment marks for the sake of just getting through it sooner and quicker while healthy, but at least completing the year.
>
> Falling ill can (looking at other people close to me) unconditionally take away 3-5 weeks out of my life and this does not sit well with graduating this summer.

34. Impact of Screen-Time

Students document the health impacts of sustained screen time.

> I get very worried about the amount of time I have spent looking at screens over the last year and how it's going to affect my eyesight - I have purchased blue light glasses but these only help a little bit.

35. Responsibility

Students are philosophical about how the pandemic has affected their own prospects and show a keen sense of social responsibility.

> Luckily I have still been able to carry on my volunteer work [ ] for citizens advice and there are several ways in which law firms are adapting to giving mini pupillage's etc.
>
> The only downside has been not being able to the Law in Sport yearly conference and chambers open days but this can be done post covid.

36. Balancing Studying with Carer Responsibilities

Many students report the emotional and financial challenges of managing study with carer responsibilities.

> I am a single parent so trying to entertain the children who all have PTSD and one who also has ADHD and ASD was sometimes challenging.
>
> Obviously, I had to try and find things for the children to do which was expensive as having been brought up in the French countryside they are outdoors kids and get bored on tablets etc.

37. Loss of Employment

A number of students express financial concerns in detailed terms.

> Financially, I have been unemployed 5 months through the pandemic on two separate occasions, one was a voluntary redundancy and the other a house move so I have had to find employment.
>
> Additionally, at the start of COVID-19 lockdown I did not have a desk or chair and would mainly have to study from the floor for the first 9 months due to financial constraints, this was difficult as I previously relied on office or library furniture.

38. Paying Tuition Fees

Students express worries paying for their tuition.

> There has been financial concerns throughout the year due to working in events which cannot be done from home.
>
> Financially it was more difficult as I was mainly furloughed after a few weeks which meant a wage cut.
>
> Also, naturally the bills go up as we are at home all the time.

For one student deferral was the only option to manage the financial burden.

> I was able to reserve a place, sort how my studies were going to be paid and secure a discretionary fee credit which if granted, I would not be incurring costs to my studies in October 2021 start.

39. Sustaining Motivation

Sustaining motivation is the second most widely documented concern after and often linked to mental health.

Keeping the motivation going was not always easy.

Without any social events – or even casual catchups with a friend over a coffee and a bite to eat – to look forward to, it has been especially hard to maintain motivation.

I was unable to study during one whole month of the course, and difficulty in restoring motivation after an extended period of illness.

I was happy to start off that way but found as it went to level 2 studies it was hard to stay motivated as some of the concepts were harder to get through than others.

Now, obviously with [tutorials] being online, [it is] harder to motivate yourself to watch and I also take a lot longer because I do not have the ability to pause, rewind, slow down the speed, etc

It has been harder to maintain motivation when the cycle often consists of getting out of bed, working, and going back into bed continuously for the whole term.

40. Sustaining Concentration

Linked with motivation, students express difficulty with concentration which makes remote study hard for them.

During the pandemic, concentration was challenging for me because of the worries about my own and my family's health.

Being at home so much has made my concentration poorer.

It has been quite difficult to find motivation to study at home, and concentrating for long periods of time without distraction is also much harder at home.

When furlough stopped but work did not start back up, this occasionally caused a concern which had a slight impact on being able to focus my full attention on studying.

41. Insecurity, Doubt and Self-Criticism

Almost all students express emotional concerns which impair their studies.

Mostly in terms of social isolation, and uncertainty about the future (in relation to the job market, when the pandemic will end etc).

The stress/pressure to get better grades affects my mental health, making my self esteem low.

The workload is very intense and once you fall behind it is difficult to catch up.

Felt more pressure.

This leads to a lot of self-criticism and self-condemnation.

42. Recognising the Gravity of the Situation

Despite well-expressed concerns, students are able to reflect on the bigger picture.

However, I do realise there are bigger fish to fry in the world than my personal woes.

43. Courage in Dealing with the Situation

Students show a toughness and grittiness in dealing with the crisis.

I just get on with it.

This in turn had an effect on my emotional state as I have had to just get on with things but I find myself having panic attacks when thinking back through the year we have had.

D. Students' Use of Technology

All students used some form of technology to sustain their studies.

> Technology was a life saver as all my studies are online.
>
> I have readily used online library resources, computers and tablets to facilitate my learning and reading.
>
> I use my phone and my laptop for work. The books on my reading list are also easier to read from and annotate online, so all my resources are exclusively technological.
>
> Online lectures and tutorials, the online library for textbooks and readings.
>
> Zoom lectures, and zoom meetings with members of our team (a substantial part of the [course] mark is based on group projects, for which we have been allocated into teams).
>
> I am studying online anyways. I have considered taking other courses because of the online availability.

44. Investing in New Technology—Students

Many students explain that they have invested in new technology to support their studies.

> The best investment was a second monitor for PC, enabling open assessment works and sources next to each other.
>
> Noise-cancelling headphones also proved to be useful.
>
> I have a colour high-speed laser printer and have printed out many articles and case law and some statutes

45. Opportunities for Skills Acquisition and Development

Many students report learnings in terms of technology proficiency and skills adoption.

> I have become a lot more familiar with using Zoom and online employment portals with my university.
>
> I started taking digital notes on my iPad rather than using notebooks, I have also attended multiple online study events whether I was able to network with students from different universities and discuss key issues in law.
>
> Utilise google calendar to compensate for lack of memory and enter deadlines in to this calendar and rely upon it for prompts for upcoming work and deadlines.
>
> Being able to improve my computer skills more general layout, which will of course be of benefit subsequently with writing essays.

46. Preference for In-person Examinations

Some students express a preference for more traditional ways of learning.

> I much prefer talking to people in person and would much rather have had closed book, in person exams; not only for the ritual and tradition, but also for the greater sense of satisfaction that it provides.
>
> I would support a return to a mixed mode of offline-online education — or perhaps a return back to traditional modes entirely after the pandemic has been dealt with.

47. Investment in Technology to Deal with the Pandemic—Institutions

Students praise their institutions where they have provided state-of-the-art online support.

> The [library team] has been superb in attempting to mitigate the loss of library access. For everything else there is Amazon.
>
> [Institution 4] is example to follow for other institutions.

48. Additional Support to Students

Students report that institutions responded with additional technical support. However, there was criticism that this was more reactive than preventative.

> This resulted in a town hall meeting [ ] where various extra things were promised to [ ] students, for example extra social events once those are possible, an extra module, and various other "gives".

49. Pre-recorded Lectures

Students cite an increased incidence of pre-recorded material.

> Tutorial recordings have also been helpful, as they explain a topic in more detail.
>
> I have watched many recorded webinars and accessed free ebooks on specific areas I am interested in, which I would not have known about in the pre-pandemic world

50. Student-led Initiatives to Achieve a Sense of Community

Students show initiative in organising their own online events.

> Have used WhatsApp extensively to develop and maintain contact with other students.
>
> I am part of an advocacy club which use Zoom for competitions etc which has always been extremely reliable.

51. Impact on Physical Health

Students express concerns about the impact of technology use on their physical health.

> I get very worried about the amount of time I have spent hunched up in front of my laptop.

52. Impact on Mental Health

Students express concerns about their mental health in response to all Key Research Questions, including when discussing the use of technology.

> I think mental-health wise, it is an incredible amount of change for young people to go through.
>
> Inevitably, this takes a toll on mental health.
>
> There has been a toll on mental health: there is no outlet from academic pressure through sports or societies, and I personally have also found that tricky to address.

E. Student's Perceptions of the Impact on Employment and Career Progression

Students are divided but mostly equivocal about the impact on employment prospects.

> No impact. In future perhaps, this pandemic has created more options as working from home will be more possible.
>
> I do not think that my experience of studying through COVID has affected any future progress in my career.
>
> I do not think this has affected my prospects. Once again I have been lucky enough to remain in a job that I genuinely enjoy and in actual fact started the job in April 2020 – the onset of lockdown etc.
>
> Because of the Covid-19 restrictions and disruption it was hard to think about starting a new career.
>
> I am not sure; I would like to think that having my studies in person would've made my learning experience much easier and more enjoyable for me, and therefore I think that I would be achieving higher, and would get better job prospects if I was studying in non-covid times.
>
> I hope this is not affected unless I get a lower grade because of lower assessment marks.

53. Value of Examination Results

Students do not voice distinct concerns about the lack of value of the resulting examination grades but do reflect on the potential impact on their career progression of delaying study.

> I did consider deferring as my marks had gone down but time is not on my side at 45 and my boss said just pass it and then you can become a solicitor, we know you work very well so we do not care about your grade.

54. Format of Examinations

Some students show a distinct preference for sustaining normalised examination procedures where possible.

> The only concerns I have had through studying through Covid-19 are the end assignments.
>
> I was pleased the find out that the [end examinations] for both modules this year went ahead. It gives a sense of finality to the course and gives the chance to really push hard in the [final examination].

55. Developing Resilience

Students demonstrate a strong sense of robustness in dealing with the crisis,

> I see it all as preparation as I believe that nothing happens without a reason.

56. Developing New Interests

Students are able to see positive aspects for their studies in the face of adversity.

> Although, I have been made redundant, unemployed twice but managed to keep going through this pandemic, I found an area of law that I would be interested in and that is publishing, having had recent experiences that has piqued an interest in this area.

57. Limited Access to Networking Opportunities

Students report undertaking online work and networking experience.

> I have also been able to do virtual work experience.

On the whole, however, more than half had concerns about the accessibility of online work experience and networking.

> This has been one of the areas I'm most worried about with regard to COVID's impact.
>
> It's also more difficult to keep track of when things are and have an awareness of them when they are online.
>
> The lack of (face to face) networking events have also made it harder to make connections and find out about the firms and industry in general.
>
> It has become a lot more difficult I think due to the fact that work experience is so hard to come by at the moment due to COVID and most jobs want you to have as much experience as possible. This is difficult when no offices are open.

58. Reduced Benefits of Online Internships/Networking

Students voice concerns about the quality of the networking interaction online.

> It's also harder to have good conversations over a video call, which has an impact when networking.
>
> It's harder to join networking events when they're held online, as they appear a lot scarier when hundreds of people are joining a zoom call.

59. Limitations of Interacting Online

When such online events are available, students hold concerns that they may not be as effective as face-to-face equivalents in terms of developing skills that are transferable to the workplace.

> Online internships are much less interactive and provide fewer opportunities for networking than a physical internship would.
>
> I think my experience has lessened my ability to talk to members of firms in which I'm interested, given the limited capacity of zoom.
>
> Normally I would be attending networking events with law firms and organised events, but the lack of those has meant I have relied more heavily on being successful in balloting for online events, as well as using the Internet to source opportunities.

60. Benefits of Technology

Some students report technology has unleashed employment opportunities.

> Being used to using Zoom and similar online tools meant that I was more relaxed during job interviews and was able in November 2020 to secure employment (not in a directly law related field) for the first time in 5 years.

61. Impact of the Pandemic on the Economy and Pool of Jobs

Wide concerns are voiced about the impact on the economy and how this may affect jobs in law.

> Negatively. The increase in number of graduates across these few years and the decrease in the number of jobs due to the pandemic and economic prospects make it a hard job market to enter into.

62. Impact on Executive Development

Post-graduate students and those on executive programmes adopt a more neutral view of the impact of the pandemic on their experience.

> I don't think it has had much of an impact, as I think a key part of what I signed up to was the "brand" i.e. the brand of [Institution 1], and the brand of an MBA; and the strength of those brands have in my opinion been untainted by the pandemic.
>
> I see the [course] very much as a professional course and part of my career, and the "university experience" is not of particular importance to me. As a result, alterations to that experience as a result of the pandemic have not had too great of an effect on me.

F. Students' Perspectives on How Higher Education Institutions Can Best Support Students Studying Remotely

Students believe that institutions have an important role to play in implementing effective responses.

> My university and its academics appear to have done all they can with the provisions put in place such as online tutorials, lectures, and some limited social events
>
> I think [Institution 4] did very well during the pandemic although it was understandably a bit confusing at the start.

63. Online Support

More than half of students endorse the need for effective online tutorials and library/resource support.

> Continue to provide access for support when required, online tutorials.
>
> Replicate what [Institution 2] is doing, especially with [online] library access.
>
> Providing good technological infrastructure eg online platforms, libraries etc.
>
> I think it's best to make sure everything required is online.
>
> Offer them group and individual tutorials and other opportunities to interact using a video based tool, such as Zoom or use the video features of Adobe.
>
> Also use the text and video facilities on WhatsApp or similar platforms. Text only forums which are awkward to find and use are unlikely to reach the majority of students as they do not use these tools elsewhere in their work/lives.

64. Institutional Flexibility in Assessment Methods

Students generally urge sensitivity and flexibility in assessing performance, in particular regarding extensions for submission of marked assessments.

I think [Institution 4] was very supportive in providing [assignment] extensions. I never used one but it gave me confidence that it is there if needed.

Maybe [end of module] extensions would be useful for persons who fall ill, but then it is difficult as a new set of [end of module] tasks need to be created.

Possibly, I would run additional [examinations] in summer for everyone who was ill during original [examinations].

Answer emails quicker, as I missed many assignments and an [examined assessment] due to being overlooked at one of the worst points of my life.

65. Support for Students' Mental Health

The most frequent area where students think institutions can offer support is in relation to mental health and well-being

Whilst it doesn't seem desirable to accept late work constantly or absent students, I think unis should be a lot gentler in their approach to students this year and offer a lot of welfare support.

Ensure that welfare [support] is available where it is needed.

Higher education institutions can make it known to students what kind of support is available so that students are aware of the support while they are in difficulty rather than when they are in crisis.

More support and learning tools could be provided for those that are struggling. Support study sessions could be put in place for moral and educational support.

Group activities could be organised for peer interaction and emotional support, such as live debates or presentations via zoom or similar platforms.

66. Sensitivity to Special Needs

Students recognise that sensitivity is needed to reflect individual circumstances.

With my disability this means that I retain very little of the richness of tutorials and struggle to remember who my fellow students are.

The only thing I feel is a shame is that the [final examinations] were cancelled. I felt there was no need to do that as we had plenty of time to complete them. I was working from home, trying to home school 3 children, one of whom has special needs and none of whom have English as there first language.

67. Assistance with Tuition Fees

Students suggest that financial support should be available in cases of need.

If possible, financial support for those who require it.

68. Planning, Response Strategies and Preparedness

Students think that institutions have an important preventative role in crisis planning and preparedness.

Universities would be better to perhaps plan future events, coinciding with the easing of lockdown for students.

The uncertainty experienced by students would be well remedied by having events to look forward to: I think the lack of structure and non-academic events to look forward to has been one of the failures of universities generally.

69. Overseas Students

Students from overseas urge institutions to take account of their needs.

Consideration of timezones for international students is helpful.

Prominent examples [of lows] would be having to return home instead of staying at university accommodation due to governmental regulations.

70. Face-to-Face Contact

Students emphasise the importance of the human factor for their effective functioning in a crisis.

Have as much face-to-face time as possible and perhaps once a week drop in sessions where students can talk about things that they need help with rather than having to wait for emails.

There is also a need for some human connection, so peer supporters and such would be a good idea.

Would be nice to feel like part of a community and this is lacking when studying remotely.

Perhaps create hang out rooms for students to socialise.

71. Effective Communication

Students see communication as a specific area for improvement.

The best way universities can support remote study is good communication.

Communication from "the top" has been poor. It would have been better for those at "the top" to have held a meeting earlier on with students in order to set out their views and thereby help to steer the ship in the right direction, including by preventing any misinformation from spreading.

The decentralised nature of communication needs to change and to become centralised. Our cohort often receives many messages per week from various members of faculty, administrative staff, and individuals purporting to be in charge of this or that.

From the student end it very much feels like whenever one individual has a piece of information that they would like to send to students, they send it; and the cumulative effect of everyone doing that every time they have information to convey is too many messages, with bits of important detail "hidden" in amongst a flurry of emails.

What would be better is for communication to come less often from one or two key individuals, and for everyone in the faculty to first send their messages to those individuals for distribution, in order that key information can be highlighted appropriately.

[Institution 4] for example has been very clear with messages and communication throughout the whole of Covid.

72. Regular Student Engagement

Students think it is vital that institutions engage with them regularly.

It is also important for HE institutions to regularly check in with students as for many institutions this form of working is new and it is more useful to catch any gaps in their approach early, but it also allows students to feel more in control of their experience as they have a say in next steps.

One way I could think of is opening up a submissions line for students directly on how they can better support them during this pandemic.

73. Recognising the Challenges of Responding Effectively in Crisis

Students express some realism in accepting the challenges of dealing effectively in a crisis, particularly praising their tutors.

> I do not really think there is much more that [Institution 4] can do. It was already online before Covid-19.
>
> The tutors throughout the whole of my degree have always been great with communication and support with queries.

74. Recognising the Uniqueness of the Situation

Students show a sensitivity to the unprecedented nature of the crisis while dealing with an ongoing and uncertain equilibrium.

> However, through no fault of the institution, there simply isn't much more to be done; the experience will not be the same – nor comparable – until normality resumes.
>
> This is inevitable and could not be avoided given the current pandemic.

75. Role of Other Support Networks

Students recognise the importance of other support networks beyond their institutions, while noting that some individuals may be more in need than others.

> Universities should be concerned with student mental health, especially with regards to those that are deprived from a friend/support circle that they would have had in normal circumstances.
>
> I personally am lucky to not have been affected, though I know a few friends who have been struggling with these issues.

References

1. Al-Hazmi, A., et al.: Knowledge, attitude and practice of secondary schools and university students toward middle east respiratory syndrome epidemic in Saudi Arabia: a cross-sectional study. Saudi J. Biol. Sci. 25 (2018)
2. Al-Rabiaah, A., et al.: Middle East Respiratory Syndrome-Corona Virus (MERS-Cov) associated stress among medical students at a university teaching hospital in Saudi Arabia.' (2020) 13 Journal of Infection and Public Health
3. Bengtsson, M.: How to plan and perform a qualitative study using content analysis. Nurs. Plus Open **2** (2016)
4. Brooks, S.K., et al.: The psychological impact of quarantine and how to reduce it: rapid review of the evidence. Lancet **395** (2020)
5. Centre for Disease Control and Prevention (CDC): Severe respiratory illness associated with a Novel Coronavirus—Saudi Arabia and Qatar, 2012. MMWR Morb. Mortal Wkly Rep. 61 (2012)
6. Coronavirus and the Impact on Students in Higher Education in England: September to December 2020 (Office for National Statistics, 21 December 2020). https://www.ons.gov.uk/peoplepopulationandcommunity/educationandchildcare/articles/coronavirusandtheimpactonstudentsinhighereducationinenglandseptembertodecember2020/2020-12-21. Accessed 9 July 2021

7. Elo, S., Kyngäs, H: The qualitative content analysis process. J. Adv. Nurs. 62 (2008)
8. Holland, J.L., Johnston, J.A., Asama, N.F.: The vocational identity scale: a diagnostic and treatment tool. J. Career Assess. **1** (1993)
9. Hsieh, H., Shannon, S.E.: Three approaches to qualitative content analysis. Qual. Health Res. **15** (2005)
10. Khalid, I., et al.: Healthcare workers emotions, perceived stressors and coping strategies during a MERS-Cov outbreak. Clin. Med. Res. **14** (2016)
11. Lovrić, R., et al.: Changes in nursing students' expectations of nursing clinical faculties' competences: a longitudinal, mixed methods study. Nurse Educ. Today **59** (2017)
12. Lovrić, R., et al.: Studying during the COVID-19 pandemic: a qualitative inductive content analysis of nursing students' perceptions and experiences. Educ. Sci. **10** (2020)
13. Irggal, M.E., et al.: Evaluation of preparedness of healthcare student volunteers against Middle East Respiratory Syndrome Coronavirus (MERS-Cov) in Makkah, Saudi Arabia: a cross-sectional study. J. Public Health **26** (2018)
14. Hassan, H.M.: Knowledge and attitude of Al-Ghad College students towards corona virus infection. Int. J. Med. Res. Rev. **4** (2016)
15. Mason, M.: Sample size and saturation in Ph.D. Studies using qualitative interviews. Forum Qual. Soc. Res. **11** (2010)
16. Palinkas, L.A., et al.: Purposeful sampling for qualitative data collection and analysis in mixed method implementation research. Adm. Policy Mental Health Mental Health Serv. Res. **42** (2015)
17. Saunders, B., et al.: Saturation in qualitative research: exploring its conceptualization and operationalization. Qual. Quant. **52** (2018)
18. Shultz, M.M., Zedeck, S.: Predicting lawyer effectiveness: broadening the basis for law school admission decisions. Law Soc. Inquiry **36**(3) (2011)
19. Stirling, B.V., Harmston, J.: Readying nurses for clinical practice: protecting students during an outbreak of Middle Eastern-Coronavirus in Saudi Arabia. Journal of Nursing Education and Practice **5** (2015)
20. Tork, H.M.M., Mersal F.A.: Middle East respiratory syndrome-corona virus: knowledge and attitude of Qassim university students. KSA Glob. Adv. Res. J. Med. Sci. **5** (2018)
21. Wong, J., et al.: Psychological responses to the SARS outbreak in healthcare students in Hong Kong. Med. Teacher **26** (2004)

Experiences from Countries

A Case of Law Teaching in Brazil During the COVID-19 Pandemic: The Response of FGV Law SP to the Pandemic

Oscar Vilhena and Marina Feferbaum

Abstract Whilst implementing a new syllabus and teaching methodologies for its undergraduate law course, the São Paulo Law School (FGV Law SP) faced the sudden shift from in-person to online learning caused by the COVID-19 pandemic outbreak, without due time to set up a proper remote learning program. With a longstanding experience in teaching methodology development, it promptly deployed a 1-week teaching training course for the faculty, aiming for a smooth transition to remote learning, by providing digital online alternatives to active in-person learning techniques, in addition to general guidelines for online synchronous learning. By the end of the first term of the pandemic, the school surveyed the students to assess its strategies. The responses brought light to the advantages of active learning over expositive lectures in remote learning during the pandemic, not only as a shift from in-person perspective, but also as pandemic-specific issues, as mental health aspects. The pandemic strategies were continuously updated in the following terms, which gave satisfactory results. The overall success in minimizing learning losses during pandemic is a credit to the maintenance of institutional structures dedicated to teaching methodology improvement and to a highly committed faculty and students.

O. Vilhena (✉) · M. Feferbaum
São Paulo Law School of Fundação Getúlio Vargas, Sao Paulo, Brazil
e-mail: oscar.vilhena@fgv.br

M. Feferbaum
e-mail: marina.feferbaum@fgv.br

O. Vilhena
Columbia University, New York, NY, USA

University of São Paulo, Sao Paulo, Brazil

Centre for Brazilian Studies, St. Antony's College, Oxford University, Oxford, UK

M. Feferbaum
Center for Education and Research on Innovation, São Paulo Law School of Fundação Getúlio Vargas, Sao Paulo, Brazil

C. Raj Kumar and S. G. Sreejith (eds.), *Legal Education and Legal Profession During and After COVID-19*, https://doi.org/10.1007/978-981-19-2568-9_6

1 Introduction

Shortly before the beginning of the COVID-19 pandemic, the São Paulo Law School (FGV Law SP) had launched a curricular and pedagogical reform of its undergraduate law program, seeking to anticipate the changes in legal professions following the evolution of digital technology and the increase in interdisciplinarity. The rise of SARS-CoV-2 as an epidemiological threat and its rapid escalation to a pandemic in the early 2020s put to the test the changes then under implementation.

New course formats, new contents and new activities still in the adjustment phase for exclusively in-person teaching were forced into the exclusively remote modality, with virtually no time for adaptation. In spite of the highly unfavourable situation, the school has managed to minimize the losses caused by the long suspension of in-person activities, mostly because of a solid experience in active methodologies and constant investment in teaching methodology with a stress on the use of digital technology in the classroom. The experience of FGV Law SP suggests that the maintenance of institutional structures dedicated to improving teaching helps to face contingencies in education.

The structuration of teaching around a learning methodology project precedes the creation of the school in 2004. Established with the mission of offering an updated legal teaching, the school chose active methodologies as the pedagogical guideline of a syllabus focused on law as the basis for a democratic society and a tool to solve complex and challenging problems, which by itself was an innovation in legal education in Brazil. The country's context helps to understand the educational project of FGV Law SP.

Generally speaking, legal education in Brazil does not cater exclusively to the legal market. With more than 1200 undergraduate courses spread over almost a 1000 schools and with almost a million enrolments each year,[1] it is the university education that offers more admissions in the country, exceeding several times the demand for legal professions, such as lawyers, judges, public defenders, police chiefs, etc. This can be corroborated by the small share of graduates who pass the Brazilian Bar Association (OAB) exam,[2] which is required for most of the regulated legal careers. So, the professional destination of most law bachelors does not require any legal qualification except as a potential professional advantage, albeit superfluous for the practice of their activity.

The search for law programs does not seem to be affected by this reality, since the number of admissions has grown a lot in the past two decades, so much so that

[1] The National Institute of Educational Studies and Research Anísio Teixeira (INEP) carries out annually, since 1995, the Census of Higher Education https://www.gov.br/inep/pt-br/areas-de-atuacao/pesquisas-estatisticas-e-indicadores/censo-da-educacao-superior. [5]

[2] According to data from the Folha College Ranking (RUF), "of the 897 institutions of higher education that had former students taking the exam, 721 (80%) have an approval rate at the OAB inferior to 25%. Were taken into account students and graduates that took the OAB exam between 2015 and 2017". Some courses that did not have graduates yet (for being very recent) were not included in the survey. https://ruf.folha.uol.com.br/2019/noticias/minoria-dos-cursos-de-direito-consegue-formar-a-maioria-dos-seus-estudantes.shtml?origin=uol. [1]

it has recently reached the first place in an offer. Not that the recently graduated bachelors do not aspire to enroll in the ranks of the OAB, for this achievement represents a sort of approval stamp for graduates. But more important than obtaining a professional license to practice law is to obtain a higher education diploma, which allows for a professional evolution albeit in a different area. Even if this reasoning is valid for other careers, the law course is an option of higher education particularly sought by secondary education graduates because it is a traditional career, whose programmatic content turns out to be quite useful in daily life, whether professional or not, representing a generic education that can be profitable even in non-legal activities. Maybe for this reason (but not establishing here a relation of cause and effect) most of the programs only care to cover the regulatory requirements, without specific goals or approaches and without institutional pedagogical projects. Most programs are thus based almost exclusively on expository lectures, based on major codes and doctrine, and learning evaluation through content exams. In this sense, offering a law program focused on law in context, with the goal to contribute to the development of Brazilian society, with a structured pedagogical project was (and still is) a distinguishing feature in Brazil.

This characteristic of the FGV Law SP undergraduate program entailed a high cost for the structuration and implementation of the curse, given the dire scarcity of national references about active methodologies in legal education. Indeed, the syllabus was conceived from scratch and the pedagogical project was adapted from foreign programs and other areas of knowledge, two years before the start of the first class. The need to adapt and improve after the inauguration demanded the creation of coordination dedicated to the theme of methodology, as well as permanent efforts to revise the methods and update the syllabus.

A key agency in the implementation of this ambitious program is the Coordination for Teaching Methodology, which started as a curatorship of active methodologies that compiled and evaluated experiences through dialogue with the faculty. Having gathered this experience, these talks were institutionalized in an agenda of periodic and permanent meetings that evolved into an agenda of faculty training courses and a public-access database of didactic materials, created to foster methodological good practices. At the same time, a research agenda for teaching and technology was set up, and a working group was formed to assess national higher education.

In 2016, FGV Law SP started the above-mentioned reform of its undergraduate program, the most profound since its inception in 2004. The goal was to conceive a program paradigm capable of dealing on one hand with the growing complexity of law, observed in the rapid increase of specialized areas and themes and concomitant rise of interdisciplinarity. On the other hand, it had to cope with the transformations caused by the advance of digital technology, already perceived in the intense automation of the management and offer of legal services, as well as the huge expectations regarding artificial intelligence. The program based on the traditional division of law exclusively in disciplines turned out to be impracticable for the new syllabus, given the lack of space in the schedule to incrementally update the programmatic content. The adopted solution was to un-discipline a part of the program, combining in-depth understanding of the foundations of several areas of law with thematic courses based on contents traditionally thought on distinct disciplines, as well as to transversally spread wider contents and goals, such as the development of instrumental skills (like soft skills) and legal discussions involving the digital technologies subjacent to traditional content. The new syllabus was implemented in 2017. It was also part of the strategy to introduce as part of our obligatory activities the participation in "projects", thought by more than one professor and incorporating several disciplines, challenging students to solve complex problems.

In the same period, the Coordination for Teaching Methodology merged with the Group for Education and Research on Innovation (GEPI) to become the Center for Education and Research on Innovation (CEPI), aiming to unify the discussions about learning methodologies with the debates about technology and the future of professions, given the need for a closer assessment of the areas of teaching and market, already incipient in the Coordination for Teaching Methodology in the researches about the degree of technological insertion in the legal area. Practically speaking, the creation of the CEPI opened a vast line of research on law and technology, which enabled more experimentation in the classroom, both regarding the new teaching methods and the programmatic content, including transversal skills.

For instance, the professors involved in the activities of the CEPI offered within the new syllabus, in the semesters preceding the pandemic, several optional project courses were carried out in partnership with LegalTech and law firms that make intense use of technology, aiming to introduce the students to the use of technology in legal practice. Those courses required that the students master technological tools (including programming activities) to be applied in real cases from partner companies, with the mission of optimizing the legal work flux. All this happened in structured sessions in the check-in/dynamic/check-out format,[3] taught with active methodologies supported by digital tools, and sometimes with meetings outside the classroom environment, including in the open air, changing the learning stimuli from one class to another.

[3] The check-in/dynamic/check-out format consists in delimiting the content dynamic with check-in and check-out activities, to prepare respectively an environment of participation and reflection, as explained in the work of the professors involved in the CEPI [4]:

"Used in the Kaospilot program, it consists in a method to stimulate the development of social and attitudinal goals. The check-in is used to generate focus and engagement in the students at the beginning of the activity, operating as an "ice-breaker" for other participative dynamics. The check-out is used to stimulate a reflection about how they leave class. Both are conducted by means of simple questions, from which the students exchange feelings, experiences or expectations and feel that they belong to the group. Some observations:

The questions do not need to be necessarily associated with what will be done in class, but it is advisable that they already stimulate the students to turn their attention to it. For example, in a class about the application of criminal law, one might ask the students "say one rule, legal or not, that you never disobey" [2].

The check-in and check-out may be used in specific moments of the course for the students to express what they feel about the class and the group.

The check-in and check-out questions must be simple, quickly answered, passible of multiple answers, and should preferably refer to something personal for the students. They might also involve the use of metaphors (e.g. "if legal teaching were a food, which one would it be?').

2 The Context of the Pandemic

When the first case of COVID-19 was identified at the end of 2019, the syllabus for the first semester of 2020 was already defined, and classes began on the 1st of February, i.e., before the confirmation of the pandemic situation in March 2020 by the World Health Organization (WHO). The restrictions set up by public administrations to counter the advance of the SARS-CoV-2 were launched during the first semester of 2020. In the case of the higher education institutions of the State of São Paulo, following State Decree no. 64.881, of 22nd of March, in-person classes were suspended from 24th of March, and remain so up to now through successive normative acts from the federative unit. The authorization for remote teaching was already in force since the publication of Ordinance no. 343, of 17th of March, from the Ministry of Education and Culture (MEC).

With the abrupt beginning of the quarantine in the State of São Paulo, FGV Law SP suspended classes for a week in order to adapt the rest of the ongoing courses to remote teaching. In the 2 days of the first weekend before this suspension, the CEPI prepared a faculty training course focused on the use of digital tools applied to active methodologies, as well as a quick reference guide to use the Zoom videoconference platform, adequate for active methodologies. During the week of suspension, the faculty was promptly trained to resume classes in the remote format, being prepared to transfer most of the methodologies in use. This was only possible thanks to the knowledge and experience accumulated in teaching and technology, resulting from the maintenance during more than a decade of an organ dedicated to the improvement of teaching activities. Indeed, at the time of the outbreak of COVID-19, the methodological repertoire of the school was developed enough to guide the institution in the response to the educational contingency that resulted from the public health emergency. We should also mention the highly favorable situation of the students, strongly qualified and with excellent conditions to realize the propositions and challenges online, such as access to a good broadband, adequate physical environment for remote learning, etc.

Thus, the emergency training paved the way for the adaptation of active methodologies to the remote format. There were those who preferred to follow the path of expository lectures, with less pressure to master digital tools, under penalty of compromising part of the pedagogical goals. However, for those more prone to active methodologies, the training enabled a less traumatic transition, preserving as much as possible the original course planning.

An opinion survey[4] after the online experience of the first semester of 2020 allowed to draw a concrete picture of the situation of the students concerning teaching in this initial phase of the pandemic. With a sample of little less than a third of the

[4] The survey consisted in a questionnaire with 31 questions destined to undergraduate (381 students), master's and academic doctorate (65 students) and professional master's students (180 students) of FGV Law SP. Of these 626 students, 194 answered the questionnaire. [3]

students, we inquired into, among others, the factors of learning encouragement and discouragement.[5] The factors of encouragement were:

(i) The use of dynamic methodologies with the promotion of debates;
(ii) The formation of smaller groups for debates;
(iii) The demonstration by the professors of concern and interest in the students' daily life;
(iv) The use of digital tools for a more dynamic interaction.

The factors of discouragement were:

(i) The use of expository methodology, when applicable, requiring student participation for evaluation purposes;
(ii) The difficulty of online interaction;
(iii) Technical difficulties;
(iv) The confusion between the domestic and learning environments during synchronous activities;
(v) The fatigue resulting from the prolonged/excessive use of screens for the classes;
(vi) The substantial increase in the amount of asynchronous activities.

The results of the survey suggest the usefulness of active teaching methods in the remote modality, confirming the institutional guideline in favour of active methodologies and the advances obtained by the CEPI in its investigation of teaching and technology. Indeed, the dynamic of the active teaching methods (that foster student participation) appears directly or indirectly in the survey as a factor that encourages participation, as opposed to the expository method, considered a factor of discouragement. Considering the factor of discouragement as potentially detrimental to attention, and therefore to learning, then active methods must prevail in remote teaching in order to reduce the losses deriving from the suspension of in-person activities.

If the encouragement of student participation (and their engagement in the course) is what we seek to minimize losses, then the use of active methods limited to videoconference may not be enough, and might even aggravate the lack of interest, for example, due to the excessive verbal participation of a few. The incorporation of auxiliary participation tools is necessary to make participative activities more dynamic.

In this sense, digital interaction tools used in synchronous classes as a complement to videoconferences in order to enable a participative dynamic allows for student participation in an alternative way to verbal manifestation. This lends agility to the reaction of the group (substantially saving time in videoconference) and prevents the occurrence of prolonged individual speeches (pointed out as discouraging). Also positively evaluated, the formation of small groups turned out to be indispensable in

[5] The factors of encouragement and discouragement to participation were compiled from question 14 of the questionnaire, with the following wording: "which other factors do you consider that stimulate or inhibit the participation in the discussions in the virtual classroom environment? (please elaborate)".

several online participative activities. Therefore, it was encouraged in faculty training for emergency remote teaching and documented in the support guide.

However, specifically for teaching during the quarantine situation, it is necessary to aggregate other strategies that value the student as an individual, working on emotional aspects of confining or social distancing, so as to minimize harms to mental health, which can be as incapacitating for learning as the use of inadequate teaching methodologies for remote teaching. Regarding this, we draw attention to the check-in/dynamic(s)/check-out format, tested by CEPI before the pandemic and transferred to remote teaching, that not only fostered student participation (according to its purpose) but also provided support to their mental health. With these techniques, we created an adequate space for the manifestation of empathy by the professor (also positively evaluated), since it is more spontaneous and not restricted to programmatic content, which prevails in the moment of the dynamic, whose main goal is to carry on with the program.

The advantages of active teaching methods in relation to the expository method in the online format are not unexpected. The videoconference platform increases the distance between professor and student, discouraging the latter's participation and impairing their attention, already affected by the fatigue resulting from the interaction mediated by the screen. In the expository format, if there is no encouragement to participation, the student might behave as a mere spectator, and could even follow recorded classes, i.e. in an asynchronous way. Conversely, in active methodologies, the progress of the class depends on the students' participation, which makes the experience less tedious, thanks also to the possibility of social interaction.

Nevertheless, it is remarkable that the increase in asynchronous content was pointed out by the survey as a factor of discouragement. It is tempting to think of the strategy of using asynchronous content to better accommodate the students' agenda, thus reducing synchronous time and perhaps screen time. If it were true, this reasoning would lead to a conclusion favorable to the use of expository methods in remote teaching. But this was not the case, and for several reasons. In the first place, the extensive use of asynchronous content only shifts screen time, with a potential increase in the case of video content. In the second place, it transfers to the students the task of programming their classroom learning, which increases the total time of the individual study. Thirdly, it decreases the opportunity of answering doubts about the content, which may become impeditive to learn topics of great complexity. Therefore, its use must be restricted to cases of necessity.

These and other issues were forwarded for a revision of teaching in the second semester of 2020, resulting in a new faculty support guide to remote teaching during the period of suspension of in-person classes. This guide contained orientations related to the three essential aspects for the elaboration of course programs: time and planning of the classes, asynchronous activities and preparation for the classes and evaluation and ethical orientations. These aspects were quoted as sensitive points in the surveys conducted in the school. It is important to mention the ethical principles that the school adopted at the beginning of the pandemic:

(i) Excellence in teaching: keeping the pedagogical principles of the course and the quality of learning;
(ii) Protection of well-being: prioritizing the physical and mental well-being of the whole academic community;
(iii) Transparency: promoting communication and transparency, enabling a greater engagement in the reflection about pedagogical practices;
(iv) Fairness: ensuring as much as possible the equality of opportunity, belonging and inclusion.

Differently from the first semester of 2020, the courses in the second semester were conceived for remote teaching, taking advantage of the beginning of the quarantine experiences. This situation led to a significant improvement in the quality of the classes for the online environment, since professors and students were more at ease with the tools to use and challenges to face after the experience of the previous semester.

At the beginning of the year 2021, the situation of the pandemic worsened again, and therefore classes continued in the online environment. Students and professors already reported a stress from the emotional impacts that the pandemic caused them, and the online environment, without any alternative, was also a factor of exhaustion. In this scenario, we intend, in the second semester, to plan in-person and optional activities for the students and to adopt classrooms with technology for hybrid teaching. All these measures shall be evaluated with a view to ensure the well-being and health of the whole community, for we do not know what the sanitary conditions will be in the next months.

3 Effects of the Pandemic on the Provision of Educational Services in Brazil

The struggle against the pandemic in Brazil has turned out to be a relatively complex issue because of the lack of a national leadership concerned with the safety of the population. This confers a predominantly political characteristic to the theme, in detriment of the technical public health measures. Consequently, each federative entity has been acting autonomously, following local criteria, by turns technical, economic, political, etc., which creates highly unstable situations regarding restrictions. Such a confusion makes the horizon of predictability too short for the development of lasting action plans by private parties, which turns the process of adaptation into a permanent activity.

The Brazilian case is singular in the world because of two factors. The first, widely reported by the national and international media, concerns the negationism within the top levels of the federal public administration, that has been acting to boycott any measures promoting the safety of public health. The second is peculiar to the state form of the country, a federative republic composed of three federative levels, i.e., the union, the states and the municipalities.

Were these circumstances not enough, the social inequality and ill-distributed economic resources are old problems of our country, that were aggravated and made even more blatant by the new challenges brought by the pandemic. Added to this, the impact of the new technologies of information and communication was already imposing significant changes to the legal professions, making possible the automatization of several activities that traditionally are the tasks of legal professionals.

Brazil, with continental proportions, has very diverse realities, with distinct local needs, but the effects of this deep change in the market were already clearly noted. The concern with the replacement of legal work by the machine and the loss of jobs, especially in the capitals and large centers, was already perceived before the pandemic. And all this, consequently, impacts the way we teach—or should teach—law.

In the particular case of higher education in the municipality of São Paulo (capital of the State of São Paulo), the sanitary measures have entailed, up to now, only an uninterrupted suspension of in-person activities, i.e., an exclusively remote teaching. "Only" refers not to the extension of the effects, but to the simplicity of the situation, since the Brazilian case is sui generis and of great complexity.

FGV Law SP has had to adapt to the restrictions set up by the public administration in an attempt to counter the advance of the SARS-CoV-2. For us, as administrators of a teaching institution and professors, this huge challenge added to those already existing challenges in the legal and educational community in the last years.

The pandemic, one of the most extreme situations that we have ever experienced, made very clear that many law schools and legal organizations were not prepared to act in a world almost totally mediated by the new technologies. In as well as the familiarity with tools and resources, most legal minds were not formatted to operate in a highly technological world—and much less to teach in the remote modality.

All these transformations imposed on law schools the challenge, with an even greater urgency, of rethinking the offered education, and adjusting it to prepare professionals to act in a way consistent with the current context, increasingly digital and uncertain. All this, without setting aside the challenges to form capable jurists, with excellent analytical capacity, knowledge of law and numerous behavioral skills' indispensable to the practice of law.

In this sense, we would like to stress that higher education also has a central role in building and fostering the basic values of justice and democracy, especially in this new digital dimension we are living in, the infosphere. We are using with even greater intensity programs, platforms and media, constantly generating and providing data that companies imperceptibly collect, putting us in a vulnerable position.

Developing this digital awareness will lead us to orient our conduct, as jurists and individuals, in favor of a digital citizenship. Especially in the Global South, where we constantly generate and provide the most private data to several companies, without being able to choose not to provide them and without any clarity as to what purposes they will be used, this must be the target of our concern and attention.

Given this complicated context, in Brazil the effects of the massification in education, the scarce reflection about whom we are educating and for what reality, and the sanitary situation that we are living in only heighten the social and historical inequalities of our country.

With the quarantine, we have had to deal with students who had to take care of other members of their families, who lost their jobs and sources of income, who have (even more) difficulties in keeping up with their studies, even more so in the remote modality, either because of their family's conditions or because they do not have a computer and/or internet access to follow virtual classes. Added to these factors, there is also gender inequality, since many women, students or professors, are even more burdened with interminable shifts of domestic work, which impairs their study and work activities.

So how should we approach the quality and preservation of the course and school year in these conditions? We cannot keep on teaching in an emergency situation without taking care of the individuals and taking into account their stories, difficulties and circumstances.

The humanization of teaching and of the professor—student relations has been one of the fundamental aspects of our experience in FGV Law SP. After more than one year of teaching totally mediated by technology and without many concrete perspectives of being able to return safely to in-person classes as before, the faculty have had huge challenges to overcome, related not only to the new teaching technologies, but to how they should teach in this context, what teaching methodologies must be applied, and how to perform researches in these conditions. We have also noted among our peers that participative teaching and active methodologies have had a much larger adoption in law schools. It seems that a significant number of faculty members convinced themselves of the advantages and adequacy of promoting a teaching centered on the student, and that teaching this way is more effective for the learning process.

But the issue is not only teaching but being prepared to contribute to solve increasingly complex economic, social and environmental problems in the regional and global reality. To provide innovative and morally responsible solutions in such circumstances is one of the vocations of legal education, improving the research performed, the teaching offered, and the excellence in the education of the graduates.

This situation involves not only the faculty, but also the fundamental support and attitude of the teaching institution. If we can relinquish educating people that only mechanically reproduces doctrines, and instead foster a more creative and reflexive professional profile, with interpersonal skills and a critical attitude, we will achieve a crucial advance. This requires putting the student at the center of learning. The idea is to empower these students and make them accountable for the society they are building, shifting from a disconnected form of legal education to a more complex learning process that links our students to the social reality in which they are immersed.

Furthermore, humanity is going through a unique and delicate moment. Preserving the health and safety of students, faculty and workers must be the priority. If hybrid teaching is one of the viable answers to this situation where social distancing is necessary, one of the basic challenges that we face is to democratize this access to knowledge and legal teaching of good quality in developing countries.

The problems related to the crisis of legal education are something that academia has been dealing with for a long time. The pandemic accelerated some processes and exposed the need to face many others, historically and deeply entwined in the formation of countries such as Brazil. If the changes in technology and its use were already causing impacts in the pre-Covid-era, they will have an even more blunt impact in the post-Covid-era. However, these transformations will not be homogeneous, in countries such as Brazil, i.e., very distinct realities, regional and according to university type.

We are witnessing profound and swift changes in the legal profession. For this reason, universities and faculty must stay connected to these transformations in consonance with the professional profile that society needs.

New pandemics or other kinds of natural or social short circuits demand resilience and adaptation of the educational system in the near future. Thus, the digitalization of courses is what the future has in stock. Hybrid teaching is a model that copes partially with these challenges, but it must be very well conducted. If on one side it is not applicable to all realities, on the other side, in-person teaching will also not be problematic for certain vulnerable groups in the short term.

The current reality leaves no doubt that reinventing legal teaching with a focus on technologies is crucial. The fact is that we were submitted to a rapid curve of apprenticeship since March 2020. Besides, we did not have time in 2020. Based on this experience, we can and should plan how to conduct and face new emergencies and how to benefit from this experience to make legal education more efficient and accessible.

So, speaking of the future of law schools and legal education in the twenty-first century requires not only that we review concepts and methodological practices, but also that we look at the basic values of democracy and citizenship. This will contribute to the construction of a more civilized digital society, with legal professionals helping to build efficient and peaceful solutions for increasingly complex problems.

References

1. Alvarez, L., Righetti, S., Gamba, S.: Minoria dos cursos de Direito consegue formar a maioria dos seus estudantes (Ranking universitário Folha 2019). https://ruf.folha.uol.com.br/2019/noticias/minoria-dos-cursos-de-direito-consegue-formar-a-maioria-dos-seus-estudantes.shtml?origin=uol. Accessed 4 June 2021
2. Centro de Ensino e Pesquisa em Tecnologia (CEPI FGV Direito SP): Ensino Participativo Online: recomendações para o contexto atual. https://direitosp.fgv.br/sites/direitosp.fgv.br/files/arquivos/fgvcepi_rec_ensinopartionline.pdf (2020). Accessed 2 May 2021
3. Comitê de Diversidade da FGV Direito SP: Mapeamento de Saúde Mental e Bem-Estar de Alunes na Quarentena [Documento interno] (2020)
4. Feferbaum, M., Klafke, G.F.: Metodologias Ativas em Direito. São Paulo (2020)
5. Instituto Nacional de Estudos e Pesquisas Educacionais Anísio Teixeira (INEP): Censo da Educação Superior. https://www.gov.br/inep/pt-br/areas-de-atuacao/pesquisas-estatisticas-e-indicadores/censo-da-educacao-superior. Accessed 4 June 2020

The problems related to the crisis of legal education are something that has been [illegible] dealing with for a long time; the pandemic [illegible] and exposed the need to [illegible] many others, historically and deeply entrenched in the formation of countries such as Brazil. If the changes in technology and business were already causing impacts in the pre-Covid era, they will have an even more marked impact in the post-Covid era. However, these transformations will not be homogeneous in countries such as Brazil, a very distinct realities, regional and according [illegible]

[illegible]

Legal Education During and After Covid-19

Achilles C. Emilianides

Abstract The methodology, objectives, and teaching methods of legal studies differ from the standard respective notions of sciences and social sciences in university curricula and research, and have often led legal studies to be considered as an isolate, albeit extremely important, field. Recent decades have seen a continuous discussion about the challenges posed to legal studies by technological innovation, new research methods, and multi-disciplinarity. The recent pandemic has abruptly led legal studies to a new era, which had been discussed for a long time: online teaching, increased usage of podcasts and online material as teaching methods, a globalized environment. The aim of this chapter is to examine how the pandemic has affected and could further influence the new landscape of legal education. The case-study for the effect the pandemic had is Cyprus, a small country with both state and private law schools, which purport to teach not only domestic Cypriot law, but also Greek continental law, and English common law. The chapter then considers aspects of legal education in a post-Covid world.

1 Introduction

Recent decades have seen a continuous discussion about the challenges posed to legal studies by technological innovation, new research methods, and interdisciplinarity. The recent pandemic has abruptly led legal studies to a new era, which had been discussed for a long time: online teaching, increased usage of podcasts and online material as teaching methods, a globalized environment. Law is a unique academic field of study. The methodology, objectives, and teaching methods of legal studies differ from the standard respective notions of sciences and social sciences in university curricula and research, and have mostly led legal studies to be considered as an isolate, albeit extremely important, field. Law remains closely connected with the legal profession, and often views itself as a professional field, more so than an academic one. Whereas, most other disciplines have introduced collaborative works

---

A. C. Emilianides (✉)
School of Law, University of Nicosia, Nicosia, Cyprus
e-mail: emilianides.a@unic.ac.cy

C. Raj Kumar and S. G. Sreejith (eds.), *Legal Education and Legal Profession During and After COVID-19*, https://doi.org/10.1007/978-981-19-2568-9_7

as the norm, legal academics still mostly view themselves as isolated researchers, who do not embrace the 'lab' or 'group' mentality, and who are skeptical of multi-authored publications. In most jurisdictions, the sole author monograph remains as the 'golden rule' for promotion, whereas collaborative or joint publications are discouraged. Even the joint publication of Ph.D. students with their supervisors, which is the norm in most other disciplines, is still viewed as an exception, with the Ph.D. student aiming to complete a single-authored monograph. Legal research and education remains predominantly national in nature, and individualized, whereas most other disciplines have grown to be globalized and depend on collectivity. In an era of technological advancement, most law texts remain, despite recent progress, hard to find, and expensive.[1]

Despite criticism, however,[2] there is little doubt that law is one of the fields that deeply affects the life of people, and is a pillar for the organization of societies. It is a highly complex field, with dozens of specializations, and connection with most other scientific fields. Hence, law remains one of the most important disciplines in a university. The question of how legal studies can become more relevant to a modern society, however, remains a topical one, and the lessons learnt during the pandemic can help towards addressing these concerns in a post-Covid world. This chapter will discuss these challenges through an assessment of the challenges faced during the pandemic by Cypriot law schools. Cyprus is an interesting case study due to its experiment of mixing legal traditions at the level of legal education. Whereas, until fairly recently Cypriot lawyers studied exclusively outside of Cyprus, mainly in the United Kingdom and Greece, in 2007 the State recognized and accredited the first University Law Department to offer a fully-fledged law degree; this was the Law Department of the University of Nicosia, a private university, which soon had its graduates admitted in the Bar.[3]

The state University of Cyprus, which had been founded in 2006, but without yet offering a law degree, immediately followed suit, as did other private Universities (European University Cyprus, Frederick University, Neapolis University Paphos, University of Central Lancashire Cyprus). The accreditation of a number of law programmes in a number of universities, both state and private, and the relative dearth of domestic students, taking into account the small population of Cyprus, as well as the fact that a significant number of Cypriot students continued to study abroad, led universities to seek students from abroad. Aiming to improve their competitiveness, Cypriot private universities have focused on offering not only a Cypriot law curriculum, but also a Greek law curriculum and, sometimes, an English law curriculum, in an attempt to attract students from Greece, as well as other countries. This has led to a rather unique co-existence of Cypriot, Greek and English law curriculum. Whereas, the state University of Cyprus offers a Cypriot law curriculum, it purports to offer Cypriot law within a comparative environment. Three other private universities, the European University Cyprus, the Neapolis University Paphos and

[1] Stolker [35].

[2] Becher [1].

[3] Ebeku [15, 16].

Frederick University offer both Cypriot and Greek law concentrations, whereas the University of Central Lancashire (Cyprus) offers an English law curriculum. One University in particular, the University of Nicosia, offers all three concentrations (Cypriot, Greek and English) to potential students. Whereas, courses of Cypriot and Greek law are in the Greek language, courses of English law are offered in the English language. Perhaps, even more importantly, academics might teach courses in both languages and in any of the concentrations.[4]

2 Response to the Covid-19 Pandemic: The Cypriot Case-Study

On 12.1.2020 the World Health Organization (WHO) confirmed that a novel coronavirus was the cause of a respiratory illness reported in Wuhan, China; the cases had first been reported to WHO on 31.12.2019. WHO declared a Public Health Emergency of International Concern on 30.1.2020, and eventually a pandemic on 11 March, 2020. The pandemic is ongoing at the time of writing of this paper, with more than 175 million confirmed cases, and more than 3.79 million confirmed deaths attributed to Covid-19, until mid-June 2021. Recommended preventive measures relied predominantly on social distancing, and hygienic measures such as hand washing, wearing face masks in public, ventilation and air-filtering. Governments aimed to restrict the effects of the pandemic by introducing extremely strict measures, including lockdowns and quarantines, travel restrictions, restriction of movement, mandatory tests, workplace hazard controls, and business closures. As a result, the pandemic has resulted in global social and economic disruption, including widespread supply and food shortages, the largest global recession since the 1930s, and an overall suspension of what was previously considered as normality, especially in western societies. Cancellation of activities included the closure of the physical areas of educational institutions, including tertiary academic institutions, and the cancellation of numerous academic events and other activities.

The Republic of Cyprus confirmed its first Covid-19 cases on 9.3.2020. On 10.3.2020, the Council of Ministers of the Republic of Cyprus introduced a number of restrictive measures aiming to limit the spread of Covid-19. These included the suspension of the function of all schools of Nicosia for three days, a prohibition to organize large-scale events until the end of March 2020, the issue of guidance to travelers, etc.[5] On 11.3.2020 the Minister of Health published an order prohibiting the participation of more than 75 persons at the same time, at closed theatres, cinemas, restaurants, bars, coffee shops, and other halls where events are being held.[6] However, on 13.3.2020 more strict measures were announced, and these included the suspension of function of gyms and sports grounds, as well as travel restrictions. On

[4] Emilianides [17].

[5] Ministry of Health [28].

[6] Ministry of Health [29].

15.3.2020 the Council of Ministers decided to impose additional travel restrictions, and to suspend the operation of a number of enterprises, such as hotels, commercial centres, coffee shops, bars, restaurants, theatres, cinemas, libraries, cultural and sport centres, hairdressers, etc.[7]

On 10.3.2020 the Minister of Education, Culture, Sports and Youth (MECSY) issued an announcement recommending the temporary suspension of all public and private institutions of higher education in the Nicosia district until 15.3.2020.[8] On 12.3.2020, the MECSY issued a further announcement clarifying that the suspension of operations solely referred to the suspension of functions necessitating the physical presence of students, and that it did not refer to the faculty, research or administrative staff of universities.[9] In view of the reference to face-to-face operations, all distance learning operations could continue. On 13.3.2020 the MECSY issued a new announcement, pursuant to a re-evaluation of the situation by the Council of Ministers. It was decided that the suspension of the function of schools and educational establishments, either public or private, would continue until 10.4.2020.[10] On 9.4.2020 the MECSY further announced that the suspension of the function of schools and educational establishments, would continue until 30.4.2020. It was further expressly clarified that institutions of higher education either public or private, would not be allowed to carry out face-to-face operations during this period.[11] Whereas, in the first announcement issued on 10.3.2020, the MECSY merely recommended the suspension of face-to-face operations of institutions of higher education, this was no longer the case in the announcement of 9.4.2020, which expressly prohibited the carrying out of face-to-face operations. It should be noted, however, that all universities had ceased their face-to-face operations after 11.3.2020. Moreover, some universities had not only suspended face-to-face operations of their students but also of their faculty and administrative staff, despite the latter not being required by the measures having been introduced. The MECSY eventually allowed the universities to carry out face-to-face studies from 11.5.2020 onwards, subject, however, to compliance with the recommendations issued by the Ministry of Health.[12] This loosening of measures was issued, however, too late in the semester for it to have any impact, and most universities opted to not resume face-to-face operations, especially in view of the strict requirements of the guidelines issued by the Ministry of Health.

Transition to an online environment entailed a number of difficulties. Many Cypriot universities had no previous experience with online learning. Faculty and students had to switch to online teaching without warning, and train in the use of electronic resources. Faculty had to further reformulate the delivery of their courses for them to become academically sound. In principle, the students received in an online environment the same number of teaching hours provided in their original

[7] Ministry of Health [30].

[8] MECSY [26].

[9] MECSY [25].

[10] MECSY [23].

[11] MECSY [24].

[12] MECSY [27].

face-to-face schedule. This was especially important for undergraduate students, who require consistency in their studies and who have not yet acquired advanced skills of independent self-learning and reflection. It should be noted, however, that a Distance Learning (DL) course is designed differently than a conventional course. The notion of DL is not restricted to teaching by electronic means but presupposes an educational philosophy consistent with a DL environment. This would be difficult to achieve, especially in LLB courses.

Each of the universities operating in Cyprus during the Spring 2020 semester, had individually prepared its own strategy on how to operate during the pandemic. However, there was from the beginning also a co-ordinated approach at the national level, in order to develop a general national framework within which all universities would operate. The Cyprus Agency of Quality Assurance and Accreditation of Higher Education (CYQAA) issued an announcement on 10.3.2020 declaring its support for the policy that other universities in the EU had adopted for indefinite online delivery of classes, so that students would be in a position to continue their studies during the pandemic. It stressed, however, that quality assurance ought to remain a priority, and that universities should maintain available all records of electronic classes and meetings.[13] On 17.3.2020 the CYQAA announced a list of tools for online delivery of courses, which is considered as options to be used by the universities. These included: Google Classroom, Learncube, Microsoft Teams, Edmodo, Moodle, Blackboard, Wizig, and Zoom. It was indicated that courses ought to continue to be offered in the same dates/times as originally scheduled and that the material ought to be available to students at any time in an electronic environment. All online courses ought to be recorded and keep attendance records.[14] On 30.9.2020 the CYQAA further clarified that recorded lecturers and examinations should be stored to secured electronic bases for a period no longer than six months; access should be provided only to authorized personnel, and for no purpose other than ensuring and monitoring the quality of the education offered. All procedures should be consistent with the GDPR.[15]

The Cyprus Rectors' Conference (CRC), which comprises of the Rectors of all Universities in Cyprus, also aimed to establish a common framework for the response of Cypriot Universities to the pandemic. On 19.3.2020 the CRC approved a Resolution, that was sent to the CYQAA. The Resolution welcomed the full compliance of all higher education institutions with the emergency measures introduced by the Government, and purporting to address the dangers posed by the pandemic, and stressed that the objective of all Cypriot universities was to complete, without delay, the spring 2020 semester, as announced to students at the beginning of the academic year. Students were reassured that their academic path and professional trajectory, as well as ensuring their health and safety, were the highest priority. The CRC announcement clarified that all universities had adopted and implemented DL mode of delivery, utilizing online and digital tools and techniques, so as to assure high quality of the education offered, with the active support and co-operation of the

---

[13] CYQAA [10].

[14] CYQAA [5].

[15] CYQAA [13].

CYQAA.[16] The Pancyprian Federation of Student Unions (POFEN) also provided input to universities, which was taken into account.

The CYQAA announced on 19.3.2020 that the interim exams should be held from distance, and recommended open-book exams, with practical questions.[17] The CRC met with the Chair of the CYQAA on 30.3.2020, and the latter extended the CYQAA's full support and commitment towards the efforts of the universities to employ also alternative methods of assessment. However, it was stressed that decisions about the final exams should be taken after thorough consideration of the matter, since there should be sufficient safeguards about quality assurance.[18] On 31.3.2020 the CYQAA acknowledged that there could not be a single policy or uniform examination method to be adopted in all fields, since different considerations apply to different courses. It was further stressed that the preferences of the instructors/examiners of the courses, as well as of the co-ordinators of programmes, should be seriously taken into account, and potentially given preference, to the extent that they did not fall below quality assurance standards. In general, the CYQAA recommended that the universities adopt one of the following alternative methods of assessment: (a) oral exams in small group of students, (b) written exam by electronic means and invigilation, or (c) open-book, or take-home exams with innovative and challenging original questions.[19] On 29.4.2020 the CYQAA further clarified that each instructor ought to be allowed to elect the alternative method of assessment, pursuant to the institutional decisions and consistent with CYQAA guidelines. Quality necessitated the introduction of specific time frame for carrying out the exams, monitoring and recording of the oral or written online exams, and identification of students who participate in the exams.[20] The Chair of the Parliamentary Committee on Education stated that there was no need to enact specific legislation on the function of universities during the pandemic, since all universities could take measures within the ambit of the existing legislative framework in order to apply alternative methods of assessment pursuant to the CYQAA guidelines. It was stressed that all universities were bound to abide by the decisions and guidelines of the CYQAA.[21]

The intention of certain universities to hold electronically invigilated exams through the Proctorio system or equivalent, was met with a negative reaction by a number of organized groups of students, who raised concern about the privacy and security of the date stored on the computer used for taking the examination. These considerations further extended to invigilation via webex and the recording of oral examinations through webex. On 10.4.2020 the CYQAA acknowledged that all procedures should be consistent with the EU General Data Protection Regulation (GDPR) regarding personal data protection.[22] Taking into account student concerns,

[16] CRC [4].

[17] CYQAA [7].

[18] CYQAA [7].

[19] CYQAA [9].

[20] CYQAA [8].

[21] Hadjiyiannis [18].

[22] CYQAA [12].

the Commissioner for Personal Data Protection (CPDP) requested information from universities about the online assessment/examinations, and the software tools utilized by the universities. On 18.5.2020 the Commissioner outlined guidelines regarding online assessment, so as to be compatible with the protection of personal data. This was complemented by the Commissioner's Opinion 1/2020, which was issued on 21.8.2020.[23] The Commissioner requested from the universities to proceed to an impact assessment whether the use of an electronic supervision programme was necessary, taking into account the existing alternatives, such as take-home exams, oral exams, or examinations in smaller groups, where this could be applicable. If the decision is to use an electronic supervision programme, then:

(a) The data requested by the programme should be only the absolutely necessary, and without any biometric identification;
(b) The data collected should not be used for any other purposes other than safeguarding the integrity of the examinations;
(c) Students should be properly informed about the prospective processing of their data, and have their questions and concerns addressed;
(d) Appropriate technical and organizational measures are taken so as to protect the personal data of students, and the provider selected ought to provide sufficient assurances for this;
(e) The data should be kept for no longer than needed, and at any event no longer than six months after the exam date;
(f) Decisions whether a student has cheated should finally be taken by the instructor concerned and not by automatic processing;
(g) Access to the student data should be restricted only to authorized personnel;
(h) Where possible, there should be pseudonymization of data.

The same considerations applied during the academic year 2020–2021, while the pandemic continued to affect societal functions. On 7.9.2020 the CYQAA issued a new set of guidelines, and advised the academic institutions to continue to use, where possible, alternative methods of instruction and learning for their conventional programmes. The CYQAA also suggested to examine the possibility of offering blended learning, as a combination of conventional and online learning of a course, including flipped teaching.[24] Some universities in Cyprus, such as the University of Cyprus, aimed to introduce blended learning techniques at the beginning of the semester; however, the deterioration of the epidemiological situation, and the introduction of stricter measures by the Government, eventually led all universities to use online instruction and learning for law courses. With regards to examinations, the CYQAA issued further guidelines on 5.11.2020, which mostly reiterated the content of its previous ones.[25]

During the 2020–2021 academic year, the government of the Republic of Cyprus continued to introduce a number of strict measures. Whereas, there was never a

---

[23] CPDP [3].

[24] CYQAA [6].

[25] CYQAA [11].

proclamation of an official emergency, or suspension of constitutional rights, executive measures were adopted as a norm during the pandemic. Lockdowns, curfews, prohibition of unnecessary movement, prohibition of access to public places, prohibition of access to places of religious worship, suspension of a number of operations, suspension of flights, closure of schools, mandatory use of masks in both open and closed places at all times, ban of assemblies in private or public meeting places, were adopted throughout the pandemic. Whereas, the constitutionality of such measures has been questioned, neither the House of Representatives, nor the courts, have so far opted to scrutinize the measures.[26] The introduction of similar strict measures not only in Cyprus, but also in other countries from where law student population hailed, led to increased difficulties for the law programmes, since unless they functioned online, their students would not be in a position to participate. However, lack of proper internet connection, hardware or software, and lack of accessibility to books and other printed material often hindered the participation of law students even with a fully online environment.

3 Challenges for a Post-pandemic Legal Education

The pandemic has raised questions about fundamental premises of the western societies. The case study analysed above, shows that the successful implementation of the response of Cypriot universities to the pandemic relied on co-ordinated collective action taken by the universities, in co-operation with the national agency for quality assurance, i.e. CYQAA. Ensuring that all students had the hardware/software required for online delivery and assessment, transposing courses that had been designed as conventional ones to online within a few days, meeting the requirements for quality assurance for online teaching and assessment, applying student authentication process, while at the same time safeguarding personal data of students, all proved significant challenges. Helpful guidelines by CYQAA, and immediate risk management and contingency academic plans taking into account potential developments and the governmental measures taken in order to prevent and/or control the pandemic, proved overall successful, despite the novelty and unexpected effects of the challenges faced.

Law schools acted immediately and were successful in limiting, to the extent possible, the wide-reaching effects of the shut-down of their physical premises. Whereas only a few decades ago offering all law courses via electronic means would be impossible, technological developments and the dedication of faculty have made it possible to continue offering all of our courses daily, with the same content as before, even though the manner in which they are offered had changed. However, teaching and learning to undergraduate students via distance learning methods has proven difficult. Law studies necessitate student participation, through questions and answers and through the development of critical thinking, as well as access to

---

[26] Kombos [20].

specialized law resources and material. The Socratic method of teaching, despite criticism,[27] remains prevalent, and this is not easily adaptable in an online environment. They further require dedicated students who meet regularly with their instructors, and deliberate with their fellow students. Most students failed to keep their cameras open during lectures, and as a result visual participation, which is of extreme significance for law studies, was limited. There are strong sentiments that these objectives of undergraduate legal education cannot be adequately offered online only, a sentiment heightened by the fact that most countries do not recognize DL law degrees. Furthermore, whereas alternative methods of assessment were in general held to be satisfactory by faculty and students,[28] personal data considerations hindered the full implementation of electronic supervision so as to restrict incidents of cheating and plagiarism.

Whereas, however, legal studies might continue to be offered predominantly in a physical environment in a post-Covid world, the academic legal life would benefit enormously from a more robust integration of technology. Not only e-books and electronic access to articles, but video and audio podcasts, should become a more permanent fixture of legal education. The lessons from other disciplines could help further advance legal education beyond its often traditional environment. Students today have grown in an era of digital revolution, and can better consume audiovisual learning material as opposed to their counterparts a few decades ago. The pandemic experience has shown that whereas legal studies are not yet ready for becoming fully online, they could properly blend online elements with the more traditional methods of teaching in order to provide for a reimagined student-centred experience.

The fact that most law schools are part of public universities, or universities funded by the State, implies that the State typically aims to introduce public interest objectives and control the legal education offered. Kogan and others have noted that the national governments in the EU insist on applying quality controls, public accountability, and connection with the market.[29] Indeed, the study of law is closely associated with the legal profession, although many countries aim to market law degrees as general degrees, prioritizing the need for legal thinking in virtually all aspects of everyday life. However, as Reichert and Tausch have noted, state intervention often restricts competition in favour of bureaucracy.[30] The question of who can take the universities, and the law schools, forward in a new era of a globalized economy is a question for debate. Whereas, the traditional view remains that academics should be the ones to lead and administer a university,[31] there is a new tendency of using more and more managers, so as to improve competitiveness, cope with the increased diversity of students and faculty, and the growing demands of consumers about the education they receive. The Cypriot case study showed that where state intervention is not unilateral, but follows careful deliberation with universities, and where

---

[27] Rhode [33].

[28] Pouyioutas [31].

[29] Kogan et al. [19].

[30] Reichert and Tauch [32].

[31] Lockwood [22, p. 124].

universities employ managers who work together with academic as leaders of their universities, the system is more willing to adapt to new challenges for the benefit of faculty and students.

Access to material remains one of the most important challenges. The digital era has allowed enhanced access to legal material, such as case law and legal doctrine. A number of specialized databases have transformed legal research. However, there are two major impediments to further progress. The first refers to the high subscription fees charged by major publishers and providers; it is difficult even for some of the largest university libraries to provide access to all sources, and this anyway creates an inherent inequality between the largest university libraries and the rest. The second major impediment refers to the peculiarities of legal studies. Due to the centrality of the monograph and of edited volumes to the traditional understanding of legal doctrine, databases consisting mainly of journals cannot substitute the need for print books. This has gradually improved in recent years; however, progress is much slower in law compared to other disciplines. Furthermore, whereas digitization of material is adequate in English-speaking sources, it is less satisfactory in other languages. Considering the still prevailing national dimension of law, English-speaking resources are not as helpful as is the case in other disciplines.

The EU has emphasized the need to invest in open access to academic content.[32] This is even more important when considering that the most important legal research work in the EU is carried out by publicly funded universities or publicly funded research initiatives, and hence the universities are effectively paying to buy back published work they had already paid to produce. A successful system of EU-wide collective negotiation by universities might lead to reduced costs, and more open access, in a manner which would still make financial sense for publishers. Furthermore, subsidizing digitization of sources in other EU official languages would facilitate access to law primary and secondary sources. This would accordingly lead to enhanced access to legal material, and would potentially improve both the delivery and content of legal education, as well as the feasibility of legal research and its interaction with teaching and learning.

4 Conclusion

As Kronman argued, law is not only about accomplishing certain things, but also about becoming a certain person, developing a good judgment and the ability to make wise choices.[33] This can only be achieved by fully living in the law, and it could be argued that living in the law necessitates physical interaction and debates with instructors and students, i.e. living the academic legal life to the fullest extent. It is suggested that the experience of the pandemic has shown that there are significant difficulties in opting for the online delivery of undergraduate law courses, together

---

[32] Directorate-General for Research and Innovation (RTD) [14].

[33] Kronman [21].

with alternative methods of assessment, and immediately adopting it as a norm in a post-pandemic environment would not be a credible option. However, the option of providing blended (hybrid) education might seem like an attractive solution in a post-pandemic society. The use of technology could improve the delivery of education and move away from the traditional techniques of legal education towards a more collaborative, societally relevant, and student-friendly pedagogical environment. Engaging the students with audiovisual and online legal material could enhance the student experience, in a manner appropriately directed to a new generation of technologically advanced students. Legal education during the pandemic has shown that engaging the intellect of students and developing their critical thinking and skepticism, as conditions of legal education[34] can also occur in an online environment, albeit not exclusively. Quality could be served by introducing a number of new teaching and learning methods used successfully in other disciplines.[35] In an era of globalization, liberalization and unprecedented technological change, law schools need to be as open-minded and innovative as possible, in order to effectively address the challenges and opportunities these developments present. The field needs to adapt, and innovate, by engaging with educational practices previously not thought possible, but which have become the norm in other fields.

References

1. Becher, T.: Towards a definition of disciplinary cultures. Stud. Higher Educ. **6** (1981)
2. Birks, P.: Editor's Preface in Pressing Problems in the Law. OUP (1996)
3. CPDP: Supervision of Distance Learning/Online Exams By Higher Education Institutions. www.dataprotection.gov.cy (21 October 2020). Accessed 9 July 2021
4. CRC: Resolution of the CRC. https://www.dipae.ac.cy/index.php/el/nea-ekdiloseis/anakoinoseis-el/505-20-03-2020-psifisma-sinodou-pritaneon (20 March 2020). Accessed 9 July 2021
5. CYQAA: Online Courses Tools. https://www.dipae.ac.cy/index.php/el/nea-ekdiloseis/anakoinoseis-el/501-17-03-2020-ergaleia-tilemathima (17 March 2020). Accessed 9 July 2021
6. CYQAA: Operation of Higher Education Institutions During the Academic Year 2020–2021. https://www.dipae.ac.cy/index.php/el/nea-ekdiloseis/anakoinoseis-el/540-07-09-2020-leitourgia-idrimaton-2020-2021 (7 September 2020). Accessed 9 July 2021
7. CYQAA: Final Exams. https://www.dipae.ac.cy/index.php/el/nea-ekdiloseis/anakoinoseis-el/509-30-03-2020-telikes-exetaseis (30 March 2020). Accessed 9 July 2021
8. CYQAA: Final Exams and Quality Assurance Safeguards. https://www.dipae.ac.cy/index.php/el/nea-ekdiloseis/anakoinoseis-el/522-29-04-2020-telikes-exetaseis-asfalistikes-diklides-poiotitas (29 April 2020). Accessed 9 July 2021
9. CYQAA: Final Exams in Emergency Situations Due to Covid. Quality Assurance Criteria and Guidelines for Alternative Methods of Assessment. https://www.dipae.ac.cy/index.php/el/nea-ekdiloseis/anakoinoseis-el/511-31-03-2020-final-exams-koronoios (31 March 2020). Accessed 9 July 2021
10. CYQAA: Indefinite Continuation of Studies Online Due to Covid-19. https://www.dipae.ac.cy/index.php/el/nea-ekdiloseis/anakoinoseis-el/498-10-03-2020-anavoli-episkepseon-distance-learning (10 March 2020). Accessed 9 July 2021

---

[34] Birks [2].

[35] Rochette [34].

11. CYQAA: Interim and Final Exams of the Fall Semester 2020–2021 in the Higher Education Institutions and Quality Assurance Safeguards. <https://www.dipae.ac.cy/index.php/el/nea-ekdiloseis/anakoinoseis-el/552-5-11-2020-endiameses-kai-telikes-exetaseis-cheimerinou-examinou-2020-2021-sta-idrymata-anoteris-ekpaidefsis-kai-asfalistikes-diklides-poiotitas (5 Nov 2020). Accessed 9 July 2021
12. CYQAA: Online Education/Exam and Personal Data. https://www.dipae.ac.cy/index.php/el/nea-ekdiloseis/anakoinoseis-el/516-10-04-2020-distance-learning (10 April 2020). Accessed 9 July 2021
13. CYQAA: Online Education/Examination and Personal Data (2). https://www.dipae.ac.cy/index.php/el/nea-ekdiloseis/anakoinoseis-el/546-30-09-2020-diadiktyaki-didaskalia-exetasi-kai-prosopika-dedomena-2 (30 September 2020). Accessed 9 July 2021
14. Directorate-General for Research and Innovation (RTD): Background Note on Open Access to Scientific Publications and Open Research Data. European Commission, Brussels (2016)
15. Ebeku, K.: Developing legal education in the Commonwealth: the case of the Republic of Cyprus. J. Commonwealth Law Legal Educ. **5** (2007)
16. Ebeku, K.: An introduction to the law Department of the University of Nicosia. Cyprus Eur. Law Rev. **9** (2009)
17. Emilianides, A.: Cyprus: 'Everything Changes and Nothing Remains Still. Ashgate Publishing (2014)
18. Hadjiyiannis, K.: Statements by K. Hatzigiannis: Decisions of the Higher Institutions to Respect the Agency's Lines. DIPAE. https://www.dipae.ac.cy/index.php/el/nea-ekdiloseis/anakoinoseis-el/517-11-04-2020-diloseis-hadjiyianni (11 April 2020). Accessed 9 July 2021
19. Kogan, M. et al.: Transforming Higher Education, 2nd edn. Springer Netherlands (2006)
20. Kombos, C.: Constitutional Improvisation and Executive Omnipotence: The Cypriot Handling of the Pandemic. https://verfassungsblog.de/constitutional-improvisation-and-executive-omnipotence-the-cypriot-handling-of-the-pandemic/ (2 March 2021). Accessed 9 July 2021
21. Kronman, A.: The Lost Lawyer—Failing Ideals of The Legal Profession. Harvard University Press (1995)
22. Lockwood, G: Management and resources. In: Rüegg, W. (ed.) A History of the University in Europe, vol. IV. CUP (2011)
23. MECSY: Additional precautionary measures on the Covid-19 epidemic. http://enimerosi.moec.gov.cy/archeia/1/ypp10554a (13 March 2020). Accessed 9 July 2021
24. MECSY: Announcement of the MESCY Regarding Measures Taken for the Prevention of the Covid-19 Virus. http://enimerosi.moec.gov.cy/archeia/1/ypp10612a (9 April 2020). Accessed 9 July 2021
25. MECSY: Clarification for Higher Education Institutions Regarding the Announcement of the MECSY on Precautionary Measures for the Prevention of Covid. http://enimerosi.moec.gov.cy/archeia/1/ypp10547a (12 March 2020). Accessed 9 July 2021
26. MECSY: Precautionary Measures Regarding Higher Education Institutions for the Prevention of Covid. http://enimerosi.moec.gov.cy/archeia/1/ypp10528a (10 March 2020). Accessed 9 July 2021
27. MECSY: Restart of Operation of Higher Education Institutions. http://enimerosi.moec.gov.cy/archeia/1/ypp10708a (8 May 2020). Accessed 9 July 2021
28. Ministry of Health: Decisions of the Council of Ministers on Covid. https://www.pio.gov.cy/coronavirus/press/10032020_6.pdf (10 March 2020). Accessed 9 July 2021
29. Ministry of Health: Order of the Minister of Health Pursuant to the Quarantine Law. https://www.pio.gov.cy/coronavirus/press/11032020_4.pdf (11 March 2020). Accessed 9 July 2021
30. Ministry of Health: Statements of the Minister of Health Following the Extraordinary Meeting of the Council of Ministers on Covid. https://www.pio.gov.cy/coronavirus/press/15032020_8.pdf (15 March 2020). Accessed 9 July 2021
31. Pouyioutas, P.: The University of Nicosia Response to the Covid-19 Pandemic (March-December 2020). University of Nicosia Internal Report (2020)
32. Reichert, S., Tauch, C.: Trends IV: European Universities Implementing Bologna. EUA Publications (2005)

33. Rhode, D.: In Pursuit of Knowledge: Scholars, Status and Academic Culture. Stanford UP (2006)
34. Rochette, A.: Teaching and Learning in Canadian Legal Education. McGill University Libraries (2010)
35. Stolker, C.: Rethinking the Law School; Education, Research, Outreach and Governance. CUP (2014)

Legal Education and Legal Profession in a Post-COVID-19 World: South Asian Context with Specific Emphasis on Nepal

Yubaraj Sangroula

Abstract The Impacts of Covid-19 are grave and widespread in the entire socio-economic spheres of society. The consequences are grave particularly in belatedly bourgeoning small economies like Nepal. The chapter looks at the impact of pandemic on students and particularly legal education in South Asia. It argues that the entire spectrum of legal education in South Asia needs to be revisited.

1 Impacts of Pandemic in Students and Its Overall Consequences

The impacts of COVID-19 are grave and widespread in the entire socio-economic spheres of society. The consequences are grave particularly in belatedly bourgeoning smaller economies like Nepal. Undoubtedly, the education sector, which imbeds future of millions of young people, suffers from unimaginably widespread impacts, particularly affecting the learning attitudes of millions of people across the globe. However, the impact is pervasive and penetrating in the regions like South Asia where 22% of the global poor population lives. The region shares only 2% of Global GDP and 1.3% of global trade.[1] The COVID-19's impact on economic growth is seen typically problematic. According to prior estimation, South Asia was supposed to march rigorously with 7.2% of economic growth rate in 2021, but the pandemic largely shattered the aspiration by pushing the same at an estimated growth rate of 4.4%, provided that the pandemic is brought to a control.[2] However, the outbreak new variant of the virus has posed further adverse situations, thus impacting every

[1] Irfan [21].
[2] World Bank [40].

Y. Sangroula (✉)
Executive Director and Professor at Kathmandu School of Law and Visiting Professor at Various Asian Law Schools, Bhaktapur, Bagmati Province, Nepal
e-mail: yubaraj.sangroula@ksl.edu.np

C. Raj Kumar and S. G. Sreejith (eds.), *Legal Education and Legal Profession During and After COVID-19*, https://doi.org/10.1007/978-981-19-2568-9_8

aspect of lives of people. The adverse impacts on economic growth may have traumatic consequences in social development sector, education sector facing the most unwanted push back.

Tangibly speaking, psychological impacts unfolded by the pandemic among students and teachers are the most serious one. Psychological impacts are inseparably connected with the economic push back. A considerably larger number of students in economically weaker countries may not be able to continue their education in future due to economic loss caused by the pandemic. Hence, many young people are vulnerable to traumatic anxieties in the post-COVID-19 situation. Particularly, smaller economies like Nepal may fail to cope with the situation because of their limited economic resources, inadequate technical expertise and technology, and paucity of infrastructure facilities, including poor public amenities. The loss sustained by students in advancing their knowledge for building a competent career is, therefore, enormously bigger, both in terms of time as well as access to the competitive global market of education.

In the present context of globalization, the necessity of building a competitive career is dependent on access to standard and professional learning. For that opportunity, students from developing countries have depended largely on the educational facilities and opportunities available in developed and some developing countries nearing to developed standards. However, the access for the same is facing almost total stagnation due to the pandemic, thus posing a situation of grim uncertainty even in future. The crippled mobility and accessibility are, therefore, major causes of traumatic psychological impacts on millions of young students. Moreover, the situation may seriously hinder the drive and prospect of socio-economic and infrastructure development due to lack of adequate human resource.

Seemingly, the rapid and alarming spread of the pandemic has resulted in a massive disruption of social life, the curtailment of mobility and the opportunity for social interactions being the gravest one. The COVID-19 forced educational institutions to shut down, thus disrupting the entire process of planning and implementation of academic activities, the disruption in operation of educational institutions being the obvious one. In this context, the worse impact of the pandemic is the closure of academic institutions. In the higher education sector, the shutdown has harshly affected the activities of empirical research, experiential learning and innovations, particularly through research activities. In the field of legal education, the spheres of experiential learning through activities like mooting, clinical endeavors based on outreach activities and strategic legal aid initiatives, and law-firm or consumer-sector internships are facing irreparable disruption, thus causing problems of knowledge deficiency and psychological degradation among masses of students and the new entrants of legal profession. An online sample survey of the Kathmandu School of Law, representing a section of ongoing and passed-out students and guardians, reveals an acute disenchantment and anxiety among students.[3]

[3] Dangal and Bajracharya [13]. The survey covered ongoing students, passed-outs and their guardians. The questionnaires included their concerns of the shutdown caused by the pandemic and its impacts on socio-economic life as well as education and employment opportunities. Except

2 Alternative Options and Effectiveness in Mitigating Adverse Impacts

The impacts of the pandemic are assessable based on various institutional studies, empirical researches and media reports. For instance, UNESCO, through an event in the 75th Session of the UN General Assembly in 2020, reflected on grave situation posed by the pandemic in education and called the international community for prompt and strong collaboration to effectively address the crisis faced by 1.6 billion students across 191 countries.[4] Admittedly, the situation is hardly improved in 2021. The new breakout of the pandemic in 2021 also poses uncertainty in 2022 and the following years. Education institutions, particularly in many developing countries, are forced to go through total shutdown of education institutions, and majority of them are even unable to apply online or distance learning option. In Nepal, for instance, reportedly only 13% education institutions are using options of e-learning, using options like online classes and distance learning during closure.[5]

In the year 2020, educational institutions across the globe tried mitigating the immediate impacts of the pandemic by applying a range of educational means, pedagogies and delivery options. Among these options, online services and programs constituted a bulk. The pandemic induced information technology sectors to develop many innovative tools for teaching and learning, thus contributing to bridge the gap of communication between institutional operation and students. However, the effectiveness of this technological innovation is far below the level of satisfaction in countries like Nepal for several reasons—this innovation provided opportunity of learning for only a small segment of students.[6] Availability of e-communication infrastructure and network and awareness as well as affordability of larger number of students to use these e-learning means and options posed obstacles in popular effectiveness of such options. Consequently, more than 80% of students in Nepal remained deprived of the opportunity to learn during the pandemic-caused shutdown.[7]

In Nepal, legal education particularly suffered adversely during the shutdown. One of the major reasons was the inadequate and impoverished infrastructure facilities and absence of adequate competent teachers in majority of law schools. The lack of effective management and institutionalized platform for teaching in law schools was equally obliterating factor. Majority law schools, based on system run by part-time teachers, failed to endorse the alternative options of platform of e-learning and teaching options. Lack of coordination between Bar and legal institutions proved equally problematic for students, because, in absence of this coordination and cooperation, students of law at the higher level failed to have an access to internship and other similar practical activities of learning. Furthermore, the university authority

a very marginal segment of the participants, the majority expressed anxieties and concerns of future, provided the situation continues for longer period of time.

[4] See UNESCO [39].

[5] Pandit [31].

[6] Dawadi et al. [15].

[7] Ibid.

and the education department of the government failed to adequately train faculties to conduct e-learning and teaching options. Consequently, only a couple of law schools had been able to continue providing learning access to law students and protect them from losing their academic year. But large majority of law students missed their academic years as well as a chance of appearing in the Bar Council Exam. This situation was not far different in other South Asian countries.[8]

The absence of a competent regulatory authority and policy for integrating e-technology in existing legal pedagogies and methodologies of education also posed an obstruction in successful operation of alternative options. Admittedly, law graduates must develop competency to meet the new challenges as well as professional competencies for successfully emerging into professional service. In physical environment, students have wider scope for this development, but, as we have opportunity to experience, the online teaching and learning do shift the emphasis from teacher to learner with the latter as customer. The relationship in this context between law professors and students is seen changing, which tends to change the entire definition of legal education. No online teaching option may, probably, be effective and reasonable if law schools take adequate caution from treating students as customers or learning users. If they fail in this precaution, the professionalism to be imparted will lose its vitality. This problem was widely observed in South Asia.[9]

Non-physical or distance learning options are entirely contingent on internet or digital-driven technological facilities. In Nepal, like other South Asian countries, the nationwide accessibility and functional strength of internet facility are seen not adequate yet. As a matter of fact, these discrepancies posed gaps both in access and quality of education imparted. In the sector of legal education particularly, problems are encountered in many forms, such as: (a) the older generation of law professors and lawyers, who are often engaged in teaching professional expertise and skills, are less aware and familiar in using online means and methods of teaching,[10] (b) a number of students living in far-flung and remote areas lacked dependable internet or digital means, (c) the lack of familiarity in online option teaching and learning method also hindered in effectiveness of communication, and (d) last but not the least, a considerably larger number of students lacked an appropriate ambience for concentrated learning at home—many households lacked learning-friendly infrastructure and social environment. Generally, the descriptions above imply that the impacts of COVID-19 in education largely differ in the situation of developed and developing countries. The impact of COVID-19 in the sector of legal education also varies in developed and in developing countries. This brief assessment leads us to argue that the alternative options may not be a helpful instrument of legal education for productive and quality teaching and learning in current South Asia, if several infrastructural, administrative and operation improvements, are friendly for learning jurisprudence as well as professionalism, are not developed.

[8] See Mallaya [27].

[9] Kumar [25] Aristovnik et al. [3].

[10] Similar problem is reported in India, See Mallaya (n 8).

3 Systemic Problems and Necessity of Paradigmatic Shift in South Asian Legal Education in the Context of COVID-19

This section will assess the history and features of some models of legal education, with a purpose of discerning some systemic errors permeating the South Asian legal education. Let us begin by a brief comparison of legal and medical professions. Juxtaposed, these two professions share similarity and difference in their professional responsibilities. Medical profession's significance and peculiarity lies in saving biological life of human beings, and this has been achieved by preventing spread of diseases, curing ailment, removing or changing affected organs of the human body and generating hope among ailing people for survival, a few to mention as examples. Legal profession, with a set of distinct peculiarities, aims at saving social life of people, in general. In this course, it prevents injustice, by abolishing the causes of discrimination and subordination, promotes equality, liberty and social justice, and defends requisites of orderly society by prohibiting breach of law and popular values of societies and humanity.

Understandably, the pandemics like COVID-19 offer ample grounds for review of the significance and worthiness of legal profession, particularly in relation to the context posed by pandemic like COVID-19. Apparently, the COVID-19 and its disastrous consequences provided medical personnel an opportunity, amidst and great danger to life, to learn new problems of medical science regarding protection of human lives. Certainly, the medical profession gained added mastery from the crises generated by the pandemic in human lives. Notably, the medical profession matured and gained added credibility. Its service gained added respect and heightened significance. Explicitly, medical professionals are now equipped with new knowledge and skills of fighting diseases. They are successful to invent new equipment and medicines necessary to protect lives of people as well as to save themselves from vulnerabilities and impacts of such pandemics.

Impacts of COVID-19 and significance of legal profession require a probe using the analogy of the COVID-19 perspectives and achievements made by the medical profession. It means that we must seek answers to some questions, empirically: What new learnings legal profession made from the disastrous consequences unfolded by COVID-19 pandemic? What roles legal profession played to mitigate the crises posed by the COVID-19 to the lives of people. Most importantly, what legal profession did to protect the lives of needy or vulnerable people facing the socio-economic disastrous of lives? Answers to these questions are encouragingly affirmative. Largely, legal profession during the COVID-19 crisis stood idle; its social responsibilities functioned in low-ebb, and general people had limited reasons to expect help from legal professionals. Lawyers through a number of writ petitions occurred in South Asian apex judiciaries demanded the Government to (a) waiver of office rents, (b) free medical treatment, (c) service of vaccination with priority, and (d) and a privileged treatment in mobility and social security services, and so on.[11]

However, examples of institutional concerns of legal professionals to mitigate the crisis of pandemic through promoting social justice or safety of general people are rare. The pandemic resulted in failure of rule of law massively in South Asian societies. Some studies reveal loss of jobs, with greater impacts on women. Women living in poverty, single spouse and essential workers, as well as those belonging to racial and ethnic minorities, are being pushed furthest to the margins.[12] Economically deprived, socially excluded and vulnerable communities suffered from isolation and barriers to using hospital and survival centers. Marginalized sections of population faced challenges accessing state's facilities, such as vaccination. State officials neglected or violated their obligations not to violate human rights, and their positive obligations to ensure the respect of these rights. According to Transparency International's report, corruption in Bangladesh during COVID-19 ranges from bribery in health clinics to misappropriated aid.[13] Cases of corruption in health services in India are widely reported.[14] Reportedly, in Nepal, the level corruption increased by 50%.[15] The institutional roles of legal professionals in these matters is dismal, unfortunately.

The difference between legal and medical education, for instance, also becomes spectacular at this point. Students of law lose ambience of environment necessary for their professional pursuit and advancement. Unlike medical professionals, law students during COVID-19 pandemic lacked professional guidance from their seniors and teachers. Spectacularly, general observations show that medical students obtained opportunity for maturing their proficiency of knowledge and skills, despite several psycho-social challenges and problems. In contrast, law students suffered from acute isolation and underwent psycho-social trauma as well as loss of opportunities to prosper professionally.

From these perspectives, the legal profession's both failures and challenges become tangibly precise. These failures and challenges, therefore, call for ambitious and wider reforms and modifications in the both legal profession and education, systemically as well as technologically. As it has been precisely evident, the conventional formalist judicial approach is seen insignificant to deliver justice during such pandemic. The crisis shows that the current judicial system of South Asia is neither pragmatic nor realist. It is neither capable of adapting the change sought by the actual circumstances. Similarly, the current conventional paradigm of lawyers–clients' relationship and dealings are proved unrealistic and impracticable to face challenges such as those posed by COVID-19 pandemic. Though adequate empirical researches to reveal accurate condition are not available yet, it is not unwise to argue that consequences posed by the inefficiency of justice system during COVID-19 like pandemic are grave. This is possible to gauze from several instances. For instance, the trials are

[11] For more descriptions of cases, See Negi [30].

[12] Bolis et al. [7].

[13] See Loh [26].

[14] See Cuadrado [12].

[15] Himalayan News Service [19].

postponed; the violation of human rights linger unaddressed; and trade and business relations are stagnated. Court users seeking justice are deprived of legal and judicial protection at all.

In Nepal, the proportion of disposal of both criminal civil cases is significantly decreased and the rights of detainees and accused are severely affected.[16] Many lawyers have become jobless, and the law-making process is stagnated due to cessation of the parliamentary functions. Altogether, the role of law and justice both in economic development drive and social transformation processes is adversely impacted, thus partly contributing to the implicit, but harmful, recession of the economy. The situation of India and other South Asian countries is similar.[17] Obviously, the impact of pandemic in human rights protection is grossly adverse.

The increasing obstacles and hindrances posed by the intermittent curfew or lock-downs have adversely impacted the entire situation general law and order. The constrained mobility of police and shutdown of prosecutorial and adjudicating institutions have suspended general peoples' access to the criminal justice service, which is directly concerned with human rights protection. Similarly, mobility constraints are hindering general peoples' access to urgent medical services, thus posing danger to the right to life. These situations have created doubts of the usefulness of the prevailing legal and judicial services in South Asia.

These unwanted impacts posed by COVID-19 pandemic raise a question needing serious reckoning. Is current legal education of South Asia capable of revitalizing or revisiting the legal and judicial professions in future? To initiate a discourse in this regard, we need to by reflecting on certain disposition of legal education and profession, particularly South Asian ones which are congenitally rooted in colonial systems. Both legal education and profession, including judicial institutions, lack substantial shift from their colonial shapes or structure.[18] Since inception during colonial era, both legal education and profession have rarely seen a paradigmatic shift to represent contemporary needs.

Nevertheless, the landscapes of global legal education and profession are diametrically changed over the years. This shift marks change from a system of mastering in legalist-centralist approach to socio-economic relevance of law and justice. But the latter's scope in South is insignificant, if not bleak. Since South Asian legal education is primarily founded on legalist-centralist approach, it is seen as incompetent to stress the social responsiveness of legal profession, thus lagging behind in transforming itself into a system of justice education. In the latter approach, the fundamental goal of laws schools is to foster social justice, particularly emphasizing the need of addressing the issues of (a) the disparity or inequality in the distribution of income, wealth, and opportunity, (b) the state of socio-economic deprivations as a cause of multiple forms of discrimination and subordination, and (c) the state of

---

[16] Himalayan News Service, 'Prisoners forgotten during COVID-19', *The Himalayan Times, (*19 May 2021) https://thehimalayantimes.com/nepal/prisoners-forgotten-during-COVID-pandemic accessed 27 May 2021.

[17] For situation of India, See Mallaya (n 8).

[18] See Sarafi [33].

regressive-status quo that permeates and hinders desired changes in the society, thus posing vulnerabilities to the violation of human rights.

Understandably, the contemporary South Asian legal education, rooted primarily in the legalist-centralist approach, is confined to breed skills and techniques of lawyers for applying and interpreting existing laws in disregard of the social contexts, realities and socio-economic development needs. As a matter of fact, it stands as an Island detached from overall general socio-economic conditions and circumcises needing legal answers and resolves. Several problems surfaced during the COVID-19 are typically associated with static or unrealistic attributes of the current model legal education in South Asia. Being largely detached from the social realities and native jurisprudence, the existing model of legal education in South Asia suffered from confusion and bewilderment concerning its role and emphasis to address crisis posed by the COVID-19—it is largely uncertain on how to mitigate the crisis posed by the pandemic and resolve impacts thereof. To be specific, legal education institutions in South Asia would largely be successful to mitigate the adverse situation had they been able to understand the interface of legal education and social justice. For instance, law schools could provide learning environment by engaging students in multiple forms of awareness-building roles as social-justice activists, using social media, television, radio, video message, and webinars. Unfortunately, the online teaching and learning option was inconspicuously and monotonously used for lectures—the one-way teaching method. This methodological err is a product of the wrong model of legal education in application.

At this very point, it is worthy to explore a brief history of different models of legal education for clarifying the methodological mistakes of South Asian model. The historical anecdotes of legal education show a persistent debate among legal scholars concerning legal study as a Science and Liberal Art. In addition, the contemporary, relatively recent, method, in the words of Joshua Krook, an Adelaide legal scholar, 'predominately emphasizes law as a personal vocational pursuit, thus requiring technical skills and set areas of expertise as key goals of the legal education.' This particular method, like many others, poses a serious fault line because it neglects the study of law as human and society-centered discipline. Indeed, this approach is potential for demise of a broader view of legal education as an intimately connected discipline with the liberal philosophy such as politics, economics, justice, and other human-centered pursuits of learning.[19] This fault line emerged evidently during the COVID-19 crisis.

This fault line is rooted in the history of British legal education beginning at the Inns of Court in London. Subsequently, it persisted in the British universities' model that stressed a strict legalist-centralist approach of teaching and learning law. The curricula and pedagogies were accordingly. This model was resented by Americans as early as independence era by saying that the goal of legal education, in opinions of Thomas Jefferson and others, was to cultivate public virtues and train statesmen, thinkers and gentlemen.[20] As a matter of fact, most American universities rejected

[19] See Krook [24].

[20] Ibid.

the strict legalist-centralist model of legal education since early twenty-ninth century. However, most law schools across the globe are neglecting such public goal of legal education. In contrast, they have embarked to dedicate their methods to serve the business interests of the powerhouses by overlooking broader intellectual interests to foster legal education as the primary instrument instilling social justice in laws and policies, thus continuously inspiring the process of social restructuring. In this course, the development of legal education has seen a paradigmatic shift from intellectual pursuit to technical legal education.

The overarching stress on technical approach resulted in the overriding formalization of legal training. The mechanically technical rules and regulations of teaching and learning, sophisticated admission requirements and formalities, lengthy subjective examination systems, peculiar grades and degrees, and so on also contribute significantly to the excessive formalization of legal education.[21] While in the recent past, the innovative clinical methods of teaching and learning have significantly contributed to relax the excess of formalization, it still suffers in developing countries. Cursory observations indicate that a kind of immutability is being reinforced or buttressed by COVID-19 posing severe hindrances in clinical methods of teaching and learning. The methods of online lectures and launching of online-friendly curriculum are mushrooming but these methods are proving more rigid, technical, and formal thereby overlooking the significance of socially contextual training and social justice. In this peculiar context, activities like externship, internship, learning through outreach and research initiatives, and socialization methods are losing their significance and a danger of legal education being insulated is in rife.

Admittedly, COVID-19 impacts have discerned that the South Asian legal education model must undergo a rapid process of paradigmatic shift. The situation facing the current teaching and learning models and methods should adopt unlearning and relearning approaches in order to successfully deal with the impacts posed by the COVID-19. To present an analogy would be worthwhile at this juncture. A building's design must pay attention to the geographical features of landscape, weather and available resources. Copying architectural design in disregard of those factors may fail to resist the typical adversities of physical environment, thus may collapse. The imported legal education may face similar adversities, and fail to cater for the needs of the society. In the context of pandemic, the analogy seems valid. South Asia has a thicker influence of Anglo-American models in legal education. The curricula, pedagogy and methods of teaching and learning adopted by South Asian legal education are less relevant to the local contexts, particularly in terms of availability of modern techniques, competent faculties, and absence of a culture of distance learning. The models adopted in the region are facing several limitations to adapt and accommodate such crises as posed the COVID-19 pandemic. The argument calls for a brief reflection on merits and demerits of different models of legal education practiced historically and debates about its contextually with the given social needs and settings. The reflection will show the relationship between broader social contexts and the relevance of the model adopted.

[21] See Girard and Laskin [18].

4 Various Models of Legal Education and Lessons to Learn

In the stage of its infancy, the modern legal education was primarily driven by a model that preferred educating students by a typical method of apprenticeship-based training. This model applied methods of imparting skills for applying existing rules of law and their interpretation. The model had a limited goal of generating competent legalist professionals by work experiences. During Rana regime, Nepal also used the same model to general legal human resources. Historically, this model was initiated and esteemed by Inns of Court in London since 1200s.[22] This model fitted the common law structure practiced in England that offered an overarching attention to the constitutional conventions and the principle of *stare-decisis*. Under this model, students would learn skills especially by observing court proceedings. Seemingly, the model ignored the need of linking law with actual life of people and the conditions of society; such an approach was meticulously considered unnecessary. Neither was jurisprudence and relevance of law with liberal art disciplines encouraged. The model continued until the English Civil War in 1642; after this period the Inns of Court as an institution of training lawyers was replaced by a model of apprenticeships in barrister's chambers,[23] which involved students observing all the work of a solicitor before maturing themselves to work as solicitors.[24]

The structure of university legal education began in England since early nineteenth century, the University College of London and Cambridge University being first and second to offer formal degree of laws, respectively. This model attached importance of learning jurisprudential principles and social contexts, but it was neither comparative and sociological. Yet, the model faced resistance from some legal scholars including A. V. Dicey. He argued that students would learn the ability to discern the facts of a case only from actual engagement in works.[25] Thus, he praised apprenticeship model and suspected the efficiency and effectiveness of the formal university model. He criticized Blackstone's view who offered significance to a cross-disciplinary model of legal education. Following the idea of Blackstone, Oxford university introduced the model of legal education teaching laws as a multi-disciplinary program. Blackstone noted that such method would train students to observe the ways the law operated in practice.[26] The colonial rule imported this model in South Asia, which still forms the primary domain of legal education. The biggest setback of this model was its overarching emphasis on analytical or legalist-centralist methods.

Paradigmatic shift in the models and methods of teaching and learning law first emerged in the U.S. during the early twentieth century. The credit for initiating the change goes to Yale and Harvard Law Schools under the leadership of Wesley Newcomb Hohfeld and Roscoe Pound, respectively.[27] As a part of the new model,

[22] See Boon and Webb [8].

[23] Ibid.

[24] AV Dicey, cited in Krook [24].

[25] Dicey [16].

[26] Blackstone [6] (Chap. 2).

[27] See Eugene Ehrlich quoted Hull [17].

Pound promoted the concept of sociological jurisprudence as an essential component of legal study. His new program emphasized the social engineering role of law, thus refuting Langdell's understanding of law as a static set of legal precepts. In succeeding years, Pound and Hohfeld pushed the idea of paradigmatic shift urging that the study of law must pay emphatic attention on social realities, philosophy, and jurisprudence. This idea had bearings on French jurist Eugene Ehrlich's ideas of living law. In his view, it was not simply enough of being conscious to a fact that the law is living, but law should be taken as an essential part of human life. He said, "... we must rather be conscious that it is part of human life ... in a sense, everything human is a part of it."[28]

The American innovations influenced many Western law schools, the project of W. P. M. Kennedy at the University of Toronto Law school being the crucial one. His initiatives brought more radical changes in the legal education of Canada, which in the past suffered from the British stereotypes. Among others, he stressed the integration of legal education with social sciences, i.e., economics, political science and sociology.[29] He stood as a staunch critic of the methods suggesting dependence on case law study on which British universities profoundly ended. This method, in his view, sticks students within history of law, thus preventing them learning the actual meaning of the rules: hence, students would be unable to discern how the rules relate to everyday life and how to develop or reform those rules to serve society.[30]

With this new approach introduced, Kennedy inaugurated a new program at Toronto Law School with specific focus on components such as history of law, legal philosophy, economics, psychology, political theories, and so on. Most importantly, his new initiatives introduced critical thinking as an essential pedagogy, thus focusing on attention to discern the situation of indeterminacy of law and fact. Consequently, this approach successfully highlighted the significance of research activities and discourse of philosophical foundations.[31] Serving the social ends thus became an inspiring goal of legal education. Under this theme, students are required to pursue a comprehensive survey of social values, which means that the understanding of social relevance or contexts and the realization of the public perception are essential components of legal education.

The South Asian legal education, however, failed to pay attention to these changes even after decolonization. Larger part of South Asian legal academia failed to realize the needs of similar paradigmatic shift in legal education. Hence, the region continued the model of training lawyers with the programmatic, pedagogical and methodological frameworks introduced by the colonial administration. Significant part of the legal system introduced by colonial rule retained legitimacy and application even after independence of South Asian nations. The judicial structure continued largely unchanged either. A number of studies highlighted that the legal and judicial system of South Asia must undertake paradigmatic shift, if they have to earn confidence of

[28] Ibid. 269.

[29] See Risk [32].

[30] Bake [4].

[31] See Risk (n 29).

people. The Malimath Committee Report,[32] 2003, for instance, says: "…The ground reality, however, is that [the] precious fundamental right is turning out to be a mere pipe dream to many millions to whom justice is delayed, distorted or denied more than its delivery in accordance with the ideals enshrined in the Constitution."

The report, in its paragraph 2.2, at pages 23 and 24, clearly identifies that the problem lies in the system carried over from colonial era. The situation of Nepal, Bangladesh and Pakistan is hardly different. The current legal education models in practice in these countries are, therefore, less concerned with the systemic failures of the legal and justice system and legal profession. Under these models, students are generally trained to apply and interpret the prevailing precepts of laws rather than preparing them for critical scrutiny of their social acceptability and implications. Regarding legal education, the National Knowledge Commission (NKC) of India, constituted in 2005 as a high-level advisory body to the Prime Minister of India, calls for changes in the approach to legal education, taking into account contemporary necessities and contexts. The commission manifestly indicates the need of paradigmatic change in the legal education system of India, which is equally true for other South Asian nations. Pointing to the lapses facing the legal education of India, the NKC stated: "…there is need for original and path-breaking legal research activities to create new legal knowledge and ideas that will help meet [these] challenges in a manner responsive to the needs of the country and the ideals and goals of our Constitution."[33]

Regrettably, though, legal education is a matter of less priority of Governments in South Asia as a whole. Neither it is a matter of priority concern for the university. Yet, the region has seen some tendency shift in all aspects of legal education in the last some decades. Taking lead, some universities dedicated to legal modern legal in India have been successful to make a breakthrough. While the influence of this change is spilled over entire South Asia, other countries are still lagging behind. In Nepal, the modernization drive began only in 1999 with the Purbanchal University effort of establishing the Kathmandu School of Law. However, this achievement owes to non-governmental sector interventions—largely, some courageous and dedicated legal academics have played a crucial role to initiate this change by establishing pioneer law schools.[34] Such law schools have adopted improved programs, pedagogies and methods; most importantly, research-based methods of learning and clinical

[32] Ministry of Home Affairs [28].

[33] Schukoske [34].

[34] In India, Jindal Global Law School, National Law School, Bangalore, Rajiv Gandhi National Law School, a few to mention, are pioneer in paradigmatic shift. In Nepal, Kathmandu School of Law played pioneer role. In Bangladesh and Pakistan, some new law schools are promisingly emerging. However, these all-new institutions often face hurdles in smooth growth and role for modernization of legal education from state's policy failure in the sector of legal education. In view of Prof. Mizanur Rehman, the main obstacle comes from failure to unlearn from colonial past. See Mizanur Rehman, 'Unlearning and Relearning: South Asia and Socio-Economic Rights', Keynote Speech at the Opening Session of the 15th International Residential School on Economic, Social and Development Rights, Kathmandu, May 24, 2021.

programs. However, bulk of legal education institutions under government undertakings lag behind inadequate standards and contextual significance. Thankfully, such law schools had been largely successful to introduce and adopt new options of teaching and learning in the disastrous crisis of COVID-19.

But the overall condition of legal education in South Asia still suffers from substandard, if not poor or deplorable. Inadequacy of vision and realization of the need for prioritizing legal education in the government education policymakers is one of the grave challenges.[35] Another serious problem relates to the absence of a common standard of curricula, pedagogy, evaluation system and teaching and learning methods. Majority of law schools in South Asia have outmoded curricula and traditional pedagogies. The insulated or one-way lecture method forms the primary method of teaching and learning.[36] Majority of legal education programs are influenced by foreign model.[37] The diverse systems copied from various foreign models produce law graduates with varying approaches, skills and notions to law and justice. In India, pre-Independence period generated number of attorneys by universities in England. Naturally, the legal profession in India witnessed a domination of those with English law degrees. The influence of English degrees, in the words of Dasgupta, an assistant professor at West Bengal National University of Juridical Sciences, Kolkata, 'had a detrimental effect on the quality of legal education in India, as rich families sent their children off to England to become barristers or attorneys, who, on their return home, were regarded as superior to those who earned their law degree in India.'[38]

In Nepal, large number of lawyers, during 1950s and 60s, earned their law degrees from Indian universities running traditional British model of legal education. That way, they were instrumental in importing British model of legal education and profession in Nepal, which continues even today. Most law schools in South Asia in early days operated legal education as part-time course, thus degrading the quality of graduates. Best among them joined the government service and bar. Hence, law schools were compelled to employ teachers from amongst them who were unsaleable in other sectors.

The lapses in innovative and knowledge production model of legal education is still a problem in larger number of South Asian law schools. The linkage of classroom teaching with research activities is persistently ignored. The University Education Commission, in India, as early as in 1948, recommended to the law schools developing research capacities in vain.[39] The report of the committee identified the research activities as a prerequisite for quality enhancement; yet, the significant number of law schools in South Asia hardly pay heed to the indispensability of

[35] Dasgupta [14].

[36] For comprehensive information: International Legal Center and Scandinavian Institute of African Studies [20].

[37] Ibid 16.

[38] Dasgupta (n 35).

[39] The University Education Commission 1948 was headed by S. Radhakrishnan, who became second president of India. This commission provided number of recommendations for the improvement of university education in India, including legal education. For detail report, See 'Introduction to the University Education Committee' [1].

promoting research as an integral part of the pedagogy for competent legal education. The situation of most law schools in Nepal and Bangladesh is typically deplorable in this regard. Overall situation of South Asian legal education, leaving some institutions as exception, is highly unsatisfactory. This problem may better have been illustrated by an analogy. In music schools, some people learn singing and other composing music and playing instruments. Understandably, students in music schools know what they have to learn—either they learn singing or playing cords. In South Asia, most law schools are unaware of what they are teaching—they are unaware if they are teaching songs or cords, indeed.

Some problems highlighted before are well deciphered and conceptualized by the study report of International Legal Center (ILC) as early 1972. It has precisely located the problems facing the legal education of developing countries in Asia, Africa and Latin America. The report is one of the few scholarly documents that has been competently reflected overall actual situation of legal education in developing countries. As one of the significant findings, the study points out the need to plan and relate legal education by every nation to the local social and developmental environment.[40] The report has taken this principle as a point of departure for reforms and enhancement of legal education in all developing countries. The report says: "The report may disturb some because its portrayal of "the present situation—the existing characteristics of legal education in many countries—is cast in critical terms, and because it seems to call for a rather drastic re-thinking of objectives and methods."[41] The report also emphasizes a principle that the development of legal education is a culture-specific phenomenon.[42] Thus, it acknowledges a fact that legal education confronts different environments in different countries. The perception and values of using formal laws and legal processes vary as well. Most importantly, the legal culture is unique to the social episteme in every country.

Over the last some years, some fast-changing societies, such as Singapore, Malaysia, South Korea and Thailand, have endorsed tendency of de-legalizing parts of the existing legal system for it being obsolete. They have largely decolonized the legal system and education. In some other countries, the trend of devolving central power to the grassroots institutions is widely acknowledged. For instance, Nepal, Bangladesh and India have generated tremendous mechanisms of dispute settlement at the local levels. Similarly, some countries have introduced a system of market-driven economy and others the socialist approach. In these varying contexts, the colonial model of legal education cannot be a suitable model even today—concept of one medicine fitting all disses is a sever obstacle in the development of legal education.

The report also rightly points out to a reality that the many aspects of legal and judicial problems in the developing countries are caused by failure to have a paradigm shift in the prevailing model of legal education. For instance, the traditional role of lawyers in most developing countries is diminishing, thus demanding the importance

---

[40] International Legal Center (n 36) 10.

[41] Ibid.

[42] Ibid.

of specialization. The role and responsibility of legal professional to promote rapid changes in the traditional social structure is equally important. Moreover, the role and responsibility of legal profession to institutionalization and workability of democracy and culture of rule of law is equally important, without what political stability may simply be a fiasco. Not the least at all, the need of developing legal profession as a vehicle for examining many problems of social change as well as new ideals of justice is indispensable. And, only the improved legal education can do this.

The situation of legal profession is also less encouraging and credible in South Asia. Arguably, it has failed to show effectiveness in dealing with increasing criminalization of politics and standardization of democratic values.[43] The corruption in justice system is reportedly rampant.[44] Particularly, the role of legal profession in disastrous situation posed by pandemics like COVID-19 is seen dismal. The courts and bars failed manifest credible and encouraging trends to prioritize a pro-active role in protecting victims and vulnerable segments during COVID-19, as recommended by the United Nations Office of the Drugs and Crimes.[45] In Nepal, the courts and bars failed to attention to the vulnerability of prison population, particularly those waiting for trial. The court's role to monitor coercive measures against detainees is reportedly ineffective either.[46] Many detainees are incarcerated for prolonged period of detention with a presence of pandemic-caused shutdown. They neglected in their roles to devise alternative options for trial during the shutdown. To conclude this section, we can argue the main reason behind all these problems lies in traditional colonial models of legal education and profession.

5 What Models May Competently Address the Impacts Created by Pandemics like COVID-19: Context of Defining Legal Education

The legal education in developing countries is far behind to cater for social needs and challenge. As per the ILC findings, some serious loopholes lie in the structure of law schools which are primarily patterned after a foreign model with limited outlooks, contents, methods and research.[47] Many law schools are excessively inspired by a private-practice-oriented approach to the study of law: one which emphasizes the study of law in relation to private commercial activity and the private affairs of more affluent persons rather than problems of the public sector or problems of the

43 For statistics and descriptions, See Ali [2], Bhargava [5]; Kashyap [23], Mitra [29].

44 See Transparency International [37].

45 UNODC [38].

46 See Kamat [22] https://thehimalayantimes.com/nepal/sc-order-on-corrective-measures-for-prisoners-remains-unimplemented accessed 9 July, 2021; NHRC 'Human Rights Situation During COVID-19 Pandemic' (2020) https://www.nhrcnepal.org/nhrc_new/doc/newsletter/NHRCNepal_COVID_Report_2020.pdf accessed 25 May 2021.

47 International Legal Center (n 36) 16.

mass of people in society.[48] Furthermore, they are too "academic" fault lines in their approach—the content of courses neither do reflect current problems confronting the legal system, nor the actual work of lawyers in everyday practice reflect on the actual problems. This problem is further worsened due to lack of a well-developed indigenous body of legal literature. It is one of the reasons, the legal education in developing countries failed to show its effective role to respond legally to the crisis of COVID-19 pandemic. In South Asia particularly, the limitations of legal profession are seen widely. The main reason is legal education's narrower indigenous relevance.

When we take reference of the local social contexts, the definition of legal education varies. German model, for instance, is mainly driven by importance to epistemology. Unlike Germany, the America model stresses on experiential model. Some Asian countries such as Japan, South Korea and China, for instance, have stressed the welfare model. The South Asian model still relies on conventional model relying on the insulated method of teaching and learning. Apparently, legal education means a science for German. For American, it is a legal business. In most Asian countries, it is a system of researching and educating legal experts on protection and welfare of people. What does South Asian model mean? It is an unanswered question yet. In Nepal, some people mockingly say that 'legal education is an instrument of boosting lawyers' paradise—earning money without social responsibility.

According to the German model, the overriding stress on analytical skills of law is the main fault line in legal education.[49] Most German professors believe that courts by following epistemological approach can turn the constitution and laws into a coherent and comprehensive ideology answering the most difficult social and political questions.[50] With this basic philosophical orientation, the post-World War German legal education has come in the shape that calls for an integrated legal education ending bifurcation between theory and practice.[51]

Within this precinct, the "Hamburg Model" provides for a five-year program. Under this, students at first year will receive a modest component of exposure to what courts and government look like. In second and third year, they devote to instructions in varieties of law such as private law, constitutional law, administrative law and commercial law. In these two years, students devote their 30% of time by attaching themselves to judges and participating in simulation (moot court) exercises and other similar activities. The primary goal is to foster elevation of legal knowledge, both theoretically and practically. In the fourth and fifth year, students are provided opportunities for greater specialization and independence. For instance, they spend 30% of their time in the fourth year in the law office where they are given responsibility to perform legal tasks.[52] Under American model, over the last several decades, the clinical pedagogy has received wider recognition as a main tool preparing students as legal professionals. For it, legal education generally means a

---

48 Ibid.

49 Casper [10].

50 Ibid.

51 Ibid.

52 Stiebeler [35] [cited in Casper (n 49)].

tool of imparting proficiency to prepare students performing legal activities independently as a professional. This model provides students an opportunity of actual representing a real client while in school, thus offering an invaluable learning experience. Experience-based learning of this sort finds its roots in the work of the early twentieth century philosopher John Dewey.[53] Under this form of clinical model of legal education, students are supposed to build ten fundamental lawyering skills. They are: (1) Problem Solving, (2) Legal Analysis and Reasoning, (3) Legal Research, (4) Factual Investigation, (5) Communications (in writing, and orally), (6) Counseling (a client), (7) Negotiation (with opposing counsel), (8) Litigation and Alternative Dispute-Resolution Procedures, (9) Organization and Management of Legal Work, (10) and Recognizing and Resolving Ethical Dilemmas.[54]

Painfully enough, South Asia fails to define its model of legal education. Except few law schools, the situation of legal education in South Asia is in quandary. Some tangible fault lines are: (1) law curricula in many university are overly theorized and lack relevance to the changing dynamics of society; neither they are reviewed and updated to contextualize, (2) several forms of programs are simultaneously going without their provinces and necessity defined—South Asia has multiple forms of law degrees offered by different universities and some of these degrees are as a part-time study of law, (3) many professors involved in teaching lack competency to teach, neither they have opportunities to upgrade their academic qualities and teaching proficiency, (4) both epistemological and clinical modalities of legal education unfamiliar in larger number of universities, thus limiting the scope of legal education as a formal model of degree rather than imparting professional competency, (6) the culture integrating empirical research is encouraged only in limited law schools, and (7) most universities lack aptitude test while admitting students—hence, legal education has become a platform for having one more degree. All these fault lines compel us to argue that most law schools in South Asia are unknown if they are teaching songs or cords.

6 Conclusion

Particularly taking example of Nepal's situation, the impacts of COVID-19 on legal education are severe. Majority of law students in Nepal, might be true in other South Asian nations, are encountering severe loss of academic year as well as learning opportunities for career development. As argued by Burgess and Sievertsen, going to school is the best public policy tool available to raise skills.[55] Undoubtedly, this assumption equally applies to university legal education, because of its professional features. Students have to work in group and clinical settings. As pointed out above, the intermittent temporary closure of law schools and working institutions prevented

[53] Dewey [11].

[54] Thomson [36].

[55] Burgess and Greaves [9].

students from (a) participation of internship and externship activities, in those institutions where teaching method are based on clinical approach and models; (b) completion of the course in time, thus blocking the usual promotion or upgradation in upper semesters or years; and (c) participation in Bar examination due to loss of time for time or completion of the course timely. Some law schools ably prevented bigger loss by jumping into alternative option of distance or online teaching methods, though many students observed that the online classes were less practical and interactive. In law schools that have bigger number of students the system of online classes was virtually impossible. Hence, most law students under three-years course modality in Nepal lost their academic calendar doing nothing.

As discussed above, an ineffective and the goal-undefined modality of legal education formed a major obstacle in implementing the alternative options of teaching. The experiences showed that one way-lecture method could not be useful in online teaching option. In this model, most students found participation in online classes as monotonous and unproductive. Besides that, number of other problems surfaced. Since lawyers' role in responding to the crisis posed by COVID-19 remained absent. A big confusion loomed on what lawyers could do in such a situation. The absence of meaningful participation of Bar in responding to the crisis largely demotivated the community law students toward their future profession. Understandably, the digital learning option in a country with bigger size of economically deprived population is prone to create inequality in access to legal education. Nepal as a low-income country has a big gap among citizens in income and wealth distribution. Many students with economically marginalized condition can benefit from Law School's library and other facilities. But when teaching activities follow the online digital mode, many students from such background fall in a trap of discrimination. Hence, it is a time for revisiting the entire spectrum of legal education in South Asia.

References

1. Introduction to the University Education Committee: http://www.kkhsou.in/main/education/education_1948.html (1948). Accessed 24 May 2021
2. Ali, M.A.: Democracy Displaced in Pakistan: Case History of Disasters of Social Pollution. Research and Development Publications, Karachi (1998)
3. Aristovnik, A., et al.: Impacts of the COVID-19 pandemic on life of higher education students: a global perspective. Sustainability **12**. https://www.mdpi.com/2071-1050/12/20/8438 (2020). Accessed 27 May 2021
4. Bake, G.B.: Legal Education in Upper Canada 1785–1889. In: Flaherty, D.H. (ed.) Essays in the History of Canadian Law. Society, Toronto, Osgoode (2012) 5
5. Bhargava, B.S.: Hawala Scam: Politics of Corruption. Arnold Associates, New Delhi (1996)
6. Blackstone, W.: Commentaries on the Laws of England. Clarendon Press (1765–1769) https://www.gutenberg.org/files/30802/30802-h/30802-h.htm. Accessed 24 May 2021
7. Bolis, M., et al.: Care in the Time of Coronavirus: Why care work needs to be at the Centre of a post-COVID-19 Feminist Future. OXFAM. https://hdl.handle.net/10546/621009 (2020). Accessed 27 May 2021
8. Boon, A., Webb, J.: Legal Education and Training in England and Wales: Back to the Future. J. Legal Educ. **58**, 82 (2008)

9. Burgess, S., Greaves, E.: Test scores, subjective assessment, and stereotyping of ethnic minorities. J. Labor Econ. **31**(3), 535–576 (2013)
10. Casper, G.: Two Models of Legal Education. (1973–1974) 13 Tenn L Rev. 41
11. Dewey, J.: Experience and Education Kappa Delta Pi 23 (1938)
12. Cuadrado, D.C.: The Ignored Pandemic Behind COVID-19. Transparency International. http://ti-health.org/wp-content/uploads/2020/12/The-Ignored-Pandemic-Behind-COVID-19-the-impact-of-corruption-on-healthcare.pdf (2020). Accessed 27 May 2021
13. Dangal, M.R., Bajracharya, L.S.: Students anxiety experiences during COVID-19 in Nepal. Kathmandu Univ. Med. J. **18**, 53–57 (2020)
14. Dasgupta, L.: 'Reforming Indian Legal Education: linking research and teaching. J. Legal Educ **59**, 3. https://jle.aals.org/cgi/viewcontent.cgi?article=1271&context=home (2010). Accessed 25 May 2021
15. Dawadi, S., Giri, R.A., Simkhada, P.: Impact of COVID-19 on the Education Sector in Nepal—challenges and coping strategies. Sage Submissions https://doi.org/10.31124/advance.12344336.v1. Accessed 27 May 2021 (forthcoming)
16. Dicey, A.V.: Can English Law Be Taught at the Universities? An Inaugural Address at All Souls College. https://archive.org/details/canenglishlawbe00dicegoog/page/n1/mode/2up (1883). Accessed 24 May 2021
17. Hull, N.E.H.: Vital schools of jurisprudence: Roscoe Pound, Wesley Newcomb Hohfeld, and the promotion of an academic jurisprudential agenda 1910–1919 (1995). J. Legal Educ. **45**(2), 236
18. Girard, P., Laskin, B.: Bringing Law to Life, pp. 80–82. University of Toronto Press, Toronto (2005)
19. Himalayan News Service: Corruption cases up by 58%. The Himalayan Times. https://thehimalayantimes.com/nepal/corruption-cases-up-by-58-per-cent (25 November 2020). Accessed 27 May 2021
20. International Legal Center and Scandinavian center of African Studies: Legal Education in a Changing World: Report of the Committee on Legal Education in the Developing Countries. http://nai.diva-portal.org/smash/get/diva2:275991/FULLTEXT01.pdf%3E (1975). Accessed 9 July 2021
21. Irfan, M.: Poverty in South Asia. Pak. Dev. Rev. **39**, 1141–1151 (2000)
22. Kamat, R.K.: Supreme Court Order on Coercive Measures on Prisoners Remains Unimplemented. The Himalayan Times (22 February 2021), NHRC 'Human Rights Situation During COVID-19 Pandemic'. https://www.nhrcnepal.org/nhrc_new/doc/newsletter/NHRCNepal_COVID_Report_2020.pdf (2020). Accessed 9 July 2021
23. Kashyap, S.C.: Institutions of Governance in South Asia. Delhi Konark Publication (2000)
24. Krook, J.: A Brief History of Legal Education: A Battle between Law as a science and Law as a Liberal Art. In Scardamaglia, A., Lake, J. (eds.) 17 (2) Legal History 30–61 (2017)
25. Kumar, V.: Clinical Legal Education During COVID-19 Pandemic: Issues and Perspectives. ILI Law Review (2020) (Special Issue)
26. Loh, D.: Corruption deepens COVID impact in developing Asia. (*Nikkei Asia,* 28 January 2021) https://asia.nikkei.com/Spotlight/Coronavirus/Corruption-deepens-COVID-impact-in-developing-Asia-report. Accessed 27 May 2021
27. Mallaya, S.P.: Contouring Legal Education in India: An Analysis of Challenges Posed by COVID-19 ILI Law Rev. (Special Issue). https://www.ili.ac.in/COVID/sp.pdf (2020). Accessed 27 May 2021
28. Ministry of Home Affairs: Committee on Reforms of Criminal Justice System (Government of India 2003) https://www.mha.gov.in/sites/default/files/criminal_justice_system.pdf. Accessed 25 May 2021
29. Mitra, C.: The Corrupt Society: The Criminalization of India from Independence to the 1990s. Penguin Books, New Delhi (1998)
30. Negi, C.: COVID-19 Epidemic: Indian Lawyers in Financial Crisis, Ignored, Depressed: In pursuit of Financial and Moral Support. SSRN. https://papers.ssrn.com/sol3/papers.cfm?abstract_id=3646300 (2020). Accessed 27 May 2021

31. Pandit, S.: Sankatma nirantar sikai. (*Gorkhaparta*, 7 May 2020) https://gorkhapatraonline.com/education/2020-05-06-13805. Accessed 25 May 2021
32. Risk, R.C.B.: The Many Minds of W. P. M. Kennedy. The University of Toronto Law J. **48**, 366 (1998)
33. Sarafi, M.: South Asian Legal History. Annu. Rev. Law Soc. Sci. **11**, 309–336 (2015)
34. Schukoske, J.E.: Legal Education Reform in India: Dialogue Among Indian Law Teachers. Jindal Glob. Law Rev. (1) (2009)
35. Stiebeler, W.: Hamburger Modell Einer Einstufigen Juristenausbildung. JuristenZeitung **25**(14), 457–461 (1970)
36. Thomson, D.I.C.: Defining Experiential Legal Education. J. Experiential Learn. **1** (2015)
37. Transparency International: Fighting Corruption in South Asia: Building Accountability. **6**. https://images.transparencycdn.org/images/2014_FightingCorruption_in_SouthAsia_EN.pdf (2014). Accessed 24 May 2021
38. UNODC: Guidance Note: Ensuring Access to Justice in the Context of COVID-19. **12**. https://www.unodc.org/documents/AdvocacySection/Ensuring_Access_to_Justice_in_the_Context_of_COVID-191.pdf (2020). Accessed 24 May 2021
39. UNESCO: UNESCO Showcases Education Reponses to COVID-19 at UN General Assembly. https://en.unesco.org/news/unesco-showcases-education-responses-COVID-19-crisis-general-assembly (23 September 2020). Accessed 23 May 2021
40. World Bank: South Asia: The Prospect of Economic Rebound in South Asia are Firming Up as Growth is Set to Increase by 7.2% in 2021 and 4.4% in 2022. https://www.worldbank.org/en/region/sar/overview (3 March 2021). Accessed 27 May 2021.

Legal Education and Legal Profession During and After COVID-19 in Nigeria

Ibibia Lucky Worika

Abstract The extent and intensity of the impact of COVID-19 differ from country to country and from one region to the other. Its devastating impact in Nigeria and across much of the world cannot, however, be overemphasized. In Nigeria, the pandemic destabilized traditional methods of legal education as well as the legal profession generally. This chapter noted the psychological impact of COVID-19 on students and parents alike and dovetailed into its tripodal impact on legal education, the legal profession and the Nigerian economy. Although there is widespread cynicism and sarcasm about the existence of COVID-19 in Nigeria, it found that, in most cases, its impact had been revolutionary. While throwing up new and sometimes herculean challenges, COVID-19 equally threw up new opportunities for legal education, the legal profession as well as the economy. The challenge is in understanding these difficulties and opportunities with a sanguine determination to take advantage of the opportunities. Neither legal education, the legal profession nor the Nigerian economy would remain the same post-COVID-19 pandemic. Traditional methods may well have, incrementally, gone for good! The future is guaranteed by adaptation to the changes wrought by COVID-19 in Nigeria and beyond.

[1] Medical News Today, "Corona virus cause: Origin and how it spreads" at https://www.medicalnewstoday.com/articles/coronavirus-causes accessed 30/06/21. On March 11, 2020, the World Health Organization (WHO) declared COVID-19 a pandemic. A pandemic occurs when a disease that people are not immune to spreads across large regions.

[2] See Nature Medicine, "Covid-19 in Africa: The Spread and Response" at https://www.nature.com/articles/s41591-020-0961-x accessed 28/06/21.

[3] See Nigeria Centre for Disease Control (NCDC), "First Case of Corona virus Disease Confirmed in Nigeria" at https://ncdc.gov.ng/news/227/first-case-of-corona-virus-disease-confirmed-in-nigeria#:~:text=The%20Federal%20Ministry%20of%20Health,in%20China%20in%20January%202020 accessed 27/12/20.

I. L. Worika (✉)
Faculty of Law, University of Port Harcourt, Port Harcourt, Nigeria
e-mail: ibibia.worika@uniport.edu.ng

C. Raj Kumar and S. G. Sreejith (eds.), *Legal Education and Legal Profession During and After COVID-19*, https://doi.org/10.1007/978-981-19-2568-9_9

1 Background and Introduction

Covid-19 had inconceivable and remarkable impact all over the world. It was first noticeable in the city of Wuhan in Hubei province of China in early December, 2019, later declared a Pandemic as it spread to the whole of Asia, Europe and the United States of America.[1] Africa was not spared.[2] In Nigeria, the impact of Covid-19 has been devastating across all sectors of society. The legal profession and, in particular, legal education was adversely affected by the pandemic.

Nigeria recorded its first case of COVID-19, which was reported by the Federal Ministry of Health on 27th February, 2020.[3] It was the case of an Italian citizen working in Nigeria, who had returned from Milan, Italy to Lagos, Nigeria on the 25th of February, 2020. Thereafter, the number of confirmed cases of infection kept rising in Nigeria and across the world. Nigeria placed a travel ban on 13 countries with high cases of the virus, the countries are; United States, United Kingdom, South Korea, Switzerland, Germany, France, Italy, China, Spain, Netherland, Norway, Japan and Iran.[4]

The Nigerian President Mohammed Buhari, in late March, 2020, declared a total lockdown of the federal capital territory, Abuja, and the commercial capital, Lagos.[5] The lockdown also included Ogun State, neighbor to Lagos. Other states, including Rivers State, wherein the University of Port Harcourt is situated, decided to follow suit, with a range of restrictions to curtail the spread of the virus. Travel on motorways between states in Nigeria was also banned. The prohibition extended to all bank branches and business premises nationwide.[6]

Inadvertently, the lockdown overlapped with the suspension of Academic activities in Nigerian universities between March and December, 2020.[7] Following the lockdown, all non-essential business activities were suspended, including legal education and operation of law firms in the normal professional course of business. The practice of Law like legal education has usually been based mostly on physical one-on-one meetings with clients.[8] The lockdown clearly made this impracticable for legal practitioners, teachers as well as students. As a result, lawyers found it both difficult and inconvenient to conduct personal interviews with new clients or review matters with existing clients. The fact that businesses and work were adversely

---

[4] CNN, "Nigeria places bans entry for travelers from 13 countries as it announces five new cases of coronavirus" at https://edition.cnn.com/2020/03/18/africa/nigeria-coronavirus-travel-restrictions-intl/index.html accessed 20/01/21. Authorities in Nigeria placed further travel ban from Brazil, India and Turkey following the growing second wave of infections from the virus. See GARDAWORLD, "Nigeria: Authorities ban travel from several countries due to rising covid-19 cases" at https://www.garda.com/crisis24/news-alerts/474026/nigeria-authorities-ban-travel-from-several-countries-due-to-rising-covid-19-cases-from-may-4-update-35 accessed 3/06/21.

[5] Denton [1].

[6] Ibid.

[7] See BBC News, "ASUU Strike Today: 2020 University Lecturers Strike Latest News Update" at https://www.bbc.com/pidgin/tori-55408139 accessed 30/01/21.

[8] See Christian B. Denton, supra note 5.

affected meant that many clients (including prospective ones) were financially devastated by the pandemic, which led to an inability to pay professional fees or engage counsel. By some fortuitous set of circumstances, it was, in retrospect, a blessing in disguise as parents would have had to struggle to keep their wards in school during the lockdowns. Considering the devastating impact of Covid 19 on legal education and the legal profession, the question that perforce arises with renewed acuity is in what ways exactly and to what extent it affected legal education and the legal profession.

2 Conceptual Framework

2.1 Legal Education

Legal education in Nigeria begins with the Joint Admissions Matriculation Board (JAMB) examinations after successfully passing the Ordinary "O" Levels examination with credit in five subject areas, including English, Mathematics and Literature-in-English. Admission into a Nigerian University with "O" Levels through JAMB normally takes five years to get a first degree, usually called a Bachelor-in-Law (LL.B.). There is a provision for Direct Entry candidates, who mostly have a first degree, a diploma or an equivalent with credits in English, Literature-in-English as well as Mathematics at 'O' level. Direct Entry candidates spend four years to get the first degree in Law (LL.B). But, the LL.B. degree still does not qualify one to practice law in Nigeria in any of the Courts of Law. In order to practice law in Nigeria, additional one year practical or vocational training at the Nigerian Law School is required to complete the legal education to qualify one to practice law in Nigeria as a Barrister and Solicitor of the Supreme Court of Nigeria.

N.J. Madubuike-Ekwe,[9] posits that,

> Legal education, simply, is the education of individuals who intend to be lawyers or who intend to use their law degree to some end either related to law (i.e. politics, academia) or business. Legal education is a system of education that produces skillful and ethical lawyers who must have, among other things, a technical competence to analyze legal issues against the background of existing law, the direction the law is or should be developing and the key policy considerations.[10]

Considering the various lockdowns across the federation, coupled with the industrial strike action by the Academic Staff Union of Universities (ASUU), the Federal Ministry of Education confirmed that all federal universities across the country lost one full academic session as a result of the industrial strike action by the Academic

---

[9] Madubuike-Ekwe [2].

[10] Ibid.

Staff Union of Universities (ASUU).[11] The implication of this was that no graduate from the nation's federal Universities could be sent to the Nigerian Law School for the 2019/2020 Academic Year during the pandemic. Authorities of most federal and even some state universities have been at a crossroads over how to manage the academic calendar to avoid overcrowding.[12]

Covid-19 impacted legal education in Nigeria generally. First, it was never anticipated. The traditional method of direct contact with students had held sway until Covid-19 took everyone by surprise. There were no preparations for online learning prior to Covid-19 and, with the industrial strike action coinciding with the period of the lockdown in Nigeria, students were forced to simply go home and wait when tertiary education would return to normal. It has never quite settled to normalcy and Universities (both private and public) across Nigeria had to grapple with the challenge of using technology to impart knowledge without necessarily making physical contact. The private Universities are clearly outperforming their public counterparts for obvious reasons.

Average tuition fees asides other payments in private universities in Nigeria are between N600,000 and N1.3 million, which is approximately between US$1500 and US$2500 respectively per academic session. In some public universities, however, the tuition is as low as N50,000 (approximately US$100) per academic session depending on the course entered for. In other words, public university education was heavily subsidized by the Federal and State Governments, which were themselves struggling with dwindling revenues from the impact of Covid-19. The National Universities Commission (NUC), estimates that there are 2.1 million university students currently.[13] Public universities with very little funding, but greater access are therefore worse hit by Covid-19 pandemic and least placed to adapt. The pandemic has unmasked substantial inequities in the education sector, generally and, legal education, in particular. While some private universities were engaging their students through online teaching, large number of students who are less privileged and in public universities were left out. Most universities lacked facilities which hindered them to partake successfully in online teaching.

---

[11] "Federal Varsities have lost one academic session due to ASUU strike" at https://guardian.ng/news/federal-varsities-have-lost-one-academic-session-due-to-asuu-strike-says-ministry accessed on 3/06/21.

[12] Nigeria has approximately 52 State Universities, 99 private Universities and 44 Federal Universities. See generally https://www.nuc.edu.ng/nigerian-univerisities/private-univeristies/; https://www.nuc.edu.ng/nigerian-univerisities/state-univerisity/; and https://www.nuc.edu.ng/nigerian-univerisities/federal-univeristies/ accessed 1/6/21; of the total 197 universities in Nigeria, 98 are public, while 99 are privately owned. But, despite the fact that private universities are more, they account for a little over five percent of the total students' enrolment, while public universities account for the bulk of almost 95%.

[13] "Nigeria's 99 private universities account for only 5% of students' enrolment" See https://businessday.ng/education/article/nigerias-99-private-universities-account-for-only-5-students-enrolment-nuc/#:~:text=Of%20the%20total%20197%20universities,while%2099%20are%20privately%20owned accessed 1/6/21.

2.2 The Legal Profession

One must be forgiven for thinking that legal practitioners with their somewhat exorbitant fees and international outlook would have anticipated Covid-19 and made adequate preparations to adapt. However, the reality is not exactly so. Most lawyers and law firms had to grapple with how to continue to provide services under the impact of Covid-19 as well.[14]

Firstly, prospective clients were reluctant to engage the services of legal practitioners for fear of their own safety in a corona virus era. Conversely, Legal practitioners had to think up new ways of appointments with their clients. The fact that private businesses were either shutting down or laying off staff as cost-saving measures meant that clients were largely financially incapacitated with the result that Legal practice was adversely affected.

It is no gainsaying that majority of lawyers in legal practice is into litigation. The conduct of litigation, especially filing of court processes in the traditional way became difficult to effect. At some point, the Chief Justice of Nigeria, Justice Muhammed Tanko had to issue a directive for the courts to be closed, which was seen as a welcome development.[15] The import of this was to leave litigants and prospective litigants in quandary with adverse impact on legal practice. Criminal prosecutions were particularly hard hit as accused persons had to be remanded in custody until the courts resumed. Admittedly, some state Chief Judges issued directives enabling the filing of court processes online. However, being a new directive with little expertise on the parts of lawyers and court registry staff in respect of online filing, the hardship on law firms and legal practice was not completely assuaged.

The conduct of litigation even with observance of covid-19 protocol took a somewhat bizarre turn. Expectedly, questions were raised on the evidential value of documents that had been filed online, but not physically seen. The fact that conducting litigation in a covid-19 era had become quite challenging meant that law firms could not easily foot their bills. In Port Harcourt, where the author is resident, quite a few law firms had to fold up their physical offices in preference for online service delivery from home as a cost-cutting measure.

Covid-19 also revealed the inadequacies of both legal education and legal practice in Nigeria. The predominant systems of physical one-on-one contact and extreme paperwork were clearly out-of-date and out of sync with recent and emergent electronic and technological trends worldwide. There is a paradigm shift to the use of emails, WhatsApp, zoom, webinar and skype in communication as well as interaction, which had never been anticipated nor frequently used by legal education institutions as well as the Nigerian Bar Association (NBA) prior to this time. These had long become the norm in other more advanced jurisdictions.

[14] Christian B Denton, supra note 5 above.

[15] Sombo [3].

3 Tripodal Impact of COVID-19

Alaba Tolulope Agbele and Emmanuel Akinbami Oyelade in their paper titled, "Impact of COVID-19 on the Nigerian Educational System: Strengths and Challenges of Online/Virtual Education"[16] examined the impact of Covid-19 on the Nigerian educational system. They noted the psychological debilitating impact on the children/university students, on families as well as teachers. They opined that:

> Most Nigerian students and other African or underdeveloped countries were more disadvantaged because most educational institutions in Nigeria still follow the traditional set-up of face-to-face lectures in the normal classroom settings.[17]

While these observations are valid, the tripodal impact of covid-19 is seen in this paper in the context of legal education, legal practice and the wider Nigerian economy and how the latter impacts legal education and legal practice.

3.1 *Impact on Legal Education*

Covid-19 disrupted legal education in the Universities as well as Nigerian Law School. At the height of the pandemic, the federal government had to close all schools and tertiary institutions, which negatively impacted on the educational academic calendar. By the time schools and universities resumed, most universities had lost one full academic session with resultant delays in graduation and, invariably, entry and graduation from the Nigerian Law School.

Covid-19 exposed the technological backwardness of the Nigerian education system, including legal education. Prior to the era of the pandemic, the Nigerian university system, in general and, legal education, in particular, was characterized by the traditional method of imparting knowledge, which consisted solely and exclusively on physical presence of the Lecturers and students. To be sure, Universities had computers and few lecturers had laptops, some with internet capability. But, these equipments were not for the impartation of knowledge through the internet. Covid-19 made it near impossible to continue with the traditional method for obvious reasons. Concomitantly with exposing the challenges of the use of technology to impart knowledge, Covid-19 equally created new opportunities in teaching and learning, which are now applied in clinical legal education. Slowly and steadily, there has been a new and renewed emphasis on e-learning, including the use of whatsApp, zoom, webinar and skype, just to mention these. While the transition has been particularly challenging for both staff and students alike, who hitherto were not used to e-learning, the experience has been worth it. Unfortunately, there are no scholarships, bursary

---

[16] 13(1) Asian Journal of Education and Social Studies 2020 pp. 26–35 at Research Gate https://www.researchgate.net/publication/346528423_Impact_of_COVID-19_on_the_Nigerian_Educational_System_Strengths_and_Challenges_of_OnlineVirtual_Education visited 29/01/22.

[17] Ibid.

schemes and financial aids to universities as a result of covid-19 with the result that students and staff have had to bear the brunt of the cost of providing smart phones, laptops and data access. The federal government through its National Universities Commission (NUC) and the Tertiary Education Trust Fund (TETFUND) has been particularly slow in meeting this challenge and, with the economic downturn, not many private enterprises have been able to fill the existing gap. What we have in most public universities therefore is an often fragmented, staggered, not so consistent or irregular availability and use of modern technology in teaching and learning. Besides, most students in public universities are impecunious and unable to provide laptops, smart phones or data to easily access online learning platforms.

Admittedly, some of the public universities are beginning to live up to the challenge of providing online learning platforms and facilities. The University of Port Harcourt Information and Communication Technology Centre (ICTC) and the World Bank Centre of Excellence is in the forefront of providing e-learning platforms. However, given the huge number of students especially in the undergraduate programmes, access is still by and large limited and inadequate.

Fortuitously, the impact of Covid-19 in terms of infections and deaths has not been as devastating as it has been in much more economically and technologically advanced jurisdictions. This has obviated the need to continue to push hard in transiting to e-learning platforms in education, generally and, legal education, in particular. It is now not so uncommon to see a gradual return to the traditional method of teaching in our universities and institutions of higher learning, which is permeating the pedagogy of learning the law especially in clinical legal education.

3.2 *Impact on the Legal Profession*

The global pandemic is increasingly impacting on the way and manner law we practice law in Nigeria. To be sure, law firms in Nigeria face challenges that are not peculiar to them. At the global level, Moore Legal Technology examined the greatest legal sector challenges and opportunities 2020–20,230 and postulated that:

> The Coronavirus pandemic has been and will be considerably changing the way that law firms operate and the way in which clients purchase legal services in future. Now, more than ever, it is critical to leverage technology not only to survive, but to prosper.[18]

In more advanced jurisdictions, Moore Legal Technology has adumbrated these challenges and opportunities into their component units. It is said that there would be new forms of legal services and new ways of delivering such services; mergers and acquisition of law firms; demise of legal aid; increased outsourcing; pricing

[18] Moore Law Technology, "The Greatest Legal Sector Challenges (and Opportunities) 2020–2023" at https://www.moorelegaltechnology.co.uk/insights/business-innovation-for-lawyers/the-greatest-legal-sector-challenges-and-opportunities-2017-2027.html visited 29/01/22.

pressures with increased client demand; blurring of the distinction between Advocates/Barristers and Solicitors as well as referral bans.[19] Covid-19 with its initial intensity brought to the fore most of these challenges and opportunities in Nigeria as well. However, given the relatively low infections and death rates, not all of these challenges and opportunities are easily noticeable. Clearly, there has been rationalization of law firms. While some are merging, others are downsizing, with few others reducing their physical presence, or folding up.[20] Some law firms have closed their physical offices and opted for online presence in consonance with the times. Litigation is getting narrower, while for legal consultancy is expanding in scope and content. Lawyers are gradually abandoning adversarial litigation and advocacy for legal consultancy and the multi-door courthouse of alternative dispute resolution.[21] The Port Harcourt and Lagos Multi Door Court Houses became busier during the pandemic.[22]

Conferences, seminars, workshops and roundtables are now being conducted through zoom, or webinar. In few cases, court sittings have been conducted online as well. Where physical presence of litigants and lawyers are still being practiced, Covid-19 protocol imposes new rules on the use of face masks and social distancing in courts. This has, invariably, placed a limit on the number of cases on the cause list. There have, however, been innovations for the development of remote justice system in some of the states in Nigeria. Ugonna Ogbuagu and Kehinde of AELEX examined this new trend and found that in three areas viz; filing of processes, service of litigation processes and the conduct of court proceedings, some Nigerian courts have had to adapt to the global pandemic.[23] The *National Judicial Council (NJC) Guidelines for Court Sittings and Related Matters in Covid 19 Period* was issued to guide the courts *inter alia* in implementing remote justice systems.[24] Also, the *Lagos State Judiciary (Remote Hearing of Cases) Covid-19 Pandemic Period Practice Direction* as well as *the Federal High Court Practice Direction 2020 for Covid-19 Period*[25] are cases in point.

---

[19] Ibid.

[20] On the implications of mergers on competition, see for example olaniwon Ajayi, 'Covid-19: Implications for Mergers and Competitors' at https://www.olaniwunajayi.net/wp-content/uploads/2020/04/COVID-19-Implications-for-Mergers-Between-Competitors-.pdf visited 29/01/22.

[21] For example, the Lagos Multi-door Court (LMDC) is said to be "…a court-connected Alternative Dispute Resolution Centre that offers a variety of Alternative Dispute Resolution (ADR) processes. The Mission of the LMDC is to supplement litigation as the available resource for justice by the provision of enhanced, timely, cost effective and user friendly Access to Justice. The Multi-Door refers to the various options available at the LMDC including Mediation, Arbitration, Early Neutral Evaluation, and Hybrid Processes."See 'Who we are' at https://lagosmultidoor.org/about-us/ visited 29/01/22.

[22] See Umegbolu [4].

[23] See Ogbuagu and Takuro [5].

[24] National Judicial Council, 'Covid-19 Policy Report: Guidelines for court sittings and related matters in the Covid-19 period', see https://njc.gov.ng/30/news-details, accessed 14/04/2020.

[25] Federal Republic of Nigeria, 'Federal High Court of Nigeria Practice Directions 2020 for the Covid-19 period', see https://thenigerialawyer.com/wp-content/uploads/2020/05/PRACTICE-DIRECTION-2020-FOR-Covid190001y.pdf, accessed 3/06/2020.

Admittedly, questions have been raised regarding the constitutionality of virtual or online court sittings. The objections rest on the presupposition that virtual court sitting does not qualify as public hearing under Section 36 (1), (3), and (4) of the Nigerian Constitution 1999 (As Amended). Section 36 (1) (3) and (4) of the Constitution is to the effect that every person shall be entitled to a fair hearing within a reasonable time for the purpose of the determination of his/her civil rights and obligations and, that such hearing must be held in public. Considering the exigencies of the times, it is not surprising that the Judiciary affirmed its commitment to the development of virtual court sitting while considering the legal challenge to the constitutionality of the new practice in *Attorney General of Lagos State* v. *Attorney General of the Federation and Anor*.[26] On 4 May 2020, the Ikeja High Court held a virtual session in Lagos, wherein it sentenced a man to death for the murder of the mother of his employer.[27] The Judge of the Court, Justice Mojisola Dada, delivered the judgment via Zoom.[28] The court proceedings, approved by the Chief Justice of Lagos State, Justice Kazeem Alogba, were in line with the *Lagos State Judiciary Remote Hearing of Cases Covid-19 Pandemic Period Practice Direction*.[29]

3.3 Impact on the Economy

Bloomberg Economics, in the most extreme of four scenarios, drawing on the experience in China, the distribution of Covid-19 cases in other countries, including estimates of risks to global supply chains as well as a large-scale model of the global economy, estimated that a total of $2.7 trillion in lost output—equivalent to the entire GDP of the U.K. to the pandemic.[30] This impact on the global economy also dovetailed into several other countries that experienced lockdowns as a result of Covid-19, including Nigeria.

The pandemic impacted negatively on Nigeria. Many Nigerians were rendered unemployed. With lower volumes of oil exports, the major foreign exchange earner,

[26] *SUIT* No. SC/CV/260/2020 Attorney General of Lagos State v. Attorney General of the Federation & Anor.; see also Lawyers online at https://cases.lawyersonline.ng/a-g-lagos-state-v-a-g-federation/ accessed 01/06/21; see also Attorney General of Ekiti State v Attorney General of the Federation *Suit No SC/CV/261/2020 Attorney General of Ekiti State v Attorney General of the Federation at Lawyers online,* https://cases.lawyersonline.ng/a-g-ekiti-state-v-a-g-federation/ accessed 01/06/21.

[27] The Guardian, "Man gets death sentence as Lagos holds virtual court session" at https://guardian.ng/news/man-gets-death-sentence-as-lagos-holds-virtual-court-session/ accessed 3/06/21.

[28] Human Rights Watch has criticized the sentencing to death of a Nigerian driver via Zoom as "inherently cruel and inhumane". See "Corona virus: Nigeria's death penalty by zoom 'inhumane' at https://www.bbc.com/news/world-africa-52560918 accessed 3/06/21.

[29] See Practice Direction for Remote Hearing of Cases in Lagos State Judiciary at https://www.aelex.com/wp-content/uploads/2020/04/PRACTICE-DIRECTIONS-FOR-REMOTE-SITTING-FOR-THE-LAGOS-STATE-JUDICIARY-003.pdf accessed 03/06/21.

[30] Bloomberg. 'Coronavirus Could Cost the Global Economy $2.7 Trillio. Here's how' at https://www.bloomberg.com/graphics/2020-coronavirus-pandemic-global-economic-risk/ visited 29/01/22.

the World Economic Forum estimated that Nigeria's economy contracted by 6.1% year on year in the second quarter of 2020.[31] With 27% of Nigeria's labour force of over 21 milliion Nigerians unemployed, it is estimated that there is a little sign of a quick recovery as the World Bank predicts that Nigeria is set for its worst economic recession in four decades.

Nigeria's economy has also been crippled by external factors too as the corona virus pandemic resulted in a near-total shutdown of economic activity around the world. The accompanying steep drop in oil prices amid a drop in global demand left Nigeria with a drastic drop in earnings given its dependence on oil as its biggest revenue source.[32]

Most commercial law firms depend on a flourishing economy with concomitant international linkages. With the near total lockdown of the economy due to Covid-19, the impact on the legal profession generally and law firms in particular can better be imagined.[33] The lockdown has since been eased but recovery has been very slow. Rationalization and downsizing have already taken place.[34] Some young lawyers have had to cope with half salaries or none at all. These developments are not likely to disappear in the twinkle of an eye or any time soon.

4 Post COVID-19: Challenges and Prospects

The major challenge of education generally and, legal education, in particular, for decades have been the inadequacy and, in some cases, absence of infrastructure in most public and private universities in Nigeria. The federal and state governments heavily subsidize education in public institutions, understandably to increase greater access in the hope that education would assist in gravitating the masses out of poverty. Despite governments' good intentions, they are unable to adequately fund public institutions effectively. The result is poor infrastructure in public institutions. While private institutions charge fees, fewer fee-paying students relative to the heavily subsidized public universities means that their return on investments is characterized by muted optimism with equally infrastructural challenges in the vast majority of them. Even with efforts to adapt to the new normal, irregular, sporadic and intermittent power supply, low internet bandwidth, a dearth of computers and other technological

[31] World Economic Forum, "Here's how Covid-19 has battered Africa's Largest Economy" at https://www.weforum.org/agenda/2020/08/africa-largest-economy-worst-contraction-in-a-decade/ accessed on 02/6/21.

[32] See the Pulitzer Centre, "The Economic Repercussions of the Corona Virus Pandemic on Nigerians" at https://pulitzercenter.org/stories/economic-repercussion-coronavirus-pandemic-nigerians.

[33] "Covid-19 Series: The Impact of the Crisis on Lawyers in Nigeria" at https://lawyersforlawyers.org/en/covid-19-series-the-impact-of-the-crisis-on-lawyers-in-nigeria/ accessed 12/12/20.

[34] See Vox, "This is the end of the Office as we know it" at https://www.vox.com/recode/2020/4/14/21211789/coronavirus-office-space-work-from-home-design-architecture-real-estate accessed on 3/06/21.

tools required by law students, legal practitioners, judges and court registrars have militated against virtual learning, online interactions and virtual court sittings.[35]

Perhaps, the greatest challenge with respect to Covid-19 in Nigeria is the sarcasm and skepticism amongst the majority of Nigerians regarding Covid-19.[36] Regrettably, this skeptical narrative discrediting the efforts of the government to manage the pandemic is being driven by both the uninformed and informed alike. Consequently, compliance has been very low on health and safety Covid-19 related guidelines. In the local markets with high population density, for example, it is not uncommon to find virtually everyone without a nose mask or hand sanitizer. Admittedly, this pessimism is not exceptional to Nigeria as can be perceived on global news channels and social media, generally. According to Emeka Oparah,

> ...the reason for this cynicism and skepticism is basically a failure in the social contract between governments and the people. Specifically, Nigerians have felt hard done by, over the years, by successive governments that have promised so much and delivered so little. So, every government official or programme is viewed with suspicion. In the case of Covid-19, many believe (and actually say) it is a scam methodically orchestrated by government officials to steal public funds.[37]

Another reason that has fueled the cynicism is possibly the relatively low incidents and death rate from Covid-19 when compared to other parts of the developed world.[38] In Africa, generally and, Nigeria, in particular, the impact of COVID-19 has been considerably lower compared to countries in the Americas, Europe, and Asia. While the demographic age structure of sub-Saharan Africa and its improved public health preparedness are seen as factors responsible for the low morbidity and mortality of COVID-19 compared to other regions of the world, the fact remains that the relatively low incidents of Covid-19 infections and deaths in comparison to other regions of the world have continued to fuel the sarcasm on whether the virus actually exist, which in turn accounts for the very low compliance with Covid-19 health and safety-related guidelines.

Brea, Brian and Bernice are of the view that "COVID-19 pandemic has revealed wide disparities in infection and recovery rates by race, ethnicity, socioeconomic

---

[35] Kenna Partners, Dispute Resolution Insights, "Overcoming the Challenges of Virtual Court Proceedings" at https://kennapartners.com/wp-content/uploads/2020/07/OVERCOMING-THE-CHALLENGES-TO-VIRTUAL-COURT-PROCEEDINGS.pdf accessed on 02/06/21; see also Kolawole Mayomi, "Nigeria: A Case for Virtual Court Hearings of Urgent Matters During the Covid-19 Pandemic and Going Forward" at MONDAQ, https://www.mondaq.com/nigeria/litigation-contracts-and-force-majeure/930796/a-case-for-the-virtual-hearings-of-urgent-matters-during-the-covid-19-pandemic-and-going-forward accessed on 02/06/21. Also, at http://www.spaajibade.com/resources/a-case-for-the-virtual-hearings-of-urgent-matters-during-the-covid-19-pandemic-and-going-forward/?utm_source=Mondaq&utm_medium=syndication&utm_campaign=LinkedIn-integration.

[36] Oparah [6].

[37] Ibid.

[38] Adams et al. [7].

status, and place of residence."[39] In Nigeria, it Covid-19 also exposed the educational as well as socio-economic divide. Children in rural and underserved communities in Nigeria, who end up studying law in universities, are being left behind as they are not equipped to adapt or transition to new online methods of learning.[40] These students most certainly prefer the traditional teaching methods and would, invariably, constitute a drag, and understandably so, on the move towards online learning. Scholarship and bursary schemes as well as provision of cost-free student online teaching platforms would help to alleviate the hardship. The Nigerian National Universities Commission (NUC) and Tertiary Education Trust Fund (TETFUND) should step in and reduce the gap. Also important is public–private partnership (PPP) in providing quality legal education in Universities.

Such gap in online capacity is also evident in the fact that not all parties may be able to effectively participate in virtual court sittings, even if they wanted to. This is the reason why some courts require both parties to agree to virtual hearing before such hearing can be scheduled for the parties. The Nigerian *Federal High Court Practice Direction* specifically provides that, where parties and lawyers in any case agree to virtual proceedings, they shall liaise with the Registrar to schedule such hearings.[41]

Going forward, Clinical Legal Education, a wholistic, "multidisciplinary and multipurpose type of legal education which seeks to develop the skills and competencies needed to strengthen the legal system…"[42] as well as other forms of online interactive learning methods should be adopted in Universities and Law Schools in Nigeria and beyond. Post covid-19, online moot court sessions, chamber attachments, online legal lectures by prominent and senior lawyers, seminars and workshops including the notion of improved practical teaching methods, such as audio-visual aids should be the norm.[43] Luckily, CLE is gradually becoming the norm in legal education in Universities across Nigeria and the Nigerian Law School. The impact of these recent and emergent trends would be felt in the legal profession with time.

[39] See Proceedings of the National Academy of Sciences of the United States (PNAS), "Pandemic Precarity: Covid-19 is exposing and exacerbating inequalities in the American heartland" at https://www.pnas.org/content/118/8/e2020685118 accessed 01/06/21.

[40] World Economic Forum, "COVID-19 has exposed the education divide in Nigeria. This is how we can close it" https://www.weforum.org/agenda/2020/06/education-nigeria-covid19-digital-divide/ accessed 08/05/21.

[41] See Part F of the *FHC Practice Directions*. See https://thenigerialawyer.com/wp-content/uploads/2020/05/PRACTICE-DIRECTION-2020-FOR-COVID190001y.pdf.

[42] Maduafor [8].

[43] See 'Oditah Advocates PPP in funding legal Education' Vanguard News, June 11, 2013 http://www.vanguardngr.com/2013/06/oditah-advocates-ppp-in-fu cited in N.J. Madubuike-Ekwe supra note 1.

5 Final Words

Although the extent and intensity of impact of Covid-19 differ from one country to the other and from one region to the other, its devastating impact in Nigeria and across the world cannot be overemphasized. The pandemic has destabilized traditional methods of legal education as well as the legal profession generally. While noting the psychological impact of Covid-19 on students and parents alike, this chapter dovetailed into its tripodal impact on legal education, the legal profession and the economy, noting that in most cases, its impact has been revolutionary. Nevertheless, Covid-19 has thrown up new challenges as well as opportunities for legal education, the legal profession as well as the economy. In quoting Sir Winston Churchill, Moore Legal Technology notes that:

> A pessimist sees the difficulty in every opportunity; an optimist sees the opportunity in every difficulty.

The challenge is to understand these difficulties and opportunities with a sanguine determination to take advantage of the opportunities. Neither legal education, the legal profession nor the economy would remain the same post covid-19 pandemic. Traditional methods may well have gone for good! The future is for those who are able to adapt to the changes wrought by covid-19 in Nigeria and elsewhere.

References

1. Denton, C.B.: The impact of covid-19 on the legal profession in Nigeria. At https://www.ibanet.org/article/93f8cd9b-d943-4a94-9303-35cc51941b5e visited 08/05/21
2. Madubuike-Ekwe, N.J.: Challenges and prospects of legal education in Nigeria: an overview. Nnamdi Azikiwe J. Int. Law Jurisprud. **8**(1). At https://www.ajol.info/index.php/naujilj/article/view/156726 (2017). Accessed 08/05/21
3. Sombo, W.: COVID-19: lawyers commend CJN for suspending court sittings (NNN, 26 March 2020) https://nnn.com.ng/covid-19-lawyers-commend-cjn-for-suspending-court-sittings/. Accessed 30/04/20
4. Umegbolu, C.: The Lagos Multi-Door Courthouse: Online Dispute Resolution in COVID-19 Era. At https://www.researchgate.net/publication/344396088_The_Lagos_Multi-Door_Courthouse_Online_Dispute_Resolution_in_COVID-_19_Era visited 29/01/22
5. Ogbuagu, U., Takuro, K.: Innovations for the Development of Remote Justice in Nigeria. At https://www.ibanet.org/article/BA479B88-55BA-43EA-9DF6-80A0FB6C3668. Accessed 1/06/21
6. Oparah, E.: Managing cynicism and unbelief in a Covid-19 era. At https://www.thecable.ng/managingcynicism-and-unbelief-in-the-covid-19-era visited 26/01/22
7. Adams, J., et al.: The Conundrum of Low Covid-19 Mortality Burden in sub-Saharan Africa: Myth or Reality? At https://www.ghspjournal.org/content/9/3/433 visited 28/01/22
8. Maduafor, N.: Clinical Legal Education and the Role of Law Clinics in Criminal Justice System. At https://www.researchgate.net/publication/340655569_THE_CLINICAL_LEGAL_EDUCATION_PROGRAMME visited 29/01/22

Teaching Law in the Time of Covid-19: Experiences from the University of KwaZulu-Natal, South Africa

Managay Reddi

Abstract The University of KwaZulu-Natal (UKZN) is a contact institution with a significant number of its students living in the University's residences during their studies. However, because of Covid-19, since March 2020, UKZN has had to migrate from contact teaching and learning to a remote, online format. This article sets out the impact of the realisation that a new normal had to be crafted to enable the academic project and academic life at the university in general and the School of Law, in particular, to continue during the pandemic. Whilst detailing the steps taken to achieve operational functionality, the writer also touches on the challenges of ensuring staff and student wellbeing during this time of a global pandemic.

1 Introduction

At midnight on 26 March 2020, South Africa went into a hard lockdown. Life as we knew it then ended when the bell tolled that midnight. The expectation at the time, somewhat naïve in hindsight, was that the lockdown and the coronavirus pandemic would be behind us in a few months.[1] Instead, sixteen months and untold tragedy later, South Africa is on the verge of a third wave of the pandemic and still in lockdown, although now at level 3.[2]

Under normal circumstances, the academic programme in South African universities begins in February and ends in December. At the University of KwaZulu-Natal (UKZN), the 2020 academic year began in the second week of February but was immediately disrupted by student protests arising from several parochial student

[1] There are five lockdown levels in South Africa with level 1 being the easiest and level 5 the strictest. A level 5 lockdown was declared in South Africa from 26 March 2020 to 30 April 2020. See also South African Government News Agency [1].

[2] The Covid-19 pandemic was declared a national disaster in South Africa on 15 March 2020. The state of disaster has been renewed repeatedly since then and is still applicable at the time of writing.

M. Reddi (✉)
School of Law, University of KwaZulu-Natal, Durban, South Africa
e-mail: REDDIM@ukzn.ac.za

C. Raj Kumar and S. G. Sreejith (eds.), *Legal Education and Legal Profession During and After COVID-19*, https://doi.org/10.1007/978-981-19-2568-9_10

issues. The disruptions lasted approximately two weeks. The Law School immediately started planning on how to address the teaching and learning time lost in the now slightly shortened academic semester. We were fairly unfazed by the situation as it was one to which we had become acclimated over the years.[3]

The 2020 academic programme then commenced in earnest at the beginning of March 2020. We were three weeks into our programme when the level 5 hard lockdown started. The result was that all academic activities at the university immediately ceased, the student residences were closed and students sent home, and the academic and support staff who could began working remotely from their homes.

In the few days between the state president's announcement of the hard lockdown and its implementation, the school leadership attempted to devise a strategy for successfully completing semester 1 of the academic programme despite the projected loss of approximately ten weeks of teaching time. The plan devised in March 2020 anticipated that come 30 April 2020, the university may be reopening and likely will operate as usual. In the light of the information at hand at the time, our anticipation was not farfetched.[4] We were wrong, however. As the pandemic evolved organically, our plans had to be revised to take account of what was quickly becoming evident—that a return to campus and in-person engagements with our students was not on the cards and would not be for a long time in the future.

This article sets out the impact of the realisation that a new normal had to be crafted to enable the academic programme and academic life at the university in general and the School of Law, in particular, to continue during the pandemic. Whilst detailing the steps taken to achieve operational functionality, the writer also touches on the challenges of ensuring staff and student wellbeing during this time of a global pandemic.

2 Devising an Emergency Teaching and Learning Plan

The South African winter is from June to August. Based on scientific extrapolations that the coronavirus infection rates were expected to increase dramatically during the cold winter months, we realised that contact teaching and learning would not be an option for the remainder of the first semester of 2020 and probably the second also. Therefore, the Law School had to rapidly devise a plan to offer all its academic programmes online, remotely. However, implementing this plan depended largely on specific measures that the central university management would have to put into place to enable the academic project to recommence but online in this instance.

Moving from contact mode to remote online teaching and learning would only be possible if the following prerequisites were achieved:

---

[3] At most South African universities, student protests are frequent, happen with regularity, and are often violent and disruptive. For an analysis of this phenomenon, See Fomunyam [2].

[4] SA News (n 1).

i. All academic and support staff were capacitated with computers and sufficient data to navigate the migration to online teaching and learning;
ii. All students were capacitated with devices and data to enable them to access materials online, engage in online lectures, tutorials and seminars, and participate in online assessments;
iii. Staff were sufficiently upskilled to successfully upload to the university's online teaching and learning platform their course materials, pre-recorded lectures and other teaching and learning aids within the applicable timeframes; and
iv. Academic staff were able to acquire the necessary skills in the short time available, to conduct all their assessments online in a continuous assessment model. Apart from the acquisition of skills necessary for conducting both formative and summative assessments online, staff also had to learn ways to ensure a level of integrity in the quality assurance of their assessments.

2.1 Steps Taken at Central University Management Level to Devise a University-Wide Emergency Online, Remote Teaching and Learning Plan

2.1.1 Practical Considerations

The University of KwaZulu-Natal's (UKZN) academic governance structure comprises 19 large schools located in four Colleges. The university's total under-and-post-graduate student enrolments in 2020 were slightly over 45,000 students. UKZN is a public institution funded mainly through the public purse. Approximately 60% of its students are funded entirely by the fiscus as their family income meets the means test for funding. A considerable number of these students' homes are in the deep rural areas of South Africa, where the infrastructure is not as developed as in the urban regions. Consequently, the rollout of online teaching and learning at UKZN would pose a challenge for several students unless the institution ensured that all of them had access to devices and reliable data.

Therefore, the university first looked to practical considerations. This it did by interrogating staff and students' information and communications technology (ICT) requirements and identifying the need to: (i) train and orient students to the new emergency mode of teaching and learning; (ii) upskill academic and professional services staff in the new work mode; (ii) identify and finance the additional resource needs of the emergency academic project, and (iv) recognise the implications of the emergency teaching plan's implementation on the various responsible divisions. The institution then resorted to geo-mapping and institution-wide surveys to assess staff and students' ICT and skills needs. Through these mechanisms and the development of a distribution strategy, subsequently emulated by several other higher education institutions in South Africa, UKZN was able to distribute, throughout the country at the height of the lockdown, 6000 computers to students without devices.[5]

Data costs in South Africa are prohibitively high. Therefore, in 2020 significant numbers of staff and students at UKZN and most other universities in South Africa were without regular, stable and adequate levels of data connectivity in their homes to enable their engagement in remote online teaching and learning. Moreover, the average normal cost of providing data to staff and students would be absurdly expensive for most universities. Consequently, at a national ministerial level, agreements were struck with several data service providers for educational institutions to negotiate the purchase of data at significantly reduced rates.

As soon as the data rollout and device distribution for those without computers or tablets had commenced at UKZN, the teaching and learning leadership of the university, together with relevant support divisions such as the ICT department, immediately developed and facilitated skills training workshops to assist staff in migrating their modules and materials to the online platform of delivery. This action was followed by the facilitation of online workshops for students to orient them to remote online learning.

Apart from the university adopting specific measures to ensure that as many students as possible would be equipped with devices, data and training, the institution's emergency teaching and learning plan also included processes for ensuring that students with online connectivity and device issues could still study, and participate in summative assessments. This aspect is discussed below.

2.1.2 Academic Considerations

(i) Adoption of new pedagogic approaches to teaching and learning

At the heart of the 2020 UKZN emergency teaching and learning plan was the motto "no student left behind." In essence, this motto meant that no student would be denied an opportunity to participate in their studies in 2020 due to contracting covid-19 or the changes in the mode of delivery of the academic programmes at UKZN. To facilitate student participation in all academic activities, the emergency plan recommended the use of a range of interactive tools such as Zoom,[6] Microsoft Teams, Skype, webinars, podcasts, and the less data-intensive means of email, SMS and social media.

The emergency plan advocated adopting the blended learning flipped classroom pedagogy and methodological approach in the online delivery of all academic programmes, including the law programmes. The blended learning methodology involves multiple iterations of the basic cycle of student learning activities, with learning resources as individuals or collaborative groups.[7] It also calls for flexible interventions and support by dynamic teaching teams, and for students to consult

[5] Gobardan [3], 7.

[6] Ibid. An interesting fact is that in the period 26 March 2020 to 31 December 2020, 95,000 Zoom meetings totalling 72 million minutes were conducted at UKZN.

[7] Cleveland-Innes and Wilton [4].

with these teachers. In addition, the asynchronous, self-directed learning inherent in the blended learning methodology required the provision of apt and responsive course and module materials online.

The requirements of the blended learning pedagogy were enormously onerous and burdened staff with having to speedily adopt novel and, in some instances, unfamiliar teaching methods and assessment practices. However, dedication to the academic project and concern that our students should not lose the academic year prompted herculean efforts from the academic staff to adapt to the new teaching methodology.

(ii) Approval by national statutory accreditation body of new teaching approaches

The Council on Higher Education (CHE) is the national statutory body that quality-assures and accredits academic programmes offered at higher education institutions in South Africa. These educational institutions are designated as either distance learning or contact institutions. In the latter case, the CHE expectation for accreditation is that students must spend a specified minimum number of the notional learning hours, in every module in a programme, in 'staff-led face-to-face campus-based structured learning activities.'[8]

The CHE had approved all UKZN's programmes, including the law programmes as contact programmes. Therefore, the migration to contactless, remote, online teaching and learning, in essence, meant that the university's programmes were being conducted in breach of their accreditation conditions. However, since remote, online learning was the only means to ensure that educational institutions could keep the doors of learning open, the CHE was approached by a consortium of affected universities for a waiver of this accreditation condition to tide over the crisis. The CHE responded appropriately by granting temporary approval of the new model of distance, online teaching and learning.

(iii) Approval by the University Senate of new assessment approaches

As is the case in all higher education institutions in South Africa, the Senate of UKZN is the body that bears responsibility for all teaching, learning, research and academic functions of the university. As an integral aspect of its duties, the UKZN Senate is empowered to make or amend any rule relating to how students are to be examined or assessed.[9]

The 2020 emergency teaching and learning plan, which proposed that all assessments take the form of continuous assessment, was an unplanned innovation. However, since none of the UKZN programmes' rules provided for assessments to be solely through continuous assessments, the adoption of this mode of evaluation would need Senate approval, failing which the integrity of the programmes would be at risk. This requirement is especially important in respect of professional qualifications like the LLB as law graduates' applications for admission to practice would be

[8] Department of Higher Education and Training [5], 9.

[9] See for instance the Purpose statement and Term of reference 3 of the University of KwaZulu Natal [6] 1–2.

under threat if either the statutory body governing legal practitioners[10] or the High Courts had doubts about the integrity of the qualification.

The UKZN Senate duly approved the changes to the modes of assessment in the various programmes.

Thus, the scene was set for the re-commencement of academic activities at UKZN on 18 May 2020 as most operational and academic prerequisites had been achieved.

3 Teaching and Learning in the School of Law During the Covid-19 Crisis

The Law School's planning for the resumption of academic activities started in March 2020. Consequently, in the seven weeks from 26 March to 18 May 2020, staff in the School of Law had worked feverishly in preparation for the resumption of academic activities. Although the Law School had managed quite early in this period to migrate its programmes and modules to the university's online teaching and learning platform and staff were equipped to restart teaching, the school could not do so because it was reliant on the central university services to assist with several operational matters such as the provision of data and devices to students. The school was also dependent on central approval and oversight bodies like the College Academic Affairs Boards and the Senate of the university to approve the academic rules waivers needed to offer our programmes in the remote online format. Consequently, the school was constrained to align the resumption of its academic operations to the framework determined by the central university services.

The academic programme resumed on 18 May 2020 with a week-long dry run to test the digital systems, technological and academic arrangements, and risk management provisions. During this week, the institution conducted tests on the readiness of its online teaching and learning platform and ICT technology to service consistently high traffic levels. The scheduling of assessments and the availability, type and functionality of the devices used by students and staff were also tested together with the adequacy of data and connectivity. At the school level, apart from testing that students could access and engage with the module materials and consult digitally with their lecturers, we also ran mock assessments. As a result, by the end of the dry-run week, staff and students in the Law School were able to approach their teaching, learning and assessments with a fair degree of confidence.

Three crucial goals featured uppermost in the minds of the school leadership and informed decision-making in 2020. These goals are discussed in detail below and were:

(i) Ensuring that the remote online mode of delivery would not compromise the quality and outcomes of the law programmes;

[10] Legal practitioners in South Africa may only practice as such if they are registered with the Legal Practice Council of South Africa.

(ii) Warranting the integrity of our assessments;
(iii) Adopting steps to ameliorate the impact on academic activities of staff members falling ill with covid-19 and assuring staff and students' wellbeing.

3.1 Ensuring Quality and Outcomes of Law Programmes

The School of Law has an enduring reputation for offering high quality and relevant legal education. Over the years, scores of our graduates have gone on to achieve great success in leading the most critical institutions in South Africa. For instance, South Africa's current Chief Justice Mogoeng Mogoeng, Judge President of the Supreme Court of Appeal Mandisa Maya, and National Director of Public Prosecutions Shamila Batohi are all UKZN Law School graduates.[11]

The CHE had recently reviewed the UKZN Law School's flagship LLB programme during a national review of the LLB qualification. The school emerged from the review as one of only three institutions whose programmes were accredited in the first round, subject to a few minor conditions.[12] The Law School has also assisted other law faculties in South Africa with their accreditation processes.

It was, therefore, important to the school to ensure that the nature of its online, remote academic activities would not compromise its reputation as a solid law school with high-quality offerings. Upskilling staff in the pedagogic and logistical aspects of its new approaches to teaching and learning would be fundamental to its goal.

Although the university had designed and conducted training workshops to acquaint staff in the use of the institution's online teaching and learning platform, the training had been generic and was intended to serve a wide range of academics from diverse disciplines. The Law School's preference for more bespoke training oriented to the professional nature of its LLB programme led it to devise its own training for staff. Consequently, a few of the academics in the school who had acquired expertise from having worked extensively with the UKZN online platform and others who were whizzes in the various forms of assessments appropriate for evaluation in law modules developed and conducted multiple workshops for the school's academic and support staff. The outcome was the creation of a handy resource portal with every possible type of training resource, including videos, audio files, useful websites and interactive exercises uploaded onto a staff training online module. This initiative proved so beneficial to staff that the school was asked to share it with the university-wide community via the institution's staff training portal.

---

[11] An interesting fact is that of the current 21 members of the Supreme Court of Appeal (SCA), eight, including both the Judge President and Deputy Judge President are graduates of the UKZN Law School. Of the nine members of the current Constitutional Court bench, three, including the Chief Justice and Deputy Chief Justice, are graduates of the UKZN Law School. This is quite remarkable as there are 17 law faculties and law schools in South Africa yet, currently, 38% of the SCA and 33% of the Constitutional Court comprise graduates of the UKZN Law School.

[12] Council on Higher Education [7].

The adoption by UKZN of the blended learning flipped-classroom approach to teaching and learning as the preferred methodology for delivering its academic programmes in 2020 meant that academics unfamiliar with this mode of instruction would need considerable help to become adept in this practice. Opportunely, in early 2019 the School of Law had embraced blended learning as its teaching approach for the future. Although staff members had then had the latitude to move to this new teaching pedagogy at their own pace, the school had run a few workshops on blended learning and supported several academics to attend a few intensive blended learning courses mounted by UKZN experts in the area.

Therefore, the unfurling of this teaching and learning innovation at UKZN in response to the covid crisis was not a teaching crisis in the Law School. Furthermore, although our teaching and learning approach had changed from face-to-face lectures to blended learning and the flipped classroom, staff members were reasonably confident that the quality and outcomes of their modules had not been compromised by the swiftness with which they had had to make the swop.

3.2 *Warranting the Integrity of Assessments*

The UKZN 2020 emergency teaching and learning plan stipulated that, in all modules where practicable, there would be no contact, in-person formative and summative assessments. In addition, the plan directed that assessments had to be continuous and conducted online.

Before 2020, except for five continuous assessment modules in the LLB programme, the assessments in all other modules offered by the School of Law were in the form of formative assessments conducted during the semester and summative assessments conducted mainly in end-of-semester examinations.[13] Moreover, no assessments had been conducted online. Thus, the challenge of shifting to online, continuous assessments was significant. In addition, the new operational framework raised two critical aspects for consideration to warrant the integrity of the assessments[14]: (i) staff had to be capacitated to formulate appropriate forms of online assessments for a proper evaluation of students' mastery of the module content; and (ii) mechanisms had to be put in place to ensure that students did not engage in dishonest practices when performing their assessments remotely.

---

[13] The total number of Law modules that had to move to continuous assessment was 98 and was made up as follows: 37 LLB modules, 12 postgraduate diploma modules, and 49 coursework Master of Laws (LLM) modules. See University of KwaZulu-Natal [8], 87, 101, 102, 112–115.

[14] These two aspects are in addition to the regular quality assurance processes the school conducts to assure the quality and integrity of its programmes. These processes have been unaffected by the transition to online teaching and learning and the change in assessments, and were conducted without problems in 2020 also.

3.2.1 Appropriate Forms of Assessments

The task of enhancing staff capacity to conduct appropriate forms of online, continuous assessments in a short time was much easier than that of developing anti-cheating strategies for students' remote, online assessments.

As mentioned earlier, a few academics with specialist knowledge of assessments and adept in online teaching and learning generously conducted assessment workshops for staff. Apart from innovative ways to conduct continuous formative and summative assessments, staff also learned of the value of innovative diagnostic assessment methods like short quizzes, journal entries and student reflections. These diagnostic assessments are especially important in remote online learning as they provide a valuable gauge and benchmark of students' progress and understanding of the learning materials. Where formative and summative assessments were concerned, staff were introduced to the benefits of novel evaluation methods like portfolios and randomised timed tests. These forms of assessments had either never or rarely been used in the school previously as the preference had been for invigilated tests, long written assignments, and summative examinations.

The LLB degree programme includes an assessed compulsory moot court programme in which every final year student participates. The programme involves students arguing complex legal matters in a high court appeal format, before academics sitting in judgment.[15] Since the moot court programme is an integral component of final year students' professional legal training, some means needed to be devised to ensure that the programme could be conducted online in 2020 and beyond if necessary. Through meticulous, detailed planning and arrangements, the School successfully ran approximately 200 moot court sessions involving around 400 final year students. The moot courts were all conducted via the Zoom platform, which worked well. Based on current projections, we anticipate that the 2021 moot programme will also be run along the same lines as 2020.

Since the onset of the pandemic, South African courts have been operating only to a limited extent. In courts with the requisite infrastructure, most civil matters are being conducted remotely via MS Teams or Zoom. Therefore, the School is pleased that its 2020 moot court programme has provided its students with valuable skills and a degree of confidence to handle online court processes, including civil trials. Since the legal profession appears to be espousing the move to digitalisation and online operations, it behoves the Law School to incorporate relevant curriculum changes to accommodate such innovations. This consideration features high on our strategic planning agenda.

[15] However, the moot court final in which the top four law students participate, is conducted before a panel of three high court judges.

3.2.2 Preventing Dishonest Conduct in Assessments

Overall, staff members were receptive to and enthusiastically embraced continuous assessment and the novel types of formative and summative assessments that could be conducted in the online, remote format. However, they still agonised over how to ensure the integrity of their evaluations such that any dishonest practice in a student's submitted assessment would be demonstrably evident. To a large extent, this conundrum informed the nature of the assessments that the academics set their students. Thus, randomised timed tests, which made it difficult for students to share answers and cheat, are featured in most modules. Long written assignments needing extensive research and deep critical analyses of the study materials also featured heavily in the Law School's assessments. Where these assessments were concerned, students had to submit their assignments for evaluation together with the plagiarism detection report generated by running the assignment through the university's plagiarism detection software programme.

Since student dishonesty in remote online assessments is a ubiquitous problem, the teaching and learning leadership of the university has been looking at various options for monitoring students during the performance of online assessments to prevent dishonest practices. However, privacy and dignity issues are important but challenging factors to navigate when considering the employment of monitoring mechanisms. Therefore, the process of finding and implementing a suitable online monitoring system is still a work in progress at UKZN.

The School of Law is alert to the possible life and career-changing, dire consequences that its graduates would face if they were found to have engaged in any dishonest practice while at university. The worst consequence is that the school could refuse to issue the graduate with a 'fit and proper' certificate, which is a fundamental requirement to register articles of clerkship or pupillage.[16] Therefore, the school is conscientious about ensuring that its students are repeatedly cautioned in every module and assessment to guard against dishonest practices like plagiarism. The Law School also ensures that in every detected instance of dishonesty, without exception, the defaulting student is prosecuted in terms of the applicable student disciplinary rules. The outcomes of these disciplinary matters are also published university-wide to act as a deterrent to any other student contemplating dishonest conduct.

[16] In South Africa, LLB degree graduates wanting to practice as either an attorney (South African equivalent of the English solicitor) or an advocate (South African equivalent of the English barrister) must first serve either articles of clerkship with an attorney or pupillage with an advocate before writing an entrance examination and being admitted to the profession. Articles of clerkship and pupillage must be registered with the relevant legal body. The LLB graduate is required to get a 'fit and proper' certificate from the Dean of the Law School to register. A similar certificate is required by the High Court when a person seeks to be admitted to the legal profession.

3.3 Continuation of the Academic Programme During Staff Incapacity and Assuring Staff and Students' Wellbeing

It is trite that covid-19 is highly infectious and that persons contracting the virus must isolate to contain its spread. It is also a trite fact that some people who contract the virus quickly become seriously ill and incapacitated. Therefore, the possibility existed that should academics in the Law School contract the virus, some could become too ill to continue with their teaching and assessing duties. It was also likely that the Law School's administrative operations could be adversely affected if its support staff were to fall ill.

3.3.1 Steps to Ensure the Continuation of the Academic Programme

In recognising the likelihood of staff falling ill, the School leadership had to devise steps to ensure that should this transpire, academic activities and the school operations would not be compromised in any way. Thus, in consultation with the staff, the leadership resolved that in every module, the staff member teaching and coordinating the module would be required to upload all relevant teaching and learning materials and assessments onto the module's online page but to keep these hidden from the students' view. The uploaded materials and assessments would only be released and made visible to students as scheduled in the module outline. The module teacher was also required to grant one or two of their colleagues and the teaching and learning leadership of the school teacher status on their module page. This status would enable the latter persons to release the materials and assessments on the relevant dates should the academic teaching the module become incapacitated by illness.

The school leadership also had to plan for the contingency of several academics becoming incapacitated concurrently and unable to conduct their assessments. This eventuality was not a burden that the remaining academics could be expected to carry as they would themselves be bearing the load of having to conduct their own assessments within the constrained time frames in which we were operating. Therefore, the leadership resolved that funds would be set aside to appoint, if necessary, temporary academic staff to assist with conducting assessments. Staff members were asked to identify suitable candidates from the legal profession or elsewhere, whom we could approach at short notice should the need arise.

Funds were also set aside for the appointment of temporary support staff if the permanent staff fell ill.

An unexpected boon of the covid-19 pandemic has been the warm and caring empathy that colleagues in the Law School have displayed in abundance towards each other. These feelings have manifested in concrete actions like stepping in to help when colleagues have been laid low by illness or their loved ones' deaths. Since March 2020, every academic in the Law School, including the dean, has on occasion stepped in to coordinate, teach, or assess in the modules of colleagues who have needed help because of the pandemic. The collective effort of the entire staff has thus ensured the success of the 2020 academic year even though it extended into 2021 and officially ended on 6 February 2021.

3.3.2 Assuring the Emotional Wellbeing of Staff and Students

During April 2020–June 2021, staff members in the Law School lost 16 immediate family members from covid and other causes. Several also took ill in this time. Staff have been working remotely, and few have been in physical contact with their colleagues. Staff members have reported over-exertion due to extreme efforts to rapidly migrate to online teaching and learning and provide additional support to their students. Several also reported high levels of stress from the constant deluge of student and other emails. Not keeping office hours has also contributed to staff exhaustion. Moreover, repeated university-wide revisions to the academic calendar to accommodate student requests and additional 'catch-up' assessments for students affected by illness or connectivity problems have all together caused staff members to suffer mentally and physically.

Mindful of the pandemic's heavy toll and the consequences on staff members, the university's human resources division has contracted with an external wellness service provider to provide staff members with a bouquet of free support services. Staff now have free access to services such as individual and group psychological debriefing and counselling, trauma counselling, psychiatric treatment, and opportunities to participate in other wellness-oriented activities. These services are ongoing since 2020 and have proved invaluable to several staff members in the school who have accessed them.

In the Law School itself, a staff Whatsapp group serves to keep colleagues in touch with each other and as a mechanism to discuss and resolve issues as they crop up. The leadership has also been meeting with staff, formally and informally, far more frequently than under normal circumstances, to stave off colleagues feeling isolated and alone. Although these meetings are held either via Zoom or Skype, they have proved an excellent way to connect with colleagues more meaningfully than via email or the telephone.

The remote online mode of working has meant that staff often feel as if they are constantly on duty as they receive emails and other types of communication from their students and the institution at all hours of the day and night. The School leadership has consequently implemented a policy that staff members do not respond to emails outside normal working hours and over the weekends. This policy has helped ease the pressure that many employees feel to respond immediately to work-related electronic communications.

The school leadership has also insisted that staff take leave whenever the opportunity arises. Therefore, colleagues are encouraged to co-teach their modules and, in so doing, free themselves from teaching and assessing duties for at least a few days at a time. Staff are urged to take leave during these times as the current university calendar makes little to no provision for staff vacation periods because of the extended academic semesters.

Student wellness features prominently in the university's strategic operations. The institution's extensive student counselling and support services migrated in 2020 to digital platforms to enable students to continue accessing the wide range of available services. Reports to the School Board from our student support services seem to indicate that more students than previously are experiencing mental health challenges. Consequently, the Law School has adopted the stance that regardless of the nature of the assistance that a student may be seeking when approaching anyone in the School, we will endeavour to either personally assist the student or put them directly in touch with the person who can help them. For instance, students with fees-related queries or financial problems often look to the school for guidance. However, no one in the school can help with such matters as the school deals with only academic and curriculum-related queries. To avert students' frustration and stress at searching for the correct people to approach or at not receiving prompt help from such persons, staff in the School directly contact the relevant functionary and connect the student to the individual.

Although all academic activities at the university, barring those that require laboratory work, are being conducted online remotely, the institution has reopened several student residences on its five campuses to accommodate those students with study-environment and connectivity problems. In this way, the institution has ameliorated the severe mental stress experienced by such students when attempting to study in non-conducive circumstances.

4 Conclusion

The covid-19 pandemic has inflicted untold pain and suffering on millions of people worldwide. The fallout of the pandemic has also been disastrous to the South African economy and has wreaked destitution upon thousands of families through job losses and the death of breadwinners. Therefore, finding something positive to say about the pandemic is difficult amid this devastation.

However, there is no denying the pandemic's influence on many positive developments at UKZN, which the writer submits will influence the nature of the institutions' future operations.

As mentioned earlier, student protests and the ensuing disruptions of the university's academic programmes were a regular feature of life at UKZN. Before 2020, because most programmes were presented in contact format, the disruptions resulted in lost teaching and learning time. However, the success of UKZN's emergency adoption of online, remote teaching and learning has made its academic programmes impervious to disruptions. As UKZN is not a distance learning institution, its post-covid academic activities will include contact classroom sessions. However, such contact will be far more limited than previously because of the adoption of the blended learning flipped classroom teaching pedagogy. This teaching method is an ideal fit with the institution's new ability to support students' asynchronous, online learning.

The move towards online continuous assessments has also spurred academics to embrace new and innovative assessment methods. Some of these methods, such as diagnostic assessments, which gauge and benchmark students' progress, are hugely beneficial in blended learning and will continue to be used post-covid.

The manner in which the Law School conducted its 2020 moot court programme provided students with a vignette of the direction in which the legal profession is moving. The school is confident that even when we revert to in-person mooting, our students' training will still include a level of skills acquisition in online trial processes and other legal proceedings.

From the perspective of the Law School, despite the pandemic's dire consequences in myriad ways, a positive consequence is that, ready or not, we have been unequivocally catapulted into the 4th industrial revolution, which we can now approach with more confidence that in the pre-covid days.

References

1. South African Government News Agency: SA to move from level 5 lockdown to level 4 (South Africa 23 April 2020) https://www.sanews.gov.za/south-africa/sa-move-level-5-lockdown-level-4 accessed 26 May 2021
2. Fomunyam, K.G.: Student protest and the culture of violence at African universities: an inherited ideological trait. Yesterday and Today 38–63 (2017). http://www.scielo.org.za/scielo.php?script=sci_arttext&pid=S2223-03862017000100004&lng=en&nrm=iso accessed 26 May 2021
3. Gobardan, K.: IPG Portfolio Report to Senate (2 June 2021)
4. Cleveland-Innes, M., Wilton, D.: Guide to Blended Learning. Commonwealth of Learning, Burnaby (2018) http://oasis.col.org/handle/11599/3095 accessed 26 May 2021
5. Department of Higher Education and Training: Policy for the Provision of Distance Education in South Africa. Government Gazette (2014)
6. University of KwaZulu Natal: Committee Charter of Senate (2012)
7. Council on Higher Education: Report on the National Review of LLB Programmes in South Africa (2018) http://www.derebus.org.za/wp-content/uploads/2019/06/CHE_LLB-National-Report_2018.pdf accessed 9 July 2021
8. University of KwaZulu-Natal: College of Law and Management Studies Handbook (2020). https://clms.ukzn.ac.za/guides-and-handbooks/ accessed 26 May 2021

Experiments in Resilience

Legal Education and Legal Profession During and After COVID-19 the Shifting Idea of Law School: Systems and Processes

Vesna Crnić-Grotić

Abstract The Faculty of Law at the University of Rijeka is a relatively young school in a relatively young university. In 2018 they both celebrated the 45th anniversary. The university has about 17.000 students, while the Faculty of Law has about 1.500 students enrolled into five years integrated legal study and three years professional administrative study. In March 2020 the Faculty signed a contract with the European Social Fund on the improvement of practical legal skills of its students including starting a legal clinic. The project included participation of students in a number of exchanges, national and international moot-court competitions and workshops for building their practical skills. The lockdown followed just two days after the signing of the contract. All activities that included physical contacts had to be stopped, naturally, and eventually only online contacts were allowed. It meant that the teachers in charge of the project had to invent new ways how to ensure its implementation. The article is describing the innovative ways how to overcome the pandemic situation.

1 Introduction

The Faculty of Law at the University of Rijeka is a relatively young school in a relatively young university. In 2018 they both celebrated the 45th anniversary. The university is a member of a new European association: Young Universities for the Future of Europe (YUFE).[1] Rijeka Law Faculty is one of four public law faculties in Croatia. There are no private law schools. University education fee is subsidized

[1] Young Universities for the Future of Europe https://yufe.eu/.

[2] The system is based on merits so students don't pay fees as long as they make at least 55/60 ECTS a year. Failing that they have to pay for the remaining number of ECTS. Stipends also partly subsidize meals for all students and lodging in student dorms. However, their availability is very limited so the majority of students either stay at home with their parents or rent privately with no state aid. Part time students have to pay fees depending on the number of ECTS they take up (between 30 and 60 ECTS).

V. Crnić-Grotić (✉)
International Law Department, Faculty of Law, University of Rijeka, Rijeka, Croatia
e-mail: Vesna.crnic.grotic@uniri.hr

C. Raj Kumar and S. G. Sreejith (eds.), *Legal Education and Legal Profession During and After COVID-19*, https://doi.org/10.1007/978-981-19-2568-9_11

by the state so it's free of charge for full-time students as long as they fulfil their obligations.[2]

The University of Rijeka[3] has around 17.000 students, while the Faculty of Law has around 1.500 students enrolled in five years of integrated legal study and in three years of professional administrative study.[4] The law student groups are made of approximately 150–200 students for lectures and about 25–50 for seminars and practical exercises. The professional study groups do not exceed 40 students. Our biggest lecture room seats 250 students while the smaller rooms have 46 and 110 seats. Every classroom has the equipment necessary for video presentations and the Wi-fi network is available throughout the premises. The teaching staff numbers 60 supported by 18 administrative and technical staff. The teachers hold various positions from assistants and postdoc assistants through assistant and adjunct professors to full-time and tenured professors.[5]

In this article, we will try to present how did the faculty cope with the sudden changes in our way of life with the pandemic circumstances.

2 The Lockdowns

When the first lockdown due to the COVID-19 pandemic was introduced in March 2020 it was imperative that the teaching goes online *asap*.[6] However, although the national internet infrastructure was available it was not solid enough to support hundreds and thousands of students and teachers, together with thousands of other users, to go online and teach in real time. The national education system had already had in place the system for e-learning called *Merlin-Moodle*[7] for online teaching and communication between faculty and students. Eventually, like the rest of the world, we discovered other platforms like MS Teams or Zoom and soon enough the national authorities ensured free use of MS Teams for all educational institutions. Real-time teaching is a challenge of itself but it provides structure for students that we thought was very important for them. It was not always possible so teachers had to teach themselves how to make recordings and video lectures.

---

[3] University of Rijeka webpage https://uniri.hr/.

[4] The two main programmes are the Integrated Undergraduate and Graduate University Study of Law and the Undergraduate Professional Study Programme in Administration Studies. In addition, the faculty runs several postgraduate and a doctorate studies. Faculty of Law webpage https://pravri.uniri.hr/en.

[5] In Croatia university teachers are required by law to advance to a higher title every five years based on their publications and other results.

[6] Decision by the Minister of Health on proclamation of epidemic disease COVID-19 was published on 11 March 2020 after the first cases had appeared. https://zdravstvo.gov.hr/UserDocsImages/2020%20CORONAVIRUS/ODLUKA%20O%20PROGLA%C5%A0ENJU%20EPIDEMIJE%20BOLESTI%20COVID-19.pdf. Accessed 20 May 2021.

[7] Merlin, System for e-learning. https://moodle.srce.hr/2020-2021/.

Another aspect of lockdown was access and availability of literature. Students were not allowed to come to libraries, sometimes they were not even able to come because the public transportation was limited and freedom of movement was restricted. Part of the literature had been available in digital form before the pandemic. In Croatia, there is a national network supporting open-access publications so that every scientific journal publicly funded is available online.[8] Furthermore, for the last 10 or more years the faculty has ensured access to some of the most important legal databases, such as Hein Online or Westlaw.[9] Students, just like staff members, have access to them remotely using Proxy and Shibboleth tools. As for digitalization of other resources, rules on intellectual property had to be observed so authors and publishers were asked to allow their books to be put online at least for the limited access by registered students. It was a rather easy exercise regarding older titles in Croatian but not so much for more recent titles or those written in English or other languages. That meant that some limited access to the library had to be organized. Special instructions were issued for physical access to the library respecting epidemiological rules, including online appointments and orders of books.

Digitization has several pre-requisites: good or at least fair quality computers, preferably with a camera and a microphone, and a good internet connection. They are not available to all students, clearly. Either for personal reasons or due to a communal problem some students were not able to participate in the online lectures. The prolonged pandemic and more or less strict lockdowns affected the financial and economic situation of many students who sometimes had to go to work to help their families. The lockdown also meant that all family members are at home competing for equipment or privacy that is very important for young people.

In addition, in Croatia in 2020 we had two devastating earthquakes in the capital city Zagreb and its vicinity.[10] Many students lost their homes and livelihood, some were put in student dormitories (evicting students who had so far occupied them!) but some of them still have to live in makeshift homes like container homes or campers with very little or no comfort and privacy. Our faculty invited those and other students with digital difficulties to come forward. We organized basic financial assistance and loaned them suitable laptops to help them overcome these circumstances.

One of the impacts of the pandemic that seems to be hitting hard on some of the world's renowned universities is the loss of foreign students.[11] That is not the case of any of the universities in Croatia due to various reasons, the language barrier being only one of them. The number of foreign students is limited apart from the students included in Erasmus+ student exchange programme.[12] These students were affected in different ways in the first lockdown: some got stranded in their own countries

[8] HRČAK—central portal of Croatian scientific journals. https://hrcak.srce.hr/?lang=en.

[9] Library of the Faculty of Law in Rijeka, online legal databases, Instructions in English. https://sites.google.com/pravri.hr/onlinebaze/legal-databases?authuser=0. Accessed 20 May 2021.

[10] The first earthquake hit Zagreb on 22 March 2020 and the next one of magnitude 6.2 followed on 29 December 2020 in Petrinja, Sisak and Glina.

[11] Marinoni et al. [1, pp. 1–50]

[12] Erasmus+ https://ec.europa.eu/programmes/erasmus-plus/about_en. Accessed 20 May 2021.

and some were stranded in foreign countries not being able to come home. As some of them tested positive or they had to go into self-isolation the university had to designate facilities for placing them and to provide assistance. Nevertheless, even in the following semester, there were some Erasmus students willing to travel to their chosen foreign universities notwithstanding the risks.[13] In order to help other students see the possibilities offered by even such limited experience and keep their interest alive we invited our students to share their Erasmus experience on social media.[14]

Another aspect of such abrupt switch to online teaching was the psychological impact on students and staff. There were many voices warning about this aspect of the pandemic. The University of Rijeka has in place the Psychological Counselling Office within the University Counselling Centre that became very active during the pandemic.[15] In the early days of the first lockdown in April 2020, the Office issued a statement on the psychological aspects of studying in the crisis situation caused by the corona-virus pandemic.[16] The statement warned about not just possible but foreseeable consequences of the pandemic on the mental health primarily of students. Social distancing as the most effective tool for fighting the virus is also one of the worst things that can happen to young people. They had to spend much more time with their family members in a rather limited space when everybody is more sensitive and vulnerable. Being separated from the peers and the colleagues from the school creates anxiety and the sense of separation but also the sense of loss of opportunities. The psychologists from the centre emphasize that young people are in a much worse position than "proper" adults because most of them have not had a chance to create their private and intimate relationships. Activities are limited and often repetitive and online learning boring and uninspiring. This also leads to depression and even suicidal thoughts.[17]

The Centre carried out research during the lockdown in the spring of 2020 on the sources of stress that students experienced during the lockdown and their effects on students' psychological and academic functioning.[18] The consequences of isolation represent the strongest stress source, followed by academic stress, the possibility of

[13] At the Faculty of Law situation in the fall semester was as follows: 16 incoming and 19 outgoing students.

[14] Faculty of Law Erasmus+ page. https://sites.google.com/view/pravri-erasmus/incoming-student-mobility. The FB page. https://www.facebook.com/pravri.uniri/. Accessed 20 May 2021.

[15] The University Counselling Centre provides students and staff of the University of Rijeka with different forms of support and counselling through its Psychological Counselling Office, Office for Students with Disabilities, and Career Office.

[16] Psychological Aspects of Studying in the pandemic caused crisis situation (*Psihološki aspekti studiranja u kriznoj situaciji izazvanoj epidemijom koronavirusa*) online leaflet published on 30 April 2020.

[17] According to the same source women and people with small children are even more vulnerable in the already risky group of young people. It is worth noting that more than 70% of law students in Croatia are young women.

[18] The sample included 923 students aged 19–28 (73% females) from different faculties at the University of Rijeka. Out of total 65% of the students changed their residence to attend university and 86.7% of them have returned back home during lockdown. The students completed Stress

infection, and family sources of stress. According to the researchers, female students are exposed to more stress, although the level of stress is smaller for students who have not changed their residence. Students who went back home during the lockdown experience more family stress and higher stress due to social isolation. The consequences of isolation make the strongest contribution to the level of depression and anxiety in students, as well as the strongest negative effect on their academic functioning.[19]

This research did not specify the results by the schools but law students are known to have psychological difficulties even in the most normal of times since law is perceived as one of the more difficult studies. We can already observe that the academic results of our students are getting worse. This is visible even more for the younger students—the first or the second year of studies. They were affected by the lockdown before they got to know the faculty and the study programme or to develop interest for the subject of study. Following only online teaching for more than a year now shows its downsides. Senior students had more personal experience and they managed to establish personal contacts with both their colleagues and the teachers before the lockdown.[20] The Faculty of Law in Rijeka is known for good personal contacts between teachers and students so these contacts were preserved in the online surrounding. One may conclude that younger students did not develop a sense of collective or belonging and it is going to be very difficult to compensate when the pandemic is over.

There was a certain ease of the restrictions imposed on public gatherings, including the different levels of education institutions during the summer of 2020 so we came "back to school" in September but it did not take long before we had to face the second lockdown in December.[21] It was somehow even more difficult to bear for the students but also for the staff as the feeling of despair became more and more present. The hope that had appeared with the vaccination soon withered with the shortage of it at the European level. As the situation is slowly improving, we are hoping that we'll get our lives back.

Source Questionnaire, Academic Functioning Questionnaire and Depression, Anxiety and Stress Scale (DASS-21). Živčić-Bećirević et al. [2].

[19] 19.6% of students express high or severe depression and 23.9% high or severe anxiety. 12.7% of the students report suicidal ideation which is more than found in general population. Ibid. Prof. Živčić-Bećirević and her team repeated the research in Spring 2021 and the results are apparently even worse. The results will be published in the next volume of *Društvena istraživanja*. http://drustvena-istrazivanja.pilar.hr/index.php/drustvena-istrazivanja. Accessed 20 May 2021.

[20] One of my 2nd year students told me how he does not know "more than five" people from his year that has 280 students!

[21] The University of Rijeka proclaimed that the ratio between the on-site and online teaching should be 60:40. However, in the lockdown the ratio was lost and all classes but some medical or laboratories exercises went online.

3 Legal Clinic Programme

In March 2020 the Faculty signed a contract with the European Social Fund on the improvement of practical legal skills of its students including starting a legal clinic for providing free legal aid. The project included participation of students in a number of exchanges, national and international moot court competitions and workshops for building their practical skills.[22]

The lockdown followed just two days after the signing of the contract. All activities that were anticipating physical contacts had to be stopped and eventually only online contacts were allowed. The challenges for the teachers in charge of the project were big and they were many—how to run such a project, what activities to plan instead of those that were planned and how to successfully reallocate the funds? The European Social Fund that gave the funds is very scrupulous about their spending.[23] In addition, it was necessary to make the students interested in the project because one of the conditions was to attract a sufficient number of students. The question is how to do it when students are not present on the faculty but only online.

According to the project, its main purpose is to "increase the employability of students of the Integrated Undergraduate and Graduate University Study of Law and Undergraduate Professional Study Programme in Administration Studies of the Faculty of Law in Rijeka by enabling the acquisition of practical skills and competencies for work". The faculty has already had several courses in its curriculum that had a strong emphasis on the practical student skills. The oldest one is the Civil Law Clinic established in 1995 that is based on the internship approach.[24] Each enrolled student has to spend a semester in local courts or lawyers' offices. Students are encouraged to spend their time actively contributing to the work of the office and at the same time work on a hypothetical case in the classroom. Students have to keep a log and write a "reflexive diary" where they have to reflect on their experience. Many students established good rapports with their hosts and were subsequently employed there. The Legal Clinic course is often used as a reference when applying for a job.

Recently, the Faculty enriched its curricula with more such practical courses based on students' internship in the field of public law, EU law and even criminal law. Needless to say, these courses faced serious problems with the pandemic since not many offices wanted to host students anymore.

The project Praxis Juris, however, had a more ambitious goal in establishing a new model of professional practice by providing free primary legal aid, and by improving the quality and strengthening the existing models of professional practice.

---

[22] Praxis Iuris—Free primary legal aid and professional practice at the Faculty of Law in Rijeka was concluded for the period from 2020 to 2023. https://praxisiuris.eu/en/about-the-project/. Accessed 20 May 2021.

[23] European Social Fund works under the European Commission. It is Europe's main instrument for supporting jobs, helping people get better jobs and ensuring fairer job opportunities for all EU citizens. https://ec.europa.eu/esf/home.jsp. Accessed 20 May 2021.

[24] The programme was encouraged by the American Bar Association/CEELI project. More on the results of the initiative. https://ceeliinstitute.org/. Accessed 20 May 2021.

Legal clinics are, of course, a well-known concept of training young lawyers in many countries. The concept was introduced in the US law schools as a method of teaching students' practical skills by providing legal services to indigent population.[25] Soon the concept was introduced in other countries as well although with a various degree of success depending on the legal framework and the concept of law schools in the country.

The free legal aid in Croatia can be provided by lawyers (advocates or barristers), registered NGOs and student legal clinics. The aid that can be provided by student legal clinics is limited to primary legal aid or to basic legal counsel. Students are no competition to lawyers, and they are not allowed to represent their clients before courts.[26] The teachers-mentors oversee the students but the clients should be aware that it is the students who provide legal counselling. Naturally, the liability insurance for malpractice is mandatory. Students should benefit from practical experience that includes direct contact with clients, so it is sometimes referred to as the live-client clinic. It enables students to improve their practical skills and competencies necessary for the future professional work. In student legal clinics students learn how to address a client, how to interview him or her in order to learn about the legal problem that the client has. To the established facts the students then learn how to apply legal institutes and regulations thus developing independence and responsibility. The hands-on approach has proven to be very efficient for practicing law. The benefit is also manifested in connecting students with employers, which will increase their employability and facilitate the transition to the world of work. There is also a wider social benefit because free primary legal aid is provided to the most socially and economically vulnerable categories of citizens. Of course, it also has to be kept in mind that students can only work with cases that are not too complex and that enable students to practice their skills.[27]

As said before, the pandemic stopped many activities planned in the project. For example, exchanges with other legal clinics in Croatia and abroad had to be postponed. All the catering services that were planned for various meetings and workshops had to be cancelled and the funds had to be spent for something else. On the other hand, the pandemic restrictions had no impact on activities connected with the making of a legal framework necessary for the registration of the legal clinic. There was also no impact on establishing contacts with NGOs who will become partners in the provision of legal aid. The faculty established co-operation with the NGOs that service homeless persons and victims of family violence.

The project foresaw the selection of students-mentors and that was one of the last activities accomplished on-site but further meetings had to go online. The selected students were to be the pillars of the future legal clinic and the project activities had

[25] American Bar Association. https://www.americanbar.org/groups/center-pro-bono/. Accessed 20 May 2021.

[26] The Law on Free Legal Aid (Zakon o besplatnoj pravnoj pomoći), *Narodne novine* No. 143/13, 98/19.

[27] The law provides that the more complex cases should be dealt with by professional lawyers in order to protect even destitute clients (secondary legal aid). Criminal cases are excluded by law and there should always be professional lawyers included, pro bono or paid by the client.

to enable them to become providers of legal aid.[28] The project was very fortunate to benefit from the participation of several Justices of the Supreme Court of Croatia including the Chief Justice. They were willing to share their vast experience with our students through online lectures and workshops. In the following months, these meetings were extended beyond students-mentors so as to include as many students as possible online. Probably there are not too many student legal clinics that are including justices of supreme courts or judges of the highest court in the country.[29]

A novelty in the project due to impossibility to have many people in one place (or to have any people during the lockdowns) was the so-called "Clinical Hubs". In the hubs students-mentors simulated the provision of legal aid to other students with a specific legal problem. Over the first few hubs, the matters covered spanned from property law through enforcement law to divorce and children's rights. Through the simulations and with the assistance of professors, students were able to work on their practical skills in small groups of their peers. That approach also helped them build their confidence before meeting real clients. Eventually, professionals were included in the hubs giving their own insights and sharing with students their personal and professional experience. It was really interesting for our students to hear from young professionals what are the differences between the scholastic and practical aspects of legal profession.

An important aspect of the project was building the competence and general skills of both students and teachers but also other staff members of the faculty. The Project had envisioned several cycles of workshops on interpersonal skills organized by Praxis Iuris team that was open for applications for Faculty students, teachers and administrative staff. Target group was students enrolled in 2nd, 3rd, 4th and 5th year of Integrated law studies. The workshop mentors were skilled practitioners having experience in similar workshops in business and private sector, introducing specific knowledge on interpersonal skills. The feedback was very satisfactory because the learned skills could be used in various aspects of professional and personal life.

Finally, the Project members came up with one more novelty format to substitute the lack of physical contact workshops having in mind that a mere transformation of lectures to online is not always satisfactory. Even more so, online activities have to correspond to this media that does not support lectures *ex cathedra* of long duration. Instead of live lectures the project leaders came up with the so-called incubators where local legal practitioners were invited to have online interactive workshops with students on specific case-law examples. This gave them the opportunity to discuss legal issues on concrete examples thus helping students better understand them. Students were also invited to write their report describing their understanding of the legal issue discussed during the incubator. The format was very well accepted by the students since it was dynamic and closely connected to real-life situations.

---

[28] The names of the students-mentors are public on the webpage of the Project. https://praxisiuris.eu/en/students-mentors-2020-2021/.

[29] The webpage of the Project includes information on all activities. https://praxisiuris.eu/en/category/activities/page/1/ and other.

All the above-described activities had that primary goal in sight: establish the live client legal clinic. In order to better prepare students for their prospective clients, the team prepared the Student Guide.[30] It explains the concept of free legal aid and its legal framework in Croatia and describes the Legal Clinic of the Faculty of Law in Rijeka. In the operative part, it guides the students through the process of providing legal aid, from receiving and interviewing clients, through legal research of the problem to finally issuing a proper legal counsel. The Guide also instructs students on how to organize the work of the clinic in terms of keeping records and avoiding conflict of interest and similar aspects of running a law office.

The student legal clinic started its work as scheduled a year after the project contract was signed. Its success will greatly depend also on the resolve of the health crisis and how enthusiastic the students will be. Regardless, the need for pro bono legal aid can only increase since the economic consequences of the pandemic will be more prominent.

4 Conclusion

The circumstances of legal studies have changed dramatically with the onslaught of the corona virus health crisis. The switch to online teaching was sudden and most of the faculty and the students were unprepared. Nevertheless, the Faculty of Law in Rijeka did its best and is still doing its best to keep the students and faculty part of the collective and be fully aware of their belonging to the community of present and future legal professionals.

Some of the lessons learned will be preserved, though, as we have learned that in online teaching there are some benefits for some and not just the part-time students. Some activities seem to be easier online without the hustle and expenses of travel and accommodation. At the same time, we can all hardly wait for the new normal to become just normal again.

References

1. Marinoni, G., Land H., Jensen T.: The Impact of COVID 19 on Higher Education around the World. IAU Global Survey Report (2020), pp. 1–50. https://iau-aiu.net/IAU-Global-Survey-on-the-Impact-of-COVID-19-on-Higher-Education-around-the. Accessed 20 May 2021
2. Živčić-Bećirević, I., et al.: How did students cope with the lockdown?', COVID-19 From Student Perspective: Impact, Analysis and Recommendations, University of Rijeka, Croatia, (2020). https://uniri.hr/wp-content/uploads/2020/11/Simpozij-COVID-V-Finalno.pdf. Accessed 20 May 2021

[30] It is published in Croatian. Priručnik za studente, https://praxisiuris.eu/praxis-iuris/wp-content/uploads/2021/03/prirucnik-za-studente.pdf. Accessed 20 May 2021.

New Landscapes on Student Exchange

Sandhya Drew

Abstract I argue that Covid-19 is likely to impact current models of internationalisation of higher education. This is because of the difficulties in physical movement of students, of a greater recognition of the potential of technology, and of greater demand for sustainable ways of educating. At present internationalisation in the Global North has too often been confused with recruitment of high-paying students. In the wake of this crisis, understanding of the term itself must be revisited in light of the purpose of universities. Another risk post Covid-19 is the risk of retreat into narrow nationalism and nationally bound perspectives on law. Exchanges of staff and students are therefore needed more than ever. Covid-19 has positively revealed the potential for transformation of international legal education and exchanges between law schools. The current model is for student exchanges to happen as parallel physical moves of students between universities, rather than direct intellectual exchange between students. Technology has enabled virtual intellectual and cultural exchange which mirrors peer work in class: online collaborative writing; breakout rooms. This new form of exchange offers access to students who might not be able to afford physical travel to access a fuller comparative conversation on law. I will draw on my own experience teaching during the pandemic. Finally, I will acknowledge that law students should expand physical horizons in study and later, work, but suggest that initial virtual cross-border intellectual exchange enhances that journey and is, of itself, a journey worth making.

1 Introduction

Once the waves of severe acute respiratory syndrome coronavirus 2 and its latest, Delta, variant have receded, they will have left us with a seismically altered global landscape. International—and sometimes infranational—travel by university faculty and students will have been reduced almost to zero. Digitalisation of knowledge exchange, learning and teaching, of legal work and of court hearings will have been

S. Drew (✉)
City, University of London, Barrister, UK
e-mail: Sandhya.Drew@city.ac.uk

C. Raj Kumar and S. G. Sreejith (eds.), *Legal Education and Legal Profession During and After COVID-19*, https://doi.org/10.1007/978-981-19-2568-9_12

accelerated beyond the wildest dreams of fans of edtech and legaltech. Flat 'we are all in this together' globalisation has peeled back to reveal inequality between and within each nation state, most brutally in the case of vaccines and medical help. Covid-19 has also revealed the fragility of the international law framework in place since the end of World War II and the economic framework of globalisation.

History has shown us that change does happen after such devastation but not always in the short-term for the good.[1] Law will have a greater national focus as each nation struggles to survive and rebuild. Differing perspectives between global North and South will be accentuated. There will be a two-tier system of the vaccinated who are able to work across borders and holiday and those who cannot. We are therefore at a crossroads of either being more connected or less connected. I will argue for greater connection and suggest some ways we can move towards this, in particular through exchange across nations.

2 What Internationalisation?

On the face of it, prior to Covid-19, universities in Britain seemed very international, with high levels of staff and student mobility. 19.6% of all students were international (EU and non-EU). This pattern has been disrupted by Covid-19. Borders have been closed. Student physical mobility programmes have been cancelled and continue to be cancelled into the autumn. International students have found themselves either stranded in a different time zone or stuck in lockdown, unable to carry out 20 h part-time they relied on and in extreme cases dependent on food banks.[2] While some mobility will return, I argue that Covid has revealed limits to current definitions of 'international' in internationalisation strategies amongst universities, at least those in the Global North, and that we must look to alternative models.

There is currently a very high level of marketisation and consequent commodification of higher education in England. This can be traced back to 1998 following the Dearing Report and the re-introduction of tuition fees for 'ordinarily resident' students (exempt since 1962) through the Teaching and Education Act 1998. Tuition fees could be charged of up to £1000 per year (£1548.31 or Rs 159,053 in today's terms). This was raised by the Higher Education Act 2004 to £3000. With effect from September 2012, the top fees rate was tripled, from £3290 to £9000 (Rs 924,327) by regulations[3] following the Browne review. In practice, 98% of universities in England and Wales now charge the top rate. The Auger Report (2019),[4] having stated as a core

[1] The Plague of 1346–53 led short to mid-term to the crack down through the Statute of Labourers 1381 on (the now rare) labourers, but long term led to the end of feudalism. See also Spinney [8]; Tumbe [11, pp. 1817–1920].

[2] Burns [1].

[3] The Higher Education (Basic Amount) Regulations 2010 SI 2010/3021 and The Higher Education (Higher Amount) Regulations 2010/3020.

[4] Independent Panel report to the Review of Post-18 Education and Funding, May 2019.

principle that 'Post-18 education cannot be left entirely to market forces', recommended a reduction to £7,500. Post Covid-19 fees for ordinarily resident students have been frozen but not reduced. In Scotland, education is a devolved issue and Scotland has no tuition fees for ordinarily resident students.

It is true that participation in higher education has expanded. The system has expanded from an elite system with a 5% participation rate in 1960, to a medium-sized system with 14% participation rate by the late 1980s, to a mass system with a participation rate of about one-third by 2000. This of course does not answer whether education is in fact happening, but few would now argue for return to education of an elite few.

However, tuition fees have made education a profitable market. The Auger Report comments that it was from 2012 that undergraduate teaching became profitable. That market has been joined by for profit universities such as the University of Law (owned at least for the moment by Global University Systems). The Higher Education and Research Act 2017 created an Office for Students to regulate access by for profit organisations to register as universities. It is now much easier to do so.

This marketisation element is particularly strong where international students are concerned. As fees for ordinarily resident students have risen, so have those for students who are not ordinarily resident, known as international students. These are not insignificant sums. Coventry University has fees at low end at £15,000 for international undergraduates. At the University of Oxford international undergraduate fees to study jurisprudence start at £29,500 per year. At City, which has a range of law courses at undergraduate and postgraduate level, the annual undergraduate fee for international students are £15,700.

The ordinary residence test was introduced by the Education Act 1962 to define eligibility for a grant by the local education authority. As the House of Lords remarked in *R v Barnet London Borough Council, ex parte Shah* [1982] 2 AC 309, it was passed in the same session as the Commonwealth Immigrants Act 1962. It may well be pointed out that the UK remains the second most popular place in the world to study, and of this I am proud. Students will no doubt get a good education in the place that they want. The cost may be mitigated through scholarships.

The real damage is the effect which these high levels of fees have had on internationalisation strategies. It has resulted in internationalisation strategies which are really simply marketing strategies. With one-fifth of students international, there is now overdependence on the large income which international students provide. Those students are recruited via agents or by setting up campuses in host countries.

This model of internationalisation does nothing to advance an international outlook in so-called 'home' students. While it has been argued that international students create a more cosmopolitan campus, this is far from borne out by the evidence. While my own university's approach is that international students are simply part of the student cohort and are welcomed in as such, in some other universities, they remain more separate, certainly at undergraduate level. Another tool to advance an international outlook in 'home' students, physical exchange, is also more accessible for those of advantaged social and economic backgrounds. In interviewing such students in my former role of Assistant Dean for Student Exchanges, I saw that the vast majority are either international students or students who have already lived their lives across borders. This current form of student mobility therefore only reaches the already mobile.

Even prior to the pandemic, many had also started to question this model of internationalisation in light of the evidence on causes of ever accelerating climate change and of the sustainable development goals. There is no discussion of alternatives in the International Education Strategy Update published in February 2021 jointly by the Department for Education and the Department for International Trade. Instead, it repeats much of the government's International Education Strategy in March 2019. In particular, it repeats 2030 as the target year by which to have increased the value of education exports (covering transnational education such as branch campuses) to £35 billion per year and the number of international students in the UK to at least 600,00 per year. India is top of the 'immediate priority areas' and a 'high-potential market'. Two paragraphs cover university to university collaboration (In the 2019 document, there is at least a Global Partnerships Sect. 3.1 which acknowledges the principle of mutual learning and partnership and a Sect. 3.2 on Global mobility and exchange).

The pandemic has revealed a strong drive to maintain income from education. As universities are currently constructed, this has protected jobs. Where jobs have been at risk, some vice-chancellors accepted temporary pay cuts to avoid redundancies. Others have not.[5]

But, like other organisations, universities will have to re-assess their purpose in the light of Covid-19.[6]

3 Purpose of the University?

By light-hearted way of discerning purpose, here is a selection of university mottos: *Education is light* (University of Dhaka); *Education is a shield* (University of Botswana); *By work, all things grow* (McGill); *The community of knowledge* (Eotvos Lorand University, Budapest); *It will last into future times* (Trinity College, Dublin); *Nourishing mother of studies* (Bologna); *Wisdom enlightens* (Colombo University); *The pen is mightier than the sword* (Keio); *Bastion of Freedom* (Leiden); *Speaking the truth in love* (Brandon); *The Lord is my light* (Oxford); *From here we derive light and sacred draughts* (Cambridge); *To serve mankind* (City, University of London); *A Private University promoting public service* (OP Jindal Global University). Many of these mottos have religious origins. Many of them date from a time when knowledge of law, as of medicine, was available only in one centre whose contents were to be promulgated or demonstrated in a lecture or anatomy theatre. Those are circumstances far removed from ours. But all of them demonstrate a sense that the purpose

[5] Stein and Greenwood [9].

[6] 'Future of the Corporation' (*The British Academy*)https://www.thebritishacademy.ac.uk/programmes/future-of-the-corporation/. Accessed 30 April 2021.

of a university is learning, through hard work if necessary, to a benefit—a light, a shield, sustenance—and that that benefit is for the community, the public good. None of the mottos selected and set out above, more or less at random, suggest that the purpose of a university is to profitably deliver a degree which has been paid for. I distinguish the purpose of the university from the purpose of a student in going to a university, which may indeed be to get the degree they have paid for, to advance their chance of a good job, or because their parents wanted them to, or to gain some independence and have a good social life. These student purposes must be heard and respected but the task of the university is to communicate its purpose to each of its students.

3.1 Sustainable Development Goals

Under this purposive approach, a better target for 2030 might be the Sustainable Development Goals (SDGs). The Times Higher Education Impact rankings[7] measure universities across the world against the SDGs. I am pleased that City was placed in the 2020 Impact Rankings. Many high-profile UK universities were not. Its partnerships for staff and student exchange are mentioned as well as its roof beehives providing shelter to endangered bees. SDG 17 underpins the other SDGs and requires global, regional, national and local partnership for all the goals. This necessarily involves reaching out beyond the defined community of paying students and paid staff.

3.2 Lessons from History

In Steven Spielberg's 1997 film Amistad, both Cinque, facing a lion in his African village and John Quincy Adams, facing the Supreme Court and the prospect of Civil War, call on the spirit of their ancestors. The insight for our times is that in a moment of crisis, we reach in and back to our own family and national history, to find a message of victory over the threat. From which comes the risk of inward-looking nationalism after coronavirus.

It is the task of those at universities to investigate, unravel and tell a truthful tale of the past. The past is a foreign country: they do things differently there.[8] For law academics, this means legal history, exploring context, rescuing cases from one-line rules which appear in textbooks as obvious and eternal, and showing how they have

---

[7] 'Impact Rankings 2020' (*Times Higher Education*)https://www.timeshighereducation.com/rankings/impact/2020/overall#!/page/0/length/25/sort_by/rank/sort_order/asc/cols/undefined. Accessed 9 July 2021.

[8] The much quoted first 11 words from Hartley [2].

contested flashpoints and could have gone the other way. The excellent Feminist Judgment Projects across the world rewrite judgments.[9]

I argue that far from retreating into national myths, now more than ever is the time to study other nations, too, and that may involve understanding their past. Sadly, comparative law is too often the forgotten sister of international law, drawing upon itself the now hackneyed accusation of comparing apples and oranges. Perhaps what underlines this accusation is the awareness that to really understand another nation, we must understand its history, including living memory history. If the past is a foreign country, the past of a foreign country must be even more inaccessible, goes the logic. Law, with its jurisdictional limits, is more prone to national isolationism than most. But it is the task of universities to carry out precisely that trans-national comparison, and draw learning from the past, as is done by the excellent Journal of International and Comparative Law edited by Professor Anton Cooray at City. In the case of national law, other solutions or frameworks are identified as possible. In the case of international law, we see its origins and its different fortunes in national law.

The alternative to nation-to-nation conversation is an internationalisation which is extractive, pithily described by Gandhi in *Hind Swaraj*, Chap. 11, where he identifies British law in India as hegemonic to Imperial Rule, as 'tightening the English grip'. This was rule by law, not rule of law. In 1920, Gandhi launched the movement for non-cooperation. In 1922 he was disbarred by the Inner Temple. And yet, the value of a transnational legal education exposed to different thinking is illustrated in *Hind Swaraj* itself. Gandhi quotes Henry Maine's work *Village Communities in the East and West.* Maine was a comparativist who saw East and West as essentially different, the East marked by static status-based societies rather than dynamic contract-based ones. Identified by Karuna Mantena[10] as an idealogue of late imperialism, he nevertheless attracted Gandhi's attention. I have argued elsewhere[11] that this was through a paper[12] on Roman Law of obligations for which Maine was then the dominant thinker and in which Gandhiji placed sixth in his Bar exams. Unlike Maine, Gandhi saw village communities as dynamic and prone to change, for example on gender equality. For Gandhi, rural communities presented a form of society, based on obligations, and he saw this difference as a model and as an answer to both colonialism and modern urban nationalism. That view was vindicated in 2020 in each step which a migrant labourer took on the long journey home. Exposure to different perspectives may lead us to reinforce our national system, but can only be a benefit.

Sometimes the term 'internationalisation at home' is used. It may be thought that this conveys little other than a sense of paradox. The French legal thinker Alain Supiot, commenting on the work of the French philosopher Simone Weil,

---

[9] Munro [6, pp. 251–61].

[10] Mantena [5].

[11] This section draws on an online lecture *Mind, Word and Deed: to what extent was Mahatma Gandhi influenced by his legal education?* given on 28 July 2020 by the author to an audience from Jawaharlal Nehru University in association with the Association of Commonwealth Universities.

[12] I am very grateful to Catherine McArdle, Librarian of Lincoln's Inn for digging out the original exam paper from the Council of Legal Education underground archive during the first lockdown. Gandhi's answer paper is sadly lost to time.

uses the term *mondialisation* (from the French word *monde* for world) in contrast to *globalisation* (author's translation):

> The problem of our time is not choosing between globalisation or retreat into national identities: we cannot ignore either the diversity of nations, nor their growing interdependence in the face of the environmental and social threats to us all. The french language allows us to bypass this false dilemma with the two words *globalisation* and *mondialisation*. To *globalise* is to labour under the rule of the market, of unlimited growth, of flexibilisation of work and of cultural hegemonisation. To *mondialise* is to establish an order which is respectful of the whole inhabited world, of human work and of the diversity of people and cultures.[13]

The linguistic gauntlet has been thrown down for us in the anglophone world. Perhaps one can distinguish between internationalisation and internationalism, between globalisation and global. Global is the word used in the Global Education Movement and in SDG4. It also appears in Jindal's full title. But the point of substance, as Weil[14] herself pointed out, is critical rootedness (*enracinement)* in a nation while being understanding and respectful of other nations. Universities are ideally placed to take this role.

3.3 Insight into the Future

A further purpose of universities must also be to offer insights into what lies two steps ahead or round the corner. On 29 January 1985, Margaret Thatcher joined Zulfikar Ali Bhutto as one of the two Oxford-educated premiers to be denied an honorary doctorate by Oxford University.[15] As excited students gathering outside the Sheldonian Theatre, we saw this as a comment on the ongoing bitter Miners' Strike. In fact, the 738–319 vote of those sitting soberly at the meeting of Congregation was driven by dons from science and medicine who were aghast at the cuts by 20% to research in those fields. We do not need to be reminded in these times how important research in science and medicine are.

Legal academics engaged in empirical research carry it out in the field, amongst people, and therefore those who have been unable to shift this research online, have had to pause it unless they have a partner local to their field work. Legal academics engaged in theoretical and doctrinal research have been able to carry on and connect with a far wider conversation online. Both have felt the demands of teaching have taken precedence over research during Covid-19.

Covid-19 has triggered deep review of current legal structures, and again the purpose of academics must be to give views to Government reviews, Parliamentary inquiries, to have in other words the role upon which think tanks are encroaching. Academics are the first point of call for comments on current dilemmas such as compulsory vaccination, or airline hijack, because we are seen as presenting an

---

[13] Supiot [10].

[14] Weil [13].

[15] Wainwright [12].

independent view. This should remain so. That independent voice in a moment of crisis can only be developed through years of research.

3.4 Education

That leaves the last, but not least, purpose: education. Herein lies a problem for universities: small size groups, of between 2 and 12 students, produce vastly superior student learning. Those of us with the fortune to be educated at Oxford or Cambridge know that this is the true enhancement of the learning we had.

As any teacher knows, the best, most stimulating, classes are those where students know they are visible, are happy to be visible, to discuss and to participate. This fundamental approach can even be seen in room layout: rows of seats ready to rote learn or circles of tables ready to discuss and challenge. Central to this approach is a vision of education as multilateral, as requiring student-student peer collaborative tasks and review. This dynamic can only be achieved in small tutorials or seminars. It is true that some lecturers achieve a strong bilateral dynamic in large lectures[16] through Socratic lecturing. In France, law lectures are regarded as an important way of modelling to student how to develop and sustain an argument or critique a doctrine. On the other hand, there were already mutterings in educational circles about whether lectures reflected a bygone era of dissemination of knowledge from one source. Covid-19 has cut through this debate. During lockdown, all universities have had to replace them with synchronous or asynchronous online sessions, often shortened into 10-min podcasts. At many universities, they show no signs of returning.

Evidence from neuroimaging shows that peer learning increases motivation.[17] This builds on empirical research by social neuroscientists on the connection between social interaction, neural reward (dopamine production) and motivation to learn. Reciprocity motivates learners, the researchers conclude, by recruiting the reward circuitry in the brain. The simple expectation of a co-operative interaction, based on past experience, recruits the social reward networks in the brain. The authors conclude that, based on neural development, peer-learning can become a useful instructional strategy at around 8.

And yet, the social aim is to promote wider participation in post-18 education. Universities in France and Italy struggle with huge cohorts. Small classes require roomy campuses or colleges. Pragmatism from widening participation calls for teaching by numbers.

The particular danger of this approach in law schools is precisely that the subject itself changes according to whether it is learnt by the student as rules to be learnt by rote and repeated or as evolving theories to be evaluated and challenged. We can teach the students the rule of law, or rule by law, or even the law of rules. Given the coming changes in the practice of law, how law is taught will be crucial.

---

[16] Michael J Sandel's Justice lectures at Harvard are an outstanding example.

[17] Ian and Guillaume [3].

4 Shifts in the Practice of Law

The most visible change to practice is the move to online work for courts, legal practitioners and law schools. Court hearings, one of the last events in which for common lawyers it seemed only in person attendance was feasible, have gone online. Working from home has increased even after lockdown as law firms have realised that staff can work at home for at least some of the time and save them costly premises. University law schools have had to move rapidly online to reach and teach both local and international students. Online conferences have permitted faculty to engage in discussion and co-writing more than before. In all cases, some elements of virtual work and study are likely to remain, they often prove cheaper in money, in time and for the planet.

Law firms have realised that allowing staff to work from home even part of the working week can relieve them of much of the costs of expensive city-centre offices.

The use of Artificial Intelligence in legal practice through legal tech has also accelerated during Covid-19, in legal research, document analysis, risk assessment in contracts and case management such as lengthy due diligence. Algorithms will be able to calculate prospects of success based on past case law. Legal secretaries have been made redundant in a number of firms. It is anticipated there will be a drop in requirement for junior solicitors. Humans will be reserved for the tasks at which they have an advantage over algorithms.

Legal education must prepare students for these changes in legal practice. The student who can use technology in a human way to identify a solution will prosper. The student who has learnt law as automatic rules for which the solution can be googled will be replaced by automation. Sophisticated human cognitive function will be key to this. Digitalisation must develop, not dumb down, learning by students. I turn now to one way this might be done.

5 And So To—Student Exchange in Legal Education

In the old landscape, student exchanges were only exchange in the sense that prisoner exchanges are exchange: *of* students rather than *between* students. Students move between universities in a parallel process for 3 months, not encountering each other. These moves were facilitated either through multilateral programmes such as the EU's Erasmus (from which Britain has now departed) or through bilateral agreements between universities via partnerships, or through funding from bodies such as the Association of Commonwealth Universities. Many students on so-called exchange only encounter other visiting students. In addition, students attended courses in English, often on subjects stripped of national perspective. Nor did students need to know the language of the country they were visiting. This is despite the existence of an excellent free-language centres, for example at my own university, City. Most

Indian students know at least two languages but Britain risks becoming a nation of monoglots.

So how and where, in the altered landscape, could student exchanges in legal education emerge?

5.1 Student Exchange of Labour

Rather than being enhanced tourists, law students should have the opportunity of internships in another jurisdiction. For many, this already happens, such as those specialising in international corporate law or for those who find placements in international governmental and non-governmental organisations. It is less common for those specialising in labour law or family law or criminal law. One challenge is the inherently national nature of legal study and qualification. Unlike the medical student or the student who goes abroad to teach their own language, even a bright law student's labour is of uncertain value to the host organisation until they qualify. Options might be work at a law clinic such as the Environmental Law Clinic set up by students at City, or a placement at court or at a research centre or even in practice in a suitable role. There ought to be a deeper level of experience of other national law systems.

The Turing Scheme[18] has been introduced for 2021 to replace the multilateral Erasmus. It funds UK students to go abroad for a period of 4 weeks or more. While this is consistent with the longer period of work I argue for below, it is not a reciprocal scheme.

The post study work visa introduced in 2021 provides international students who have completed a degree in the UK to stay for 2 years after their degree.

Some more promising avenues for our—exchange—purposes are contained in the Migration and Mobility Partnership Memorandum of Understanding (MOU), signed in February 2021.[19] The MOU recognises a variety of migration and mobility such as 12-month student internships (paragraph 3), exchanges of young professionals for up to 24 months. These provisions apply to 18–30-year-olds. If this MOU results in more specific provisions, this could enhance a fuller bilateral exchange. Further initiatives may emerge from a UK-India Trade Agreement, currently in discussion.

Universities in partnership could also make representations to their professional bodies on mutual recognition of law degrees.

All this might enable longer, practical, exchange visits along the lines of medical electives, and set within the law degree.

---

[18] 'Turing Scheme' (*Government of UK*) https://www.turing-scheme.org.uk/. Accessed 9 July 2021.

[19] 'MoU on the migration and the mobility partnership between Indian and the United Kingdom' (*UK Government*, 4 May 2021) https://www.gov.uk/government/publications/migration-and-mobility-partnership/mou-on-migration-and-mobility-partnership-between-india-and-the-united-kingdom. Accessed 26 May 2021.

5.2 *Student Exchange of Dialogue*

How do we prepare our students for the above physical exchange work abroad? I suggest that one important opportunity forward is building into our courses an element of direct online dialogue with students from another jurisdiction. This can be to discuss a common area of international law, or it can be a comparative of an aspect of national law or practice. The move to online work over the past year has shown that this can be done. This dialogue is sometimes called telecollaboration, sometimes collaborative online international learning, sometimes virtual exchange. [7] discusses its merit as a pre-physical mobility programme in the context of language learning. For law, comparative study might be one term or online intercultural exchange. This would permit exchange across jurisdictions such as Britain and India, but also with students from civil law jurisdictions with very different approaches in law. At the early undergraduate stage of building knowledge, the exchange could be directed to a precise task. As O'Dowd comments, this is not a replacement for physical mobility.

Until Brexit, the EU Erasmus Scheme had been the main mechanism for student mobility across the European region. Students at City, including international students from India, had been able to hop across to France and get some exposure to studying at a university in a civil law jurisdiction. The UK has now left Brexit but continues to be a member of the Bologna Process.[20]

On 19 November 2020,[21] the 48 Ministers of Education issued the Rome Ministerial Communiqué 'from' Rome, Annex II of which sets out guidelines addressing inequalities and point 8 of which recommends blended mobility.

8. International mobility programs in higher education should be structured and implemented in a way that foster diversity, equity and inclusion and should particularly foster participation of students and staff from vulnerable, disadvantaged or underrepresented backgrounds
Guidelines: International experiences through learning mobility improve the quality of learning outcomes in higher education. Public authorities and higher education institutions should ensure equal access for all to the learning opportunities offered by national and international learning and training mobility programmes and actively address obstacles to mobility for vulnerable, disadvantaged or underrepresented groups of students and staff
Besides further support to physical mobility, including full portability of grants and loans across the EHEA, public authorities and higher education institutions should facilitate the use of information and communications technology (ICT) to support blended mobility and to foster internationalisation at home by ***embedding international online cooperation into courses***. Blended mobility is the combination of a period of physical mobility and a period of online learning. Such online cooperation can be used to extend the learning outcomes and enhance the impact of physical mobility, for example by bringing together a more diverse group of participants, or to offer a broader range of mobility options

[20] This is a meeting of Ministers of Education aimed at comparability between higher-education qualifications. Harmonisation has been slowed down but degree recognition is being worked towards.

[21] 'EHEA 2020 Rome ministerial Conference 2020' (European Higher Education Area and Bologna Process 19 November 2020) ehea.info. Accessed 9 July 2021.

I conclude that virtual exchanges are one way to meet the challenges thrown at us by Covid.

5.2.1 Digitalisation with Human Faces and Voices

Covid has accelerated moves in universities towards digital learning. Lecturer voice is muted. The unit of learning can be put online by any lecturer. It increases the automated quality of education. This is entirely consistent with the high level of marketisation of higher education in Britain which I have described. But, as I have suggested, automation in thinking about law and legal rules is a dangerous thing. Moving online for a video, learning from powerpoints, is not using automation intelligently. It is reducing students (and faculty) to automatons for whom the law is a series of rules under which outcomes can be predicted automatically.

If the peer group approach sketched out above is applied to international exchange, it can be an extremely exciting activity. Virtual exchange should not be viewed as only an emergency tool to be used during Covid-19. As faculty, we have seen how, across distance, we can engage and discuss online easily and widely. Students should be able to learn the same. But the activity has to be very carefully designed so as to enhance conversation and exchange between students. We are using technology to bridge a distance which could not otherwise be travelled, even post Covid-19.

In July 2021, my counterpart (for International Collaborations) at Jindal, Professor Malvika Seth, and I devised and delivered a two-week pilot virtual Summer School on Human Rights and Business. This is a subject where differences of perspective and interest as between Global North and South can be obscured. 50 undergraduate students selected from each university engaged on a virtual platform in groups of 5 over 10 days on a joint project, and during that time also attended seminars on cutting edge topics such as evolving human rights, the changing corporation, labour rights, the environment, and vaccines. We recruited speakers from each university and indeed from neighbouring juridisdictions (respectively Pakistan and France). These speakers were leaders in their field reflecting on their subject. As a summer school, there was no assessment. Through a random process, each small group chose a theme such as equality or freedom from torture or freedom to trade, and worked together towards a 15-min presentation. Feedback from the students was extremely positive and anecdotal evidence is that students stay in contact. Another City-Jindal virtual event is planned in 2022.

There are clearly different ways in which such a project could be set up by universities: as a summer school, as a one-day workshop, as a regular class within a module, or it could lead to a resurgence of the comparative dual degree (such as the one I teach on at the University of Paris Nanterre): law combined with another national law or law combined with a language. Whatever the form chosen, virtual exchanges are in my view best taken early in the law degree if they are to be effective in creating lawyers with strong truly international thinking in the post Covid-19 world.

I have mentioned above the evidence from neuroscience of peer-group learning and suggest that the same benefits can occur to a class with students in another room and jurisdiction if the project is carefully designed. This does not even require complex technology if that is not available. During autumn 2020, I had to move classes for my LLM students at the University of Paris Nanterre online. I set up clear preparation for the online class. Most of them had cameras which did not work, and I was reduced to seeing only myself on screen. However, the discussions we had on labour law through the medium of voice alone were some of the most engaged ever, and certainly far superior to students sitting in rows of desks robotically writing notes of my lecture.

5.2.2 New Landscapes

I have set out some proposals for the world of student exchanges post Covid-19 which, in my view, are consistent with the international partnerships approach enjoined us by the SDGs. If the aim of a law school is to develop freedom of thought in its students by teaching them to examine the past, present and future of law, the airwaves might be a good place to start.

References

1. Burns, J.: International students turn to food banks in lockdown BBC News https://www.bbc.co.uk/news/education-53552831 (29 July 2020). Accessed 9 July 2021
2. Hartley, L.P.: The Go Between. Hamish Hamilton, London (1953)
3. Ian, C., Guillaume, D.: Towards a neural basis for peer-interaction: what makes peer-learning tick?' 6 Frontiers in Psychology https://doi.org/10.3389/fpsyg.2015.00028 (2015). Accessed 9 July 2021
4. Mantena, K.: Alibis of Empire. Princeton, UP (2010)
5. Munro, V.E., Feminist judgments projects at the intersection. 29 Fem Leg Stud, 251–61. https://doi.org/10.1007/s10691-020-09428-0 (2021). Accessed 9 July 2021
6. National Committee of Inquiry into Higher Education. Dearing Report (1997)
7. O'Dowd, R., Virtual exchange: moving forward into the next decade Comput. Assist. Lang. Learn. **34**(3), 209–24 (2021). https://doi.org/10.1080/09588221.2021.1902201.Accessed 9 July 2021
8. Spinney, L., Pale Rider: The Spanish Flu of 1918 and how it changed the world. Random House (2017)
9. Stein, J. Greenwood, G.: University vice-chancellors quietly bump salaries back up. The Times. UK. https://www.thetimes.co.uk/article/university-vice-chancellors-quietly-bump-salaries-back-up-5nhzwj5gc (22 May 2021). Accessed 30 May 2021
10. Supiot, A., Mondialisation ou globalisation? Les lecons de Simone Weil. College de France (2019)
11. Tumbe, C.: The Age of Pandemics 1817–1920: How they shaped India and the world. Harper Collins (2020)
12. Wainwright, M.: From the archive: Oxford votes to refuse Thatcher degree. The Guardian. https://www.theguardian.com/politics/2010/jan/30/thatcher-honorary-degree-refused-oxford (30 January 2010). Accessed 9 July 2021
13. Weil, S.: L'Enracinement. Gallimard (1943)

Law School Accreditation During COVID-19: Transparency, Agility and Trust and the Australian Experience

Pip Nicholson

Abstract The global coronavirus pandemic of 2020–2021 has wreaked havoc on universities around the globe, radically impacting staff and students, while concurrently provoking bedrock questions about universities also. While law schools have been quick to respond to the health requirements of legal education in a Covid-19 world, they have had to simultaneously ensure that the education provided retains the accreditation standards set well before Covid-19 became a global phenomenon. This brief paper suggests that there are three central attributes of the Australian accreditation processes, evident from a reflection on accreditation in the Australian states of Victoria and New South Wales, which enabled the law schools to respond to Covid-19 with minimal disruption: transparency, agility and trust. The paper also suggests that it was the building of an accreditation system based on those three attributes, prior to the onset of Covid-19, which allowed the accreditation system to hold-up under the intense pressure produced by the global pandemic. As a result, the paper notes that the Victorian and New South Wales models of accreditation hold lessons for other Australian and international jurisdictions.

1 Introduction

Covid-19 has wrought change at every level of legal education, for both educators and regulatory bodies. Whilst this is clearly seen in the changing ways in which law schools now teach (online course offerings, changes to assessments, virtual clinics, etc.), it is also true in relation to the broader academic and professional contexts within which law schools and regulatory bodies operate. One critical context concerns law school accreditation. While law schools have been quick to respond to the health requirements of legal education in a Covid-19 world, they have had to simultaneously

I am deeply grateful to Nick Boyd-Caine for his invaluable assistance in the preparation of this paper.

P. Nicholson (✉)
Melbourne Law School, University of Melbourne, Parkville, Australia
e-mail: p.nicholson@unimelb.edu.au

C. Raj Kumar and S. G. Sreejith (eds.), *Legal Education and Legal Profession During and After COVID-19*, https://doi.org/10.1007/978-981-19-2568-9_13

ensure that the education provided retains the accreditation standards set well before Covid-19 became a global phenomenon.

This paper considers the ways in which regulatory bodies and academic institutions have successfully adapted their accreditation processes in response to Covid-19, with a focus on the jurisdictions of Victoria and New South Wales within Australia. It suggests that there are three central attributes of the Australian accreditation processes in these two jurisdictions that enabled them to respond to Covid-19 with minimal disruption: transparency, agility and trust. The paper also suggests that it was the building of an accreditation system based on those three attributes, prior to the onset of Covid-19, which allowed the accreditation system to hold up under the intense pressure produced by the global pandemic. As a result, the paper recommends the Victorian and New South Wales models of accreditation, noting that they could be considered by other Australian and international jurisdictions.

2 Admission into Legal Practice

The completion of a degree or diploma of law does not, in and of itself, enable a person to enter into legal practice in Australia. Rather, a further process exists by which an individual may seek admission into the Australian legal profession. The objective of such a process is to protect both the administration of justice and the interests of clients, by ensuring that those eligible for such admission 'have the appropriate academic qualifications and practical legal training…and are fit and proper persons to be admitted'.[1]

The admissions process varies across Australia's states and territories. As a federation, Australian states and territories have traditionally regulated accreditation and admission. In 2014, Australia's two most populous states, New South Wales and Victoria, sought to streamline their admissions frameworks by creating the Legal Professional Uniform Law scheme. This regulatory framework provides a uniform admissions process, open to all Australian jurisdictions. Whilst the goal is for all states and territories to adopt the Uniform Law scheme, to this point, it only applies in New South Wales and Victoria.[2] The Uniform Law scheme operates under the auspices of the Legal Services Counsel and Commissioner.[3]

Completion of this admissions process requires the fulfilment of a series of criteria. Relevantly here, one criterion is the satisfaction of the specified academic qualification prerequisite.[4] 'Specified academic qualifications' are those tertiary academic courses in law that are deemed to provide a legal education sufficient to enable people to pursue practice within the law. 'Accreditation' then, the topic of this paper, is the

[1] *Legal Profession Uniform Law (NSW)* 2014, s 15(a)–(b).

[2] Western Australia has indicated an intention to join the scheme as early as 2022: https://www.lpbwa.org.au/Uniform-Law. Accessed 9 July 2021.

[3] 'Legal Services Council', *Legal Services Council and Commissioner* (Web Page, 26 April 2019).

[4] Ibid.; *Legal Profession Uniform Law 2014*, s 17(1)(a).

process by which tertiary law courses are reviewed and deemed suitable to satisfy this 'specified academic qualification' criterion.

3 The Process of Accreditation

The accreditation process is undertaken by the designated local regulatory authority in each State.[5] In Victoria, the designated local regulatory authority is the Victorian Legal Admissions Board ('VLAB').[6] To receive accreditation, a law course must include the equivalent of at least three years' full-time study of law and allow law students to acquire and demonstrate appropriate understanding and competence in various areas of legal knowledge.[7] These areas of legal knowledge are colloquially known as the 'Priestly Eleven' subjects and are listed within the statutory rules relevant to admissions (see Appendix 1).[8]

As with the admissions process, accreditation has historically been non-uniform, with the individual local regulatory authorities applying individual standards to those institutions seeking accreditation within their respective jurisdictions. One aspect of New South Wales and Victoria's attempt to introduce a Uniform Law scheme has been the creation of a single accreditation standard. The Legal Services Counsel and Commissioner include a Law Admissions Consultative Committee ('LACC'), which, since 2009, has been developing a standard that it hopes both law courses seeking accreditation and local regulatory authorities will adopt.[9] Unsurprisingly, the standard has been adopted in New South Wales and Victoria, and courses seeking to be accredited must demonstrate compliance with the standard to the local regulatory authority.[10]

4 Uniform Accreditation Standard

The intention of the accreditation standards is to provide clear guidance on the evidence required to satisfy each element of accreditation. Individual standards relate to the nature, duration, content, learning outcomes, prescribed area of knowledge,

---

[5] Ibid.; *Legal Profession Uniform Law 2014*, s 29.

[6] The VLAB currently consists of Bernard Teague AO (Chair), David Habersberger QC (Deputy Chair), Suzanne McNicol AM QC, Caroline Counsel, and Magda Karagiannakis. Members are appointed for a period of three years and may be reappointed: *Legal Profession Uniform Law Application Act 2014* (Vic) s 21(3).

[7] *Legal Profession Uniform Admission Rules 2015*, r 5(1)(a)–(c).

[8] Ibid., sch 1. See Appendix 1.

[9] Law Admissions Consultative Committee [2].

[10] See for example: Victorian Legal Admissions Board [5]

and assessment of a law course.[11] Accreditation successfully received is intended to last for an interval of at least five years between reviews, though this is to be determined by the local regulatory authority.[12]

4.1 Nature of the Law Course

An accredited course must be a tertiary academic course in law. However, it does not need to lead to a degree in law; for example, tax law subjects undertaken during a commerce degree may be credited as relevant study. Rather, it must be a 'coherent sequence of units of study leading to the award of a qualification' in law.[13]

4.2 Duration of the Law Course

As discussed above, the course must include the equivalent of three years' full-time study of law. However, both part-time and accelerated course modes may be offered. The respective law schools have control over the breadth and depth of content, teaching methodology, use of technology, and assessment.[14]

4.3 Learning Outcomes of the Law Course

An accredited course must allow students to acquire and demonstrate an appropriate understanding and competence in the relevant area of knowledge, including both specific and generic skills that will assist a student in the practice of that area of law (see Appendix 2).[15]

4.4 Content of the Law Course

Accredited courses must include teaching or other instruction on at least the areas of knowledge specified in the statutory rules; the Priestly Eleven subjects. This requirement is substantive rather than formal. The institutions can determine how the areas

[11] Law Admissions Consultative Committee [3].

[12] Ibid., 3.

[13] Ibid., 6.

[14] Ibid., 7.

[15] Ibid., 8.

of knowledge are taught (whether across single or multiple subjects), what they are called, etc.[16]

4.5 *Teaching of the Law Course*

The course must be taught by people qualified to teach in the particular area of knowledge. However, the methods, content, and resources used are decided upon by the respective law schools.[17]

4.6 *Assessment of the Law Course*

Assessment must demonstrate that students have an appropriate understanding and competence in each prescribed area of knowledge and have acquired the relevant specific and general knowledge and skills. Accredited courses may be pass/fail or graded.[18]

5 Satisfaction of the Uniform Standard

An academic institution seeking accreditation must demonstrate to the local regulatory authority adherence to each of the standards set out above. Often, this will require a detailed explanation of the manner in which the course has been both constructed and conducted. In satisfying the standard concerning course content, an academic institution will likely describe each element of each prescribed area of knowledge, mapping the ways in which that knowledge is taught through the course as an individual block and as part of a larger body of knowledge, along with the teaching formats used, teaching hours proposed, and specific and generic skills developed.[19] Where showing that the relevant course is equivalent to three years' full-time study, institutions must demonstrate how part-time or accelerated programs are equivalent to their full-time counterparts, and how teaching and/or assessment methodologies achieve a similar outcome.[20]

Institutions seeking accreditation are provided the opportunity to make comprehensive submissions detailing their satisfaction of the standards. Where sufficient evidence as to the satisfaction of the standards is provided within submissions,

[16] Ibid., 9.
[17] Ibid., 10.
[18] Ibid., 12.
[19] Ibid., 9.
[20] Ibid., 7.

accreditation may be attained 'on the papers', with no further investigation needed. The local regulatory authority can also conduct its own assessments of the courses. In Victoria, this is done by the Academic Course Appraisal Committee ('ACAC'), a sub-committee of the VLAB. In 2019–2020, for example, the ACAC commissioned external assessors to review a series of courses offered by La Trobe University. Whilst this process involved consideration of a detailed submission provided by La Trobe University, it also included site visits to various La Trobe University campuses and interviews with staff, resulting in accreditation being awarded for each course for which it was sought.[21] Similarly, when Melbourne Law School last sought accreditation, in 2017, an onsite visit was conducted by the VLAB-appointed external assessor.[22] Interestingly, in NSW there is an assumption, at least since 2018, that accreditation will proceed on the papers, absent the regulator identifying a particular inquiry s/he wishes to make on site. When consulted about the 2017 Melbourne Law School accreditation process, the then Dean noted the streamlined process in NSW and its benefits over site visits unless they were clearly focused.

6 Accreditation During Covid-19

The above model of accreditation has been put under significant stress by Covid-19. However, and despite this stress, the central strengths of the model have meant that both the local regulatory bodies and tertiary institutions have been able to cooperate to ensure that accredited courses have continued to be taught, with the minimum degree of disruption possible. In particular, the agility and transparency of the accreditation system have been critical in responding to the unprecedented impact of Covid-19. This can be demonstrated by the way in which the Melbourne Law School worked with VLAB to ensure ongoing accreditation of its courses throughout 2020.

6.1 Risks Posed by Covid-19

The first confirmed case of Covid-19 in Australia occurred in late January 2020.[23] By late March, State governments began closing 'non-essential services'. Universities, including the University of Melbourne, made the decision to stop 'in-class' teaching, opting instead to move courses to an entirely virtual format. Whilst there were many challenges arising from this transition to a new pedagogy, the concern relevant to this paper was ensuring that such a move did not threaten the ongoing accreditation of Melbourne Law School's JD.

---

[21] Victorian Legal Admissions Board, *Annual Report* (Report, 2019–2020) 12.

[22] *Review of the University of Melbourne JD Course* [4].

[23] Hunt [1].

6.2 Engagement Between VLAB and Melbourne Law School

Indicative of its proactive approach regarding accreditation, VLAB approached Melbourne Law School in March 2020 in relation to the challenges to accreditation presented by Covid-19.[24] VLAB indicated its understanding of the 'unprecedented nature' of Covid-19 and the requirement for universities to respond rapidly to the evolving situation. VLAB recognised that course delivery, including assessment, would likely need to be modified, and committed to working with Melbourne Law School to ensure that such modifications would reach the standards required for accreditation. In turn, VLAB requested that Melbourne Law School document the changes to courses it intended to make, advise VLAB of those changes, and ensure the breadth and depth of the virtual course offerings matched those of their face-to-face teaching. VLAB moved early to contact Victorian law schools, reaching out to MLS on 16 March 2020, and in advance of some other states and territories in Australia.

Having determined the manner in which it would provide virtual teaching for the JD, Melbourne Law School then contacted VLAB in April 2020 (a little over a month after the initial letter from VLAB), to demonstrate its compliance with the accreditation requirements, specifically in relation to the changes wrought to the courses offered in Semester One, 2020.[25] Melbourne Law School identified the 'duration of the law course', 'content of the law course', 'teaching of the law course' and 'assess[ment] of understanding and competence' as the standards most at risk under the proposed changes to its courses and made submissions as to why those standards would continue to be satisfied.[26] In relation to the 'content of the law course' standard, for example, Melbourne Law School explained how its changed approach to non-core content and use of virtual moderated tutorials and Discussion Board software ensured that the Priestly Eleven requirements would continue to be met. Similarly, in relation to 'assessing understanding and competence', Melbourne Law School described how proctored in-person examinations would be replaced by take-home online exams, and the rationale behind the time allocated and structure of such exams, to ensure an equivalent standard of assessment.

In addition, Melbourne Law School provided a summary of every subject being offered in Semester One, a summary of the changes required to shift each subject from a face-to-face class to one that was wholly virtual, and any changes to the assessment regime of that subject. These were accepted by VLAB, and accreditation continued for Melbourne Law School's modified offerings. The work involved in creating the adapted courses, and then documenting changes for VLAB, was considerable. The then Deputy Dean, the Associate Dean for the *Juris Doctor*, and a research associate spent three weeks meeting with subject co-ordinators and teachers, working through the proposed changes to subjects, and collating the information to be provided to VLAB.

---

[24] Letter from Deborah Jones to Pip Nicholson (16 March 2020).

[25] Letter from Pip Nicholson to Deborah Jones (20 April 2020).

[26] Ibid., 1–2.

Given the Stage 4 lockdown in Victoria required all restricted workplaces (which included universities) to work from home wherever possible, teaching continued virtually at MLS for much of 2020 (and remains much disrupted across 2021).[27] As of mid-2021, Melbourne Law School had notified VLAB of its proposed teaching arrangements to the end of 2021, with the need to further update VLAB given recent lockdowns.

7 Insights from the Operation of the Accreditation Process During Covid-19

A number of insights arise from the operation of the accreditation process during Covid-19, and the case study offered concerning VLAB and the Melbourne Law School. Key during this period was the fact that the standards by which accreditation was achieved were transparent. The standards were understood by both VLAB and Melbourne Law School, as was the requirement of Melbourne Law School to ensure that those standards were maintained, and the manner in which Melbourne Law School proposed to ensure their maintenance. Had there been confusion as to the standards themselves, or the manner in which they were to be satisfied, it is likely that the accreditation of courses during the period in which tertiary institutions fundamentally changed their teaching structures would, at the very least, have been called into question.

Relatedly, the history of transparent and well-established standards allowed for institutions to demonstrate their compliance with those standards in a Covid-19-safe manner. Whilst site visits are an option open to the assessment of accreditation, they are not inherently necessary. Where an academic institution provides sufficient written evidence that it has satisfied the standards, accreditation can be determined 'on the papers'. Whilst this system has historically allowed for greater efficiency, particularly when compared with one that requires the accreditation body to attend and interview members of the academic institution, this efficiency also produced a health and safety dividend in relation to Covid-19. Accreditation officers from VLAB were not required to attend Melbourne Law School at a time when infection rates were increasing and there was still uncertainty as to the manner and likelihood of transmission of Covid-19. Given Victoria was under an increasingly restrictive lockdown from March 16, the absence of a need for site visits was critical. Rather, the detailed information provided by the Melbourne Law School was deemed sufficient, and accreditation was retained.

A parallel takeaway to that of transparency is that the structure of the accreditation process provided sufficient agility for both the local regulatory body and academic institutions to act with haste in ensuring that accreditation was retained. The process

[27] Just as MLS was to resume predominantly campus-based or Blended Synchronous Learning in its JD program, 3 states in Australia (New South Wales, Victoria and South Australia) went into lockdown requiring we once again teach virtually.

allowed for different accredited academic institutions to determine changes to their course structures that fit the individual needs of the students and the institution, while also maintaining accreditation. Similarly, the process empowered VLAB to contact academic institutions directly and indicate the minimum requirements for retaining accreditation. Such agility is obviously necessary in a world beset by a once-in-a-century phenomenon, such as Covid-19. However, that agility has greater use beyond responding to such unusual circumstances. The greater movement of international students, changing funding regimes, and demands of professional markets mean that academic institutions generally, and law schools in particular, are required to constantly consider and evolve their course offerings. Regulation in such an environment is particularly difficult, as the changing demands of students and markets risk outpacing the capacity of regulators to respond to such demands. Regulatory bodies therefore need to ensure that the systems they administer have sufficient agility to respond to a wide range of potential challenges, be they known unknowns (fluctuations in international student movements) or unknown unknowns (Covid-19). Such agility within the accreditation system in Victoria and New South Wales has been demonstrated during Covid-19 but is also likely to be used in a variety of ways in a post-Covid-19 regulatory world. This might be in response to other broad-ranging public health emergencies. It will also be of ongoing relevance as law schools test the benefits identified in virtual teaching and produce new pedagogical approaches to teaching law not previously considered by existing accreditation regimes.

The importance of trust between the regulatory bodies and the academic institutions that they regulate has been bedrock to accreditation throughout the pandemic. This trust is the third critical attribute, along with transparency and agility of both law schools and accreditors in Victoria and New South Wales. In this instance, there was significant trust placed in the regulatory authority that the accredited institutions would be able to both respond to their own specific student and institutional needs, while also maintaining the standards required for accreditation, without the regulatory body having to prescribe actions to be taken. Similarly, there was trust from the academic institutions that the regulatory body was willing to both give them time to consider how to respond to Covid-19 and work with them to ensure that accreditation standards were met, and accreditation itself maintained. Each of these characteristics, transparency, agility, and trust, is both reliant on and informs the existence of the other two attributes. It is clear then that such a process, and the broader admissions system, was crucial in ensuring that Melbourne Law School, and Victorian and New South Wales academic institutions more broadly, were able to respond to Covid-19 quickly and efficiently, in a manner that assured their current and future students of the ongoing accreditation of their tertiary studies.

8 Conclusion

Covid-19 has forced fundamental reconsiderations of the ways in which regulatory bodies and academic institutions operate to provide legal education. As law schools have changed the ways in which legal education is provided, so too have regulatory bodies reconsidered how to review and accredit such education in a Covid-19 world. It has come as a great comfort then to both academic institutions and regulatory bodies in Victoria and New South Wales that one area in which the impact of Covid-19 has been significantly cushioned is the accreditation of law courses. In large part, this has been the case because the key elements of the pre-existing accreditation regime allowed for both regulatory bodies and the academic institutions to work together to ensure accreditation was retained, even as law schools were forced to fundamentally change the ways in which they delivered legal education. Those key elements were in-turn; the transparency of the system, which allowed for regulatory bodies and law schools to understand clearly what was expected of them, even as they worked to respond to Covid-19. Agility, not previously tested, allowed for both regulatory bodies and the law schools to change the ways in which they sought and considered accreditation, without changing the underlying standards and expectations of that accreditation. And trust played a key role in enabling the regulatory bodies and law schools to work together to ensure that accreditation was maintained in unique and challenging circumstances. These elements were built into the accreditation system, which takes as its focus the teaching of substantive legal precepts. The system maintained its focus and continued to operate, despite the pandemic. In Victoria, and as this example demonstrates at Melbourne Law School, we benefitted from dealing with a practical, purposeful regulator, which targets its accreditation transparently. It is a model of accreditation which has much to recommend locally and globally.

Appendix 1—Priestly Eleven Subjects

The following subjects make up the Priestly Eleven subjects and are listed as required academic areas of knowledge in Schedule 1 of the *Legal Profession Uniform Admission Rules 2015* (NSW):

- Criminal Law and Procedure;
- Torts;
- Contracts;
- Property;
- Equity;
- Company Law;
- Administrative Law;
- Federal and State Constitutional Law;
- Civil Dispute Resolution;
- Evidence; and
- Ethics and Professional Responsibility.

Appendix 2: Learning Outcomes of Law Courses

The Tertiary Education Quality and Standards Agency ('TEQSA') identifies a series of specified learning outcomes for each course of study, encompassing both discipline-related and generic outcomes, including:

- specific knowledge and skills and their application that characterise the field(s) of education or disciplines involved;
- generic skills and their application in the context of the field(s) of education or disciplines involved;
- knowledge and skills required for employment and further study related to the course of study, including those required to be eligible to seek registration to practise where applicable; and
- skills in independent and critical thinking suitable for life-long learning.[28]

Appendix 3: Council of Australian Law Deans Review of Legal Education in Australia

In November 2020, the Council of Australian Law Deans considered the content of the Stage One Report in its expert review of legal education in Australia. The Council agreed that the Stage One Report should include:

- a comprehensive description of the current system of legal education in Australia and its regulation, including:
  - the distinction between the academic requirements for admission, the practical requirements for admission, and the regulation of continuing professional development for lawyers;
  - the role of LACC and the various admission authorities;
  - the Uniform Admission Rules and the approaches adopted in other states and territories, the Prescribed Areas of Knowledge ('Priestley Eleven'), the Threshold Learning Outcomes for Law, the LACC Standards, the CALD Standards, and the PLT Competency Standards; and
  - the relevant provisions of the Higher Education Standards and the AQF;
- the background and history of that system;
- the current context of legal education in Australia, with an emphasis upon the factors driving the need for change in the current system of regulation;
- a comprehensive review and summary of the relevant literature relating to:
  - the competing conceptualisations of the role of law schools and the purpose of legal education; and

[28] *Tertiary Education Quality and Standards Agency Act 2011* (Cth) Part 1.4(2).

  - academic support for and academic critique of the current system of regulation, including the scope and impact of the Priestley Eleven;

- a comparative evaluation of the systems of regulation and accreditation in key overseas jurisdictions; and
- a list of options for a reimagined system of legal education regulation in Australia, from conservative to progressive and even radical. These might (or might not) include retaining the current system, revising/expanding/contracting the Priestley Eleven, replacing the Priestley Eleven with an entirely new list of prescribed areas of knowledge, and reimagining the present system of regulation entirely by developing a model law school curriculum, abandoning the distinction between the LLB/JD and PLT, adopting a 'bar exam' model, and/or some other option presently unanticipated.

References

1. Hunt, G.: First confirmed case of novel coronavirus in Australia. Department of Health Web Page. https://www.health.gov.au/ministers/the-hon-greg-hunt-mp/media/first-confirmed-case-of-novel-coronavirus-in-australia (25 Jan 2020). Accessed 9 July 2021
2. Law Admissions Consultative Committee, Accreditation standards for Australian Law Courses (Report, July 2018)
3. Law Admissions Consultative Committee, Accreditation standards for Australian Law Courses (Report, July 2018) 6
4. Review of the University of Melbourne JD Course (Final Report, 2 October 2017) 24
5. Victorian Legal Admissions Board, Annual Report (Report, 2019–2020) 12

The Impact of the Pandemic on Legal Profession

Covid-19 and Courts: How "Remote" Should the Future Be?

Sabrina Shizue McKenna

Abstract Various courts in the United States, including those in the State of Hawai'i of the United States of America, temporarily closed in March of 2020 in response to the Covid-19 pandemic. Although it was initially anticipated that courts would be reopened relatively quickly, when it became apparent this could not happen, many courts, including those in Hawai'i, began utilizing "remote" videoconferencing platforms for various types of court proceedings. Some court administrators suggest that some remote court proceedings should become permanent. This chapter discusses the Hawai'i experience with remote court proceedings then discusses advantages, impediments to, and concerns regarding such proceedings. The author concludes that although some types of court proceedings are particularly suited to be conducted remotely, court leaders need to consider social science studies regarding the effects of remote appearances on credibility and demeanor determinations to make informed decisions. The author also concludes that, despite concerns, remote appearances by parties and witnesses should be permitted for access to justice purposes, but that judges should be educated on the possible effects of remote appearances on their credibility determinations.

1 The Pandemic's Closure of Hawai'i Courts

On March 16, 2020, Chief Justice Mark E. Recktenwald of the Supreme Court of the State of Hawai'i issued an Order in response to the emerging Covid-19 pandemic.[1] In

[1] *See* Chief Justice Mark E. Rectenwald, 'Judiciary's response to the COVID-19 outbreak' (Supreme Court of the State of Hawai'i, 16 March 2020). https://www.courts.state.hi.us/wp-content/uploads/2020/03/031619_scmf-20-152_In_Re_COVID-19.pdf. Accessed 9 July 2021. Hawai'i became the 50th state of the United States of America in 1959.

The views expressed are of the author alone and are not those of the Supreme Court of the State of Hawai'i or the Hawai'i Judiciary.

S. S. McKenna (✉)
University of Hawaii, Manoa, HI, USA
e-mail: Sabrina.S.McKenna@courts.hawaii.gov

C. Raj Kumar and S. G. Sreejith (eds.), *Legal Education and Legal Profession During and After COVID-19*, https://doi.org/10.1007/978-981-19-2568-9_14

the Order, Chief Justice Recktenwald noted that on March 5, 2020, Hawai'i Governor David Ige had declared a state of emergency in Hawai'i and that the World Health Organization had since designated the Covid-19 outbreak a global pandemic.[2] The Hawai'i Department of Health had also urged all people in Hawai'i to prepare for the possible community spread of Covid-19 and to take steps to avoid potential transmission, including avoiding public gatherings.

Consistent with the recommendations of these public health authorities, and pursuant to his authority as Chief Justice under Hawai'i statutory law, Chief Justice Recktenwald ordered that, with the exception of emergency and time-sensitive matters, in-person appearances for civil, family, and, to the extent possible, criminal dockets would be limited starting Tuesday, March 17, 2020. The Order also postponed all oral arguments in appellate cases scheduled to take place before May. The Order further directed administrative judges of the courts of Hawai'i's four counties to devise plans to significantly reduce the need for in-court appearances, including postponing court proceedings as appropriate. In addition, it prohibited entry into judiciary buildings of those with a fever, cough, or other respiratory symptoms and those who had traveled outside Hawai'i in the past 14 days or had close, prolonged contact with a person who had or was suspected to have Covid-19. The Order, however, created specific exceptions for those needing to enter judiciary buildings to file documents[3] or to participate in domestic violence restraining order hearings. Judges also had discretion to schedule other urgent matters to take place in-person.

The March 16, 2020 Order was set to expire on Thursday, April 30, 2020. At the time of the Order's issuance, neither Hawai'i nor the world knew how devastating the impact of Covid-19 would be and how long it would last. Just four days after the initial Order, on March 20, 2020, Chief Justice Recktenwald was compelled to issue another order, the Order Directing Courthouse Closures. This Order noted that on March 17, 2020, Governor Ige had directed people to avoid gatherings of more than ten people, consistent with federal recommendations. Based on the Chief Justice's March 20, 2020 Order, entry into judiciary buildings by judiciary employees became severely restricted; for months, only extremely essential judiciary employees were allowed to enter, and other staff were required to work remotely, using technology such as email, virtual private networks, and videoconferencing platforms.[4] Thus, from March 23, 2020, to April 30, 2020, Hawai'i judiciary facilities were almost completely closed off to entry; the only exceptions were for extremely essential judicial employees, participants in domestic violence restraining order hearings, and

[2] This happened on March 11, 2020.

[3] As a practical matter, this would only be for self-represented litigants and for family court matters. In Hawai'i, as of the end of 2020, all appellate and non-family court criminal and civil proceedings had already converted to online filing, which all attorneys are required to utilize. Hawai'i's family court proceedings are scheduled to convert to online filing within a few years, after which only self-represented litigants will be permitted to manually file court documents.

[4] In this chapter, the term "remote" court proceedings are often used to refer to court proceedings using videoconferencing platforms, such as Zoom or WebEx.

those who needed to file court documents. After that, court proceedings slowly and cautiously resumed using remote videoconferencing or other technology, or through live appearances.[5]

2 Remote Court Appearances in Hawai'i Courts

2.1 Introduction

Before Covid-19, beginning in 1996, a few courtrooms in Hawai'i became equipped with videoconferencing connections to correctional centers in order to arraign criminal defendants who were in custody due to the inability to post bail or due to an order disallowing the setting of bail. Some civil trial courts had permitted trial testimony using the technology in those courtrooms.[6] The Hawai'i Judiciary also had an existing contract with a video remote technology company that was being used to connect members of the judiciary located on different islands for administrative or educational conferences. However, there had been little, if any, use of videoconferencing technology for court proceedings other than criminal arraignments of defendants in custody.

In the first few weeks after the March 23, 2020 closure of Hawai'i judiciary facilities due to Covid-19, very few in-court proceedings took place, other than the domestic violence restraining order hearings discussed above. In addition to the existing court caseload and normal new filings, however, Hawai'i law enforcement officials began issuing thousands of criminal citations for violations of state or county quarantine or mask mandates instituted due to the pandemic.

As it increasingly became clear that the effects of Covid-19 would continue and the backlog of cases would only grow exponentially, on April 17, 2020, Chief Justice Recktenwald issued an "Order Regarding the Committee on Operational Solutions."[7] He appointed a committee of judges and the President of the Hawai'i State Bar

---

[5] Various orders and information relating to Covid-19 and Hawai'i courts are available at https://www.courts.state.hi.us/covid-19-information-page. Accessed 9 July 2021.

[6] In October 2001, after the September 11, 2001 terrorist attacks, followed by a dengue fever scare in Hawai'i, and after a medical malpractice civil jury trial had already begun, an expert witness residing on the east coast of the United States, who was to testify for the plaintiff, refused to fly to Hawai'i to testify in-person. The author was the presiding trial judge and suggested using the videoconferencing technology that had, since 1996, connected a courtroom in the Circuit Court of the First Circuit on O'ahu with the O'ahu Community Correctional Center for video arraignments in criminal cases. This was the first time a witness testified in a trial via videoconferencing in Hawai'i state courts. *See* Nelson Daranciang, 'Civil trial greets real-time video: An expert witness testifies live on camera in a malpractice case' *Honolulu Star-Bulletin* (5 November 2001). http://archives.starbulletin.com/2001/11/05/news/story6.html. Accessed 9 July 2021.

[7] *See* Chief Justice Mark E. Rectenwald, 'Judiciary's response to the COVID-19 outbreak: Order regarding the committee on operational solutions' (Supreme Court of the State of Hawai'i, 17 April 2020). https://www.courts.state.hi.us/wp-content/uploads/2020/04/041720_scmf-20-152_InReCOVID-19_ORD-Com-on-Op-Solutions.pdf. Accessed 9 July 2021.

Association "to examine and accelerate the Judiciary's capacity to conduct matters remotely as appropriate and to plan for the safe and timely return to normal operations." Thus, Hawai'i courts began exploring adjustments that would allow for some court proceedings to resume.

This chapter focuses on one of those adjustments: the utilization of videoconferencing platforms to conduct "remote" court proceedings.[8]

2.2 *Hawai'i Supreme Court Oral Arguments*

Because it appeared that in-person court proceedings would not be able to resume for some time, in May of 2020, the Hawai'i Supreme Court resumed oral arguments, using a videoconferencing platform, with live-streaming and closed captioning. YouTube links have been provided on the Hawai'i Judiciary's website so the public can observe these arguments.[9] Thus, since May of 2020, anyone in the world has been

[8] Not discussed, therefore, are temporary protocols or adjustments due to Covid-19 that would probably only be in effect during the pandemic, such as health screenings of those entering courthouses, including the conducting of temperature checks; masking and social distancing mandates; placement of hand-sanitizers by entry-ways and in other locations; installation of plexiglass to protect staff, judges, and witnesses; and significant additional special disinfecting wipe-downs of surfaces. Also not discussed is an adjustment the author also views as having important access to justice implications: staggering of start times for court proceedings, to minimize the number of people within a court building or a specific courtroom at a certain time. In Hawai'i some courtrooms routinely schedule all matters to begin at either 8:30 a.m. or 1:30 p.m. In the author's view, this makes sense for courtrooms that handle certain matters, usually criminal matters, in which one or two attorneys represent the government or all defendants, for many short hearings. In the author's view, however, such scheduling practices do not make sense when many attorneys representing different parties are required to sit in a courtroom for many hours. In the United States, many attorneys bill their clients by the hour. This means that in some courtrooms, various clients are being billed many thousands of dollars just to have their attorneys sit around and wait for their cases to be called. This creates an access to justice issue, as clients have limited budgets for legal representation. Thus, clients can exhaust their attorneys' fees budgets just for having their attorneys sit around and wait. Whether or not attorneys are billing their time by the hour, however, when attorneys are waiting around, they are not able to work on other matters. This also affects access to justice. Therefore, with the exception noted above, the author strongly believes all courts should schedule matters at appropriately staggered times to avoid attorney wait time.

[9] *See* Hawai'i State Judiciary 'Oral Arguments Schedule'. https://www.courts.state.hi.us/courts/oral_arguments/oral_arguments_schedule. Accessed 9 July 2021. These video remote oral arguments have continued regularly since May of 2020. Only the Chief Justice, the bailiff, and court clerk are situated in the actual courtroom. The other four justices, including the author, participate remotely from their own chambers using computers with cameras and microphones. Attorneys participate remotely, usually from their own offices. These oral arguments are conducted similarly to live proceedings. The main difference in Hawai'i is in the remote oral arguments, the four associate justices manually raise their hands or use the "raised hand" reaction function and wait for the Chief Justice's acknowledgment before posing questions to attorneys. This differs from live oral arguments, in which all justices independently pose questions. The author understands that some other state appellate courts continue to have justices independently ask questions during remote oral arguments, instead of waiting to be acknowledged by the chief or presiding justice or judge.

able to observe the oral arguments of our court. The technology allows observers to see and hear the justices, and through closed-captioning, read the attorneys' arguments and the questions posed by the justices.

2.3 *Trial Court Proceedings*

From the spring of 2020, Hawai'i trial courts also resumed some hearings through use of remote videoconferencing technology.[10] As discussed by Chief Justice Recktenwald in his January 27, 2021 State of the Judiciary Address,[11] the Hawai'i Judiciary went from essentially no use of Zoom or WebEx in March of 2020, to conducting more than 128,000 trial court proceedings on those platforms statewide between August and December.[12] As also noted by the Chief Justice, for those without internet access, the Judiciary helped ensure that the digital divide would not be a barrier to justice, by opening a remote hearing kiosk in the Supreme Court Law Library, as well as by creating a guide to online access and a map of free Wi-Fi hotspots.[13]

Thus, in many trial courtrooms across Hawai'i, some proceedings are now being conducted via videoconferencing platforms. Some trial court proceedings, however, are not amenable to being conducted remotely, and have remained on hold. Under Hawai'i constitutional law, defendants charged with crimes have the right to be present in the courtroom and confront the witnesses against them. Thus, unless a defendant waives this constitutional right, in criminal cases, evidentiary proceedings involving witnesses cannot be conducted remotely. And even in civil cases, which do not implicate the constitutional right to confrontation, jury trials were completely suspended until recently because they require bringing many people together. With the increased percentage of Hawai'i's population becoming vaccinated[14] and with

[10] It appears some Hawai'i trial judges have also expanded upon or begun the use of telephone conference calls to conduct short status conferences or hearings. From May 4, 2020, the United States Supreme Court has been conducting its oral arguments through telephone conference calls. *See* Williams [7].

[11] Hawai'i Senate, 'State of the judiciary address' (27 January 2021). https://www.youtube.com/watch?v=QX85omB8UTw. Accessed 9 July 2021.

[12] Statistics were not kept until August 2020. As of March of 2021, this number has increased to almost 200,000 proceedings.

[13] Information regarding remote hearings and links for various courtrooms are available on the Hawai'i Judiciary's website at https://www.courts.state.hi.us/remote-court-hearings-via-zoom-or-webex. Accessed 9 July 2021.

[14] As of May 24, 2021, 65.3% of Hawai'i's population had received at least one vaccination dose and 46.9% were fully vaccinated, compared to 49.5 and 39.9% of all Americans. *See* State of Hawai'i 'Hawaii's Economic Improvement Accelerating' (*News*, 26 May 2021). http://dbedt.hawaii.gov/blog/21-18/. Accessed 9 July 2021.

the number of new Covid-19 cases declining,[15] jury trials resumed in Hawai'i state courts in November 2020, but only by using a few large courtrooms for the jury selection process to ensure adequate social distancing. This has limited the number of jury trials that can proceed.

3 The Future of Remote Proceedings in Courts

3.1 Advantages of Remote Proceedings

Before the Covid-19 pandemic, the Conference of Chief Justices (of U.S. states and territories) encouraged U.S. judges to "promote the use of remote audio and video services for case hearings and case management meetings" in civil cases as part of a broader set of reforms to promote access to justice.[16] The Conference of Chief Justices has called for combining video proceedings with enhanced services for self-represented litigants, including internet portals and stand-alone kiosks to facilitate access to court services, simplified court forms, and real-time court assistance over the internet and phone.

The Brennan Center for Justice report regarding the "Impact of Video Proceedings on Fairness and Access to Justice in Courts"[17] points out that videoconferencing technology can reduce the time and expense associated with traveling, transportation, childcare, and other day-to-day costs that individuals incur when they go to court. The report also highlights costs associated with going to court for relatively low-stakes proceedings, such as for minor traffic infraction proceedings, which can be avoided through remote court proceedings.

These advantages of video conferenced court proceedings have also been seen in Hawai'i. As Chief Justice Recktenwald pointed out in his January 27, 2021 address, Hawai'i has actually seen court appearances increase for online traffic infraction hearings, as many people welcome the convenience of appearing remotely through computers or smart phones at home or at work, rather than having to incur the time and expense associated with traveling to a brick-and-mortar courthouse or having to arrange for care for children or family members.

And with respect to oral arguments before the Hawai'i Supreme Court, remote arguments have also had the advantage of not requiring attorneys, especially attorneys that reside on other islands, to incur the time and expense of traveling to the courthouse in Honolulu. Also, through online links making the arguments easily accessible to the public, many people, especially those living on other islands, have

[15] *See* Google search, 'COVID cases in Hawaii graph'. https://www.google.com/search?q=covid+cases+in+hawaii+graph&rlz=1C1GCEU_enUS864US864&oq=covid+cases+in+hawaii+graph&aqs=chrome..69i57j0i22i30l3j0i390l4.8263j0j4&sourceid=chrome&ie=UTF-8. Accessed 9 July 2021.

[16] *See* NCSC [3].

[17] *See* Bannon and Adelstein [1].

been able to observe oral arguments, some probably for the first time. For example, for one argument in a case arising out of the island of Maui, there were about 500 observers, hundreds more than could have been accommodated within the actual courtroom.

The reality is that not only in Hawai'i, but throughout the world, people are becoming more and more accustomed to doing business online, and for some types of proceedings, remote court proceedings make eminent sense.[18]

3.2 *Impediments to, or Concerns Regarding, Remote Court Proceedings*

There are, however, disadvantages or impediments to remote court proceedings, some of which are not apparent at first blush. First, as pointed out above, without an effective waiver of a defendant's constitutional right to confront witnesses, remote proceedings are not possible in evidentiary proceedings in Hawai'i criminal cases. For other types of proceedings, although there may not be constitutional prohibitions, there are other concerns that should be considered.

For example, an article regarding "[t]he legal and technical danger in moving criminal courts online" by Jason Tashea[19] points out that "[i]n the rush to manage the fallout of the pandemic, courts overlooked a body of evidence showing that virtual hearings are connected to potential constitutional violations and worse outcomes for defendants." According to this article, a 2014 study concluded that defendants in Baltimore, Maryland, were denied their constitutional right to counsel when appearing over video during a bail hearing because attorneys were denied the ability to speak with their clients.

This article also points out that in-person testimony is seen as more believable than virtual testimony for various reasons, including technology connection issues, an inability to assess non-verbal cues, and also because videoconferencing technology can filter out voice frequencies associated with human emotion.

Professor Tashea also explains that 82% of defendants facing state court felony charges qualify for public defender representation, which means they are from an income group with less access to the technology and high-speed internet required to attend a virtual courtroom. According to him, "[w]hile virtual hearings are touted as a way to improve access for individuals in rural America, that will never happen as long as poor, rural Americans lack equitable access to the internet." Hawai'i also has significant issues regarding internet connectivity for certain socio-economic communities.

---

[18] One recent article also points out the possible benefit of initially allowing potential jurors to appear remotely to ascertain whether they have medical, financial, scheduling, or other hardships with respect to jury duty. *See* Ratzan [4].

[19] *See* Tashea [6].

The Brennan Center for Justice report[20] also discusses issues with remote court proceedings. This report posits that while some U.S. court leaders suggest making expanded use of remote technology permanent, there are still important questions about how litigants' rights and their access to justice may be impacted.

According to the Brennan Center, one study examining the use of closed-circuit television for bail hearings in Cook County, Illinois, found that judges imposed substantially higher bond amounts during video proceedings; this study caused the county to voluntarily return to live bail hearings.

The Brennan Center discusses another study examining the use of video technology in immigration proceedings, which found that detained respondents were more likely to be deported because they were less likely to take advantage of procedures that might help them, such as applying for relief and obtaining counsel. This study also highlighted problems in effective and confidential communications with counsel.

The Brennan Center also points out that in addition to the "digital divide" issues highlighted by the Tashea article, people with disabilities may also require special technology in order to engage in remote court proceedings. The report also discusses challenges faced by self-represented litigants in navigating the legal system, especially for those who do not speak English or have limited English proficiency; the report discusses a research finding that approximately 30% of litigants in immigration court who used an interpreter appeared to misunderstand what was happening, either due to misinterpretation or inadequate interpretation.

The Brennan Center concludes that "although videoconferencing technology has been a valuable tool during the Covid-19 pandemic, existing scholarship suggests reasons to be cautious about the expansion or long-term adoption of remote court proceedings."

A law review article by Susan Bandes and Neal Feigenson also provides critical information for courts considering use of remote court proceedings; it provides extensive analyses and details on how evaluating demeanor online differs from in-court credibility determinations.[21] As explained by the authors, whether or not such emphasis is justified, the U.S. court system relies heavily on a person's in-court demeanor to evaluate credibility and make decisions.[22] Pre-pandemic experiences with partly virtual hearings, such as parole or asylum hearings in which an applicant

---

[20] *See* Bannon and Adelstein (n 17).

[21] Bandes and Feigenson [2, p. 1275].

[22] The authors discuss the capital sentencing hearing of Dzhokhar Tsarnaev, the Boston Marathon bomber, "whose body language, including his beard-fiddling and his tendency to lean back in his chair, was perceived as arrogant and inappropriately informal" and point out that although "there is no evidence that remorse can be accurately assessed via facial expressions, jurors tend to believe they are well equipped to make just such an evaluation in a matter of life or death" and that judges and the media are not exempt from these beliefs. The authors point out studies showing "that judges and other fact-finder's employ cues to complex states like remorse in an inconsistent or even contradictory manner, so that one judge may rely on a given behavior as indicative of remorse while another believes the same behavior indicates lack of remorse."

appears via videoconference, already indicated that witnesses and litigants are evaluated more negatively in virtual courts than in in-person hearings or trials. Additional studies have shown it is harder for decision-makers to empathize with those testifying on screen. The authors indicate this could be due to reduced eye contact, as many online participants look at the screen to see how their words are being received and because the images of others' faces are more interesting. Viewers may construe this apparent lack of eye contact or the shifting of the eyes back and forth as signs of uncertainty or even dishonesty. Also, an online speaker's sense of uncertainty about whether they are being paid attention to and understood can affect demeanor while testifying, which decision-makers may then construe as a lack of confidence or lack of interactivity, either of which may be misread to indicate diminished credibility.

These authors also point out an extremely important concern regarding videoconference appearances on perceptions of credibility: "Reading demeanor across racial lines is particularly fraught." According to the authors, "this is in part an artifact of selective empathy–the difficulty we all have attending to and interpreting cues from members of other cultural, racial, or ethnic groups." Empathy is negatively affected by difference, and the problem is greatly exacerbated when the subject is Black, in part due to "perception of a linkage among blackness, criminality, and dangerousness." In terms of difference, the authors also point out that "juvenile status and mental or emotional disabilities can confound the evaluation of demeanor."

The authors also point out other differences that can negatively impact credibility perceptions. Connectivity issues not obvious to others can cause delays in responding. Fidgeting due to discomfort, reduced confidence while testifying due to the lack of supportive friends or family members in the courtroom, distractions and increased anxiety caused by seeing oneself on screen, and the casual, familiar environment of the home or office resulting in dress or behavior inappropriate in the physical courtroom, can all negatively affect perceptions of credibility.

The authors also point out how cognitive demands on decision-makers participating in extended remote proceedings can also affect demeanor evaluations. A judge's ability to concentrate on a witness or party can be affected by the simultaneous on-screen appearance of other participants, offering a constant source of distraction. The authors posit that the increased mental effort judges are required to allocate to the virtual courtroom may bias their impressions of witnesses' and parties' demeanors, especially if they find it hard to watch and listen due to poor video or audio quality.

The article also points out that judges may be unaware of how features of the videoconferencing medium influence their evaluations and decisions. Movie directors know that showing faces in close-ups allows audiences to identify emotions more easily, but faces that appear too close can be perceived as occupying personal space, which can be regarded as inappropriate, annoying, or threatening. Also, witnesses whose faces appear smaller can be perceived as less important. Camera angles can also affect credibility evaluations; for example, filmmakers are taught that high-angle shots tend to make the person depicted appear smaller or weaker, while low-angle shots make the person seem more significant and powerful, and studies have found that faces seen from below are perceived more positively than faces seen from above.

The authors also discuss the importance of the feeling of co-presence that exists in the courtroom, the sense of being together with others in the world, and that this feeling is difficult to achieve in a remote proceeding, especially when real-time audio and video are impaired or disrupted. Also, "reciprocation of gaze" is generally important for feeling engaged with another, but genuine eye contact is not possible in a remote proceeding. The authors stress that the diminished sense of co-presence affects a judge's ability to empathize with a witness or party. In other words, physical co-presence is critical to empathetic engagement, but cannot happen in a remote proceeding.

Courts considering remote proceedings need to carefully review these issues in evaluating what type of court proceedings should allow remote appearances and steps to take to mitigate the kinds of concerns discussed in this section.

4 The Future of Remote Court Proceedings

In Hawai'i, the Judiciary's Committee on Operational Solutions is currently studying whether remote court proceedings should continue after the pandemic for certain types of proceedings, and will undoubtedly consider concerns regarding remote proceedings revealed by various studies and articles, including those above. As remote court proceedings proliferated worldwide due to Covid-19, additional studies will be published analyzing the advantages and disadvantages of such proceedings.

Although there is good reason for caution, however, there appear to be certain types of proceedings for which remote court proceedings should probably continue after the effects of the pandemic have completely or largely subsided.

The first is appellate oral arguments that only involve attorneys making legal arguments. In the U.S., such oral arguments do not involve witness credibility determinations, which is a significant area of concern regarding remote hearings. Although the default should be in-person oral arguments, remote oral arguments should be allowed if at least one attorney who would have to travel some distance to the courthouse expresses preference for a remote hearing. If a remote oral argument is allowed, however, the court should require that all attorneys appear remotely. The perception of unfairness of having one attorney argue in the courtroom while another argues remotely is, in the author's view, too strong to allow that to occur. A court itself should also have discretion to order a remote oral argument even if not requested by an attorney.[23]

[23] For example, in Hawai'i, when any one of the five justices is not available by reason of retirement or recusal for a conflict of interest, that justice is replaced by a general jurisdiction trial court judge who sits as a substitute justice by designation for a specific case. Before Covid-19, because oral arguments were almost always conducted at the Hawai'i Supreme Court's courtroom on the island of O'ahu, only O'ahu judges were appointed as substitute justices. After remote oral arguments were instituted in May 2020, however, judges from the other islands were also able to be appointed as substitute justices. In the author's view, this practice should continue and. as such, oral arguments in cases involving substitute justices from other islands should be conducted remotely.

The second type of proceedings for which remote proceedings should be considered to be allowed to continue after the pandemic is for relatively low-stakes proceedings, such as minor traffic infraction proceedings, for which the maximum penalty is almost always a relatively minor monetary fine.[24] In these cases, a litigant should have the option of appearing remotely or in person in court for a scheduled hearing. The Hawai'i experience during the pandemic shows that many litigants prefer being able to appear remotely for such proceedings through use of their home or work computers or their smartphones, without incurring the time and expense associated with travel, transportation, childcare, or other possible costs.

The third type of proceeding which, in the author's view, remote proceedings should be allowed is for pre-trial or post-trial status conferences or hearings involving attorneys arguing legal or procedural issues only, in which an attorney, who would have to travel some distance to the courthouse, expresses preference for a remote hearing. Again, if a remote oral hearing or conference is allowed, however, due to the perception of unfairness, this author believes the court should require that all attorneys appear remotely. A recent article, however, also points out the importance of in-person conferences even for status hearings, as "court conferences are invaluable in how they get lawyers in the same room to build relationships and connections with one another."[25] The article aptly points out that court systems cannot handle the volume of cases presented without settlements and that "[i]t is much easier to talk about a case and settle a matter with someone if you have seen them face-to-face, interacted with them, and forged a connection with them."

The real issue regarding the future of remote court proceedings is whether they should be permitted for evidentiary hearings that require witness credibility determinations. The studies and articles discussed above show serious concerns regarding credibility determinations when witness testimony is received through remote technology. Importantly, judges or jurors may not be aware of how remote proceedings can affect their witness credibility determinations or their assessment of the strength of a party's case. Thus, in this author's opinion, remote proceedings should be considered for evidentiary hearings or trials only in special situations. These situations could include when a litigant, witness, or even an attorney, would have to travel some distance and bear significant costs to get them to a courthouse, or where a witness is not able to be subpoenaed to appear in a court, but is important to a party's case, and is willing to testify remotely from another location.[26]

In other words, in this author's opinion, remote proceedings involving evidentiary matters should only be allowed to provide access to justice, whether in civil

[24] The author fully recognizes that this is a vague term, and that the amount of a "relatively minor monetary fine" differs from person to person, but the litigant should be able to make that determination and decide whether to appear in person.

[25] *See* Rothman [5].

[26] In the U.S., a court could consider whether to allow such live remote testimony or to instead require the witness to appear through a videotaped deposition. Remote testimony would appear to have the advantage of being adjusted to be more relevant or responsive to evidence that has been received up to that point in a trial.

or criminal cases,[27] where costs or logistics would prohibit presentation of evidence important to a party. In a jurisdiction like Hawai'i, the most remote populated land mass in the world, even inter-island travel is conducted by air, and at significant cost. In the author's view, the default for evidentiary hearings, even in civil cases, should always be for live testimony, not only due to the concerns expressed in the studies above, but also due to the technological glitches that invariably arise in remote proceedings, the difficulty of conducting side-bar conferences with attorneys, problems with authenticating exhibits, and the requirement of providing public access to court proceedings, which are complicated when various attorneys and witnesses are in different locations. Courts should carefully consider these concerns and possible mitigation measures before allowing remote proceedings.

5 Conclusion

The Covid-19 pandemic caused many courts throughout the world to turn to videoconferencing for some types of court proceedings. Remote technology allowed many courts to continue critical, essential work. As courts consider the future of remote court proceedings, however, they should consider social science studies regarding effects of remote court appearances, particularly those affecting credibility and demeanor determinations. There are some court proceedings not involving witness or party credibility determinations for which remote court appearances should be allowed. But remote court appearances should be allowed even when witness or party credibility are at issue, if they are a means of achieving access to justice that otherwise would not exist. In recent years, judges in Hawai'i and in other jurisdictions are being educated on the effects of cognitive biases, including implicit or unconscious biases based on various socio-economic categories. Judges should also be educated regarding the effects of remote appearances on perceptions of credibility and demeanor. If parties and litigants are permitted to appear via remote videoconferencing, courts should also provide instructions regarding connectivity, audio, lighting, camera angle, gaze, appropriate attire, and other issues that may affect perceptions of their credibility.

[27] In the U.S., due to a criminal defendant's constitutional right to confrontation, such remote testimony could only be proffered by the defendant, unless the defendant waives the right for a government witness.

References

1. Bannon, A., Adelstein, J.: The impact of video proceedings on fairness and access to justice in court. Brennan Centre (2020). https://www.brennancenter.org/our-work/research-reports/impact-video-proceedings-fairness-and-access-justice-court. Accessed 9 July 2021
2. Bandes, S.A., Feigenson, N.: Virtual trials: necessity, invention, and the evolution of the courtroom. Buff L Rev **68**, 1275 (2020)
3. NCSC: Call to action: achieving civil justice for all. https://www.ncsc.org/__data/assets/pdf_file/0029/19289/call-to-action_-achieving-civil-justice-for-all.pdf. Accessed 9 July 2021
4. Ratzan, S.: Pandemic-era jury trial innovations may be here to stay. LAW 360 (2021). https://www.law360.com/articles/1386079/pandemic-era-jury-trial-innovations-may-be-here-to-stay. Accessed 9 July 2021
5. Rothman, J.: In-person court conferences should not be completely eliminated. Above the Law (2021). https://abovethelaw.com/2021/05/in-person-court-conferences-should-not-be-completely-eliminated/. Accessed 9 July 2021
6. Tashea, J.: The legal and technical danger in moving criminal courts online. Tech stream (2020). https://www.brookings.edu/techstream/the-legal-and-technical-danger-in-moving-criminal-courts-online/. Accessed 9 July 2021
7. Williams, P.: Supreme Court makes history with oral arguments by phone. But it's business as usual for justices. NBC News, Washington (2020). https://www.nbcnews.com/politics/supreme-court/supreme-court-makes-history-oral-arguments-phone-it-s-business-n1199446. Accessed 9 July 2021

The New Normal in the Legal Profession: Embracing Technology

Shreeyash U. Lalit and Raveena Lalit

Abstract The Indian legal profession was pushed to a challenge when it had to cope with the pandemic yet ensure that there were no hindrances in access to justice. This chapter will explore how Indian courts have adapted to technology during the pandemic and the possible way forward in this technological shift for the profession in the long run. It will reflect on aspects such as live-streaming of court proceedings, the Supreme Court's e-committee and their initiatives, e-filings, virtual appearances and how these changes have impacted those in the bar and the bench over the last year. For instance, live-streaming has been seen as a welcome initiative, with the Supreme Court on the brink of finalising procedures in relation to live-streaming of its proceedings as well. It aims to comment on the possibility of a sustained adoption of aspects such as use of AI, virtual appearances and e-filings, in a post-pandemic world.

1 Introduction and Background

The Indian legal landscape has largely been paper-heavy and driven by traditional modes of operation. Until recently, lawyers were expected to file their submissions in print versions, physically with the registry of any court. This necessarily meant bulky paper-books for each matter and no centralised system to manage them.

Until before the pandemic, technology was used sparingly across the legal profession in India despite the fact that the computerisation of courts project commenced in 2010. The primary technological headway until before the pandemic was limited to the case information system project. Court websites were used to upload notices, rosters, cause lists, final judgements, daily orders and provide the status of a pending

S. U. Lalit (✉)
14 Setalvad Chambers, Opposite Supreme Court of India, Delhi 110001, India
e-mail: office@lalitchambers.com

R. Lalit
Shardul Amarchand Mangaldas & Co., Amarchand Towers, 216 Okhla Ph. III, Delhi 110020, India
e-mail: raveenasethia@gmail.com

C. Raj Kumar and S. G. Sreejith (eds.), *Legal Education and Legal Profession During and After COVID-19*, https://doi.org/10.1007/978-981-19-2568-9_15

case, among other information.[1] Similarly, technology was also used by way of the National Judicial Data Grid which identifies case pendency, providing consolidated figures of pendency in all trial and appellate courts as the statistical data is automatically updated every day and contains pending civil and criminal cases segregated into categories up to 2 years, between 2 and 5 years, between 5 and 10 years and more than 10 years.[2]

Virtual courts, and associated processes, have found recognition and regulation in jurisprudence too. In *State of Maharashtra v. Dr. Praful Desai,* the Supreme Court allowed video conferencing for the recording of evidence.[3] Courts have allowed video conferencing on health conditions[4] and geographical distance.[5] However, parties cannot resolve matrimonial conflict through video conferencing,[6] barring one case where it was allowed in January 2021.[7]

As of April 2017, only four High Courts across the country (Delhi, Bombay, Madhya Pradesh, and Punjab and Haryana) had adopted e-filing of cases.[8] Further, only limited strides were made using technology to advance access to justice using technology. For example, the vulnerable victim protection programme in Delhi used video conferencing to protect vulnerable victims of heinous crimes such as rape or young children from facing the accused, prior to the pandemic. E-filings were permitted only for arbitration matters in Delhi District Courts.[9] In addition, only one High Court actually initiated live-streaming of court proceedings prior to the pandemic, stating that a matter which had national ramifications should be streamed live.[10]

Therefore, despite the need of the hour and realisation that legal proceedings should be streamlined using technology, limited strides were made. The pandemic has proven to be a litmus test for Indian courts in terms of adopting and adapting to technology, while making courts more accessible to all. The pandemic has also proven to be a blessing in disguise, as courts have been forced to undertake video conferencing as an alternative to regular open-court hearings, thereby reducing the latent inertia and reservations that judges and lawyers had towards virtual proceedings.

E-filings have been permitted in several courts across the country, which have eased the administrative process for litigants and lawyers. For example, earlier, while affidavits and documents would need to be couriered by a litigant from his/her remote location to the lawyer's office; now, the litigant only needs to scan and send them online. This has greatly eased the burden and helped streamline e-filing procedures.

---

[1] Reference [12].

[2] Reference [38].

[3] *State of Maharashtra v. Dr. Praful Desai* (2003) 4 SCC 601.

[4] *Alcatel India Limited and Anr. v. Koshika Telecom Limited* 2004 (76) DRJ 524.

[5] *Bodala Murali Krishna v. Smt. Bodala Prathima* AIR 2007 AP 43.

[6] *Santini v. Vijaya Venkatesh* (2018) 1 SCC 62.

[7] *Anjali Chauhan v. Navin Chauhan Review Petition* (Civil) 472 of 2018.

[8] Reference [17].

[9] Jain [27].

[10] Reference [3].

Virtual hearings have been adopted across a large number of courts, with several High Courts and District Courts issuing standard operating procedures (SOPs) to regulate the manner in which these proceedings should be conducted. With these SOPs and through trial-and-error, over time, the manner in which these proceedings should be conducted has also become more efficient. Live-streaming of court proceedings was also initiated on an experimental basis and may be implemented across the board in time. In other words, during the pandemic, courts found a way to use technology to their advantage in terms of administrative tasks and for conducting hearings.

These measures have collectively transformed the manner in which legal submissions are recorded, and proceedings take place—changing the landscape from a predominantly traditional model to an evolving, technology-driven one. However, there's still a long way to go in terms of using technology to its full capacity in legal proceedings, while balancing the interests of all parties and ensuring that there's no compromise in access to, or deliverance of, justice.

The sections below highlight the in-ways made during the pandemic and provide recommendations on the way forward in terms of implementing technology further across the legal profession.

2 E-filings, Court Proceedings and Resources

The initial significant procedural changes to take place during the pandemic were the introduction of e-filings across several courts and introduction of virtual hearings. These changes have helped significantly transform the manner in which legal proceedings take place and have helped provide a primer to better assimilate how technology may be used in the long run to streamline and digitise filings and proceedings. However, there is still a long way to go before a long-term and sustainable system is set to provide continuity to the progress made during the pandemic. Further, India is not yet at a stage where access to technology is available at the grassroot level. As such, while the pandemic has made small strides towards cost-effective access to justice, several impediments remain.

2.1 E-Filings

The Supreme Court has introduced a very comprehensive system of e-filings, detailing the format to be followed for various types of cases. Given the file sizes, it has introduced a system whereby the file can be uploaded in parts, under different headings.[11] This has made the filing system easier across the board.

[11] Reference [16].

Similarly, the Delhi High Court has also constituted a dedicated e-filing portal and an FAQs page to answer questions in relation to e-filings.[12] Recently, it even directed that caveat be filed electronically across District Courts.[13] District Courts across the country have also adopted e-filings, with the third phase of the e-filing project underway.[14] The e-filing portal, since 12 April 2021, allows for electronic recording of oath, digital signing of documents, filing multiple applications together and exchange of files across advocates.[15]

From lawyers and litigants, e-filings have resulted in greater access to justice, given that a litigant may share documents with his advocate electronically from anywhere, and the advocate may be able to draft and file pleadings at any time and from a different location.

The primary issue for judges is that physical files need to be scanned and added to the electronic record in order to provide a streamlined process of virtual hearings, which is perhaps why courts such as the Bombay High Court require both physical as well as e-copies of a petition/application to be filed with the Registry, since 2011.[16] The Rajasthan High Court requires that physical copies also be supplied along with the electronic filings, till such time as all the requirements of paperless courts are achieved.[17] However, due to the second wave of the pandemic, the Rajasthan High Court relaxed the requirement by mandating that the hard copies may be filed within seven days of regular court functioning.[18]

Madras High Court has recently formulated the Madras High Court E-Filing Rules, 2020 which clearly define and set out the procedures and practice directions for electronic filing.[19] The Madras High Court does not mandate physical filing of hard copies along with electronic filings.

Tribunals like NCLAT required that hard copies be accompanied with electronic filings in accordance with the procedure under the NCLAT Rules, 2016.[20] Recently, the Bombay High Court issued notice on a petition requiring the NCLAT to do away with the requirements of filing hard copies.[21] As a result, the NCLAT had to release a notification which temporarily relaxed the requirement of filing hard copies.[22]

In addition, for certain matters, records are only available physically in remote grassroot-level government departments or offices. Access to such records is limited,

---

[12] Reference [19].

[13] *Tarang Gupta v. District and Sessions Judge (HQ), Tis Hazari's Court* WP (C) 5746/2021.

[14] Ministry of Law and Justice, 'Justice Chandrachud inaugurates Judgments & Orders portal and e-filing 3.0 module' (*Press Information Bureau, Government of India,* 12 April 2021). https://www.pib.gov.in/PressReleasePage.aspx?PRID=171115. Accessed 9 July 2021 [35].

[15] Reference [18].

[16] Reference [24].

[17] Reference [20].

[18] Reference [40].

[19] Reference [34].

[20] Reference [37].

[21] Kashyap [30].

[22] Reference [39].

given that there has not been any consistent practice of saving electronic copies of files over the years. This has proven to be an impediment to filings, given that the underlying records are inaccessible during the pandemic to substantiate the same. Therefore, there is still a long way to go before a holistic system of filings and access to underlying documents is established.

2.2 Court Proceedings and Resources

During the pandemic, several courts instituted measures to conduct virtual hearings, using a myriad of portals such as Zoom, Microsoft Teams, Vidyo, Jitsi, etc. A link for the virtual hearing of the day is uploaded on the website of the court or circulated to advocates whose matters are listed on a given day, and court proceedings take place through these portals.

Over time, through trial and error, virtual proceedings have been streamlined by the Supreme Court to ensure minimal interruptions.[23] Advocates appearing for a certain matter are able to direct the bench to any filed submission or update through screen sharing, if required, as an attempt to create the same impact one would have had, upon handing over a note or document to the bench during a physical hearing. As recounted by Justice Pratibha M Singh, the split screen option and the screen sharing option have been a great boon for lawyers and judges alike.[24]

The Supreme Court in *Prashant Bhushan and Anr.* noted that.

> [T]he total number of sittings that the various benches had from 23.3.2020 till 4.8.2020 is 879. During this period, the Court has heard 12748 matters. In the said period, this Court has dealt with 686 writ petitions filed under Article 32 of the Constitution of India,[25]

and the number has only grown substantially since then with all categories of matters being listed for virtual hearings as courts have learned to better adapt to the change in proceedings. According to the Law Ministry, the Supreme Court is a world leader, having conducted 52,353 virtual hearings as of February 2021.[26] District Courts have heard approximately 45.37 lakh cases while High Courts have heard 20.60 lakh cases during the pandemic as well.[27]

At the same time, it must be acknowledged that the pendency of cases has surely increased. From the statistics available on the Supreme Court website,[28] as of 1 April 2020, the Supreme Court was facing a pendency of 61,142 cases with 41,286 admission matters and 19,856 regular hearing matters. However, that number has increased by 10% in the whole year. As of 1 May 2021, the Supreme Court is facing

---

23 Reference [6].

24 Reference [28].

25 *Prashant Bhushan and Anr.* (2020) SCC Online SC 407.

26 Thakur [46].

27 Ibid.

28 Monthly Pending Cases: Supreme Court. https://main.sci.gov.in/statistics. Accessed 9 July 2021.

a pendency of 67,898 cases with 49,015 admission matters and 18,883 regular hearing matters.

Judges have also commenced referring to their e-resources to locate precedents and cross-refer to citations in pleadings. This is a shift for most members of the judiciary, who traditionally prefer physical copies of legal journals.[29]

Similarly, prior to the pandemic, there was a physical limitation in terms of access to counsel. In most cases, a local advocate would be briefed to appear in a matter, given that the advocate would have to physically file any submission and appear before the court. However, during the pandemic, an advocate situated in any part of the world may be briefed on a matter by a litigant from any other part and be able to effectively appear before any bench.[30] This has significantly aided in providing additional access to courts, and broadened the horizon for several advocates, who have appeared across jurisdictions in the past year.

While virtual hearings have resulted in ensuring that there is no impediment in terms of 'work as usual', they have surely restricted an advocate's ability to effectively utilise his oratory. During the second wave, only extremely urgent matters relating to public health and safety, law and order, and criminal proceedings, etc. have been taken up, restricting access to justice for other litigants.[31] Several judges,[32] lawyers[33] and administrative officials have also been victims of COVID-19, due to which there have been multiple challenges for the courts to deal with, while ensuring that there is a continuous, accessible platform for access to justice.

There have also been issues with the virtual hearing links being shared with third parties. In November 2020, the Supreme Court has cautioned advocates against sharing links with outsiders.[34] The Delhi High Court has also been categorical that links cannot be shared with other persons.[35] Despite that, there have been several issues as was recently seen when Delhi High Court imposed costs of INR 20 lakhs on Juhi Chawla for having shared the virtual hearing links with her fans.[36]

This would lead us to the larger question whether virtual hearings ought to be live-streamed, however, as is evident from the aforementioned issues, there is still a long way to go for virtual hearings and proceedings to provide a systematic response to transforming the legal profession. There is a need for proper guidelines and rules to ensure victim protection, access to justice, balance of convenience and sanctity of procedure. These issues will also be discussed in the sections to follow.

---

[29] Khanna et al. [31].

[30] Dave and Vyas [10].

[31] Reference [1].

[32] Dutt [11].

[33] Reference [2].

[34] Reference [5].

[35] Reference [25].

[36] Gunasekar [22].

3 Live-Streaming

One measure taken during the pandemic was live-streaming of court proceedings, on an experimental basis. On 26 October 2020, the Gujarat High Court became the first court to live-stream judicial proceedings, through its YouTube channel.[37] In less than 40 h, the stream which was recording the proceedings before Division Bench No. 1 (comprising of Chief Justice Vikram Nath and Justice J.B. Pardiwala) was viewed 106,342 times and was 'liked' 3900 times. A press release was issued by the Gujarat High Court stating that the live stream was on a trial basis, with the modalities being considered.[38] Subsequently, the proceedings of 27 October 2020 were also live-streamed through YouTube.[39] Within 7 h of being streamed, the video was viewed 24,647 times and received 1100 likes.

Following the Gujarat High Court's initiative, Attorney General for India, Mr. K. K. Venugopal also urged the Supreme Court of India to consider live-streaming its proceedings, in light of the judgement in *Swapnil Tripathi v. Secretary-General, Supreme Court of India* (Swapnil Tripathi).[40] In response, erstwhile Chief Justice of India S. A. Bobde noted that he is in favour of live-streaming on a principle basis but is sensitive to the practicalities that surround it.[41] As of 9 April 2021, news report suggested that the Supreme Court e-committee is also on its way to finalise rules for live-streaming.[42]

While the initiative has been welcomed, as is visible through the commendations it has received, and statistically, from the substantial number of 'likes' the videos on YouTube have received, certain questions on technological feasibility and potential misuse remain.[43]

3.1 An Overview of the Decision in **Swapnil Tripathi**

While the issue of video conferencing as an effective tool for dispute resolution was mired in controversy, the Supreme Court had the occasion to consider the question of live-streaming of regular open court proceedings in *Swapnil Tripathi*. The question that arose before the Court was whether the case proceedings in the Supreme Court, which were of '*constitutional importance having an impact on the public at large or a large number of people*', could be live-streamed in a manner which would be easily accessible for public viewing. The Court considered the position on live-streaming in

[37] Reference [21].

[38] Reference [26].

[39] Ibid.

[40] *Swapnil Tripathi v. Supreme Court* (2018) 10 SCC 628.

[41] Thomas [47].

[42] Ojha [41].

[43] Sethia and Lalit [45].

several other jurisdictions, and observed that the requirements of an open court and public access to justice could be traced to Articles 19(1)(a) and 21 of the Constitution.

Notably, while the majority judgement held that the Supreme Court Rules, 2013 would have to be suitably amended in order to provide for a regulatory framework; the concurring judgement of Justice Chandrachud went a step further to provide the requirements of such live-streaming procedures. It provided a list of matters that would be excluded from live-streaming, such as matrimonial disputes, cases involving sensitive issues as in the nature of sexual assault, cases concerning juveniles, etc. Furthermore, it also provided the manner of conducting live-streaming, including the requirement that live-streaming should be done with a delay of two minutes, in order to stop any broadcast that is embarrassing or prevent administration of justice. It also laid down the technical specifications for live-streaming, including the fact that discussions among judges on the bench, or instructions given to administrative staff, or notes taken down by the judge, should not be filmed.

However, what is important to note is that both the majority as well as concurring judgement held that the Supreme Court would have exclusive IP rights, including copyright over the broadcast. Therefore, any reproduction, rebroadcasting, transmission, publication, republication, copying, storage and/or modification of any part(s) of the original broadcast of court proceedings would stand prohibited. The rationale behind permitting live-streaming of proceedings and guidelines chalked out in the *Swapnil Tripathi* decision may be adopted on a wider scale.[44]

3.2 *Position of Courts in Other Jurisdictions and Possible Models That May Be Adopted*

Live-streaming/recording of judicial proceedings is a concept well-recognised in various jurisdictions. The High Court of Australia publishes audio–visual recordings of full-court hearings heard in Canberra, on its website.[45] The terms of use provide that the audio–visual material does not constitute the official record of the Court. This appears to be a measure adopted by the court to prevent misinterpretation of the recordings. Unlike the live-streaming adopted by the Gujarat High Court where the proceedings in every matter called for the day are recorded, the High Court of Australia publishes recordings on a case-by-case basis, and the content of the recordings mostly comprises the submissions made by the parties. The content of the coverage is vetted and recordings are posted usually within a day or two of the hearing.

The Brazilian Supreme Court allows live video and audio broadcast of court proceedings, including the deliberations and voting processes by the judges in court.

---

[44] Ibid.

[45] Reference [23].

The proceedings are streamed through a television channel[46] and radio channels that are managed by the court.

The Canadian Supreme Court allows broadcast and live-streaming of its proceedings. Every archived webcast[47] is accompanied by a summary of the proceeding and also has options to hear the proceedings in French or English. The live-stream and recorded archives are available on the Cable Public Affairs Channel (CPAC),[48] which also broadcasts proceedings in houses of parliament. The CPAC describes itself as '*Canada's only privately-owned, commercial free, not for profit, bilingual licensed television service*'.[49]

The U.K. Supreme Court has issued a practice note which allows for hearings to be live-streamed on its own website with a delay of around one minute and also has a YouTube channel which shows selected broadcasts from the live stream. However, the permission of the President and the Justices of the Supreme Court must be obtained on each occasion.[50]

Therefore, while the initiation of live proceedings has been a welcome step, there are various models from which features may be borrowed to provide a more suitable and sustainable model of ensuring transparency in proceedings and access to justice for the general Indian public.

4 Supreme Court e-committee and Use of Artificial Intelligence

The immediate judicial responses to the COVID-19 pandemic in India included suspending the limitation period and extending interim orders and bail condition orders. Guidelines for holding court hearings through video conferencing, standard operating procedures for urgent hearings and e-filings were adopted to meet the challenges posed by the pandemic. Apart from these, several initiatives were taken by the Supreme Court e-committee and AI committee.

The Supreme Court e-committee was constituted to oversee and implement the e-courts project in India. The e-committee was established in 2004 through an order of the Ministry of Law and Justice in pursuance of a proposal received from the then Chief Justice of India. The e-courts project is a pan India initiative monitored and funded by the Department of Justice, Ministry of Law and Justice, Government of India.

The e-committee has evolved in terms of its roles and responsibilities over the last fifteen years. The objectives of the e-committee include[51]:

---

[46] Reference [43].

[47] Reference [7].

[48] Reference [9].

[49] Reference [8].

[50] *Swapnil Tripathi v Supreme Court* (2018) 10 SCC 628.

[51] Reference [12].

- The Interlinking of all courts across the country.
- IT enablement of the Indian judicial system.
- Enhancing judicial productivity.
- Making the justice delivery system accessible, cost-effective, transparent and accountable.
- Providing citizen-centric services.

During the pandemic, this committee has made vast strides in terms of implementing procedures driven by technology to facilitate access to justice for lawyers as well as litigants, such as[52]:

- Formulating a mobile application.[53]
- Development of a free and open-source software-based case information and management system.
- E-service centres in court complexes.
- Virtual courts for petty traffic offences have been inaugurated with options of either admitting the petty offence and online payment of fine or with an option to contest the case if not admitted.
- Development of a National Judicial Data Grid as a national repository of data relating to pending and disposed of cases in all district, taluka courts and High Courts of the country.
- Introduction of GPS-enabled software application NSTEP to tackle the delay in service of summons.

Phase III of the e-courts project, which commenced post-April 2021, has aimed to transform the legal landscape significantly. Apart from procedures regarding e-filing and providing a common portal to make such filings across courts, the Phase III project also announces the establishment of an intelligent system that enables data-based decision-making for judges and registries when scheduling or prioritising cases and allows for greater predictability and optimisation of the capacity of judges and lawyers.[54]

Importantly, the e-committee, in its Phase III vision document, addresses the key issue in terms of technological adaptation, a discussion that seems to be driven due to the pandemic:

> COVID-19 has amplified the need to strengthen digital capabilities and has provided the stepping stone to an unprecedented opportunity for change...Given the large, diverse and constantly evolving needs of different users and the constant evolution of technology, administration of justice must not just remain as a sovereign function, but evolve as a service: to mitigate, contain and resolve disputes by the courts and a range of public, private and citizen sector actors. To achieve this, it is critical to adopt an 'ecosystem approach' that supports scale, speed, and sustainability. Rather than focus on developing all the solutions itself, Phase III will curate the right environment and infrastructure for solutions to emerge rapidly from

52 Reference [15].

53 Reference [14].

54 E-committee Supreme Court of India (n 51).

> the ecosystem to create a multiplier effect for change. It can achieve greater adoption and impact by leveraging the collective strength of the ecosystem.[55]

It has provided certain measures such as constituting the Digital Courts Technology Office and improving hardware solutions to bridge this technological gap, and hopefully, with infrastructure support, it may be possible to digitise the processes further.

Similarly, the Artificial Intelligence (AI) committee of the Supreme Court was constituted in 2019. The use of technology to translate Supreme Court languages is also underway to ensure better access to information. The aim is to now use AI to aid legal research for judges. with the objective of reducing pendency and enhancing the efficiency of the system.

In the last two years, the Supreme Court's AI committee has already launched and piloted a neural *translation* tool (SUVAAS), and more recently, a court *administration* tool (SUPACE). In view of this, it becomes abundantly clear that the talk of integrating AI into the justice system is not a futuristic endeavour, decades from now.[56] According to Manthan Trivedi:

> SUPACE is one of a kind solution that is fully customisable and behaves uniquely like its user. The AI within it adapts and adopts user behaviour based on incremental usage of the platform. This is one of the first examples of mass customisation in the world.

These initiatives certainly seem to suggest that the Supreme Court is increasingly looking into integrating AI and technology to deliver justice more effectively.

5 Recommendations and Way Forward

Firstly, by virtue of Article 145 of the Constitution of India, the Supreme Court is required to pronounce judgements in open court. This mandate is also followed in section 327 of the Criminal Procedure Code, 1973 (CrPC) as well as section 153B of the Code of Civil Procedure, 1908 (CPC). However, going by the experience of Indian courts with virtual hearings, it is not possible to countenance the idea that virtual courts are not 'open courts'.

Secondly, every litigant faces heightened costs during the process of litigation. This was also observed by the 128th Law Commission Report in 1998, which noted that costs of litigation were 'back-breaking' for the ordinary litigants. Examples of such costs associated with litigation include costs related to filing, advocate fee, summoning of a witness, travel costs to observe the matter, etc.[57] In this backdrop, virtual hearings and proceedings offer a more cost-effective mechanism to provide access to justice. Needless to say, there must be adequate measures in place to ensure that technology is used in the most efficient yet responsible manner.

---

[55] Ibid.

[56] Jauhar and Misra [44].

[57] Reference [32].

5.1 *Infrastructural Access, Development and Need for a Dedicated Platform*

The key impediment to ensuring that technology is used in a sustained model for legal proceedings is lack of access to the internet and infrastructure to access e-courts, and e-filing systems. Only 40% of the Indian population has access to the internet and 30% lack basic literacy, and nearly 90% lack digital literacy.[58] Therefore, to ensure that these steps taken during the pandemic sustain, it is imperative to ensure digital access and digital literacy across the board, for advocates, litigants, judges and administrative staff. For instance, it has been recommended that consumers themselves should be able to argue consumer redressal disputes.[59] However, this can only be achieved in a scenario where there exists a high level of literacy and digital literacy.

Simultaneously, infrastructure and technology should also be developed to ensure that virtual hearings take place using a common, customised tool for video conferencing, especially catering to courts. Technology should be used to create a platform such as *Zoom* or *Teams* for courts which allows juniors and assisting counsels to assist the arguing counsel in a matter and provide for instantaneous secure file sharing as well. Courts should appoint nodal officers to look into technology adopted and constitute committees with experts to facilitate real-time implementation of suggestions to make the technology better.

AI may be used to undertake certain administrative tasks such as patent examinations or scheduling hearings, registration of deeds and creating cause lists. Further, computational tools can be used to expedite justice delivery for traffic challans and motor vehicle compensation claims.[60]

5.2 *Live Streaming—Recommendations and Challenges*

As the authors have stated earlier,[61] the courts should consider a mechanism by which they can collate the arguments in each matter, so as to create a single, consolidated recording covering the substantive hearing of that particular matter. This will greatly enhance the accessibility and educational value of the recording, as any person interested in proceedings of a particular matter heard over several days, will not be required to go through the cumbersome task of reviewing several hours of live stream comprising all daily matters taken up by the court. Further, courts can take a cue from the Canadian Supreme Court, for instance, which provides a summary of each case along with a link to the recording. This adds to the educative value of the archive,

58 Kapoor [29].

59 Sekhar et al. [42].

60 Sengupta, Jauhar and Mishra (n 56).

61 Sethia and Lalit (n 43).

apart from increasing accessibility to people, who can understand the background and issues involved in a short paragraph.

There may be concerns with respect to the privacy of the parties in certain criminal proceedings involving rape, sexual assault, juveniles, etc. It may be prudent to obtain the consent of these parties prior to live-streaming or recording proceedings in their matters. Live-streaming should make justice accessible but should be limited to the extent that it compromises the identity or sensitive nature of parties/proceedings in certain cases.[62]

As identified in *Swapnil Tripathi,* the court should retain IP rights over the live stream but could consider facilitating comprehensive compilations of the recordings by legal reporters. The court may add a further clarification that the proceedings should not be misrepresented by way of portraying incomplete or piecemeal parts of the live stream, to ensure that people do not misuse the footage.[63]

5.3 Use of Video Conferencing in Civil and Criminal Proceedings

5.3.1 Civil Trials

Unlike the onerous nature of criminal trial proceedings, civil trials do not require the physical presence of the parties except in accordance with Order X of the CPC. Under Order X of the CPC, the trial court can, with a view to understand the matters in controversy, propose to orally examine the parties. Such oral examination can also be greatly aided through the use of virtual hearings and video conferencing.

In this context, there are several judgements of the High Courts which deal with the manner and procedure in which witnesses ought to be virtually examined on commission. After the pronouncement of *Praful Desai (supra)*, the Karnataka High Court in *Twentieth Century Fox Film v. Nri Film Production Associates*[64] also passed certain guidelines to ensure the sanctity of the evidence proceedings. These guidelines were also adopted by the Calcutta High Court in *Amitabh Bagchi v. Ena Bagchi.*[65] Therefore, there are sufficient safeguards already present, which have been further augmented with the advent of technology, and civil trials, as such, do not require any amendment in the statute or regulations.

---

[62] Ibid.

[63] Ibid.

[64] *Twentieth Century Fox Film v Nri Film Production Associates* AIR 2003 Kant 148.

[65] *Amitabh Bagchi v Ena Bagchi* AIR 2005 Cal 11.

5.3.2 Criminal Trials

If virtual hearings have to be the new normal in criminal trials, it is extremely crucial for the Parliament to consider amendments in the provisions pertaining to the attendance of accused persons and commission of witnesses. It is well settled that the object of granting bail to an accused person is to ensure his presence during the trial and ensure that he is answerable to justice. However, in certain situations, where travel for an accused becomes difficult, technology can come to the aid of the accused person as well as the trial court.

There have been several situations where an accused person is facing trial in multiple jurisdictions and multiple courts. In *Hani Nishad v. State of UP,*[66] the Supreme Court was faced with a situation where an accused person was facing 31 criminal cases. Considering these facts, the Supreme Court permitted the petitioner to file one personal bond which would hold good for all 31 cases. In the context of investor fraud cases, the Supreme Court has held in *State of Punjab & Anr. v. Rajesh Syal,*[67] and *Narinderjit Singh Sahni v. Union of India & Ors.,*[68] that each individual investor is entitled to maintain a separate FIR which would culminate into a separate charge sheet. In such situations, the accused person faces untold harassment as he/she has to travel to different jurisdictions to physically attend the proceedings in trial courts.

Fortunately, sections 205[69] and 317(1)[70] of the CrPC permit the trial court to dispense with the requirement of personal attendance at the stage of issuance of summons or at the stage of trial if the attendance is not necessary in the interests of justice. However, it is not possible to view these sections in isolation.

Under section 273 of the CrPC,[71] evidence can only be taken in the presence of the accused person '*except as otherwise expressly provided*'. The only two exceptions which are '*otherwise expressly provided*' are sections 299(1), CrPC and 317, CrPC.

[66] *Hani Nishad v State of UP* SLP (Crl) No 8915/2018.

[67] *State of Punjab & Anr. v Rajesh Syal* AIR 2002 SC 3687.

[68] *Narinderjit Singh Sahni v Union of India & Ors* WP (Crl) No 245/2000.

[69] Section 205, Criminal Procedure Code (CrPC): (1) Whenever a Magistrate issues a summons, he may, if he sees reason so to do, dispense with the personal attendance of the accused and permit him to appear by his pleader; (2) But the Magistrate inquiring into or trying the case may, in his discretion, at any stage of the proceedings, direct the personal attendance of the accused, and, if necessary, enforce such attendance in the manner hereinbefore provided.

[70] Section 317(1), CrPC: At any stage of an inquiry or trial under this Code, if the Judge or Magistrate is satisfied, for reasons to be recorded, that the personal attendance of the accused before the Court is not necessary in the interests of justice, or that the accused persistently disturbs the proceedings in Court, the Judge or Magistrate may, if the accused is represented by a pleader, dispense with his attendance and proceed with such inquiry or trial in his absence, and may, at any subsequent stage of the proceedings, direct the personal attendance of such accused.

[71] Section 273(1), CrPC: Except as otherwise expressly provided, all evidence taken in the course of the trial or other proceeding shall be taken in the presence of the accused, or, when his personal attendance is dispensed with, in the presence of his pleader.

a. Section 299, CrPC[72] states that the witnesses can be examined in the absence of the accused person only if he "*has absconded, and that there is no immediate prospect of arresting him*".

b. On the other hand, Section 317, CrPC permits the trial court to dispense with the attendance provided that it "*may, at any subsequent stage of the proceedings, direct the personal attendance of such accused*". Furthermore, the said order under Section 317, CrPC can be passed only with the subjective satisfaction of the trial court, and if the Court feels that the personal attendance of the accused is "*not necessary in the interests of justice*".

Therefore, unless there is a finding that the personal attendance of the accused is '*not necessary in the interests of justice*', then it may not be possible for the accused to seek virtual hearing and attend the trial court proceeding remotely. Therefore, not only the statutory provisions relating to the requirement of personal attendance of the accused person, but also the bail bonds required to be executed under CrPC[73] would have to be suitably amended in order to accommodate virtual presence of an accused person during the trial court proceeding.

The Supreme Court, in the case of *Basavaraj R. Patil v. State of Karnataka,*[74] answered the question as to whether an accused needs to be physically present in court to answer the questions put to him by the court while recording his statement under section 313, CrPC. The majority opinion of the Supreme Court was answered in the negative, wherein it held that section 313, CrPC had to be considered in the light of the revolutionary changes in technology. Therefore, it was held that it was not necessary for the accused person to answer the questions under section 313, CrPC by remaining personally present in court.

Considering these facts, video conferencing may provide a great avenue to ensure that evidence is recorded in the presence of the accused without mandating physical attendance of that person. Such an initiative could lead to lower costs and administrative hassles while ensuring effective access to justice. The obvious drawback of the accused person not being subject to the jurisdiction of the trial court could also be solved by ensuring that he submits to the local police station every week. However, the same would again require suitable amendments in section 273, CrPC and the bail bond provisions to accommodate these aspects.

In so far as remote examination of witnesses is concerned, the Supreme Court has already made it very clear in *State of Maharashtra v. Dr. Praful Desai*[75] that it is not always necessary that the witness needs to be examined in the physical presence of the accused, and when a witness is being examined on commission, it would be the

---

[72] Section 299(1), CrPC: If it is proved that an accused person has absconded, and that there is no immediate prospect of arresting him, the Court competent to try, or commit for trial, such person for the offence complained of may, in his absence, examine the witnesses (if any) produced on behalf of the prosecution, and record their depositions and any such deposition may, on the arrest of such person, be given in evidence against him on the inquiry into, or trial for, the offence with which he is charged, if the deponent is dead or incapable of giving evidence or cannot be found or his presence cannot be procured without an amount of delay, expense or inconvenience which, under the circumstances of the case, would be unreasonable.

[73] Form No 45, Second Schedule, CrPC.

[74] *Basavaraj R Patil v State of Karnataka* (2000) 8 SCC 740.

[75] *State of Maharashtra v Dr Praful Desai* (2003) 4 SCC 601.

duty of the officer who is deputed to ensure that there is no tutoring or prompting during the examination.

However, there are several practical issues that arise during the virtual examination of witnesses. One such situation was faced by the St. Joseph County District Court in Michigan, US, where upon the interruption of the prosecutor, it was understood that the accused person was in the same apartment as the complaining witness, and therefore was clearly intimidating her.[76] In order to prevent such ordeals, sufficient statutory or regulatory practices must be developed in order to ensure that witnesses feel safe and secure while giving testimony.

Furthermore, in so far as victims are concerned, virtual hearings may also be a great tool in ensuring that certain victims, such as those involved in a rape case/POCSO offences, child labour or other sensitive matters, are able to record their statements through virtual conferencing and not be subject to physically facing their accusers or feeling distressed due to the make-up of the court environment.

For example, in Delhi, Vulnerable Victim Deposition Centers were opened in 2013[77] with a view that this would prevent witnesses from turning hostile and enable them to fearlessly give testimony without being intimidated by the physical presence of the accused persons. With the use of technology, depositions of vulnerable witnesses can be conducted with ease by masking the identity of the accused person on the video conference, which can enable the witness to furnish her deposition fearlessly. This would not only substantially save the administrative costs but would also reduce the mental ordeal on the part of the witnesses.

Therefore, while the pandemic has provided a much-needed impetus to adopt to technological advances in the legal profession, there is still a long way to go in terms of utilising technology to its fullest, based on our own experiences with it in the past and by learning through other jurisdictions.

References

1. All rise. IBLJ (2020). https://law.asia/virtual-courts-opens-doors-arbitrators. Accessed 9 July 2021
2. Five more Supreme Court advocates-on-record pass away from COVID-19. In: Bar and Bench, 13 May 2021. https://www.barandbench.com/news/litigation/five-more-advocates-on-record-pass-away-from-covid-19. Accessed 9 July 2021
3. In a first, calcutta court allows live streaming of hearing on youtube. NDTV (13 Feb 2020). https://www.ndtv.com/india-news/in-a-first-calcutta-high-court-bench-allows-live-streaming-of-case-hearing-on-youtube-2179383. Accessed 9 July 2021
4. Now, witnesses won't have to face accused. Times of India (13 Sept 2013). https://timesofindia.indiatimes.com/city/delhi/now-witnesses-wont-have-to-face-accused/articleshow/22532008.cms. Accessed 9 July 2021

[76] Li [33].

[77] Reference [4].

5. SC cautions advocates for unauthorised sharing of links of virtual court hearings. The New Indian Express (7 Nov 2020). https://www.newindianexpress.com/nation/2020/nov/07/sc-cautions-advocates-for-unauthorised-sharing-of-links-of-virtual-court-hearings-2220750.html. Accessed 9 July 2021
6. Standard operating procedure for Ld. Advocate/party-in-person for e-filing, mentioning, listing and video conferencing hearing' Supreme Court of India (4 July 2020). https://main.sci.gov.in/pdf/LU/04072020_153040.pdf. Accessed 9 July 2021
7. Archived webcasts. Supreme Court of Canada. https://www.scc-csc.ca/case-dossier/info/webcasts-webdiffusions-eng.aspx. Accessed 9 July 2021
8. Cable public affairs. https://www.cpac.ca/en/about-cpac/. Accessed 9 July 2021
9. Cable public affairs channel. https://www.cpac.ca/en/programs/supreme-court-hearings/. Accessed 9 July 2021
10. Dave, S., Vyas, M.: Pandemic brings windfall for lawyers as courts go digital Economic Times (10 Apr 2021). https://economictimes.indiatimes.com/news/india/top-lawyers-rake-it-in-as-courts-move-online/articleshow/81998707.cms?from=mdr. Accessed 9 July 2021
11. Dutt A.: Lokpal member justice Ajay Kumar Tripathi dies of Covid-19. Hindustan Times (3 May 2020). https://www.hindustantimes.com/delhi-news/lokpal-member-justice-ajay-kumar-tripathi-dies-of-covid-19/story-WGfoGbbojmRmsPC2IBTevJ.html. Accessed 9 July 2021
12. E-committee Supreme Court of India, 'Draft Vision Document for Phase III of e-Courts Project' (20 Apr 2021). https://ecommitteesci.gov.in/inviting-suggestions-on-the-draft-vision-document-for-phase-iii-of-ecourts-project/. Accessed 9 July 2021
13. E-committee Supreme Court of India, 'Case Management through CIS 3.0 Report' (Aug 2018). https://doj.gov.in/sites/default/files/CIS%203.0%20final_0.pdf. Accessed 9 July 2021
14. E-committee Supreme Court of India, 'e-Courts Services Mobile Application-Manual' (2021). https://ecommitteesci.gov.in/publication/e-courts-services-mobile-application-manual/. Accessed 9 July 2021
15. E-committee Supreme Court of India, 'The Courts and COVID-19: Adopting Solutions for Judicial Efficiency' (July 2020). https://ecommitteesci.gov.in/the-courts-and-covid-19-adopting-solutions-for-judicial-efficiency/. Accessed 9 July 2021
16. E-filing manual, 'Practice Directions for E-Filing (Phase-II) in The Supreme Court of India'. https://main.sci.gov.in/php/FAQ/5_6246991526434439183.pdf. Accessed 9 July 2021
17. E-filing service only at four high courts in India, *The Times of India* (10 April 2017). http://timesofindia.indiatimes.com/articleshow/58100660.cms?utm_source=contentofinterest&utm_medium=text&utm_campaign=cppst. Accessed 9 July 2021
18. E-filing Services, 'Electronic filing of cases in the court'. https://filing.ecourts.gov.in/pdedev/index.php. Accessed 9 July 2021
19. E-filing, High Court of Delhi. http://delhihighcourt.nic.in/efiling.asp. Accessed 9 July 2021
20. Guidelines for e-filings, Rajasthan High Court (8 April 2020). https://hcraj.nic.in/hcraj/Allfiles/eFilingNotification.pdf. Accessed 9 July 2021
21. Gujarat High Court, 'Live Streaming of Court Proceedings of First Court of High Court of Gujarat' (26 Oct 2020). https://www.youtube.com/watch?v=WpqQWBERB_Y. Accessed 9 July 2021
22. Gunasekar A, '"For Publicity": Juhi Chawla's 5G Case Dismissed, Court Says Pay 20 Lakh' NDTV (5 June 2021). https://www.ndtv.com/india-news/juhi-chawlas-suit-against-5g-rollout-dismissed-by-court-for-publicity-2456486. Accessed 9 July 2021
23. High Court of Australia, 'Audio-visual recordings of Full Court hearings heard in Canberra' (30 June 2020). https://www.hcourt.gov.au/cases/cases-av/av-2020-06-30. Accessed 9 July 2021
24. High Court of Bombay, 'Practice note no. 31: Introduction of e-filing proceedings' (25 Aug 2011). https://bombayhighcourt.nic.in/writereaddata/practfiles/PDF/2011-08-25pnote-31.pdf. Accessed 9 July 2021
25. High Court of Delhi, 'FAQ's on Video Conferencing'. https://delhihighcourt.nic.in/pdf/FAQVideoConfrencing.pdf. Accessed 9 July 2021

26. High Court of Gujarat, 'Order of Honourable the Chief Justice - Experimental Live Streaming of First Court Proceedings' (26 Oct 2020). https://gujarathighcourt.nic.in/hccms/sites/default/files/miscnotifications/PRESS%20RELEASE%20-%20Order%20of%20Honourable%20the%20Chief%20Justice%20-%20Experimental%20Live%20Streaming%20of%20First%20Court%20Proceedings.pdf. Accessed 9 July 2021
27. Jain A, Now district court in Delhi launches e-filing for arbitration matters, test Run On' (LiveLaw, 24 May 2019). https://www.livelaw.in/news-updates/now-district-court-in-delhi-launches-e-filing-for-arbitration-matters-test-run-on-145254. Accessed 9 July 2021
28. Justice Pratibha Singh, 'A judge's experience of hearings through video conferencing' Bar and Bench (14 May 2020). https://www.barandbench.com/columns/video-conferencing-experiences. Accessed 9 July 2021
29. Kapoor, A.: Online justice and the pandemic: impact on procedure. In: The Peninsula (19 May 2021). https://www.thepeninsula.org.in/2021/05/19/online-justice-and-the-pandemic-impact-on-procedure/. Accessed 9 July 2021
30. Kashyap, N.: Bombay High Court issues notice on plea for directions To NCLAT for enabling e-filing & doing away with physical filing. LiveLaw (12 Jan 2021). https://www.livelaw.in/news-updates/bombay-high-court-nclat-e-filing-notice-issued-168278?from-login=189769. Accessed 9 July 2021
31. Khanna, V., Kaul, P., Chaudhary, A.: The trial of technology in Litigation: a virtual experience. Bar and Bench (15 May 2020). https://www.barandbench.com/columns/the-trial-of-technology-in-litigation-a-virtual-experience. Accessed 9 July 2021
32. Law Commission of India: One Hundred Twenty-Eighth report on Cost of Litigation (1998). https://lawcommissionofindia.nic.in/101-169/Report128.pdf. Accessed 9 July 2021
33. Li, D.K.: Virtual court hearing takes turn after prosecutor spots assault suspect in victim's home. NBC News (11 Mar 2021). https://www.nbcnews.com/news/us-news/virtual-court-hearing-takes-turn-after-prosecutor-spots-assault-suspect-n1260698. Accessed 9 July 2021
34. Madras High Court: E-filing rules Tamil Nadu. Government Gazette (2020). http://www.hcmadras.tn.nic.in/Madras%20High%20Court%20eFiling%20Rules_2020.pdf. Accessed 9 July 2021
35. Ministry of Law and Justice: Justice Chandrachud inaugurates Judgments & Orders portal and e-filing 3.0 module. Press Information Bureau, Government of India (12 April 2021). https://www.pib.gov.in/PressReleasePage.aspx?PRID=171115. Accessed 9 July 2021
36. Mishra, D., Chanchani, M.: For the first time, India has more rural net users than urban. The Times of India (6 May 2020). https://timesofindia.indiatimes.com/business/india-business/for-the-first-time-india-has-more-rural-net-users-than-urban/articleshow/75566025.cms. Accessed 9 July 2021
37. National Company Law Appellate Tribunal: Revised standard operating procedure for ld. advocate/authorised representative/party-in-person for hearing/mentioning the matter through virtual mode (3 Jan 2021). https://nclat.nic.in/wp-content/uploads/2021/01/Revised_SOP_03.01.2021.pdf. Accessed 9 July 2021
38. NJDG: National judicial data grid (district and taluka courts of India). https://njdg.ecourts.gov.in/njdgnew/index.php. Accessed 9 July 2021
39. National Company Law Appellate Tribunal: Notice 112/2021. New Delhi (24 May 2021). https://nclat.nic.in/Useradmin/upload/15694893960b4d6871f023.pdf. Accessed 9 July 2021
40. Rajasthan High Court: Notification PA/RG/Misc./2020 (19 April 2021). https://hcraj.nic.in/hcraj/hcraj_admin/uploadfile/latestupdates/notification_1904202175.pdf. Accessed 9 July 2021
41. Ojha, S.: Supreme Court E-committee finalizing rules for live streaming: Justice Chandrachud. Live Law (9 April 2021). https://www.livelaw.in/top-stories/supreme-court-website-judgments-e-filing-30-172386. Accessed 9 July 2021
42. Sekhar, R., et al.: Re-imagining consumer forums. Vidhi Centre for Legal Policy (25 Feb 2021). https://vidhilegalpolicy.in/research/re-imagining-consumer-forums/. Accessed 9 July 2021
43. STF: Pleno—Direito exclusivo ao ICMS sobre importação de gás da Bolívia—COM AUDIODESCRIÇÃO' (24 Oct 2020). https://www.youtube.com/watch?v=9P1U2tlaVSY. Accessed 9 July 2021

44. Sengupta, A., Jauhar, A., Mishra, V.: Responsible AI for the Indian Justice System—A strategy paper. Vidhi Centre for Legal Policy (15 April 2021). https://vidhilegalpolicy.in/research/responsible-ai-for-the-indian-justice-system-a-strategy-paper/. Accessed 9 July 2021
45. Sethia, R., Lalit, SU.: Gujarat HC tests livestreaming judicial proceedings for first time, but are Indian courts ready yet? News18 (30 Oct 2020). https://www.news18.com/news/opinion/gujarat-hc-tests-livestreaming-judicial-proceedings-for-first-time-but-are-indian-courts-ready-yet-3023915.html. Accessed 9 July 2021
46. Thakur, P.: SC is global leader in virtual hearings, says law ministry Times of India (17 Feb 2021). http://timesofindia.indiatimes.com/articleshow/81070044.cms?utm_source=contentofinterest&utm_medium=text&utm_campaign=cppst. Accessed 9 July 2021
47. Thomas, A.: Live-streaming court proceedings open to misuse: CJI Bobde' Hindustan Times (26 Oct 2020). https://www.hindustantimes.com/india-news/live-streaming-court-proceedings-open-to-misuse-cji-bobde/story-HmZ5cu168Rb5IsnwvAo9QK.html. Accessed 9 July 2021

The Way Forward

A Blueprint on Global Legal Education: The European Perspective

Soledad Atienza and Sonsoles Arias

Abstract This chapter is based on the report "Blueprint on global legal education" by the International Bar Association and the Law Schools Global League that outlines the main trends and challenges that legal education faces globally. In this chapter, the coordinators of the report describe the quantitative and qualitative research methodology used to develop the report and reach the conclusions from the analysis, including the main key trends, challenges and opportunities emerging globally in current legal education, with a particular focus on Continental Europe. The key trends identified in global legal education include internationalization, technology and the development of new skills, while one of the main challenges identified is the regulation of legal education and the legal profession, an aspect that could hinder internationalization and innovation. Special mention should be made of legal education in the COVID-19 era. Since the outbreak of the pandemic, new challenges in legal education have arisen and need to be addressed.

1 Project Description. Scope of the Project

The International Bar Association, the organization that represents the global legal profession, has worked intensely on a study of the trends that are shaping the future of legal services, specifically focusing on the impact of globalization and technological disruption.[1] With the aim of connecting the findings on the legal profession to legal

[1] The results of the work, which identify a number of key drivers of change, can be found here IBA Task Force on the Future of Legal Services. https://www.ibanet.org/Task-Force-on-the-Future-of-Legal-Services.aspx. Accessed 29 March 2021.

S. Atienza (✉) · S. Arias
IE Law School, Madrid, Spain
e-mail: soledad.atienza@ie.edu

S. Arias
e-mail: Sonsoles.arias@ie.edu

C. Raj Kumar and S. G. Sreejith (eds.), *Legal Education and Legal Profession During and After COVID-19*, https://doi.org/10.1007/978-981-19-2568-9_16

education, the IBA embarked on an ambitious research project called "Blueprint on global legal education",[2] in conjunction with the Law Schools Global League.[3]

The purpose of the report is to determine the key trends and challenges in global legal education, identifying best practices from different academic institutions around the world that can be of practical use to law schools, bar associations and professional legal services firms. The blueprint offers an original categorization of law schools, based on current trends in legal education and the legal profession, which allows each academic institution to recognize its own category. This can be of use for those seeking to achieve a better understanding of the situation of legal education in different regions. The report also offers a detailed description of the principles, activities and elements that are included in each category and universities can therefore easily understand what each category entails and evaluate the cost and risks of moving from one category to another.

The report identifies the best practices applied by some institutions, which may be of inspiration to those trying to deal with the same challenges. In addition, the blueprint shows where some of the opportunities lie for the future development of legal education.

The key goals of the report are:

- To understand how globalization, technology and the fourth industrial revolution, among other drivers, affect legal education globally.
- To identify the challenges that are common to legal education around the world, while recognizing the significance of the local context (cultural, regulatory, historical, etc.) in which they take place.
- To identify and understand the main solutions to these challenges applied by law schools, globally and specifically in official degrees.
- To identify the main challenges still present and the negative consequences of non-adaptation.
- To develop common/shared solutions to the challenges, while recognizing the need for locally sensitive solutions.
- To generate a compendium of best practices, per jurisdiction.
- To generate a model or blueprint to assist law schools to navigate the paradigm change.

This global report was undertaken by representatives of the Law Schools Global League and, for the purposes of the project, the following regions chosen:

- Region I: United Kingdom and Ireland[4]

[2] The report was presented at the IBA annual conference in November 2020 and can be found here: Ref. [3].

[3] The Law Schools Global League brings together 25 law schools that share a strong vision on the need to promote a global approach to legal education, research and impact upon society; Law Schools Global League. https://lawschoolsgloballeague.com/. Accessed 29 March 2021.

[4] This region was selected as an independent region, due to its relevance in legal education. The research was carried out by the University of Edinburgh, Dr. Verónica Ruiz Abou-Nigm.

- Region II: United States and Canada[5]
- Region III: Continental Europe[6]
- Region IV: Southeast Asia and Australia and Hong Kong[7]
- Region V: Latin America[8]
- Region VI: Asia and Russia[9]
- Region VII: Africa.[10]

The scope of this project is intended to be as broad as possible and include as many regions as possible to achieve a large geographical sample, rather than focus in depth on one specific region. The scope also endeavours to reflect the richness of the sector in order to include a diverse sample of law schools and institutions. The broad geographical scope of the project has allowed us to perform a truly global analysis. Even if each region varies in terms of quantity: number of universities, number of law schools, number of lawyers, numbers of bar associations, for the purposes of this research, the quantitative analysis remains under the same parameters and the same number of law schools was analysed per region.

This chapter describes the "Blueprint on global legal education" project and attempts to shed some light on the issue of the current challenges facing legal education. The project offers a global approach to the issue, although with the intention of offering a deeper vision in one region. For this article, we focused on the region of Europe and, under the current circumstances, also on issues that are of relevance for legal education in times of COVID-19.

2 Research Methodology. A Qualitative and Quantitative Analysis

To carry out the project, the research was distributed into four main phases. First, we carried out a study of all the literature on legal education and selected and analysed hundreds of law school websites worldwide. We then launched an open survey of all law schools, bar associations, legal organizations and other institutions to identify the

[5] This region's analysis was conducted by Dr. Ana María Zorrilla Noriega, from the *Instituto Tecnológico Autónomo de México* (ITAM).

[6] IE University (Spain) was responsible for the European analysis, which was conducted by Dr. Sonsoles Arias.

[7] Dr. Michael Legg from the faculty of Law of the University of New South Wales carried out the study in this region.

[8] The Latin American region was analysed by the Universidad de los Andes. The research was conducted by Dr. Eleonora Lozano. Fundação Getulio Vargas, conducted the Brazilian study, which was coordinated by Dr. Marina Feferbaum.

[9] Jindal Global Law School carried out this region´s analysis. The research was conducted by Prof. (Dr.) S.G. Sreejith. The Chinese research was specially conducted by the China University of Political Science and Law (Dr. Liu Kunlun). Furthermore, the Russian perspective was analysed by the Higher School of Economics University (Dr. Maria Filatova).

[10] University of Cape Town. Dr. Kathy Idensohn.

main challenges they face in legal education today. Finally, we conducted multiple surveys of deans and senior members of selected law schools.

2.1 Literature Research

The literature on legal education and the challenges it faces today is abundant, not only at a global level, but also specialized in different regions and countries. The analysis of literature used the following methodology: Firstly, we researched several databases, all gathered from the same engine: Worldcat Discovery.[11] The compilation of scientific literature included the fundamental term of "legal education" and three population terms: Globalization/Globalisation, Challenge/Challenges and Trends.[12]

A selection was then made of the academic articles and papers that were really useful for the purposes of the study. The selected documents were read by the research team, who identified and conceptualized the most relevant challenges and trends that were referenced in each document and had an impact on global legal education.[13]

2.2 Webpage Analysis

Along with the analysis of the existing literature on legal education, we analysed the websites of a large number of law schools around the world. The purpose of this study was to discover what trends and challenges they are currently facing, based on the information presented by law schools on their websites. It is important to note that this second phase of the project is a quantitative analysis and therefore differs in this respect from the literature survey. The information and descriptions collected on the websites show how the law schools describe themselves and the information

[11] Worldcat https://ie.on.worldcat.org/search?lang=en&queryString=&scope=. Accessed 29 March 2021. The search results are limited to the English language, but not to country of origin. Papers were also limited to those published from January 2010 to December 2019, to obtain the most up-to-date studies of the challenges and trends in current global legal education. The study sample was limited to global legal education and also the main regions and countries. Finally, the search was limited to documents including legal education with a significant impact on the population sample.

[12] These key words and inclusion criteria were then used to research into the following databases and journals, among others: ABI/INFORM, IEEE, JSTOR, OECD, PsycARTICLE, SAGE Knowledge, SciELO, ScienceDirect, Taylor and Francis Journals, Wiley Online, WorldCat.org, OCLC catalog of books.

[13] The list of papers that were finally analysed by the research team have been included in Annex i of the report, See IBA (n 2) 104–113. For identifying the different trends and challenges, a hierarchical diagram was used: It starts with all the diverse trends and challenges we found in the document and then branches and groups them together according to conceptual similarities (in common or similar trends or challenges), from generalities to specifics. The results of the literature research can be found in the final report IBA (n 2) 15–24.

they intend to convey publicly about themselves. Even so, this information is very useful and will help to supplement the analysis carried out in the other phases of the project.

A selection of 60 law schools was made for each of the seven regions into which the project was divided. Taking into account the existing rankings at a global, regional and local level, a total of 420 law schools were selected, whose web pages would be the subject matter of the study.[14] The aim was to analyse a diverse group of law schools, in regional terms as well as in terms of ranking and a number of law schools were therefore chosen from the top, medium and low positions, thus combining different rankings.

All the information collected was classified according to four major thematic blocks considered today as major challenges in legal education: globalization, technology, skills and diversity. Within each of the topics, a categorization was made in different levels (from the lowest to the highest)[15] according to the information presented by the law school on that particular topic on its website. Thus, for example, if the law school described itself on its website with little information on the topic of globalization, the law school would be categorized with low level of globalization.[16]

The results of the website analysis are highly illustrative, both globally and by region[17]: firstly, law schools mostly show a low level across the four elements (globalization, technology, skills and diversity) on their websites. In addition, a limited number of law schools present themselves on their website with a high level in all the categorized topics: 4% show a high level of globalization; 12% show a high level of technology; 28% show a high level of skills; and 10% of law schools show a high level of diversity (see p. 34 of the report).

2.3 Survey

Along with the study of existing literature on legal education and the analysis of websites, a global survey was also conducted, where law schools, bar associations and other legal institutions could give their opinion on the main challenges facing legal education today.

---

[14] Among the variety of rankings used for the selection of law schools globally, we used those published by Times Higher Education (THE), World University (Law) and The Complete University Guide League Tables (Law) in 2019. See Annex ii IBA (n 2) 114-119. In addition, for each specific region, local or regional rankings were also taken into account. For example, for the UK & Ireland, the ranking published by The Complete University Guide. https://www.thecompleteuniversityguide.co.uk/league-tables/rankings?s=law was also taken as a reference. In addition, in some regions, more law schools were included to provide diversity in terms of location (rural/regional) or not ranked and higher education specialists also consulted in the region (i.e. Southeast Asia, Australia and Hong Kong). See IBA (n 2) 115.

[15] Four specific levels were designed for this categorization: low, medium, high and top.

[16] On the methodology followed to categorize law schools according to their different levels, see pages 27 and ff. of the report.

[17] IBA (n 2) 33–43.

2.3.1 Survey Sample

The analysis draws on data collected from November 2019 to April 2020,[18] when 521 law schools, bar associations and other legal institutions in more than 70 countries responded to the survey. For the purpose of the report, we only used responses from 369 respondents. The remaining ones had to be discarded, as they were empty and did not provide any relevant information. Of the 369 users, 213 registered as law schools, 47 as bar associations, 33 indicated that they were legal institutions and the remaining 76 registered in the survey as "other institutions".[19]

2.3.2 Survey Data

The survey asked respondents about the new challenges facing legal education today. It was divided into eight main thematic blocks: user general information, globalization, employability skills, multidisciplinary programmes, technology, regulation of legal education, resources and challenges. A total of 68 questions were included[20] on the level of internationalization of law schools, the enrolment situation faced by international students and the faculty in law schools, the use of technology by law schools (i.e. only as a tool or as content in their programmes), the situation of access to the legal profession in the region, etc.

2.3.3 Research Findings and Key Learnings

The research findings and key learnings obtained from the surveyed law schools shed a great deal of light on the current challenges facing legal education.[21] For example, in relation to globalization and internationalization, there is an intention to become more international, although most law schools have not yet reached this point. There is a need to increase curricula, faculty and students. Regarding employability skills, many law schools teach employability skills. Not many law schools include management skills in their law programmes. With regard to technology, about one quarter teach online, although a new situation has arisen due to COVID-19.[22] Regulation is seen as a constraint to internationalization and a minor constraint in terms of increased use of technology. In terms of regulation, a new situation has also arisen as a result of COVID-19. In terms of resources and competition, there is not much competition outside law schools, but there is increased economic/cost pressure

[18] Start date: 29 November 2019. End date: 2 April 2020.

[19] Therefore, 57.72% of the respondents were law schools, 12.73% were bar associations, 8.94% were legal institutions and 20.59% were other institutions.

[20] IBA (n 2) 119–120. For the design and development of the survey, we took into account the criteria proposed in Diamond [4].

[21] IBA (n 2) 65–66.

[22] On the effects of COVID-19 on technology and legal education, vid. Chapter 4 of this work.

on law schools. Ultimately, the survey results show that resources, technology and internationalization are the biggest challenges facing legal education today.

2.4 *Interview of Deans or/and Senior Members of Law Schools*

Following the lines designed for the survey, interviews of senior members or deans of law schools were conducted globally. In this phase, a qualitative analysis was conducted. The purpose was to complete the information received from the survey, the analysis of the websites and the study of the literature, as well as to obtain first-hand information on the main concerns and obstacles that law schools are currently facing.

To this end, approximately 15 law schools were selected in each of the regions where the interview was to be conducted.[23] The questions were also divided into the following eight topics: globalization/internationalization, technology, regulation of legal education and the legal profession, resources, employability-related skills and multidisciplinarity and new market players and challenges.[24]

All responses and observations made by the deans and senior members of the law schools were analysed in aggregate and compiled in an executive summary for each region. In this way, the results obtained could be analysed on a regional basis.[25]

3 Analysis Results. A Special Approach to Europe

The different results obtained in the four phases of the project can be analysed globally, but it is also possible to carry out an interesting study in each of the regions.

---

[23] The interview participants are listed in Annex iv of the report see IBA (n 2) 122–127.

[24] All the questions asked are listed in Annex v. See IBA (n 2) 128–129. In relation to globalization/internationalization, for example, the deans or senior members were asked how the law school approaches internationalization; what activities or projects it develops to promote more international legal education; or whether it has a strategy to offer more international legal education. In relation to technology, the deans or senior members were asked whether the law school offers combined programmes (partly in person and partly online); whether its faculty employs the use of technology as a teaching tool; or whether the law school has joined forces with the legal profession or the public administration (for example, the judiciary) to develop legal tech tools or to discuss legal tech needs, among other issues. They were also asked whether the law school faculty is involved in research projects concerning law and technology and, if so, whether it could describe them. Questions related to the regulation of legal education and the legal profession focused on the regulatory frameworks governing access to the legal profession in the law school's jurisdiction and whether higher legal education is an obstacle to the development or innovation in the law school. They were also asked whether these regulatory frameworks limit the provision of more international legal education at their law school.

[25] IBA (n 2) 69–82.

In the particular case of continental Europe, the main results obtained and the key findings of the analysis are of interest.

3.1 Literature Research

The literature on the main challenges facing legal education in Europe is abundant. Authors such as [1] stress the importance of Law schools offering their students relevant education to enable them to face the difficulties in the late modernity.[26] Difficulties such as the increase in technological possibilities, the de-mystification of science and globalization are highlighted by scholarship.

The constant transformation to which law schools are subject today as a result of European integration and globalization inevitably provokes 'new challenges to legal education and calls for a new generation of European law graduates'.[27]

Other authors, such as J. Goldsmith and Faulconbridge and Muzio [2], point out the difficulties that lawyers encounter when entering the legal profession. For example, they state that the control over the regulation of the legal profession through bar associations is a barrier to a constant globalization trend.[28]

In this phase of the project, as indicated in the previous section, we performed a quantitative and qualitative analysis of all the existing literature in the continental European region on legal education and its main challenges. From the papers analysed at a global level, those focusing exclusively on continental Europe were extracted and provided the following results[29]:

- The biggest challenge facing European law schools is globalization/internationalization.
- In addition, one of the major concerns in addition to the above is the teaching of the new skills necessary to adapt to new times.
- Along these lines, the different gaps and obstacles to access to the legal profession are considered a current challenge in legal education.
- Multidisciplinarity in the legal education, technology as a tool and law programme content and the implementation and development of a Legal Clinic are also relevant challenges facing European Legal Education.

---

[26] Van Rossum,[1, pp. 245, 247].

[27] Kornet [5, pp. 313–339].

[28] Goldsmith [6, pp. 441, 443]. The problem of globalization in legal education in Europe is a long-standing one. *See* Faulconbridge and Muzio [7, pp. 317–321].

[29] IBA (n 2) 22, 24.

3.2 Webpage Analysis

For the analysis of the websites, 60 law schools across Continental Europe[30] were selected, based on the reference of the different university rankings published in 2019 and 2020 for the European region.[31] The methodology for the extraction of the data was explained in the previous section, classifying it into four main thematic blocks (Globalization/Internationalization, Technology, Skills and Diversity) and evaluating it at several levels (from low to high), according to the greater or lesser extent the website defines the law school in these four main topics.

The analysis of the websites in Continental Europe yielded the following results[32]:

- The vast majority of the websites analysed (68% of the total) define law schools with a low level of globalization/internationalization. This means that law schools in Continental Europe do not include relevant information on internationalization on their websites. They merely describe themselves on their websites as international law schools with an international mission and vision; open to diversity and international students, but do not elaborate on further characteristics that would qualify them as having a high level of globalization/internationalization.
- A large majority of law schools (72%) do not define themselves on the websites as institutions that teach their students a wide range of skills. On the contrary, they present very little information in this regard. Only 28% of law schools present the skills that students acquire in their programmes on their websites.
- In relation to the level of technological innovation, 81% of law schools do not define themselves on their websites as highly technological or with legal tech programmes.
- Neither do they show on their websites an adequate level of diversity in their communities.

The results of the website analysis clearly show that in Continental Europe: the level of information provided on the degree of globalization, skills, technology or diversity of law schools is low or non-existent, compared to the actual situation.

---

30 Annex ii see IBA (n 2) 114.

31 The criteria used to select universities for the European region was the same as that used for the rest of the regions: geographical spread, diversity in ranking (top, medium and lower-ranking law schools) and different age of the schools (before/after 1992). The main rankings used to select the universities were Times Higher Education (THE); World University (Law) and the Complete University Guide League Tables (Law).

32 IBA (n 2) 37, 43. Interestingly, the results are very similar to those obtained for US/Canada and Latin America.

3.3 Interviews

The participants in the interviews were senior members or deans of law schools in the European region, as well as directors of the most important bar associations in Spain and France. The majority of the interviews were conducted in person—both online and face-to-face—between January and May 2020. Some of the interviews were also answered by completing the questionnaire in writing.[33]

The purpose of this phase of the project was to be able to complete or clarify the information collected and obtained in the previous phases. Questions were therefore asked in relation to: globalization; technology; regulation and liberalization of the legal profession; resources in legal education; skills related to employability and multidisciplinarity; and new players and challenges in the market. However, a more direct and personal approach was given to senior members or deans of law schools.

The interviews yielded the following aggregate results[34]:

- Globalization is considered a reality, but the scope of strategies and achievements differ, depending on the intention of the institution and external elements such as regulation. In relation to the programmes, international content has increased and so has the methodology of comparative law, civil law and common law, as well as global law. With respect to the relations between law schools and other institutions or universities, there is a greater offer of joint or dual degrees with international law schools and exchange programmes for students, faculty and staff.
- In relation to technology, there is a clear initiative to implement technology, not only as a tool for legal education, but also as content in law programmes, either through mandatory courses, elective courses or programmes totally focused on technology (master's degree in legal technology).
- Regulation of law and legal education: there are obvious restrictions and barriers imposed upon access to the legal profession, although not all programmes are official and therefore not all are affected by regulation. An important insight conveyed by participants was that, despite the serious difficulties posed by the regulation of legal education and the legal profession, there is always room for innovation.
- Resources: there is a clear division between private and public law schools (most countries have both public and private schools; although in some countries all law schools are public). Resources are considered a major constraint to internationalization, technology integration and active teaching methodology.
- In relation to multidisciplinarity, most interviewees stated that there is a gap between legal education and the legal profession, but legal education should not only be vocational and practice oriented. They also advocated that multidisciplinarity is an unstoppable trend, as all degree programmes are multidisciplinary and some multidisciplinary programmes allow students to take non-law

[33] The participants in these interviews are listed in Annex iv of the report see IBA (n 2) 122–127.

[34] The complete results of the interviews can be seen in IBA (n 2) 73–74.

subjects. The interviewees also considered that multidisciplinary courses are not programmes, yet they are already planning to convert them into law programmes.
- Finally, regarding new market players and challenges, it is true that Continental European law schools compete with other law schools, but this situation may change. For example, there are law firms offering in-house legal training to non-law graduates. There are also legal institutions other than law schools that offer online legal training. At the same time, there are some programmes open to non-lawyers, such as tax, compliance, technology and innovation programmes.

4 Legal Education After COVID-19

The pandemic has clearly been a disruptive element in all areas, including the field of legal education. The emergence of the pandemic has brought about many changes in the day-to-day operations of law schools, intensifying existing challenges and creating new ones.

With the advent of COVID-19, a new section had to be introduced to the project to analyse the impact of the pandemic on legal education, incorporating these new trends and challenges.[35]

After the qualitative analysis of all the articles published so far, it was observed how the main key challenges facing legal education in the midst of the pandemic are mainly: technology, law student skills, regulatory gaps and several other challenges related to healthcare and issues that could affect the more personal sphere of individuals in legal education.

- *Technology*. Online teaching has been the most relevant challenge faced by law schools during the closures adopted in a large number of countries due to the pandemic. Thus, technology positioned itself as the first and essential challenge with the arrival of the pandemic and technology not only as a teaching tool, but also as part of the very content to be introduced in law programmes. The qualitative leap that this challenge has required with the arrival of the pandemic and the confinements derived from it is of an enormous scale.

  In relation to technology as a tool for conducting distance learning, the main problems arising from this new form of teaching have been, for example: the need to explore new options for distance learning, the lack of face-to-face teaching, the existence of gaps in the accessibility of distance work by disadvantaged and disabled students, the implementation of e-learning as a platform for teaching, as well as online examinations, etc. Perhaps the biggest challenge that law schools have faced after the advent of COVID-19—and which affects, of course, all branches of higher education—is being able to ensure equal access to education.

[35] See the last section of Chapter 2 of the report (pages 83 and ff.). The literature on the subject is scarce, so we analyzed the main articles and Ed-ops published to date in the different media. Some interesting articles have recently been published on the topic. See, for example, Sandoval et al. [8, p. 367]. See also Dobrila [9, pp. 130–137].

In addition, due to the pandemic, certain law schools have seriously considered the possibility of including technology, not as a single tool in the teaching of law, but also as a new subject in legal studies (legal tech).

- *New skills for law students.* Along with technology, consideration should also be given to introducing new skills for law students after COVID-19, as it is clear that students now have to prepare for the practice of law in a way that is quite different from the pre-pandemic situation. Legal education needs new skills to prepare students for the world of legal services.[36] Some of the new skills highlighted are: agility; creativity; cognitive flexibility and collaboration. It should also be noted that programmes must include project management, processes, data analytics, design, business basics, mathematics, programming, forecasting, risk management and leadership; in a new multidisciplinary, integrated, platform-driven, capitalized, data-driven, problem-solving and client-focused marketplace.
- *Gaps in the regulation of legal education and the legal practice.* The current pandemic has also highlighted issues and challenges that law schools should address in terms of regulating both the teaching of law and the practice of law. For example: providing online training for all those preparing to practice law in light of the shift to online learning; similarly, the regulator's position on the teaching of law programmes, the time and cost involved in law school curriculums, faculty structure and the transition from degree awarding centres to life-long learning centres should be reviewed. Undoubtedly, one of the major post-pandemic gaps that law students must deal with is the precarious job market they will face in the wake of the pandemic's economic downturn.
- Finally, new important challenges have arisen in the wake of COVID-19, which affect in a greater way the particular individual sphere. The students and faculty members' mental health is evidently one of the most serious problems that law schools now have to deal with as a new challenge, including stress and other psychological disorders due to COVID-19. Remote teaching can also become a familiar problem that can thus be extrapolated to the academic environment. In addition, there is a need for a culture committed to prioritizing emotional intelligence, cultural awareness, collaboration and compassion, principles that are not a priority in our current legal culture.

5 Conclusions

The conclusions of the report gather the most relevant trends in legal education globally, as well as the main challenges that law schools are currently facing. In addition to these findings, the report defines various levels of accomplishment for each one of these trends and proposes a number of recommendations for development and growth that range from less complex to more sophisticated activities.

[36] See, for example, new skills set provided during the pandemic for the clinical legal education in Welgemoed [10, pp. 1–31].

The most relevant trends include globalization, technology, skills and regulation of legal education and the legal profession. The key challenges described are the regulation of legal education and legal profession and resources.

5.1 *Globalization is the Key Trend in Legal Education*

What do we refer to when we talk about globalization in legal education? The literature analysed showed that the main topics and elements that the academic and professional legal community refer to when they talk about the globalization of legal education are the following:

> Comparative methodology, Cultural globalization, Dual legal training, US and UK Legal Education as a pattern, Europeanization, Importance of multicultural education, Institutional and State-motivated globalization, Internalization of law schools and the legal career, Common law as a pattern, international firms & law students, Globalization per region, Diversity, Equity, International law as its own system rather than a single course, Transnational legal education.

The vast amount of literature on this topic, in addition to the web page review, the survey responses and the interviews show that there is an intention in the legal education community to become more international. Nevertheless, most law schools have not achieved full internationalization and many detect a need to increase the international element in their curriculum, faculty body and student body.

Under the category of globalization, we created a series of levels that correspond to the different elements and activities that law schools can offer. They show how growth in internationalization can be achieved by an academic institution.

A Low Level of internationalization means that the law school has very limited international activity. A medium level means that the school has an international faculty and international students.

A high level requires not only an international faculty and student body, but also international activities and content in the Law programmes, which include the following elements, listed in order of simple to more complex:

> Exchange programmes, international summer courses, participation in international competitions, programmes that include courses with an international approach, comparative law courses, international PhD/SjD, international dual degrees, comparative law methodology.

The maximum level is the top level and is the most sophisticated level of internationalization that only some law schools achieve. It requires having implemented a full internationalization process and programmes that allow graduates to obtain legal qualifications for more than one jurisdiction (multijurisdictional) or other complex elements, such as international accreditation. From a simple to a more complex level, the elements are the following:

> International internships, international research projects, international networks, two jurisdictions qualification.

5.2 Technology

Technology was a transforming element in higher education already before COVID-19 and the analysis shows that this is the second trend in the legal education debate. Recently, under COVID-19, the development of technology for education at large, including legal education, has been unprecedented.

In the literature review, the terms and elements that arise as those most mentioned in the area of technology and law schools are:

> Use of technology in the Legal Practice, Impact of technology in Legal Education, Internet and Law, Legal Technology and its outcomes in the legal market, Needs for the evolution of legal education.

Due to the current pandemic, technology as a tool to offer education has become necessary for academic institutions and the debate among legal academics continues in relation to the following topics:

> Exploring new options for remote learning; Lack of face-to-face teaching; Switch to online teaching immediately; Live-streaming lectures; Increased exam flexibility; Gaps in the access to legal advice or legal training; Technology as an operational lifeline.

Different levels of use of technology in legal education were identified from low to high. A low level includes law schools that have no clear or distinctive elements of technology. A medium level refers to law schools that use technology as a teaching tool, including online/combined programmes, online webinars, online conferences, online examinations, online teaching.

A high level describes schools that use technology as content in their programmes, as opposed to the use of technology as a tool, as mentioned above. Law schools considered to be at this level are those that include the following practices:

> Law & tech focus. Legal tech; Courses on technology (Programming, technology); Preparation of students for future online litigation; Programming skills; Interactive online teaching combined with interactive online activities.

5.3 New Skills Set

The analysis proves that there is a new skill set which legal education academics and professionals are considering. A relevant conclusion is that many law schools describe themselves as schools that teach skills for employability, but very few include management skills in their curriculum. The debate on a new skill set includes the following topics:

> Global society in addition to a global economy, Employability and the future, Globalization/Legal skills for the international practice of Law, International skills for practice, new Legal skills for a globalized practice, Legal skills for the practice of law, Professionalization of Curricula, Reforms in Legal Education & New Skills, New spaces to learn, new skills.

We defined two levels of the development of skills set in academic institutions, low and high. A low level refers to law schools that include in their programmes basic skills, such as legal skills, writing skills and oral skills. A high level includes more sophisticated skills, such as:

> Employability related skills: mediation, sociology, cultural diversity, management, entrepreneurship, communication, leadership, client-orientation and technology. Professional skills. Practice-orientated skills; Vocational skills; Analytical and critical skills. Skills in the new legal market: Client-friendly communications, commercial understanding, financial literacy, networking, teamwork, collaborative problem solving, legal tech skills, project management, adaptability, resilience.

5.4 Regulation of the Legal Education and the Practice of Law

Regulation is a key topic in the current debate on legal education, as it is usually considered a limitation to internationalization and innovation. To a lesser extent, also considered as a limitation to the increasing use of technology, or at least before COVID-19, is the extensive regulation of the access to the legal profession, both locally and regionally, and many legal educators consider the regulation of legal education as a constraint to growth in globalized training, which is the principal trend in the discipline.

In addition to these trends (globalization, technology, skills and regulation of legal education and the legal profession), the report identifies the key challenges for legal educators: the regulation of legal education and the legal profession and resources. Regulation represents a trend in legal education, as it is the main topic of debate and one that shapes the model of legal education for academic institutions while, at the same time, appearing to be a challenge due to the limitations that it poses for law schools. One very interesting finding is that even in this reality, certain law schools find ways to achieve flexibility, which allow them to become more international.

Resources are a limitation to internationalization and the inclusion of technology, in particular at a time when many academic institutions consider that there is an increase in the cost of teaching and increased economic pressure on law schools.

To conclude, we can summarize that the main areas of focus in the legal education community are internationalization, technology, skills, regulation, diversity and COVID-19. These areas will define the future development of law schools.

Diversity of students and faculty members is seen as an increasing challenge in legal education in most regions. Not only in terms of internationalization, but also diversity in its different variables: diversity in terms of location (rural/regional), gender diversity and cultural diversity.

The **COVID-19 pandemic** has disrupted the previous needs in the legal education sector. Technology becomes the first and main trend for legal education. Globalization/internationalization now appears behind the other trends. Other challenges such as mental and physical health and equality in the access to legal education have emerged due to the pandemic.

References

1. Van Rossum H, ‘Lawyers, law schools and social change – defining the challenges of Academic legal education in the late modernity’ IJLP **25**(3) (2018)
2. Faulconbridge, J., Muzio, D.: Legal education, globalization and cultures of professional practice. Geo. J. Legal Ethics (2009)
3. IBA Commission on the Future of Legal Services: Blueprint on Global Legal Education (2020). https://www.ibanet.org/MediaHandler?id=B372104C-690D-4EEE-B7F2-47A18C563E38. Accessed 29 March 2021
4. Diamond, S.S.: Reference guide on survey research. In: National Research Council (ed.) Reference Manual on Scientific Evidence, 3rd edn. The National Academies Press (2011)
5. Kornet, N.: English-medium legal education in Continental Europe: Maastricht University´s European Law School—Experiences and challenges. In: Arzoz, X. (eds.) Bilingual Higher Education in the Legal Context: Group Rights, State Policies and Globalization. Martinus Nijhoff, Leiden (2012)
6. Goldsmith, J.: The core values of the legal profession for lawyers today and tomorrow. Nw J Int Law Bus **28**(3) (2008)
7. Goldsmith, P.: Globalization: the European experience. J. Legal Educ. **46**(3), 21 (1996)
8. Sandoval, C., et al.: Legal education during the COVID-19 pandemic: put health, safety and equity first. Santa Clara Law Rev **61**(2) (2021)
9. Dobrila, M.C.: Legal aspects regarding online learning process for students at university and digital education in the European Union: Different life, challenges and the ability to continue education during the pandemic caused by Coronavirus (COVID-19). *Revista* Romaneasca pentru Educatie Multidimensionala **12**(2) (2020)
10. Welgemoed, M.: Clinical legal education during a global pandemic—Suggestions from the trenches. The perspective of the Nelson Mandela University. PELJ **23** (2020)

Potential Changes in Law School Teaching in Central Europe After the Pandemic

Martin Škop

Abstract The text responds to the current pandemic crisis and its manifestations in law schools in Central Europe, especially in the Czech Republic. It identifies three positive factors of distance learning and modern technologies in law education: legalisation, democratisation and modernisation. These factors are due to possible socioeconomic changes and changes that may accompany a post-pandemic society. Furthermore, the text identifies two negative factors: lack of socialisation and discipline. All of these factors must be taken into account when planning strategies to reflect societal change. Next, the text discusses one of the classical tools, fiction, for which new perspectives in legal education are now opening up.

1 Introduction

In 1983, the American constitutionalist Robert Cover recalled one of the basic ideas of legal theory: that law consists only in small parts of formal legal institutions (such as norms, regulations, etc.). It is much more composed mainly of the narratives that give it meaning, contributing significantly to creating what we can call the legal world[1] and it is the narrative[2] that defines the interrelation between law and society. Through narratives, the formal system becomes the system that regulates society—a system involved in social cohesion. Law cannot be reduced to the words of the legislation, just as a play cannot be reduced to the words in a script. At least for a reason, that law touches people's lives and affects people's destinies. Therefore,

[1] Cover [5, pp. 4, 5].

[2] Almog [1, pp. 89–103].

This text is the result of a research activity supported by the Grant Agency of the Czech Republic, reg. no. GA19-12837S "Law in literature: a qualitative analysis of the image of law in fiction at the turn of the nineteenth and twentieth centuries".

M. Škop (✉)
Faculty of Law, Masaryk University, Veveří 70, 611 80 Brno, Czech Republic
e-mail: skop@law.muni.cz

C. Raj Kumar and S. G. Sreejith (eds.), *Legal Education and Legal Profession During and After COVID-19*, https://doi.org/10.1007/978-981-19-2568-9_17

it is possible to understand the law as a system, an environment, or even a world intimately connected to the conventional understanding of the society in which it exists, or perhaps to understand it as a product of social conventions. Its cultural foundations are the fundamental determinants of the shape of the law, including its practical application. Law, society and culture cannot be separated from each other. Without an understanding of these contexts, the law can only be treated minimally.

Robert Cover is not the only one who has explored the meaning of the relationship between law and society. Stanley Fish, like Cover, attached great importance to so-called interpretive communities.[3] Their action is already centred before the moment of reading—in writing. According to Fish, writing is already determined by one style (i.e. one text), and thus there is no barrier to understanding texts when they are read. Here too, we encounter social determinants affecting the reader's comprehension of the text. And, therefore, how legal texts will be constructed and interpreted. Texts cannot exist independently, and they must be linked to particular methods of writing and interpretation: methods based on a specific society and a specific culture. And it is the awareness of this connection that can be the cultivation David Hume wrote about, and that is gained through practice[4] through learning about society and improving the skill of reading texts.

The social relevance of law and its connection to the community is also reflected in James Boyd White's assertion. In his view, the law is an artificial language[5] based on a common language. It is a language that must be learned. And this is in conjunction with the ethical standards of a particular society. Indeed, the law is not reduced to mere forms but is necessarily linked to moral content. White also argues that law is a culture of argumentation and interpretation.[6] In law, values and form must be linked. Without values, the law becomes an administrative apparatus moving inexorably towards the commodification of human beings and their lives. The allure of this approach lies in its simplicity: only objects are regulated. Its unacceptability lies in its detachment from the social foundations and respect for humans. The role of the state is strengthened, interfering in all private spheres of man.[7] On the contrary, the overemphasis on values leads to relativisation and the impossibility to find a consensus. In complex social relations, it is essential to find certainty: to anticipate the consequences of specific actions. Gustav Radbruch, among others, was aware of this when he included legal certainty among the purposes in law.[8]

Let us, therefore, accept the thesis that law is a social skill (language) that enables us to find simple solutions to complex social problems. It is not a solution that is ideal under all conditions but a predictable solution and allows the cohesion of society. A lawyer should understand the culture and be aware that law is a tool of last resort to deal with problems. The formal and value aspects of law must be skillfully integrated.

---

[3] Fish [6, p. 171].

[4] Hume [8, p. 274].

[5] White [21, p. 201].

[6] White [20, pp. 415–445].

[7] Rose et al. [13, p. 84].

[8] Wilk [24, p. 108].

A lawyer must be able to distinguish between good and wrong solutions to conflicts arising in interpersonal relations. Law schools play an indispensable role in what law is. They are in a different position from parliaments, courts or administrative authorities. Law schools shape future lawyers and alert them to what to pay attention to. They prepare future lawyers to read and write. They shape the context in which lawyers will use the artificial language that is the law.

The current pandemic situation, which has affected the whole world, shaped the law into a prohibitive instrument whose dominant narrative is restriction. At the same time, it has affected all levels of education. In the Czech Republic, primary and secondary schools have been closed for almost a year. Higher education institutions were closed for even longer. Teaching was carried out in a distance (synchronous) form using computer communication platforms. Schools were forced to accept the conditions and limitations to which almost all forms of interpersonal communication were subjected. Although this was and is a trend that cannot be ignored and will become part of our lives, it cannot be viewed only with optimism. It is essential to learn from and adopt the suitable tools and disregard what harms interpersonal communication. This paper, therefore, focuses below on how modern teaching elements can be promoted in legal education and how law (and legal education) can be linked to what is inherent in it. The text focuses on the production of texts and their interpretation, i.e. understanding texts and identifying the social context in which the law is situated.

My perspective is European and focuses on legal education as it is usually practised in Central and Eastern Europe. This view cannot be used to generalise the overall (world) view of legal education. That would be unacceptable. This view strongly determines my knowledge and experience, and any findings and conclusions must always be related to this situation. I believe, however, that just as Central and Eastern European law schools need to learn from and be inspired by other parts of the world, my perspective may be interesting for others.

2 Connection of Law and Society

This text is about nothing more than connections between law and culture in a narrower sense and attributing to law meanings inherent in society. It is undoubtedly essential, to begin with a reminder of the necessity of linking law and culture in law schools. Law is a part of society and, despite its artificiality (we said above that it is an artificial language), it cannot be separated from society. In the course of practice, or by a kind of unconscious process of imitation with the absence of epistemic reflection, there is no longer enough room for this. In the fast-paced sequence of events of everyday legal work, there is no time for this. Schools are precisely where interpretive skills should be honed, and basic methodological (in the broadest sense) approaches to understanding law, and its sources and contexts should be introduced. Schools also have a stake in how the current situation will be interpreted in the future. What happens in society after the crisis is of great importance. How society processes the crisis (pandemic), and its associated stories are crucial for subsequent regulation.[9] And in this interpretation, the approach of schools is essential.

In this paper, I'll lean towards the conservative view. A concept that does not deny the importance of current or modern trends in law school teaching. A conception that also reflects the debate about the importance of lectures. Although I do not believe that lectures are entirely useless: by this, I do not mean the reading of one's scripts, i.e. the classical "Vorlesung", but a lecture mapping current knowledge that does not necessarily have to be expressed in writing. The new concept of lectures should be closer to the audience. Undoubtedly, the use of available electronic aids—video lectures, interactive teaching text, educational games, clinical teaching, etc.—may prove beneficial. I do not suppose that their benefits can be overlooked, nor do I presume that these modern trends should be stopped.

On the contrary, the more forms legal education embraces, the more information it will retain in students and facilitate their path to understanding law as a social phenomenon. At the same time—and perhaps despite this—it is still essential that legal education includes work with (coherent) texts. Pedagogical work leads law students to acquire basic indispensable skills (even if they sound pretty bland), i.e. reading and writing. I will therefore focus below on the benefits that working with text can have. These didactic aids (the book) are old, and their use has become commonplace. Recall that this is not about reading specialist legal texts. That is indispensable, but not surprisingly so.

Beyond the pedagogical and didactic aspects, this paper will also focus on other social factors that a change in legal education can bring. The change that the current crisis may have brought about in its nature. Here, we can identify at least three positive factors that the current situation offers us: legalisation, democratisation and modernisation. At the same time, however, there are at least two interventions (factors) of a more negative nature: socialisation and discipline. These are all factors of legal education that should not go unnoticed and should form the basis for further discussion.

All five factors mentioned above are due to distance learning. I anticipate that the distance form of legal education will play an increasing role, although I hope not as fundamental as it is in these days of what we call lock-down. Therefore, it is essential to use positive elements to improve legal education so that graduates are familiar with what law is and respond to the challenges posed by the present day. The harmful factors must be minimised and possibly used as arguments why legal education should not be absorbed entirely by distance or electronic forms.

3 Identifying Positive Factors

Law schools cannot isolate only the abstract process of learning. Law schools are not just didactic tools that serve in memorising the names and numbers of laws and the

[9] Carmichael [4, p. 146].

names of court decisions. If we have accepted the thesis above that law is not merely a form, then legal rules and precedents are not what law can be reduced to. Therefore, we now turn to other aspects of legal education. Therein the current pandemic crisis may have benefits, albeit at a cost that is often drastic because the pandemic has taken its toll on the life and functioning of all societies.

Legal education—like any other education—should have been presented more as "opening doors". It is not primarily about discipline but about making knowledge accessible. It is not right to force students to memorise strings of words. It is necessary to awaken a desire for knowledge that will accompany them throughout their lives (in law, too, lifelong learning is an essential standard). Law is a vast field whose boundaries are challenging to know. Within the limits of the law, there is also an endlessly fascinating, complex and complicated world. Law schools should awaken in students a desire to explore this world. That is why "opening the door": to make knowledge accessible, to show the sources of knowledge and how law can be learned and worked with. The educator should motivate and prepare students to want to go further and enter the law themselves. It is not appropriate for the situation outlined to resemble the concept presented by Franz Kafka in his short story *Before the Law*. An educator is not a doorkeeper who gives a man from the countryside enough advice on standing in the face of the law. Let us imagine it somewhat differently. The educator–doorkeeper is the one who urges entry so that the student (the one seeking admission) has a chance to enter the law. So that the student has an opportunity to know the law. So that the student has the motivation to explore the law further.

One of the three factors mentioned above is legalisation. Access to higher education, and especially to legal education, should be the same for all, and only the skills, knowledge and abilities of the applicants should be decisive. However, this statement is only valid in theory. Cultural and social determinants also play a role in access to education. Not everyone can afford to pay tuition fees (if the law school in question requires tuition fees—I note here that in the Czech Republic, studying at public universities is usually tuition-free). Other cultural and social determinants may also determine whether an applicant does not get an education at such a school. The barrier to studying at a university may also be since the applicant prefers other activities for her livelihood. Or that she does not have enough time and opportunities to do so due to her busyness (e.g. due to social conditions). Expensive tools (computers, books, etc.) can also play a role.

The electronic form of education is not without costs on both sides: creating content and its consumption. I'll leave aside the costs on the law school side. They are an essential factor but not the deciding factor in this approach. However, the costs on the side of the students (applicants) may be lower as the development of computer technology continues to advance. With it, the cost of technology is falling. In the case of the Czech Republic, universities also have scholarship programmes that enable students to equip themselves with technology. This barrier, although perceptible, can thus be overcome.

Moreover, it is a one-off investment that is offset by access to legal education. Since students can access the materials anytime and anywhere, there is no need to be present at school at fixed times. Learning can thus be more relevant to their needs and opportunities. If students have to work while in school, they can combine a challenging legal education with work that is not competitive. Student success rates can also increase. This form of schooling closes the gap between students due to their socioeconomic backgrounds.

The process of democratisation is related to this. Thus, law schools can be opened to students (applicants) from economically disadvantaged social classes (for instance, students with limitations that do not allow social contact). As we have seen above, the law is linked to society. It should apply to all members of the community, regardless of origin, status or social background. To be functional, the law must be interpreted and used by people from every social class. Only in this way can hidden and unjustified inequalities be exposed.[10]

However, distance education, which is synchronous and allows teachers to transmit their experience and knowledge to students directly, offers access to students who could not be physically present in the classroom. Indeed, some of the students are unable to participate in the lessons because, for example, they are unable to attend school. This distance learning format gives them the opportunity and allows them to participate in a simplified form of teaching that is not as costly. In this way, legal education can reach other social classes which usually have difficulty accessing education because of their social insecurity. This democratisation of law schools gives the law a perspective it can sometimes miss. It will broaden not only its use but also its legitimacy. Its education will extend to all social groups. It will also enrich the school curriculum with a new perspective that will not take place in the classic schemes of a divided society. Bringing the law closer to all social groups and making it less influenced by existing socioeconomic limits enables the development of a society based on education and is a condition for further development.

The fourth positive factor is modernisation. Although the law is more of a tool for preserving society and can maintain the state quo, it is undeniable that society is changing. And this must be matched not only by a change in law and legal thinking but also by a change in legal education. The worldwide restriction (recall that in the Czech Republic, universities were closed for fifteen months) was also linked to the development of modern technology in teaching. These communication platforms have enabled remote access and tools that complement traditional education (e-books and textbooks, distance learning, audio–visual supplements, etc.). Law schools must prepare students for the world they are about to enter.[11] The post-pandemic world will be different—other forms of interpersonal communication will develop than immediate physical contact.

Just as the world will change (has changed), so will the law and legal education. Even the current situation (in the Czech Republic) is connected with a rapidly evolving legal system, to which the classical forms of education cannot respond flexibly. It is, therefore, necessary to focus on electronic formats, the revision of which may be more manageable. In addition to broader availability and potentially lower costs, it will also allow flexibility in their preparation. Concentrating on traditional

[10] Kennedy [9, p. 591].

[11] Nussbaum [12, p. 269].

forms will no longer make sense, as students' attention spans have changed, and practice also requires slightly different knowledge and skills. This change is also related to the emphasis placed on modern (contemporary) legal issues, which have so far, in many cases, escaped the classical curriculum. Current capital markets, intellectual property protection and government computerisation are just some areas that will require more attention from law schools. Modernisation trends cannot be resisted but must be appropriately integrated into the necessary classical legal knowledge and skills. Therefore, the current situation should be a lesson that problems can be solved, and solutions must benefit the future, even when the crisis has passed.

In understanding law in terms of language, performance and persuasion, the so-called legal imagination is invaluable:[12] the ability to work with the abstract mental constructs on which law is built. By knowing the legal imagination, we can better understand what law is, what place it occupies in society, and what forms it takes. Understand the law in a broader context. It is also relevant to turn our attention to the context in which law exists. To know the law correctly, it is not sufficient to study only legislative documents (e.g. laws, generally binding decrees, treaties or instructions), but it is necessary to place it in context. Here we can quickly get to literature. Through literature, lawyers may better understand justice and legal texts because they will better understand the society in which they will use them. As we have said above, the law expresses values, ideas and (perhaps in part) justice, and these are the basis of the culture from which law emerges. So is artificial literature. The possibility of knowing law through its interconnectedness with culture and society, which is related to the exploration of the (legal) imagination, arises from the fact that human life has to do with images. In addition to the real world, there is a world of mental images of reality that is as significant and influential as the real world.[13]

If we admit that there is a change in the nature of society, we are accepting a shift in context. It is then necessary for the legal imagination to reflect these changes. Law schools must therefore be prepared for the fact that law exists and operates in a different context. And law schools must prepare their students for this. Therefore, this modernisation is due to the change in the nature of society, the difference in socioeconomic conditions, and the values that the law expresses. This goal can be achieved both by new forms of teaching and by the change of content influenced by the legalisation and democratisation of law and law teaching.

4 Identifying Negative Factors

Among the factors of legal education that we have identified as negatively affected by the current distance education, we include socialisation and discipline. Therefore, we will focus on those phenomena and consequences that have been affected by the current crisis to diminish their benefits and thus influence the relevant factors of legal

[12] White [19].

[13] Le Goff [10].

education. These negative factors illustrate that not all consequences of the current nature of legal education are positive. They also identify what needs to be improved or where there are unbridgeable gaps detrimental to law school students.

The first negative factor is socialisation. Law is a social discipline and manifests itself in the life of society. Law is made and used by people, which means that it has a social dimension. Law schools associate lawyers with law students. Students learn how to think about law, how to talk about law, and how law manifests itself in society. Thus, socialisation takes place in law schools, where students are introduced to the world of law. Law also has an experiential dimension. By being present in statutes and judicial decisions and society's life, it is necessary to cultivate this experience.

When distance learning occurs, the importance of socialisation is reduced. The transmission of experience by distance (electronic) learning is possible but does not reach all relevant elements. It isn't easy to transmit experience in a literary way—although this is one necessary way. Literature is an essential condition, not a sufficient one. I do not deny that fundamental legal knowledge is acquired by practice—legal practice is a skill. But law schools cannot resign themselves to creating the conditions for the subsequent honing of skills. We have also seen that the law manifests itself in people's lives. That is why it is necessary to meet people. This social integration is also the purpose of law schools, where students and teachers learn to argue; to respond to the claims and arguments of others. Students learn to respect others and to hone their social intelligence. Without direct contact, however, this isn't easy. By not physically meeting people, their ability to respect others can be diminished. Therefore, it is essential to also focus on the social and socialisation dimension of legal education.

The second negative factor is discipline. Discipline undoubtedly has rather negative connotations. Nevertheless, a lawyer needs to subordinate his or her personal preferences to the search for law, truth and justice. This subordination is the fundamental ethos of the legal profession. By resigning to the pressure to seek values and giving in to personal preferences, we may leave to social coherence and respect for other people and their problems. Law is not a subjective discipline. It expresses the objectified values and principles of society, and law students must be guided to this at all times. However, as in the case above, discipline is complex in the constraints imposed by the global pandemic. By dropping the routine and interacting and meeting other people in a natural setting, perceiving the social dimension of law may be affected. Law can then be understood only as a subjective element. This subjectification of the concept of law may lose sight of the need to seek a balance between the interests of the individual and those of society.

5 Fiction and Teaching Law

Having looked at the positive and negative factors of the current form of law school education, we turn to whether other tools can be used to reinforce the cultural identity of the law while at the same time fostering respect for society and care for people.

To strengthen the cultural identity of the law, a more conservative tool can be used: fictional literature. It is a traditional tool, but one that currently lacks the aura of necessity. Let us now turn our attention to what literature in the teaching of law schools can be helpful. Two answers are pretty straightforward—to help students learn to read and write. The practice of the legal profession is, to a large (vastly predominant) degree, linked to the written word. Submissions, decisions, regulations, commentaries, etc., are most often found in written form. It is a text that needs to be understood. And then, it is necessary to write a text of one's own. But can literature be used for something else? It can—at the very least to address questions of understanding law concerning a particular society and maintain the symbolic role of law. Although the law is a social phenomenon, and it is necessary to deal with people (the socialisation factor), it is required to work with literary descriptions of human action in addition to performative elements.

Other elements that can be more easily conveyed through beautiful literature undoubtedly include "cultural cultivation". In 1907, the American legal academic John Henry Wigmore published an article titled "A List of Legal Novels",[14] containing a list of literary works that lawyers (and especially law students) have to read. This list—despite its later modifications[15] and the edits and additions made by other authors[16]—still points in the same direction. A lawyer has to be a cultivated person. Lawyers make decisions about people's lives; they participate in shaping people's destinies. Therefore, such a person should know the culture in which she pronounces her decisions and is a worthy representative of it. According to Wigmore, this cannot be achieved without knowledge of literature. Eugene Wambaugh, his intellectual predecessor and colleague, thought similarly about the relationship between law and literature.[17] For him, knowledge of works is not on the list of duties, and it is up to students to decide for themselves whether they will become familiar with the fine literature they choose.

Nevertheless, Wambaugh did not doubt that a proper and educated lawyer could not be indifferent to literature—even if it were merely an artistic description of the legal environment.[18] An element that neither Wigmore nor Wambaugh reflects, but which is undoubtedly related to legal education, is the ethical element. One may even assume that by cultivation, they both mean precisely the inclination to understand the law in a moral context. That is to say, what Jeanne Gaakeer points out, who wants to return the association of law and literature to its value roots: to achieve intellectual and ethical goals and to be able to empathise with the perspective of others.[19] All this in addition to the understandable use of fiction to improve interpretive skills. As stated above, literature is a suitable element for enhancing these skills, but it is

---

[14] Wigmore [22, pp. 574–93].

[15] Wigmore [23, pp. 26–41].

[16] Weisberg [17, pp. 17–28]; Weisberg and Kretschman [18, pp. 94–103].

[17] Wambaugh [16, pp. 28–31].

[18] Ibid 31.

[19] Gaakeer [7, p. 186].

insufficient. Reading alone is not enough. Even though many activities will move to the online environment, we will still be meeting people there.

The literature helps students prepare for real practical cases or real clients whose theoretical characters can draw from the fictions. In doing so, Wigmore identifies with what was familiar, even if it had not been subjected to scholarly reflection: stories punctuate law.[20] They are necessary for understanding and constructing a coherent world that makes sense to people and can only act meaningfully. Works such as Thomas Mann's novel "Death in Venice", Albert Camus' novel "The Plague" or Karel Čapek's drama "The White Disease" describe our present too sharply and show the possible folds of human thinking in the face of the epidemic. At the same time, the narrative is an essential precondition for the reproduction of law and a mediator of its effect on society. These are the social conditions of the law, and their transmission must occur already in law schools. Stories and narratives are also crucial for the image of law itself, reinforcing its acceptance in society. From narratives, potential addressees and future lawyers (and any other lawyers) can learn to know the law and how to deal with it.[21] Well-crafted learning materials that support the above factors must be able to present a strong narrative.

Artificial literature—or sufficient knowledge of it—can help lawyers understand how they create certain reality images, including identifying important elements. Again, this is a tool that should be started in school. The literature offers lawyers or, more specifically judges procedures for drawing a perfect picture composed of the essential elements. A picture that is not a perfect copy of reality but captures the important elements of the reality being described. Thus, Benjamin Cardozo emphasised writing—writing is used to communicate the facts essential to the factual findings. Cardozo's approach is very close to the notion of narrative coherence, which the Scottish legal philosopher Neil MacCormick understood as a test of truth in the case of facts that are difficult (or even impossible) to observe directly.[22] The means of proof and the evidence produced, and the general body of knowledge accompanied by a narrative form of cognition become crucial here. Exaggeratedly, the question is not whether it is true but whether it matches the recipient's expectations. What matters, then, is that it feels true. Their form (in Cardozo's terms) can give the content such a ring that it affects reception. Form, of course, is related to persuasiveness.[23] And both are amply present in fiction. It contains methods and techniques that can then be capitalised on in the composition of legal texts. A truly functional decision gains meaning only by its power. It is a document in its own right, standing up both to evaluate the parties and the evaluation to which its surroundings subject it. By cultivating their literary skills, lawyers can craft their decisions more persuasively. This composition is about combining facts, arguments and clarifications and the appropriate use of decorative elements.

[20] Brooks [2, p. 1].

[21] Schwarz [14, p. 213].

[22] MacCormick [11, p. 245].

[23] Cardozo [3, pp. 492–493].

6 Conclusion

As William Shakespeare expressed long ago through Hamlet, "The time is out of joint". Human society is facing a crisis that takes a toll on human life, health, social solidarity and coherence, and property. Fundamental rights and freedoms are affected. Constraints are therefore also affecting law school education. At the same time, we can say that a return will be difficult. Yet, it will not be impossible. Therefore, it is necessary to reflect on the present and identify the strengths and weaknesses of the current process of teaching law.

Above, I have identified the positive and negative factors of legal education under the current constraints. The positives must be exploited, the negatives must be eliminated, or at least their influence marginalised. This may give room for the cultivation of legal education and the improvement of law schools in Central and Eastern Europe, especially in the Czech Republic.

At the same time, it is possible to use classical tools and form the cultural identity of law as a starting point for the meaning of law and its role in society. Artificial literature is a classical tool that develops the ability to write and read, strengthen legal imagination, and create the understanding of rank, as is customary in a particular society. Thus, as a recurring element of legal education, beautiful literature offers tools for dealing with the crisis.

References

1. Almog, S.: As I read, I weep—In praise of judicial narrative. Okla City U L Rev. **26**(2) (2001)
2. Brooks, P.: Narrativity of the Law'. Law and Literature **14**(1) (2002)
3. Cardozo, B.: Law and literature. Yale Law J. **48**(3), 492–493 (1939)
4. Carmichael, A.G.: The Last past plague: the uses of memory in renaissance carmichael epidemics. J. History Med. Allied Sci. **53**(2) (1998)
5. Cover, R.: The Supreme Court, 1982 Term—Foreword: Nomos and Narrative. HLR, **97**(1) (1983)
6. Fish, S.: *Is There a Text in This Class? The Authority of Interpretive Communities*, HUP (1980)
7. Gaakeer, J.: The future of literary-legal jurisprudence: mere theory or just practice? Law and Humanities **5**(1) (2011)
8. Hume, D.: Of the standard of the taste. In: Green, T.H., Grose, T.H. (eds.) *The Philosophical Works of David Hume*, vol. III, Longmans Green and Co, (1875)
9. Kennedy, D.: Legal education and the reproduction of hierarchy. J. Legal Educ. **32**(4) (1982)
10. Le Goff, *L'imaginaire Médiéval : Essais*, Gallimard (1991)
11. MacCormick, N.: Coherence in legal justification. In: Peczenik, A., Lindahl, L., Van Roermund, B. (eds.) Theory of Legal Science Proceedings of the Conference on Legal Theory and Philosophy of Science, Springer (1983)
12. Nussbaum, M.C.: Cultivating humanity in legal education. Univ. Chicago Law Rev., **70**(1) (2003)
13. Rose,N., O'Malley, P., Valverde, M.: Governmentality. Ann. Rev. Law Soc. Sci., **2** (2006)
14. Schwarz, C.: Sentences to "Storification ": a trial on legal narratives. In: Grabher, G.M., Gamper, A. (eds.) *Legal Narratives: European Perspectives on U.S. Law in Cultural Context*. Springer (2009)
15. Smejkalová, T.: Story-telling in Judicial Discourse. Comparative Legilinguistics **5** (2011)

16. Wambaugh, E.: Light reading for law students. The Law Bull. State Univ. Iowa **2** (1893)
17. Weisberg, R.H.: Wigmore's "legal novels" revisited: new resources for the expansive lawyer. Northwestern Univ. Rev. **71**(1) (1976)
18. Weisberg, R.H., Kretschman, K.L.: Wigmore's "legal novels" expanded: a collaborative effort. The Maryland Law Forum **7**(2) (1977)
19. White, J.B.: *The Legal Imagination*, Little Brown and Company (1973)
20. White, J.B.: Law as language: reading law and reading literature. Texas Law Rev. **60**(3) (1982)
21. White, J.B.: *Justice as Translation: An Essay in Cultural and Legal Criticism*, University of Chicago Press (1990)
22. Wigmore, J.H.: A list of legal novels. Illinois Law Rev. **2**(9) (1908)
23. Wigmore, J.H.: A list of one hundred legal novels. Illinois Law Rev., **17**(1) (1922)
24. Wilk, K.: *The Legal Philosophies of Lask , Radbruch and Dabin*, HUP (1950)

Legal Education and Legal Profession During and Beyond COVID-19 Building Bonds Between Academia and Practice

Suzanne Rab

Abstract Professor Suzanne Rab, professor of commercial law and practising international barrister and mediator offers a unique perspective on the challenges of digitisation and legal education in a post-COVID-19 world. Operating at the conflation of academia and practice Professor Rab explores the following themes using a blend of case study experience from the UK and from a comparative perspective: (1) the future of legal education in changing times; (2) the practitioner perspective and the digitised courtroom; (3) the academic experience and lived in experiences through COVID-19; (4) the role of online learning; (5) the implications for continuing legal education; (6) blended approaches to executive learning; (7) the impact on specific legal practices areas; (8) diversity and accessibility; (9) new world approaches to assessment of performance; and (10) humanising our legal education for the digital generation.

Keywords Legal education · Practitioner · digital courtroom · COVID-19 · online learning · executive learning · diversity · accessibility · inclusion · human rights · assessment tools

1 Introduction

Universities have been the bedrock of knowledge creation, development and exchange for centuries. In a changing society, they can form a transformational role in shaping communities and nations into knowledge societies and economies founded

---

The insights presented in this chapter are drawn from her professional and academic roles. The views expressed are personal.

S. Rab (✉)
Serle Court Chambers, London, UK
e-mail: SRab@serlecourt.co.uk

University of Oxford, Oxford, UK

Imperial College London, London, UK

Brunel University, London, UK

C. Raj Kumar and S. G. Sreejith (eds.), *Legal Education and Legal Profession During and After COVID-19*, https://doi.org/10.1007/978-981-19-2568-9_18

on shared and enlightened interests. In 1915 Rudyard Kipling in his poem Gehazi spoke 'of knowledge which is profit in any marketplace'. The words were expressed at a time when international air travel, let alone space voyage was in its infancy, before globalisation of human rights and before artificial intelligence (AI), nanotechnology, autonomous vehicles, smartphones and multi-media devices became a reality for increasing numbers of the world's population. This was a time before video conferencing entered our living rooms, before online delivery of groceries and before contactless payments. It was before the United Kingdom's withdrawal from the European Union in January 2020. It was before the biggest twentieth century public health crisis (Spanish flu in 1918 and 1920) broke out.

In a rapidly changing world, it is and has been an imperative for lawyers to continuously refresh their knowledge and keep current with developments in law, technology and society. In 2021 the coronavirus disease (COVID-19) continues to wreak economic and human havoc on an international scale and where virtually no region or people are untouched. While digitisation has allowed some aspects of pre-pandemic life to continue during the most severe lockdowns and social distancing, this is not without a cost. Access to reliable, and high-speed internet and multi-media devices is not ubiquitous. Even where these are available the loss in human experience can be palpable.

At the time of writing in London in late March 2021, the author sits at home in the third tranche of COVID-19 lockdown and approaching the anniversary of the first such nationwide measure on 23 March 2020. Until 29 March 2021, a 'stay at home order' remains in place in England and Wales except for certain specific and limited purposes. As a practising barrister and university law professor, the author has lived through the experience of trying to combine (juggle) a busy commercial law and regulatory practice with online court hearings, virtual arbitrations and mediations, as well as online teaching.

This chapter observes the legal industry's changing demands and expectations with respect to the areas of law which have called for more attention in the wake of the pandemic, and the skills required from the legal professionals that deliver them. The author explores what role can legal and particularly executive education play in supporting legal professionals in building this knowledge base and skillset. Operating at the conflation of academia and practice, the author explores the following themes using a blend of case study experience from the UK and from an international comparative perspective: (1) legal education in changing times; (2) the practitioner perspective and the digitised courtroom; (3) the academic experience and lived-in experiences through COVID-19; (4) the rise of online learning; (5) the rise of new areas of legal education; (6) the implications for perennial pedagogic themes including continuing legal education (CLE), blended approaches to executive learning, diversity and accessibility and approaches to assessment of performance; and (7) humanising the pursuit of knowledge and legal education for the current and next generation. This chapter also serves as a companion chapter to Chap. 5 by the same author which provides a qualitative study of the perceptions and experiences of law students studying in the time of COVID-19.

2 Legal Education in Changing Times

This chapter can only highlight some of the main themes emerging. The trajectory in terms of the implications for legal education in changing times is becoming clearer; even if the endpoint is yet to be determined. To set in context what follows, it is useful to map out a selection of pervasive themes which are explored in the remainder of this chapter.

First, certain areas of law will boom (Sect. 6). The world has changed over the course of a few months and there is no escaping this phenomenon and, with changes in the world, come changes in law, specific areas of law that are more important than ever. Areas of law which were previously underexplored that may see growth include legal technology with a new need to have digital solutions; litigation, with companies in disputes with customers over cancellations and delays; insolvency with the inevitable economic dip, as well as mental health law and family law.

Second, legal proceedings may take longer while social distancing measures are still in place and in dealing with the backlog (Sect. 3.1). This in turn opens up opportunities for efficiency-enhancing technology solutions supporting virtual as well as physical trials including video conferencing, live streaming and e-bundling.

Third, a new style of working is emerging (Sect. 3). It is an exciting time to embark on a career in law. The industry is facing turbulence much like society and law students who embrace this will be a part of a newly shaping legal industry.

Fourth, these trends can be expected to have a levelling effect (Sect. 7). Law students in the waiting may not have the same battle as their predecessors in trying to change and adapt old behaviours, systems and traditional ways of working. Instead, they will likely be part of a new dynamism that has the potential to effect radical and positive change in the profession.

Fifth, there will be more focus on emotional intelligence. This brings more emphasis on the client/customer and the ability to adapt to the plethora of technological shifts that will come while firms explore different platforms to meet the new demands of their clients (Sect. 3.2). There are more firms endorsing flexible working arrangements and work/life balance both during and in the aftermath of the height of the pandemic. This reflects a recognition that what Silicon Valley discovered years ago has resonance beyond that environment and that at least some old ways of onsite working are unsustainable. This can only be good for future lawyers who should have greater prospects of being able to balance their home life with work in a way that the legal industry had not previously experienced.

Sixthly, technological skills are more important than ever. One does not have to be an expert in quantum computing to appreciate the significance of IT literacy for the new generation of lawyers. Gone are the days where a dictaphone and a secretary were the standard toolkit of a practising lawyer. Future lawyers will therefore need to demonstrate that they can work with a multiplicity of software and hardware with agility. They will need to show their digital as well as legal acumen in order to contribute to a wider use of existing and evolving technology.

Finally, studying through the pandemic shows resilience and this is a skill that is increasingly valued by employers. The brutal reality is that the 2020/2021 cohort of law students—wherever they are in their legal careers—has had an experience unlike anything that has gone before. In these unprecedented times, gaining work experience and networking has become more difficult. Those law students who are able to do this demonstrate to their employers that they are able to transcend the limitations of their experience and are able to maximise effectiveness during a time of crisis.

3 The Practitioner Perspective

3.1 The Rise of the Digital Courtroom

The legal sector like others had to adapt in short order to the restrictions imposed by lockdown. In England and Wales, as early as March 2020 courts were using technology to allow participants to attend hearings remotely in a move that has tested the ability of the justice system to meet the exigencies of the pandemic. The move towards a more digitised court environment has long been considered.[1] Yet it was the 'real-life experience' of the pandemic that forced the imperative.

In 2016, Lord Justice Michael Briggs evaluated the potential for online courts, noting that the antiquated and inefficient IT systems in operation at that time were in dire need of an overhaul.[2] That observation might now seem prescient.

The case of *National Bank of Kazakhstan & Anor v The Bank of New York Mellon & Ors*[3] is an early example of how technology was deployed in a virtual hearing. The claimants were the National Bank of Kazakhstan and the Republic of Kazakhstan. The dispute concerned the freezing of US$ 530million by the Bank of New York Mellon in response to an order of the Belgian court. The trial was listed for seven days starting on 23 March 2020. In anticipation of a lockdown, the judge directed the parties to attend a hearing on 19 March 2020 and against the defendants' submissions that the trial should be adjourned. This case may be considered to be a pivotal decision and symptomatic of a 'no nonsense' approach to moving to full virtual trials in appropriate circumstances and which has characterised the experience that followed. On 24 March 2020, the Supreme Court conducted its first-ever remote hearing.[4] The

[1] Susskind [33].

[2] Briggs [18].

[3] *National Bank of Kazakhstan & Anor v The Bank of New York Mellon & Ors* [2020] EWHC 916 (Comm).

[4] *Fowler (Respondent) v Commissioners for Her Majesty's Revenue and Customs* [2020] UKSC 22.

first judgment to be handed down remotely was *Elgizouli (Appellant) v Secretary of State for the Home Department (Respondent)*.[5]

One year on, it is fair to say that courtrooms have undergone an overnight digital transformation to engage in virtual hearings in approximately 85% of civil cases that would otherwise have involved an in-person hearing.[6] However, the experience has not been without its technical hiccups.

The legal profession's response is largely focused on leveraging technology-based solutions to keep the wheels of justice moving. There is no doubt that responses to the pandemic have tested the courts' digital preparedness. Even before the pandemic, the courts were using video links in appropriate circumstances which do not necessitate a physical hearing. The system was not starting from scratch. However, there are concerns about the capacity of video links to meet increased demands, especially if they are being used for evidence.

The author's experience of civil matters as advocate including before the Administrative Court and Technology and Construction Court in London is that judges are flexible about technology choices. In one case, Skype for Business was the parties' choice but other technology choices, such as Zoom, Microsoft Teams, Ayotree, Adobe Connect and Starleaf were considered. Confidentiality concerns have been expressed over Zoom but those may reduce with the deployment of its new end-to-end encryption.

Document management in a virtual trial environment has forced consideration of electronic bundling solutions. In one case in which the author was involved where an online hearing was conducted at the peak of the pandemic in the UK, document bundles had to be prepared at short notice. Correspondence was duplicated. Normally, the parties would have produced a chronological bundle of correspondence, but the judge was fairly relaxed about the more 'home-made' approach.

The pandemic has seen the growth of comprehensive commercial virtual trial solutions comprising services such as video conferencing, live streaming, e-bundling and transcription. Providers including Epiq Global and Opus2 have developed their pre-pandemic offerings to cater the increased demand. There is a multiplicity of other providers, upwards of 100 offering services in the UK. As yet, the courts in England and Wales have yet to declare a provider of choice. There is some reason to suppose some reticence in so doing, not least to preserve a level playing and competition and to minimise the risk of being wedded to a particular provider in a dynamic environment. It may be anticipated that the emphasis will be on functional equivalence where factors such as reliability, security, confidentiality and comprehensiveness will govern technology choices. However, there are examples in other jurisdictions where the court has named a preferred provider, most notably the Singapore Supreme Court has identified Epiq Global as its chosen platform for audio and transcription services.[7]

---

[5] *Elgizouli (Appellant) v Secretary of State for the Home Department (Respondent)* [2020] UKSC 10.

[6] Valkov and Gillett [34].

[7] Reference [10].

It may be asked whether and to what extent these developments signal a seismic shift to technology-supported courtrooms from which there is no turning back. Even before the pandemic, the types of cases which were well-suited and could benefit from technology were relatively easy to spot, for example, complex commercial cases which are document-intensive and often with a financial or fraud element where the number of witnesses, documents and jurisdictions tends to be multiplied by several orders of magnitude. At the same time, such cases are precisely the types of cases where lawyers consider it necessary to cross-examine in person (for example, in fraud cases evidence as to alleged dishonesty may be crucial and it is essential to see the whites of the witness' eyes in a physical setting).

At the more grassroots level, jury trials in the Crown Courts have had to grapple with a changing situation. They were subject to the initial embargo but as early as May 2020 important jury trials restarted at the Central Criminal Court (the Old Bailey), Manchester, Bristol and Cardiff. Inevitably, though, the 'stop-start' approach to lockdown in the UK has meant that despite some initial reopening, there have been progressive returns to more restricted environments. Special arrangements needed to be in place to ensure hygiene, appropriate distancing and compliance with the other relevant guidance for the safety of court staff, jurors, witnesses and legal professionals. It is undeniable that the effective administration of justice is fundamental but the way it is delivered has to be consistent with the health advice given in other sectors. The safety of all concerned must be paramount at this uncertain time.

As more hearings are conducted in person, there is also an issue about ensuring equality of arms between parties who are represented at a hearing in person and those represented remotely and consideration needs to be given as to whether that is as effective. The author can speak of at least one anecdotal example in a recent case where the whole hearing was held by teleconference where one of the parties needed to self-isolate.

While the official reporting may tell a narrative of a seamless transition to online where this is deployed, the anecdotal experience of advocates reveals a more nuanced picture. In the author's experience, the practical experience can be quite mixed and some trials will not be suitable for an online hearing. In a recent civil case in which the author was involved as advocated in Spring 2020, the judge, counsel and clients all participated from home or their offices. There were some initial teething issues with technology which took almost an hour to resolve. Some parties could not join via the Skype link. After about twenty minutes the judge took over and initiated an immediate Skype meeting using his judicial account. The hearing was set down for a day but went on until about 17:00 h; somewhat longer than the physical equivalent. This reflected some lost time at the start and the need for structured breaks at the direction of the judge. There were reporting restrictions, so everyone was asked not to share images or make any recording. Solicitors were tasked with preparing a note to be put on the Court website once agreed by the parties.

With any process of technology adoption and deployment, each case will be managed according to its circumstances. The teething troubles have been immeasurably reduced. For the foreseeable future at the time of writing, the author predicts that virtual hearings will not be mainstream when more normalised times return.

The oral tradition of advocacy in England and Wales, and which revolves around physical hearings and the art of cross-examination, is what has made these courts a destination of choice. However, it is an expensive choice. The corollary is that access to justice may be hindered. The pandemic has shown that technology can and does yield efficiencies which would have been scarcely credible only eighteen months ago and this is here to say. The move to virtual environments is not a linear move to the mainstreaming of virtual hearings but, rather, a transition to a more hybridised courtroom with digitised functionality. This embraces what technology has to offer in supporting, or in some cases replacing, a face-to face interaction.

Despite the exigencies of the pandemic, the courts of England and Wales have remained open for business, albeit in a more digitised form and having had a dose of realism. In the London commercial courts in 2020/21, there were 292 cases and 1336 litigants, a substantial increase from last year, where there were 198 and 808 respectively.[8] This suggests some resilience not only in addressing the immediate situation of the pandemic, but some cause for optimism that the attractions of litigating in the jurisdiction will continue.

3.2 *Technology and Access to Justice*

Advances in technology, brought to the fore during and in the wake of COVID-19 reignite the debate about how such developments may remove barriers connected with access to justice. This question is explored with reference to the situation in England and Wales.

The technological advances observed build on the field of artificial intelligence or 'AI' as a discrete phenomenon which has its origins in a workshop organised by John McCarthy held at Dartmouth College in 1956.[9] The aim of the workshop was to explore how machines could be used to simulate human intelligence. Various disciplines contribute to AI including computer science, economics, linguistics, mathematics, statistics, evolutionary biology, neuroscience and psychology. A useful starting point is a definition offered by Russel and Norvig where, for example, AI is defined as computers or machines that seek to act rationally, think rationally, act like a human or think like a human.[10]

AI is therefore characterised by four features. First, acting rationally: AI is designed to achieve goals via perception and taking action as a result. Second, thinking rationally: AI is designed to logically solve problems, make inferences and optimise outcomes. Third, acting like a human: this form of intelligence was later popularised as the 'Turing Test', which involves a test of natural language processing, knowledge representation, automated reasoning and learning. Fourth, thinking like a human and inspired by cognitive science, Nilsson defined AI as 'that activity devoted

[8] Reference [28].

[9] See further Ref. [3].

[10] Russell and Norvig [30].

to making machines intelligent, and intelligence is that quality that enables an entity to function appropriately and with foresight in its environment'.[11]

An effective civil justice system supports and upholds the rule of law where the law must be fair, accessible and enforceable. However, there are well-documented barriers to accessing justice. In England and Wales, the Legal Services Research Centre (LSRC) commissioned a series of surveys between 2001 and 2011 involving more than 5000 participants to explore whether they had experienced problems in accessing justice. Cost is a major barrier where the LSRC found that less than 30 per cent of individuals who recognised that they had a legal problem sought formal advice.[12] There are other non-financial barriers including mental health problems, immigration status and discrimination.

AI and other advances in technology have been used extensively in legal practice and provide opportunities to deliver and access legal services in ways previously unimaginable and represent the nearest that the legal world has come to science fiction.

Predictive analysis draws on big data[13] to forecast the outcome of a case and advise clients whether to proceed, effectively substituting an individual lawyer's experience, assessment and intuition. Decisions founded on such tools could result in outcomes which are much cheaper than pursuing cases with limited prospects of success. However, the use of predictive analysis to access whether an outcome is likely to be successful may be inaccurate because of a number of factors. The number of cases decided out of court means that predictive analysis based on reported cases will cover a small subset of actual disputes. The accuracy and value of AI rely on how software is programmed and machines learn bias based on past experience. These examples can distort the data collected. Relying on predictive analysis to advise clients whether to proceed (potentially, saving time and money if a case is unlikely to be successful) may be flawed due to lack of a statistically significant dataset. Inconsistencies in algorithms could mean that critical data is not being collected. The software may not be able to work out the finer subtleties and variations involved in some cases. In such cases, relying on predictive analysis to advise clients may be flawed because it misses the 'human factor'.

Virtual solutions do allow cheaper access to ADR and a number of innovations can be observed where online solutions (whether mediations, arbitrations or hybrid early neutral evaluations). Advances in technology have unleashed automated document generation or information provided via chatbots in order to provide free or cheaper access to legal information.

New means of searching for law are emerging. ROSS intelligence was developed to free up lawyers' time so they could devote this to other tasks, potentially pro-bono. DoNotPay represents another channel for delivery of free legal advice. This chatbot was invented in the UK by Joshua Browder and by March 2017 assisted users

---

[11] Nilsson [26].

[12] Pascoe Pleasence and others [27].

[13] The term 'Big data' has been coined for the aggregation, analysis and increasing value of vast exploitable datasets of unstructured and structured digital information.

to overturn 200,000 parking fines in London and New York.[14] There are however practical limitations of chatbots regarding more complex areas of law. Lawyers may be unable to audit the accuracy of forms submitted online (and update them when required).

While it may be difficult to contemplate at least at the current times that machines will replace lawyers, developments in technology have the potential of reshaping some parts of legal practice. While this raises a number of legal, moral and ethical issues this phenomenon opens up new vistas and opportunities. For consumers of legal services these innovations allow greater and more diverse access to legal services.

Given the need to be well versed with technology to engage in effective outcomes, it may be asked whether and to what extent it would be useful in technology-led dispute resolution, for members of the judiciary to have legal technology programmes. Related to this is the question of how can the judiciary leverage support of law schools to develop such executive learning programmes.

COVID-19 has shown the legal sector lags in terms of digitisation despite its aims to bring the sector into the digital age. Law Schools that have developed online learning will be able to transfer their head-start to support the judiciary but there also needs to be an investment in systems. While that is happening, support can be given in the area of legal technology skills training. This will support at the skills level but also assist with overcoming any technology phobia or reticence. On the whole, in the author's view the experience in England and Wales has been positive in terms of the alacrity of the judiciary to embrace technology.

A related issue in terms of capacity building and skills adoption concerns access to the underlying technology and infrastructure. The ideal of high-speed internet access within and across the jurisdiction is not universal. COVID-19 has revealed the disparities in access to affordable, consistent and reliable internet within and between nations.[15] Not only the judiciary but most lawyers and clients in India do not have access to high-speed internet. Where courts do not have the infrastructure for online hearings this simply means that trials do not take place, adding to backlogs. There are anecdotal examples of cases being filed using WhatsApp. The judiciary and practitioners can perhaps work with not just law schools but engineering/software departments to initiate online filing software pilots and then have relevant executive programmes around this.

4 The Academic Lived-In Experience

A central thesis of this chapter is the role that academia and practice can play in supporting the emerging and next generation of lawyers. As a practising barrister

[14] Goodman [21].

[15] Reference [8].

and university professor, the author has experience in responses to COVID-19 in the academic and professional practice legal communities.

As the author moves to the first anniversary of home working, the reflections below document one individual's experience of working under lockdown and social distancing over the period. It is hoped that this will contribute to the wealth of experience coming out of the pandemic. The reflections here may also serve as inspiration to others to contribute to the learnings gained and, in so doing, chart pathways for ongoing continuing development of the nexus between the academic and professional practice of law. The world is connected in ways we have not previously imagined; the pandemic has shown that as academics, lawyers, citizens and human beings we do not and cannot operate effectively in silos.

4.1 The Academic Perspective

4.1.1 Elasticity of Time

As in many sectors, the provision of higher education is characterised by multiple formats and where pure online courses and remote learning options compete with more traditional campus-based or traditional physical formats.

The Open University (OU) in the UK has a long history of embracing the culture that is necessary for online tutoring.[16] The OU was founded in1969 and is the UK's only university dedicated to distance learning, and it is the only UK university to have a significant presence in all four nations.

The OU reacted with some agility when the UK Prime Minister announced the most stringent lockdown measures on 23 March 2020 because it was largely set up to work online. The author as an OU associate lecturer mainly teaches law online with the OU supplemented with face-to-face tutorials. The latter were moved to 'online equivalent'. The changes that needed to be made to the underlying substantive content were relatively minor given that there was already in existence functionally equivalent online content.

The author's perception of institutions that had already developed online offerings is that the need to move all teaching online was more like an institutional opportunity than an existential threat. However, this has not been the experience of all academic institutions and particularly those which were set up wholly or mainly around a campus environment. While technology issues can be easier to resolve, the willingness of people to change their mindset in embracing new ways of working can be more difficult.

The author has seen a huge change, for example, in relation to delivery of summer schools or in-person events that she has designed and delivered at academic institutions or with commercial organisations. Very early on in the pandemic it became apparent that these were no longer going to be viable in their original format as they

[16] Reference [13].

depended on face-to-face social and cultural interaction over a sustained period. This was the case for a summer school of two weeks' duration which the author would have delivered in June 2020. Historically the programme attracted delegates from India, China, Hong Kong, Eastern Europe, Latin America as well as the UK. It was perhaps inevitable that this had to be postponed until 2021. Notwithstanding the expected lifting of all social distancing restrictions by the end of June 2021, conversion to a virtual format was almost inevitable also for 2021. While there is reason to be optimistic about the roll-out of vaccines, prudence suggests some caution about a return to 'business as usual' for 2021 at least.

The experience has shown that while a lot of teaching can be brought online without significant loss to the user experience, some delivery formats cannot be replicated in quite the same way. The author did conjecture whether such courses could be reinvented for online delivery. While this was possible at the margins for the more limited duration content-based presentations, there was really no substitute for visiting the Supreme Court, mock trials in wig and gown and the dining halls of the Inns of Court. These ingredients have no online proxy and remain integral to a full summer school experience for those seeking more than textbook legal learning and intimate connection with legal places and personalities. The advances in the area of virtual reality[17] may, however, change the assumption that a virtual teaching environment is a close but imperfect approximation of reality in the coming years.

The author has also seen that when there are fewer options for learning and teaching, people who up to now may have been more reluctant to put themselves 'out there' (i.e. with an online academic presence) seem to be more willing to do so. The author has observed more and more academics and others publish work online whether it is a short thought-piece or webinar. There has also been cross-fertilisation of knowledge between academia and the legal profession where the author has delivered over 80 webinars for professional clients in the twelve months since the first UK lockdown. She has seen even more interest from university colleagues who have asked for use of her content as part of their lectures. The remarkable insight from this is not the sheer scale and audacity of some of the requests. It is the willingness of the participants to share without obvious personal gain and in ways that would not be contemplated on this level before the pandemic. Although some are more reticent, the author observes greater reciprocity among academics to share their work with peers.

While academics have had to confront the reality of moving all or most of teaching work into their homes, there have been changes in the mix, variety and the volume of work. The author observes that in general the academic workload has continued for employed staff and, in many respects, increased. There have been changes in the type or weighting of work. Where online teaching existed pre-pandemic this has continued without material changes. With the physical equivalent being shifted

[17] Virtual reality is a simulated experience that can be similar to or completely different from the real world. Applications of virtual reality include entertainment (e.g. video games) and education (e.g. medical or military training).

online, there is a need to rethink the design of content and delivery to overcome the challenges of sustaining attention and motivation in such format.

The author has experienced increased requests from students for structured individual support sessions. Such requests are sometimes fuelled by insecurities of studying in a pandemic and having to consider whether to be assessed on coursework to date, or defer. More individual support sessions were conducted using video conferencing technology such as Skype or Zoom, whereas before the pandemic a mobile call was generally the preferred option.

The frequency and number of video-conference meetings have increased yet their duration has reduced and they tend to end much earlier in the working day. It may be questioned whether the notion of the 'working day' has any tangible significance where the boundaries of time zones and 'always-on' technology have blurred the demarcation between home and office. As time spent online increases, so does the potential for screen fatigue which can act as a strong incentive to limit discussions to the essentials.

The author has questioned whether the move to operate virtually might be at the loss of valuable social interaction that takes place between colleagues in those all too important 'water cooler' conversations outside structured meetings. On the whole, she observes a positive development as colleagues and students seem more open to reaching out and connecting to inquire about personal welfare and for no particular reason. It is as though they are trying to replicate the randomness of interaction that would otherwise take place before a physical meeting starts.

The author observes a new language etiquette develop where emails sent at the start of the pandemic no longer started with 'I hope you are well'. The tone changed to a more sombre, yet realistic recognition of the reality. Even twelve months on, an email might say something like 'I thought I would check in with you to see how things are with you?' In the early stages of lockdown, it was rare to see an email that did not conclude without the salutary 'keep safe'. As greater cause for optimism mounts that the worst is behind, it may be asked whether the need for these exhortations has waned. However, this is tempered by the resurgence of the virus and its variations which has exposed the fragility of the situation and the ability of the public health system to cope. It is hoped, nonetheless, that the newfound cause for concern for others does not itself become a casualty of COVID-19.

4.1.2 Beyond Emotional Intelligence

The pandemic has highlighted the significance of emotional intelligence in all spheres of life. The author's emotional reactions to working in the time of COVID-19 have fluctuated. At the outset, when measures were more relaxed in the UK, the immediate personal impact seemed somewhat remote.

This all started to change in the middle of March 2020 when it became increasingly likely that the UK would need to impose tougher measures. Even before the 23 March 2020 UK escalation, the higher education and professional organisations with which the author has connections were preparing response plans with varying degrees of intensity. Almost overnight, the author's own professional Chambers went from level 0 (lower intensity) to level 3 (higher intensity) and, with it, working from home for all. This brought with it a mix of emotions, ranging from incredulity, loss and anxiety about the ability to sustain business during and potentially beyond lockdown. The author's professional drive and motivation is to plan and organise several weeks, even months in advance. This is obviously unrealistic in the evolving and unprecedented situation.

Over time, the situation has evolved as more information and clarity has emerged and with it, the emotional journey has been less of a rollercoaster. The transition can be likened to a 'Gestalt cycle of experience'.[18] It is a continual cycle of contact and withdrawal with and from ourselves and our environment. In Gestalt, the self is not seen as a static thing but rather as a continually evolving process that is defined and illuminated by how a person makes contact with his or her environment. This frame of reference can be viewed as a familiar analytical construct when dealing with uncertainty. It reflects the range of changing contexts and emotions in seeking to adjust to the new reality and constantly reassessing one's place in it.

By the twelfth week of the first UK lockdown, digital learning communications at higher education institutions and in other learning environments became almost normalised. Whereas the OU's whole business model is built for distance learning, the author observed that this phenomenon has now become mainstream across more traditional campus-based universities in her experience set. Some of the anticipated concerns about online being the only or main method of communication have dissipated. There are technology glitches and design issues but these can be fixed over time. There also emerged more tolerance on the part of colleagues for any technology issue that might prevent a person connecting at all, or in uninterrupted manner. Time is precious but colleagues will understand if their coworker may be sharing bandwidth with other users and this impedes their ability to maintain a seamless connection.

More traditional or 'bricks and mortar' learning institutions have had to embrace the online reality that organisations built around distance learning have pioneered from the start of their history. Some will be successful in implementing the changes but others will struggle if they are not technologically ready or culturally prepared. The transition is already happening but echoing the theme of the incomplete Gestalt cycle of experience, the endpoint is yet to be determined.

In this environment, the prospects for personal self-directed learning are enhanced. There are also manifold opportunities for academia to connect more with the business world of legal practice than previously. The author has presented as a guest lecturer at numerous online seminars organised by other universities which have been more open to internal and external participants on subjects as diverse as data protection, cyber-security, social media regulation, intellectual property and competition law. An example is the programme hosted by Jindal Global Law School 'Reimagining &

[18] Gestalt psychology, gestaltism or configurationism is a school of psychology that emerged in the early twentieth century in Austria and Germany as a theory of perception that was a rejection to the basic principles of Wilhelm Wundt's and Edward Titchener's elementalist and structuralist psychology.

Transforming the Future of Law Schools and Legal Education: Confluence of Ideas During & Beyond COVID-19' and which has provided the springboard for this chapter.

There is now a greater recognition that some of the positive interchanges and, particularly the exchange of ideas, should not cease with the end of lockdown. The academic community has shown that as tutors, citizens and human beings there is the will, technical ability and capacity to engage more fulsomely and make allowances for people who are not quite yet up to speed. It is hoped that with some careful ex-post evaluation and an openness of mind the legal community has the humility and foresight to look beyond itself and will be able to take remote connecting to even greater levels going forwards. For the academic study of law, this begins with engagement with lawyers in practice, the judiciary and ultimately consumers of legal services. In so doing, it is imperative not to lose sight of the fact that it has not been easy for everyone.

4.1.3 Precarity of Work

2020 started as a good year in the author's academic and professional practice with a full academic programme of teaching across the LLM in law, a two-week intensive summer school, an overseas teaching and business visit and three external conferences, in addition to numerous other speaking engagements.

Almost overnight the shape of the portfolio of academic work changed. With exams cancelled, there was immediate loss of examination marking. While the loss of marking income did not affect the author personally in a material way, it is an important source of revenue for some tutors during the summer and this income stream reduced or vanished with changes to assessment models. The pandemic has exposed the economic vulnerabilities of part-time workers and self-employed consultants in academia and elsewhere.

Events that revolve around physical interaction were cancelled quite early on. While some participants showed their commitment by electing to transfer their bookings to a future presentation, serious questions are being asked about the viability of summer schools and largescale gatherings in the future. This has much wider implications for universities where the summer school business is a key source of funding.

There has also been an impact on teaching initiatives which involve physical interaction. An example in the author's experience is a project involving 'Street Law'. Street Law has a long and respected history dating back to 1972 when students at Georgetown University, Washington DC were introduced by their tutors into the community to provide rights-based learning material to members of the public. The aim was first, to provide the audience with information on rights and responsibilities and second, to develop the students' grasp of the law, legal procedures and lawyering skills in an applied context. Street Law is based on three core concepts or variations on a theme being: knowledge (belief), capacity (skills) and community. In the USA, Street Law has been used in a wide range of institutions since its inception. It has also been the catalyst for similar initiatives worldwide including in South Africa. Street Law in the UK is less developed but recent initiatives in particular those undertaken by the Law Societies in Ireland and Scotland have led to increased interest in the concept.[19] It is beyond the scope of this chapter to provide a detailed and exhaustive summary of the Street Law initiative and its historical evolution and application. A succinct summary of its motivation, advantages, methods and benefits is provided by Grimes.[20] While the pandemic may have put on hold or reshaped traditional Street Law initiatives, it is suggested that this area is ripe for reassessment with the return to more normalised teaching patterns.

At the same time, the author saw valuable overseas academic and professional work disappear with no immediate prospects of reinstatement. A visit to Hong Kong in June 2020 to deliver a week-long programme of lectures to local regulators and universities was jettisoned. With 14 days of mandatory quarantine either side, this was not viable. As the prospects of a return to overseas travel became more remote, the parties moved to online delivery defying geographical and time zone differences. This was due in no small part to the strength of the relationships that were forged during a pre-pandemic personal visit but others in similar situations may not have been so lucky. In short, that one physical meeting may be necessary at the outset to build the foundational relational ties that endure.

The new reality has forced academics and others to seek new ways of sustaining and generating work and research opportunities. With the loss of some teaching projects, the author has seen others emerge and many of which have been born out of the pandemic itself. She has been appointed on a number of additional research projects including audits of curriculum resources on mental health and inclusiveness where funding was released during the pandemic, as well as a support programme for full-time intensity students (Sect. 7.3).

When the author's week-long mediation training and accreditation programme due for delivery in its physical format in April 2020 was in jeopardy, it was converted into an online version, practically over a weekend. This raised issues of cost against expectations that an exclusively online programme should be cheaper than the physical equivalent. However, the online functionality brought with it economies of scale which allowed for delivery to more people at a lower price per user. The platform has since been used to deliver real-life online mediations. This is part of the greater convergence between academia and practice which COVID-19 has brought to prominence.

[19] Arthurs and others [16, pp. 118–241, 17, pp. 19–81].

[20] Grimes [22, pp. 273–84].

4.2 Case Study Experience

The pandemic has provided the context for real-life experiment and innovation. This section outlines a number of projects where the author participated in her capacity as a university tutor and researcher.

4.2.1 Documenting 'Lived in Experiences'

The research team set out to investigate the 'lived in' experiences of academic tutors and the impact this may have on higher education. Using data collected pre-COVID-19 as a baseline, the objective was to compare data collected during the COVID-19 pandemic to understand the perceived impact in relation to the three areas documented above (Sect. 4.1). The author was an autoethnographic study participant and the insights summarised in Sect. 4.1 reflect a series of daily dairy entries over the period May–June 2020.

4.2.2 Online Student Support Forum

There has been a significant increase in full-time law students over the past few years and now approximately 44% of OU law undergraduates are studying with a full-time study commitment. The OU strives to give the best possible support to every student and to provide tailored support to meet individual needs. In recognition of this, the OU wanted to provide a platform with dedicated support for full-time students. While studying full time has many benefits, it is recognised that it can also come with some distinct challenges such as lack of time, study-related stress and distance learning isolation. The OU provided students with dedicated full-time study support through an online forum. This was not intended to replace the roles of academic tutors but, instead, provided an additional resource which students can draw on to exchange views with other students. The forum was monitored by dedicated lecturers to support students at different levels in their law degrees (corresponding to years 1, 2 and 3 of a law degree at a campus-based university).

4.2.3 Online 'Drop in' Sessions

As well as the forum, the OU offered online events which gave students opportunities to socialise with other students, while also addressing useful topics to support learners in their studies and careers. These sessions were informal and were not intended to duplicate or replace subject-matter tutorials which continued in an online format.

To illustrate the variety of themes one session covered the challenges of full-time study online (November 2020). This was an opportunity for students to discuss their queries and concerns balancing study with other commitments, typical worries and how to deal with them. Another session covered how to use feedback (January 2020). The session was an opportunity for students to engage with feedback and help them answer such questions as: (1) what to do with feedback; (2) separating feedback from grades; and (3) an action plan on making effective use of feedback. Yet another session sought to look ahead to a career in law whether as a solicitor, barrister and other routes (March 2021). The author led the session supported by careers staff building bridges between the academic and practitioner environments and which has been a core theme of this chapter.

4.2.4 Curriculum Audits (Mental Health and Diversity)

In universities, there is a growing focus on creating and maintaining a diverse and inclusive learning environment and curriculum. This challenge is set against well-documented disparities in performance among students from certain groups (often referred to as the 'awarding gap').[21] There is comparatively less evidence on the causes of such disparities and what concrete action can be taken to seek to remedy the imbalance.

There is no question that conscious and unconscious impediments often persist even once the awarding gap problem has been recognised. Yet the literature is still in its infancy and finds that addressing the symptoms may be poorly targeted when the issues are ultimately multifaceted and contextual. There is also a level of discomfort in categorising people as for example 'BAME' (i.e. Black, Asian and minority ethnic, a UK demographic) because the outcomes among the segments can often be very divergent in different contexts.

The author was an auditor of curricula materials from the mental health and BAME perspectives across law and business. These disciplines were selected as they exhibit features which by their nature present challenges for diversity and inclusion. Recognising the magnitude of the issues, many of which have been given added impetus by COVID-19, the aim of this project was to consolidate institutional initiatives in this area and seek to improve the curriculum from the perspective of mental health and diversity/inclusion.

In Law studies, the primary and secondary materials (laws, cases, textbooks) may reflect cultural norms and traditions that would now be seen as offensive. For example, the earliest written legal source on marital rape in the UK appeared in a 1736 treatise entitled History of the Pleas of the Crown by Sir Matthew Hale, a former Chief Justice of the Court of King's Bench in England. Hale argued that 'the husband of a woman cannot himself be guilty of an actual rape upon his wife, on account of

[21] University College London has collated a collection of guides, case studies and other resources to inspire and advise on ways to reduce the BAME awarding gap and embrace inclusivity. D'Reen Struthers, 'Resources to help close the awarding gap' (University College London (UCL) Arena Centre for Research-based Education) <https://www.ucl.ac.uk/teaching-learning/education-strategy/1-personalising-student-support/bme-attainment-project/resources#Diversifying> accessed 20 March 2021.

the matrimonial consent which she has given, and which she cannot retract'. This remained the legal reality until a landmark court judgment in 1991.[22]

Contrastingly, in Business Studies the curriculum may be based on Western approaches to management and industrial organisation (capitalism). Values and approaches respected in one culture but which are not universal (e.g. a focus on collaborative learning) may raise tensions within the curriculum.

The audits comprised three stages. Stage 1 (pre-audit) involved development of the audit tool, establishing the audit team, initial awareness training, training in use of the audit tool and identification of tutorial materials to be audited. Stage 1 (audit of tutorial materials) involved a first stage sampling of materials for review, initial feedback on results and further audits of additional materials by way of sensitivity testing. Stage 3 (post-audit) involved a review of results and key findings and recommendations, and where appropriate, revision to existing materials and preparation of new materials, culminating in an assessment of how findings could be deployed wider in the organisation.

The following key themes emerged across the review of Law materials:

(1) Idiom: the use of idiom may be exclusive (e.g. 'fancy dress' may not translate across different cultures);
(2) Shared experiences: examples drawn from a shared culture may be divisive (e.g. cricket on a Sunday afternoon);
(3) Language: may be offensive or create a 'them and us' culture (e.g. 'foreign');
(4) Reinforcing stereotypes: e.g. criminal law where the suspect is from a BAME group;
(5) Case study characters: names, genders and roles need to be carefully scrutinised to avoid perpetuating stereotypes or 'tokenism';
(6) Western pedagogy: skills that are predicated on self-directed learning and active student engagement may be valued in western pedagogy yet this is not universally shared and may put students who have studied in other environments at a disadvantage;
(7) Lack of alternative examples: the course content may not lend itself to alternative examples without compromising the learning experience (e.g. Law involves controversial subject matter which needs to be confronted in its raw form to accurately depict the content, e.g. the frequency of stop and search among certain groups);
(8) UK v Europe v Rest of World: the risk of compartmentalism (e.g. references to 'other countries' may carry overtones of cultural superiority or academic imperialism);
(9) Segmented vs. holistic approaches: the curriculum must be viewed in its individual components as well as holistically and where issues with individual case studies may be addressed or even exacerbated when viewing the content in context;

[22] *R v R* [1991] UKHL 12.

(10) Cross-cutting diversity: age, culture, disability, gender, language, race, religion, sexual orientation or other aspects of identity must be assessed individually and from an intersectional perspective (e.g. a case study showing a black male does not necessarily engage a student who shares those attributes but who has other characteristics that are not also reflected);
(11) Over-compensating: e.g. a scenario where the characters are all from the same ethnic group may not reflect society or inclusiveness and may reinforce cultural isolation;
(12) Beyond content: the paper-based curriculum materials are a starting point only due to e.g. information asymmetry (the tutor does not necessarily know the student's characteristics) and the manner of delivery is critical to ensuring that a culture of diversity is promoted.

These projects examined the tutorial materials in a largely paper-based format. They do not address the fundamental issues about the root cause of the awarding/attainment gap and how other initiatives in an institution and beyond might address it. The author's experience from soundings at institutions in her experience set and among regulators shows how individual perceptions of the general 'opportunity and outcome problem' diverge.

While tackling the range of issues (root causes and how to address them) needs attention, it is the issue of what can be done to narrow the gap and who should be responsible that is most challenging and which this project did not address. Related measures such as institution policies, procedures process and guidance on equality, diversity and inclusivity as well as support to individual tutors on how to deliver inclusive tutorials are also relevant as part of the wider engagement. Areas for future inquiry and which have cross-institutional significance could include: (1) comparative performance (across years, within the institution and across other institutions); (2) qualitative assessment of student experience (e.g. through interviews or focused groups); (3) the challenges of distance learning where the student's characteristics may not be known to the institution/tutor and which is brought into sharp focus by the pandemic; and (4) the institutional and personal challenges of revising materials once issues have been identified (e.g. perspectives of subject-matter experts who may resist change).

5 The Rise of Online Learning

The legal profession is notoriously demanding and time-intensive. Significant investments, typically measured in years, are made by a student at the academic, vocational and continuing legal education (CLE) stages. With time being a luxury that lawyers cannot afford, and physical campuses being temporarily in lockdown, the pandemic has forced reassessment of how law schools can leverage technology to provide legal professionals easy and flexible remote access to executive education programmes. At the same time, there are some limitations of online learning.

As a point of clarity, online learning covers a variety of formats starting with basic asynchronous programmes or e-learning which allows a learner to 'click through' content at their own pace but without a bilateral or multilateral exchange with tutor or other learners. This may be contrasted with synchrounous learning that takes place in realtime with a live tutor and, potentially, using breakout rooms and other multi-media engagement (e.g. document share, screen share and webtours). This modality can resemble or even improve on the experience of a physical delivery in a seminar threatre or classroom.

The benefits of online learning are many. First, this provides an opportunity to use (imposed) social distanced time to focus without distractions. Second, online learning can be delivered and consumed at a fraction of the cost of travelling to location-based events saving time and money. Third, it is possible to deliver even greater quality user experience using state-of-the-art technology with no compromise on the physical equivalent. Finally, there is the flexibility to learn anywhere, anytime and to suit more individualised needs and schedules.

It may be asked whether online can genuinely deliver a functional equivalent to face-to-face. The author's experience of designing and delivering mediation training and accreditation provides a case study vignette. In her view, the use of virtual breakout rooms testifies to the power of this learning method which can simulate the physical equivalent. Beyond training, online mediations are an alternative dispute resolution technique in itself so training over an online platform allows trainees to build the nexus between classroom learning and practice. There are also benefits of screen distance which may overcome student apprehension and allow them to be more confident in expressing their own views in a chatbox, breakout room or use of an emoji in a way that would not be achieved as easily or at all in a large lecture room.

The limitations of online as a single education platform must be acknowledged. First, remote learning programmes without direct human contact has costs in human terms and particularly for longer duration programmes.

Studying for full-time students has been particularly hard during the pandemic. Without any social events—or even casual catchups with a friend over a coffee—it has been especially hard to maintain student motivation. The author has the privilege of teaching in a campus-based university which is relatively unique in having a high ratio of tutor–tutee engagement in more normalised times. This tutorial system had to move online. Although there was no reduction in the size of the tutor groups, the loss of physical contact brought its toil. Technology has been useful in terms of pre-recorded lectures, online tutorials, additional research and catching up with friends and colleagues. However, this rather misses the point where the academic endeavour is founded on the shared experiences of self and others who prefer talking to people in person and would much rather meet face-to-face, in person interactions; not only for the ritual and tradition, but also for the greater sense of intellectual and personal satisfaction that it provides.

Second, as the quality of technology improves and becomes more affordable so too will the learning product face commoditisation. This contemplates at least four future scenarios for online learning depending on the relationship between market concentration, cost and market differentiation.

In Scenario 1, ('Spoilt for Choice') there is a diverse and wide variety of products and services offered through multiple players providing a range of online and physical alternatives at different price points. In Scenario 2 ('Price War') the market moves to the lowest price as the lowest common denominator. In Scenario 3 ('Winner Takes All') providers who can deliver at scale are able to grow their share. Over time, this is likely to lead to a diluted value proposition and less choice as later adopters fall by the wayside because they are not price or value-competitive. In Scenario 4 (Loss-leader), providers who have the scale and cash resource are able to offer their products at below cost. While this can bring immediate-term consumer benefits in terms of lower prices, over time the market may converge to Scenario 3.

It is too early and beyond the scope of this chapter to predict where the future of online learning in higher and executive education will be and whether the pandemic has forced a seismic shift from which there is no going back. The early experience seems to suggest a more nuanced picture at least for longer term programmes. Anecdotally, there is demand for more sophisticated, adaptable and bespoke solutions and not 'off the shelf.' This suggests that higher and executive education institutions can do well to partner with external organisations with ready-made solutions in terms of courses and online delivery capability. In turn, they will be bringing their wealth of subject-matter expertise to the design of fit-for-purpose and adaptable content.

6 The Rise of New Areas of Law[23]

As the courts pivot towards increasing the use of online hearings, consideration should be given to the inevitable emergence of COVID-19 specific legal disputes arising from the public health crisis. Encompassing supply-chain issues, interruption of live entertainment events, and employment matters, a range of legal disputes have emerged as a product of the pandemic itself. Dealing with these issues will require unprecedented adaptability and innovation by the courts and the legal profession for many years to come.

The pandemic crisis is also a classic representation of how dynamic the judicial landscape is. The courtroom has seen a transition in the type of cases in the last few months: cases of increased commercial disputes, cyber-fraud, domestic violence data-privacy breaches are some visible changes which courtrooms can anticipate in a post coronavirus world. Given the transition in subject matter expertise required by lawyers, this raises a question as to what existing and new areas of law should form the basis for legal education.

This section will first consider some of the many predictable flashpoint issues arising from the second-order effects of the pandemic and which threaten to spill-over

[23] Material in this section is informed by an article by the same author published by the Practical Law Company ('COVID-19: resolving legal disputes through virtual mediation', 24 April 2020).

into legal disputes. It also examines what appears to be increasing demand for legal services in areas of law which are burgeoning quite apart from, but coincidentally with the shifts in law, technology and society that are documented in this chapter. It is evident that some of these areas of legal practice do not automatically fall into the categories of new or old but they are growth areas. The focus of analysis is on the UK experience.

6.1 Commercial Contracts and Supply/Production

Government regulations aimed at flattening the COVID-19 infection curve inevitably lead to businesses finding it impossible or extremely difficult to perform their contractual duties. For example, Company A might not be able to deliver promised raw materials to Company B as all 'non-essential' travel has been prohibited. Alternatively, Company C might not be able to deliver products due to a strained supply chain where the wholesale suppliers on whom they depend are unable to operate. Tesla, for example, revealed in March 2020 that it had to install older processors in its cars due to a strained supply chain, sparking concerns about potential consumer disputes.[24]

Whether disputes will arise within the scope of supply and production contracts depends largely on the underlying contractual framework. Each case will turn on its own facts. Parties affected by the pandemic may find relief if their contractual agreements include 'Force Majeure' clauses. In the absence of such protective clauses, many businesses will find themselves in breach of their arrangements unless they can rely on general doctrines such as that of frustration.

Force majeure

Force majeure clauses are provisions within contracts which, if successfully invoked, have the effect of relieving, either temporarily or permanently, one or both parties' from performing their legal obligations. The doctrine has previously lent itself to cover acts of God,[25] strikes,[26] trade embargoes and abnormal weather.[27]

Unlike civil law systems, under common law, the doctrine is based on contract law and will be construed on the basis of specific provisions within the contractual relationship to the extent possible. Generally, the party seeking to invoke the force majeure clause will have to satisfy the court that the event has prevented it from performing its obligations despite it having taken 'reasonable' steps[28] to mitigate its impact. Disputes can therefore arise if parties try to invoke force majeure clauses to

[24] Reference [11].

[25] *Matsoukis v Priestman & Co* [1915] 1 KB 681.

[26] *Lebeaupin v Richard Crispin* [1920] 2 KB 714.

[27] *Coloniale Import–Export v Loumidis Sons* [1978] 2 Lloyd's Rep 560.

[28] *Rhodia International Holdings Limited & Another v Huntsman International LLC* [2007] EWHC 292.

escape liability where they might have failed to fulfil their legal obligations regardless of the effects of COVID-19, or where they can perform their obligations albeit this will be more onerous or costly in the wake of the pandemic.

It should be noted that relief under force majeure clauses is difficult to invoke as the courts strenuously scrutinise issues of causation.[29] In current circumstances, however, due to the unprecedented nature of the occurrence and its rapid escalation, COVID-19 may allow more successful claims of force majeure.

Frustration of contract

In the absence of a force majeure clause, parties unable to fulfil their contractual commitments may rely on the doctrine of frustration. Frustration discharges parties from their contractual obligations where performance becomes impossible or circumstances are so 'radically different' that it becomes unfair to hold the parties to their legal obligations. Central to the test here is what is meant by 'radically different'.[30]

The doctrine of frustration is invoked very rarely, as the courts are committed to uphold the integrity and certainty of contracts. However, usual obstacles in the way of frustration may not apply here as circumstances could indeed be regarded as radically different for those contracts that were entered into prior to the pandemic. It should also be noted that the change must be 'unexpected'. At first sight, this might seem to be satisfied given the unforeseen emergence of COVID-19. However, much will depend on the circumstances of the contract at hand. For example, on 31 December 2019 China reported a cluster of cases of pneumonia in Wuhan, Hubei Province and a novel coronavirus was identified. On 30 January 2020, the Director-General of the World Health Organization declared the novel coronavirus outbreak (2019-nCoV) a Public Health Emergency of International Concern. Interesting questions arise as to when this development was or could have been anticipated with implications for contracting parties seeking to claim their contract was frustrated.

Frustration may, however, be undesirable as it brings all obligations of both parties to an immediate end upon occurrence of the frustrating event. This may be contrasted with the operation of a force majeure clause where the parties would typically know, with greater certainty, that an obligation is suspended or excused. Take a newly opened restaurant for example, whose launch date of 25 March 2020 was postponed by the UK lockdown announced just days earlier. The restaurant required a new fit-out and has invested thousands of pounds in construction, marketing and advertising. It has also received catering orders even before the official launch. In this case, depending on which payments have already been made, frustration of the contract would leave the affected party without any sort of repudiation or notice. Hence, an innocent party's losses may pile up without them having the opportunity to mitigate them.

Ultimately, whether parties can successfully rely on a force majeure clause or claim that a contract has been frustrated will depend on the language and provisions of the contract itself and all the circumstances. Each case would have to be evaluated

---

[29] *Classic Maritime Inc. v Limbungan Makmur Sdn Bhd & Anor* [2018] EWHC 2389.

[30] *Davis Contractors Ltd v Fareham Urban District Council* [1956] AC 696.

on its own merits. For example, whereas there will be instances where performance is genuinely impossible, a more complex situation will arise where a party seeks to renege from its supply obligations which become unduly onerous or difficult to perform but not impossible. This situation is unlikely to be covered by force majeure and will typically expose the party to a claim for breach. Alternative contractual protection may be provided through clauses that excuse performance for a material adverse effect. However, their interpretation can be expected to be contentious where little thought will have been given in advance to the type of situations these would hypothetically cover.

6.2 Entertainment and Sports

The lockdown caused most, if not all, live entertainment events to be postponed or cancelled indefinitely. This includes the football calendar which was postponed. This has huge financial implications for clubs that are no longer generating revenue through tickets, matchday sales and merchandise. Players' salaries weigh heavily on clubs' finances, for example making up 50% of revenues in the Bundesliga and close to 60% in the Premier League. Therefore, laying off or furloughing non-playing staff will not provide comprehensive financial relief, with more needed by way of players agreeing pay cuts and wage deferrals.

A spirit of sacrifice has certainly been demonstrated by players across different leagues agreeing to timely wage cuts.[31] However, disputes emerged in instances where players refused to accept a salary sacrifice. Cameroonian midfielder Alex Song initiated an unfair dismissal claim against Swiss club FC Sion after his contract was terminated along with nine others who refused a reduction in their wages.[32]

As political and social pressure mounted on clubs not to place staff on furlough or lay-off non-playing staff, there may be a greater push towards player wage cuts. This has the potential to cause more disputes than are reported, especially with fringe players that will suffer far more than high earners.

The entertainment industry is also ripe for disputes. What happens when organisers cancel or postpone events for which they had already sold tickets and entered into various supply contracts such as with ticketing platforms, promoters and advertisers? Legal disputes arise as obligations can no longer be performed at all or in the manner originally anticipated.

Again, whether disputes arise depends largely on the terms and conditions contained within the contracts surrounding the event. For example, if Organiser X can no longer hold a concert for which tickets have been sold and performers have entered a contract to perform, disputes may arise if fans demand a refund or when Organiser X seeks to refuse to refund any advance payment paid made to the performer. Ticketing terms and conditions and contract clauses will have to be

[31] Ames [15].

[32] Reference [1].

analysed to see if such a crisis has been provided for. Disputes arising within the entertainment and events industry have an additional goodwill element. Planners will want to preserve their relationships with performers and fans. This makes these disputes uniquely tailored towards a mediated solution which provides scope for 'out of the box' solutions preventing from a complete breakdown of the relationship.

6.3 Employment-Related Disputes

Governmental restrictions on the movement of people and closure of businesses pose a host of potential legal problems for both employees and employers:

Potential disputes with employers

As businesses suffer the economic costs of the pandemic, many are forced to lay-off workers or reduce their contract hours or pay. These terminations and curtailments will have to be dealt with very carefully taking account of the underlying employment contract and new regulations such as the Coronavirus Job Retention Scheme. Employers need to be wary of taking steps such as unilaterally reducing wages or working time, non-payment of wages and selective dismissals.

It is possible to manage necessary furloughs and lay-offs without inviting disputes. Where lay-offs are necessary, it might be tempting to terminate low-performing staff, if the reasoning is objective and defensible but employers should proceed with caution given the potential objections. A reconciliatory approach which takes all stakeholders into confidence, considers alternatives and does not resort to mass lay-offs as the default response is also vital.

There is a lot to be said for companies taking a long-term view of the crisis and not rushing into lay-offs. Investing in retaining the workforce can put businesses in a strong position to gain a competitive edge after the pandemic when others are reeling from dwindled resources and capacity and need to build-up their skill-set. Employee morale and confidence boosted as a result of such steps can also be a huge asset for companies taking a strategic view. However, for a cash-constrained business this may not be a feasible option forcing them to take steps that contain the seeds of future disputes. Where furloughing is necessary, decisions must be made without any discrimination and employees must consent to being furloughed in order to minimise the potential for any disputes. This will inevitably bring some tough choices.

Dealing with the effects of the virus also raises novel health and safety concerns for employers. This specially affects essential workers who are more exposed to their need for close physical contact as part of their essential duties. It is not inconceivable that employers will claim that employees have been exposed to the virus at work due to inadequate protection. However, such claims will face an evidential hurdle given how difficult it may be to prove causation. In any event, businesses will still need to be vigilant about assessing risks and putting required prevention and protective mechanisms in place. This could incorporate methods of social distancing at the workplace including the use of screens as well the more obvious provision of Personal Protective Equipment and washing facilities.

Non-essential workplaces will have to be equally vigilant with their social distancing policies and ensure that staff have the capacity to work from home. Failure to ensure this can lead to non-essential workers having to come into the office and compromise on social distancing.

Potential disputes with employees

An employer-to-employee relationship is fundamentally contractual in nature and, therefore, like every contract, is built upon trust and confidence. Working remotely poses problems for the employers with decreased supervision and IT information being shared across home devices instead of work computers.

Any misconduct on an employee's part such as violating confidentiality or misuse of company information would usually be a breach of contract. Non-essential employees flouting social distancing measures and coming into work may also interfere with the employer's health and safety responsibilities and raise questions as to whether the employer has complied with its legal obligations to other members of staff.

6.4 Public Law Disputes

The virus has led to unprecedented peace-time restrictions on public liberty and enjoyment. The Coronavirus Act 2020 (Coronavirus Act) prohibited public gatherings, restrained free movement and allowed for enforced closure of businesses. It did so without directly compensating businesses for the ensuing economic losses, albeit other support schemes have been put in place to alleviate the economic burden on business.

The Human Rights Committee examined[33] these regulations in the light of the Human Rights Act 1998 (HRA 1998) to assess if they are compatible with rights under the European Convention on Human Rights (ECHR) rights. According to the Committee quarantine and self-isolation has a potential impact on Article 8—the right to liberty and Article 2—the right to life, while a ban on public gatherings interferes with Article 11—freedom of assembly and association. School closures raise the issue of potential conflict with the right to education under Protocol 1, Article 2. Moreover, it has been argued that restricting people's ability to work and closing businesses without compensation is contrary to Protocol 1, Article 1—right to peaceful enjoyment of property and has a disproportionate effect on self-employed individuals and smaller businesses.

Public law jurisprudence has established exceptions where the state can limit the use of property without providing direct compensation.[34] The HRA1998 also

[33] Reference [12].

[34] *Grape Bay Ltd V AG of Bermuda* [2000] 1 WLR 574.

allows limitations on the right to the peaceful enjoyment of possessions provided that the restrictions are proportionate and strike a fair balance between the rights of the individual and the general public.

In the current circumstances, courts may be inclined to take the view that the Coronavirus Act strikes a fair balance between individual rights under the HRA 1998 and general public interest. In addition, whereas direct compensation has not been provided, the government announced multiple stimulus packages including initially a measure worth over £300 billion to support businesses through the economic hardship.[35]

While few would question the need for resolute action in the immediate term, the longer lockdown lasts, the more likely it is that these assumptions are to be challenged. Private groups and the Opposition decried a lack of an exit strategy[36] within the lockdown, which could conceivably have been used as a basis for a public law challenge. It is reasonable to say that the appetite to challenge the government will have increased as a result of the applicants' success in cases arising from EU withdrawal.[37]

A further area of potential disputes in the public law arena arises out of challenges to government contracts awarded under relaxed public procurement procedures. On 18 March 2020, the Cabinet Office published Procurement Policy Note 01/20. PPN 01/20 provides that, in the exceptional circumstances of the COVID-19 outbreak, authorities may need to procure goods, services and works with extreme urgency. Claims by dissatisfied bidders who lose out on lucrative contracts to supply the National Health Service for example may be anticipated where they can establish the contracts were awarded in violation of procurement rules. While the time limit for court challenges to awards made at the height of the pandemic may have expired, these measures may be expected to be the subject of wider public inquiry as the dust settles on the immediate crisis and there is greater pressure for accountability over past decisions.

6.5 Data Protection

The evolutions in technology charted in this chapter bring a number of benefits, including improvements in economic outcomes, enhanced human decision-making, increased levels of productivity and potential solutions for complex and pressing economic and social problems. At the same time, technology and AI in particular present a number of potential challenges that will need to be confronted if the full benefits are to be realised. Not least, there is a challenge in ensuring that policy,

---

[35] Harding and Ashworth [23].

[36] Reference [5].

[37] *R (on the application of Miller) and anor v Secretary of State for Exiting the European Union* [2017] UKSC. 5; *R (on the application of Miller) v The Prime Minister, Cherry and others v Advocate General for Scotland* [2019] UKSC 41.

laws and regulations governing systems enabled by AI are relevant, adequate and proportionate.

While it is beyond the scope of this chapter to provide a full assessment of existing legal regimes that interact with technology, the interaction between data and machines will continue to be at the forefront of global, regional and national legal and regulatory developments.

The overarching legal basis for data protection in the EU is mainly contained in the General Data Protection Regulation[38] or 'GDPR' subject to national law provisions and derogations where permitted by the GDPR. The GDPR entered into force on 25 May 2018.[39] The GDPR is a development of EU data protection law first adopted in 1995.[40] It may be viewed as evolutionary rather than revolutionary, even though it contains some noticeable innovations.

There are features of EU data protection law under the GDPR that contribute to ensuring the accountability of AI systems. These include: (1) a preventative, process-oriented approach which restricts the way in which personal data is collected and processed in order to prevent 'data power' in the hands of the data controller, (2) strengthening of the rights of individuals to obtain information about how their data is being processed and for what purpose and to object to such processing under certain circumstances, and (3) enhancement of sanctions against data breaches. This increased emphasis on data processing 'harm' may be expected to represent a more substantive approach.

Given that the experience of GDPR implementation is still recent, it is probably not realistic to expect a wholescale revision in the near future. However, useful work could be done to inform appropriate and targeted policy-making and with insights that could shape development of similar laws internationally. First, there is a need for clarification of the goals of data protection regulation potentially through a survey of its origins and implementation in different countries and emerging enforcement trends so as to discern best practices against those goals or determine whether other goals may be more appropriate (e.g. focusing more on data processing 'harm' as opposed to data procedures). Second, COVID-19 highlights the real-world problems in AI use cases which may not be caught and whether these are consistent with the underlying purpose of the regulation and, if not, whether the regulation needs to be changed or improved (e.g. track and trace measures). Third, there is a question as to the identification of possible initiatives that may be pursued voluntarily by the industry to address any such gaps and which may include exchange of data relating to vaccine availability and performance as well as the impact on particular groups. This aspect is particularly important in balancing the risk of regulatory overreach against the need to win over the hearts and minds of individuals and regulators.

---

[38] General Data Protection Regulation (Regulation (EU) 2016/679).

[39] Following the UK's withdrawal from the EU on 31 January 2020, the GDPR is retained in UK domestic law now the transition period has ended, but the UK has the independence to keep the framework under review. The 'UK GDPR' sits alongside an amended version of the Data Protection Act 2018.

[40] Directive 95/46/EC on the protection of individuals with regard to the processing of personal data and on the free movement of such data.

6.6 Social Media Regulation

The surge in social media has revolutionised the twenty-first century, making significant changes to communication.

Facebook, YouTube and Instagram represent the major social networks with 2.7 billion, 2 billion and 1 billion users, respectively. Against the backdrop of COVID-19, PricewaterhouseCoopers reports[41] in 2020 that Apple and Microsoft saw market capitalisation increases of $469bn (42%) and $344bn (29%), respectively, closing the gap with Saudi Aramco. Amazon became the fourth public company with a + $1tn market capitalisation as of June 2020. Alphabet was close, with market capitalisation of $966bn, which has since moved above the $1tn mark. Market capitalisation is only one metric, yet these companies find themselves in a position where they have enormous power and control over the flow of information which has the potential to influence most aspects of civil society, including the electoral process.

The detailed regulation of social media is beyond the scope of this chapter. In the author's view, this area of law is worthy of examination in detail in executive education programmes.

There has been criticism that the social media sector has been hugely under-regulated, in areas such as facial recognition, AI, algorithms, use of data, among others and prompting an inquiry as to why have lawmakers been slow to put legislation into action. New laws and regulations at the interface between technology and social media face equally vocal opposition. Technology firms are disruptors by their nature—they are offering new innovations that are bound to come up against regulatory issues in their attempts to push boundaries. Regulation of social media using traditional and new regulation is likely to be a fertile area for governments, regulators and providers of legal education.

The areas that are likely to be engaged include: antitrust or competition law; data protection and privacy; regulation of content and, relatedly, imposition of *ex ante* obligations on social media companies to prevent harmful practices.

In the area of antitrust alone, technology companies face scrutiny on both sides of the Atlantic. In the USA, the Department of Justice[42] has filed an antitrust lawsuit against Google and the Federal Trade Commission[43] has its own antitrust investigation into Facebook. The European Commission has launched an antitrust investigation into Amazon, accusing the online retailer of using business data to gain an unfair advantage over retailers on its platform.[44] The European Commission has also imposed penalties on Google of more than €8bn over competition issues in a series of antitrust investigations,[45] and ordered Apple to repay €13bn in taxes to the

---

[41] PricewaterhouseCoopers [29].

[42] Reference [7].

[43] Reference [6].

[44] Reference [2].

[45] *Google Search (Shopping)* (39,740) Commission Decision 4444 [2017] OJ C9/11; *Google Android* (40,099) Commission Decision 4761 [2018] OJ C402/08; Google Search (AdSense) (40,411) Commission Decision 2173 [2019] OJ C369/04.

Irish government amounting to unlawful State aid.[46] Both companies appealed those decisions, but the battle to police the internet and the technology firms that occupy this ecosystem continues.

6.7 Cyber Security

The threats arising from online communications being intercepted by hackers or disclosed through negligent management are many. Data protection laws, including under the GDPR will generally require that personal data is kept secure, especially where the data is sensitive such as medical history. However, security threats in the technology/AI environment are multiple and transnational, and stem from negligence on the part of businesses dealing with customer data, to criminals, terrorists, and even other governments.

The UK Cyber Security Centre has defined cyber security as 'how individuals and organisations reduce the risk of cyberattack' and where its 'core function is to protect the devices we all use (smartphones, laptops, tablets and computers), and the services we access—both online and at work—from theft or damage'.[47]

In an age of surveillance, cyber security regulation may be expected to form part of the curriculum of executive education programmes. This is an area which is evolving and where education programmes would usefully: (1) explore the threat landscape and some of the security challenges posed with the advent of AI and information and communications technology; (2) develop a critical understanding of the key features of cyber security law in key areas (privacy and data protection, cybercrime, cyber-war and cyber-terrorism and surveillance and cybercrime investigations). Of relevance to these issues, for example, is the recent case of *Big Brother Watch and Others v. United Kingdom*[48] concerning the right to a fair trial under Article 6, privacy under Article 8, freedom of expression under Article 10 and non-discrimination in the enjoyment of the rights guaranteed under Article 14 of the ECHR.

7 Perennial Themes Revisited

It is beyond question that COVID-19 has forced individuals, businesses and governments to change their usual ways of living and working in a manner thought unimaginable before its inception. As the prospects of a steadier state begin to appear, it is useful to reflect on the implications for some enduring themes in legal education and to ask whether the experience is a temporary aberration or a shifting of paradigms.

---

[46] Reference [9].

[47] Reference [14].

[48] Big Brother Watch and others v United Kingdom (Applications Nos. 58170/13, 62,322/14 and 24,960/1513, September 2018).

7.1 *Continuing Legal Education*

Continuing Legal Education (CLE) for lawyers enables lawyers to constantly evolve in knowledge, competence and efficiency, which in turn improves legal professional standards and leads to increased public confidence in legal professionals and the justice system as a whole. Given the role of lawyers as agents of this change, this raises a question as to whether CLE should be a matter of choice, or a mandatory requirement. There is a related question of how CLE is best delivered.

In the UK, there is less emphasis on CLE hours and more on flexibility and meeting continuing learning and skills acquisition that meets individual requirements. For example, from 1 November 2016, solicitors in England and Wales no longer need to count continuing professional development hours. Instead, they must now reflect on the quality of their practice and identify any learning and development needs. They can then address these needs to make sure their knowledge and skills are up to date and that they are competent to practice.[49] The concern is that if CLE is reduced to clocking up hours it becomes box-ticking. The upside is that lawyers who invest in CLE on a voluntary basis are doing it because they want to and as a source of competitive differentiation.

An underexplored issue concerns the relationship between legal education at the academic and/or vocational stage and employability skills. This may be contrasted with the legal education of active legal practitioners. This area has been considered by Street Law and similar projects.[50] Here law students take part in practical work experience as part of their law degree for academic credit. These experiences may be distinguished from purely voluntary pro bono initiatives where students participate in law clinics or similar initiatives where they give advice to the public. Cantatore finds that pro bono legal experience obtained for academic credit can also be of significant benefit to students as it promotes such characteristics as altruism, community service and enhanced work ethic 'in addition to developing practical workplace skills, communications skills and increased self-confidence'. However, Cantatore acknowledges that further research was needed to determine whether students leave their clinical experience with enhanced workplace skills.

7.2 *Blended Learning*

The disruption caused by COVID-19 has reshaped not only how university education is delivered and consumed during the height of the pandemic but it compels a consideration of whether such adaptability as seen at a time of crisis has more enduring

---

[49] The Solicitors Regulation Authority toolkit provides useful information and resources to help solicitors adopt this new approach to continuing competence. 'Continuing competence' (*Solicitors Regulation Authority*) < https://www.sra.org.uk/solicitors/resources/cpd/tool-kit/continuing-competence-toolkit/ > accessed 20 March 2021.

[50] Cantatore [19, pp. 147–72].

application. It may be asked what are the possible steps and strategies law schools should employ in deploying a blended programme on a sustainable basis. Such planning becomes relevant considering the fact that such a deployment is happening against an overall decline in the legal profession.[51] This in turn raises the question of how to provide the right orientation in Law Schools to equip professionals to apply their skills effectively in the workplace.

This suggests that the emphasis should be on teaching transferable skills that are relevant to law as well as other disciplines. An example of this approach is the learning programme designed and delivered by the author at Brunel University London. The Practical Skills for dispute resolution is part of an immersion programme on international comparative competition and regulatory law. Beyond textbook learning, this programme includes: interview skills, handling information requests, advocacy, mediation, mock board rooms and a mock trial. The mix of theory and practice simulations and role play can put students in real and challenging situations so that they can apply their skills in practice. Given that executive legal education for programmes of shorter duration may be expected to have an online component this can be contextualised by engaging members of the judiciary, business leaders and practitioners with leading academic profiles to bring enhanced credibility.

7.3 *Diversity and Accessibility*

The implications of COVID-19 for diversity and accessibility have been discussed in Sect. 4.2.4 above. Post-graduate or executive programmes are likely to cater to a more diverse demographic where students comprise individuals with varied attributes in terms of length of work experience, or professional background. Such courses would exhibit elements of heterogeneity unlike a homogeneous regular cohort of law students. In these situations, there is a challenge of developing a teaching methodology to benefit the whole cohort.

While the business case for diversity in law schools is familiar, translating this into practice is another. There is a need to create an inclusive curriculum and put students in a position where the learning is accessible as well as inclusive. Insights from curricula audits from the mental health and BAME dimensions (Sect. 4.2.4) show that this is not straightforward. While accepting that such audits do not address the reasons for the awarding/attainment gap which is a topic meriting much deeper study, useful design considerations include first, background research on course attendees (during the booking process) which can help refine the course selection and delivery. Consideration should be given to incorporation of scenario-based case studies into

[51] Revenue generated by the UK's legal sector is down 12% compared to 2019, as the impact of lockdown on firms began to emerge. Jemma Slingo, 'Legal industry revenue drops to four year low' (*The Law Society Gazette*, 14 July 2020) <https://www.lawgazette.co.uk/news/legal-industry-revenue-drops-to-four-year-low-/5104995.article> accessed 20 March 2021.

the programme which can then be diverse in subject matter and distributed according to professional background.

The experience in a desert-based education system called *Mahdara* provides inspiration for how such programmes can be delivered effectively in diverse user environments.[52] In the Middle East, this model of teaching involved students studying their own materials at their own pace in the same class with the same tutor. This learner-led approach can be facilitated using technology and could be a blended model that suits executive courses perfectly.

Further research and analysis could cover the relationship between diversity and inclusiveness in such programmes. There is always value in taking quantitative outputs and then using them to frame further qualitative enquiry through interviews and focus groups. The mere process of initiating and publishing the results of a detailed research and scrutiny exercise will further move diversity and inclusion issues into the public consciousness and up the political and regulatory agenda. In so doing, this would reignite discussions about whether individual institutions or others need to do more to attract students from diverse backgrounds into higher education. This, in turn, could potentially lay the groundwork for solid regulatory recommendations that might emerge from a qualitative approach to inform better outcomes. This recognises that the underlying issues are endemic and complex and cannot be solved by one institution alone.

7.4 Assessment Methods

The assessment methodologies in executive education programmes demand differential approaches given the more varied demographic of participants. This raises a question as to how to set expectations and standards for assessing the participants of such executive courses.

Adults learn in different ways and show their abilities in different ways. By its nature, executive education focuses on knowledge and skills that are transferable into practice. The workplace (for present purposes, the practice of law) is not looking for technocrats and practical skills will be increasingly important. This suggests that practitioners, employers and the judiciary as ultimate consumers of the outputs from such programmes, should have an involvement not only in the design of the courses but also the resulting evaluation methods. In this context, the author speaks to her dual roles as academic and practitioner in providing the nexus between academia and the practice of law. She has designed multiple executive programmes and delivered them into the public and private sector. Many of these underwent rapid transformation to adapt to the challenges of COVID-19. Some innovations such as increased online options for evaluation including recorded practical role plays are likely to remain a permanent feature of these programmes.

---

[52] Ladjal and Bensaid [24].

Insights from Street Law and similar initiatives can also provide a focus on how the very process of teaching law can build skills that lawyers can use in the workplace (Sects. 4.1.2, 4.1.3 and 7.1). Although these initiatives are aimed at law students rather than working professionals they exemplify the learning by doing philosophy that underlies the success of executive programmes that provide transferable skills.

Consideration could be given to the lawyer effectiveness factors identified by Schultz and Zedeck (2011). Grouped into eight broad categories, these factors are: intellectual and cognitive; research and information gathering; communications; planning and organising; conflict resolution; client and business relations/entrepreneurship, working with others; and character. A summary of these factors is provided in Appendix 1.

Executive programmes can also be informed by other research that identifies the legal skills, professional competencies and characteristics that make lawyers successful. Gerkman and Cornett report on the results of the Foundations for Practice survey which surveyed more than 24,000 lawyers in all 50 US states from a range of backgrounds and practice areas. The authors postulate that the answers pose opportunities and challenges both to schools that educate lawyers 'and the employers that ultimately hire them'.

First, lawyers need character (The Character Quotient). 76% of characteristics relating to this element (e.g. integrity, work ethic, common sense and resilience) were identified by the majority of respondents as necessary upon leaving law school. This finding builds on the understanding of what makes people—not only lawyers—successful where it is accepted that some threshold intelligence quotient (IQ) is needed. In recent years, it has become accepted that a favourable level of emotional intelligence (EQ) is also required. The study suggests that lawyers also require some level of character quotient (CQ). Second, the findings suggest that successful entry-level lawyers are not merely legal technicians but they are successful where they have a much broader blend of legal skills, professional competencies and characteristics that comprise the whole lawyer (The Whole Lawyer). Of particular relevance to executive education and its focus on employability the authors conclude that:

> When law schools educate students toward learning outcomes developed with feedback from employers and employers hire based on what they say they want, we will see law school graduates with high character quotients who embody the whole lawyer, we will see the employment gap shrink, we will see clients who are served by the most competent lawyers the system can produce, and we will ultimately see public trust in our system expand.

8 Humanising Legal Education

Information and access to information are critical to knowledge acquisition and human development. Lockdown and social distancing during and in the wake of COVID-19 have meant that information technology devices have taken on a new or increased significance. Computers have kept the wheels of business and social discourse turning, and for many, they have been the main or only source of information on everything from the weather to the availability and safety of vaccines.

This umbilical attachment to technology in the thirst for information, knowledge and connection raises questions about the need for a new equilibrium between protecting individual freedoms and wider national interests in the context of the global digital information society. This balance has to be struck and moderated with particular regard to the rights to respect for human rights including private and family life, home and correspondence, the peaceful enjoyment of possessions, freedom of thought, conscience and religion, and freedom of expression. More specifically, this freedom of expression includes the right to receive and impart information and freedom from discrimination in the exercise of such rights, while recognising that the exercise of these rights carries duties and responsibilities.

The ECHR and other international human rights instruments set out minimum conditions for the legitimacy of any interference with individual rights. Broadly stated any interference with fundamental rights must be prescribed by law and necessary in a democratic society in the interests of national security, public safety, the economic wellbeing of the country, for the prevention of disorder or crime, for the protection of health or morals, or for the protection of the rights and freedoms of others.

It is hard to dispute that there has been a seismic shift in the development of technology prior to and ongoing through COVID-19. This shift has in some respects allowed for mitigation of some of the worst shocks of dealing with the immediate public health crisis, yet it raises a question as to how, if at all, this has affected our humanity.

December 2018 saw the inauguration of The transHuman Code in Shenzhen, China. This was presented as: 'informing and engaging all citizens of the world about the dynamic influences of technology in our personal, communal and professional lives, The TransHuman Code was formed to redefine the hierarchy of our needs and how we will meet them in the future'.[53] Further endorsement followed with the 'The TransHuman Code Davos Gathering of Minds' during the World Economic Forum in January 2019. Among the innovations unveiled at this event were the world's first digital 'person', the first digital book signing and the first autonomous flying 'taxi'. The authors of The transHuman Code also introduced a transHuman Code Manifesto. In May 2019, the Organization for Economic Cooperation and Development (OECD) published the first, internationally agreed principles on human-centred, trustworthy AI which respects human rights and democratic values agreed by the OECD countries.[54]

Knowledge (whether formal education or posing as 'fake news') where the labour or endeavour that generated it is cheap, where it propagates ideologies that are not aligned with the cherished values of the rule of law and where it is used for profit or political oppression, is a threat to our very humanity. While the internet transcends the nation-state, the protection of human rights remains largely a matter for individual state autonomy and perhaps remains the next existential threat beyond COVID-19.

---

[53] Moreira and Fergusson [25].

[54] 'Recommendation of the Council on Artificial Intelligence' (*OECD Legal Instruments*, 22 May 2019) <https://legalinstruments.oecd.org/en/instruments/OECD-LEGAL-0449> accessed 20 March 2021.

9 Conclusion

COVID-19 has provided a catalyst for reimagining the relationship between the academic and professional practice of law. The 2020/2021 cohort of law students was always going to face unprecedented difficulties by not having had the opportunity to learn and sit exams in the conventional manner. Now, more than ever, it is important to maintain standards and confidence in the robustness of the education system and to equip lawyers of the moment and of the future with skills that are transferable to the workplace. This applies as much to undergraduate courses as it does to executive education. Otherwise, the qualifications are not worth the paper they are written on and lose their currency in the battle for talent at universities and, ultimately, in the legal profession.

There are also opportunities for academia to connect more with the legal business world of practice than previously. For law professionals, the emerging new(ish) normal is an opportunity to reinvent a legal practice. The imposed physical isolation has encouraged interdisciplinary working in a way that happened less frequently pre-pandemic. There is greater recognition that some of the positive interchanges and, particularly, the exchange of ideas should not cease with the end of lockdown. The academic and legal community as tutors, citizens and human beings has the will, technical ability and capacity to engage more fulsomely.

These changes were probably coming anyway. The public health emergency has forced us to reassess how we relate to each other, in an academic, business and personal environment. Many have found opportunities for personal development and heutagogy (self-determined learning). Whether these insights are sufficiently embedded to flourish beyond the current crisis situation will be the next interesting development to follow.

The inequities highlighted or intensified by COVID-19 have affected almost all areas of everyday life and education. These include the compulsory shut-down of education institutions; homeschooling within multiple learner households without access to dedicated devices or reliable internet; and domestic situations which do not support effective online learning. These imbalances will have to be addressed as part of sustainable education programmes at all levels: in schools, in higher education and executive learning. It is hoped that our humanity and what it means to be human are not lost in this process.

Institutions which are witnessing this interaction and students and legal and other professionals who plan to pursue executive legal education, will inevitably need to operate with uncertainty. In this environment, the prospects for personal self-directed and flexible learning are enhanced. 'Chaos is a ladder' is an iconic line from a speech in the third season of *The Game of Thrones*.[55] This provides a clarion call to action where, out of chaos, comes the ladder of opportunity: 'Many who try to climb it fail, and never get to try again—the fall breaks them. And some are given a chance to climb, but they refuse'.

---

[55] Game of Thrones is an American fantasy drama television series created by David Benioff and D. B. Weiss for premium television network, HBO.

Appendix 1—List of 26 Effectiveness Factors

Factors Identified as Important to Lawyer Effectiveness

1. **Intellectual and Cognitive**
   Analysis and Reasoning.
   Creativity/Innovation.
   Problem Solving.
   Practical Judgment.
2. **Reasoning and Information**
   Researching the Law.
   Fact Finding.
   Questioning and Interviewing.
3. **Communications**
   Influencing and Advocating.
   Writing.
   Speaking.
   Listening.
4. **Planning and Organising**
   Strategic Planning.
   Organising and managing One's Own Work.
   Organising and Managing Others (Staff/Colleagues).
5. **Conflict Resolution**
   Negotiation Skills.
   Able to See the World Through the Eyes of Others.
6. **Client and Business Relations/Entrepreneurship**
   Networking and Business Development.
   Providing Advice & Counsel & Building Relationships with Clients.
   Developing Relationships within the Legal Profession.
7. **Working with Others**
   Evaluation, Development and Mentoring.
8. **Character**
   Passion and Engagement.
   Diligence.
   Integrity/Honesty.
   Stress Management.
   Community Involvement and Service.
   Self-Development.
   Source: Adapted from List of 26 Effectiveness Factors in Shultz and Zedeck (Shultz and Zedeck (2011)).

References

1. Alex Song claims 'unfair dismissal' following FC Sion sacking. *sky sports* (2020) https://www.skysports.com/football/news/11095/11965405/alex-song-claims-unfair-dismissal-following-fc-sion-sacking. Accessed 20 Mar 2021
2. Antitrust: Commission sends Statement of Objections to Amazon for the use of non-public independent seller data and opens second investigation into its e-commerce business practices. (*European Commission*, 10 November 2020) https://ec.europa.eu/commission/presscorner/detail/en/IP_20_2077. Accessed 20 Mar 2021
3. Artificial Intelligence, Emerging Opportunities, Challenges, and Implications, Highlights of a Forum Convened by the Comptroller General of The United States (*GAO*, 28 Mar 2018). https://www.gao.gov/products/gao-18-142sp. Accessed 9 July 2021
4. Continuing competence: (*Solicitors Regulation Authority*) https://www.sra.org.uk/solicitors/resources/cpd/tool-kit/continuing-competence-toolkit/. Accessed 20 Mar 2021
5. Coronavirus: Stop treating public 'like children' and reveal exit strategy, say senior MPs: S*ky News* (18 April 2020) https://news.sky.com/story/coronavirus-stop-treating-public-like-children-and-reveal-exit-strategy-say-senior-mps-11975154. Accessed 20 Mar 2021
6. FTC Sues Facebook for Illegal Monopolization: (*FTC*, 9 December 2020) https://www.ftc.gov/news-events/press-releases/2020/12/ftc-sues-facebook-illegal-monopolization. Accessed 20 Mar 2021
7. Justice Department Sues Monopolist Google For Violating Antitrust Laws: (*The United States Department of Justice*, 21 October 2020) https://www.justice.gov/opa/pr/justice-department-sues-monopolist-google-violating-antitrust-laws. Accessed 20 Mar 2021
8. Pay the wi-fi or feed the children: Coronavirus has intensified the UK's digital divide: (*University of Cambridge*) https://www.cam.ac.uk/stories/digitaldivide. Accessed 20 Mar 2021
9. State aid: Ireland gave illegal tax benefits to Apple worth up to €13 billion, (*European Commission*, 30 August 2016) https://ec.europa.eu/commission/presscorner/detail/en/IP_16_2923. Accessed 20 Mar 2021
10. Supreme Court Audio Recording and Transcription Services, (*Supreme Court of Singapore*) https://www.supremecourt.gov.sg/services/court-services/audioandtranscriptionservices. Accessed 20 Mar 2021.
11. Tesla downgraded Model 3 chip in China thanks to coronavirus, *BBC News* (4 March 2020) https://www.bbc.co.uk/news/technology-51736405. Accessed 20 Mar 2021
12. The Government's response to Covid-19: human rights implications, (*UK Parliament,* 2020) https://committees.parliament.uk/work/218/the-governments-response-to-covid19-human-rights-implications/. Accessed 20 Mar 2021
13. The history of the OU, (*Open University*) http://www.open.ac.uk/about/main/strategy-and-policies/history-ou. Accessed 20 Mar 2021
14. UK Cyber Security Centre, (*National Cyber Security Centre*) https://www.ncsc.gov.uk/section/about-ncsc/what-is-cyber-security. Accessed 20 Mar 2021
15. Ames, N.: Arsenal's first-team players set to agree 12.5% salary cuts within 48 hours. *The Guardian* (17 April 2020) https://www.theguardian.com/football/2020/apr/17/arsenal-first-team-players-set-to-agree-125-salary-cuts-in-next-48-hours. Accessed 20 Mar 2021
16. Arthurs, S., et al.: From zero to 60: building belief, capacity and community in street law instructors in one weekend. Int. J. Clin. Legal Educ. **24**(2) (2017)
17. Arthurs, S., et al.: From zero to 60: building belief, capacity and community in street law instructors in one weekend. Int. J. Public Legal Educ. **1**(1) (2017)
18. Briggs, M.: *Civil Courts Structure Review: Final Report* (2016)
19. Cantatore, F.: The impact of pro bono law clinics on employability and work readiness in law students. Int. J. Clin. Legal Educ. **25**(1) (2018)
20. Gerkman, A., Cornett, L.: Foundations for Practice: The Whole Lawyer and the Character Quotient. (*IAALS,* 26 July 2016) https://iaals.du.edu/publications/foundations-practice-whole-lawyer-and-character-quotient. Accessed 20 Mar 2021

21. Goodman, J.: Law Society Gazette, DoNotPay 'chatbot' scales up to 1000 legal queries. (*The Law Society Gazette*, 12 July 2017) https://www.lawgazette.co.uk/practice/donotpay-chatbot-scales-up-to-1000-legal-queries-/5061967.article. Accessed 20 Mar 2021
22. Grimes, R.: Legal Literacy, Community Empowerment and Law Schools—Some Lessons from a Working Model in the UK' (2003) 37 The Law Teacher
23. Harding, L.T., Ashworth, L.: Rishi Sunak unveils £330bn bailout to save British economy from coronavirus. *The Telegraph* (17 Mar 2020) https://www.telegraph.co.uk/business/2020/03/17/markets-live-news-coronavirus-pound-euro-ftse-shares-flights/. Accessed 20 Mar 2021
24. Ladjal, T., Bensaid, B.: Desert-based Muslim religious education: Mahdara as a model. Religious Educ., **112**(5) (2017)
25. Moreira, C., Fergusson, D.: *The TransHuman Code*, Greenleaf Book Group Press (2019)
26. Nilsson, N.J.: *The Quest for Artificial Intelligence: A History of Idea and Achievement*, CUP (2009)
27. Pleasence, P., et al.: *CIVIL JUSTICE IN ENGLAND AND WALES* (Legal Services Commission and Ipsos MORI, 2011) https://webarchive.nationalarchives.gov.uk/20130403062303/ http://www.justice.gov.uk/downloads/publications/research-and-analysis/lsrc/2011/civil-justice-wave1-report.pdf. Accessed 20 Mar 2021
28. Portland Commercial Courts Report (2021)
29. PricewaterhouseCoopers: Global Top 100 companies by market capitalisation (July 2020) https://www.pwc.com/gx/en/audit-services/publications/assets/global-top-100-companies-june-2020-update.pdf. Accessed 20 Mar 2021
30. Russell, S.J., Norvig, P.: *Artificial Intelligence: A Modern Approach*, 3rd edn, Pearson (2010)
31. Shultz, M., Zedeck, S.: Predicting lawyer effectiveness: broadening the basis for law school admission decisions. Law Soc. Inquiry **36** (2011)
32. Slingo, J.: Legal industry revenue drops to four year low, (*The Law Society Gazette*, 14 July 2020) https://www.lawgazette.co.uk/news/legal-industry-revenue-drops-to-four-year-low-/5104995.article. Accessed 20 Mar 2021
33. Susskind R, *Online Courts and the Future of Justice* (OUP 2019)
34. Valkov, A., Gillett, F.: Keeping justice going: the UK Commercial Court's swift move to virtual trials, (*Law Society of England and Wales*, 23 October 2020) https://www.lawsociety.org.uk/en/topics/coronavirus/keeping-justice-going-the-uk-commercial-courts-swift-move-to-virtual-trials. Accessed 20 Mar 2021

The manufacturer's authorised representative in the EU is Springer Nature Customer Service Centre GmbH, Europaplatz 3, 69115 Heidelberg, Germany. If you have any concerns regarding our products, please contact ProductSafety@springernature.com

Printed and bound by CPI Group (UK) Ltd, Croydon, CR0 4YY
30/09/2026
02225246-0015